# Constitutionalism and American Culture

# Constitutionalism and American Culture

## Writing the New Constitutional History

Edited by
Sandra F. VanBurkleo,
Kermit L. Hall, and
Robert J. Kaczorowski

Foreword by Stanley N. Katz

University Press of Kansas

Published by the University Press of Kansas (Lawrence, Kansas 66049), which was organized by the Kansas Board of Regents and is operated and funded by Emporia State University, Fort Hays State University, Kansas State University, Pittsburg State University, the University of Kansas, and Wichita State University.

Library of Congress Cataloging-in-Publication Data

Constitutionalism and American culture : writing the new constitutional history / edited by Sandra F. VanBurkleo, Kermit L. Hall, and Robert J. Kaczorowski

p. cm.

Includes index.

ISBN 0-7006-1153-3 (cloth : alk. paper) — ISBN 0-7006-1154-1 (pbk. : alk. paper)

1. Constitutional history—United States. 2. Culture and law—History. I. VanBurkleo, Sandra F., 1944- II. Hall, Kermit III. Kaczorowski, Robert J.

KF4541 .C5895 2002

342.73'029—dc21

2001005036

British Library Cataloguing in Publication Data is available.

Printed in the United States of America

10 9 8 7 6 5 4 3 2 1

The paper used in this publication meets the minimum requirements of the American National Standard for Permanence of Paper for Printed Library Materials Z39.48-1984.

# Contents

# Foreword

Stanley N. Katz

In a famous essay in the 1963 *American Historical Review,* Paul L. Murphy urged historians that it was "time to reclaim" their rightful role as interpreters of the history of American law, "a vital area for which [they were] responsible."[1] Murphy was concerned because lawyers and judges were using history instrumentally to bolster their a priori contemporary political and legal goals. The result was "law office history," serving the goals of clients and ideologies rather than Clio, the muse of history. It was time, Murphy chided us, for the historians to reassert their professional right and duty to historicize constitutional law.

Murphy was not alone in condemning the inaccurate, obtuse, and sometimes perverted use of history in the courtroom. Other historians, political scientists, and many lawyers agreed. More important, the early 1960s were the time at which American legal history was emerging as a respectable field for law school scholarship and teaching, under the lead of Willard Hurst (University of Wisconsin Law School), Mark DeWolfe Howe (Harvard Law School), and others. This was the moment when modern approaches to the historical study of American law were beginning to take hold, the time at which the academic legal profession, at least, was paying attention to historians and to serious historical work.

But that had not always been the case, for historians had characteristically been treated rudely by their law school counterparts. Paul Murphy and my other constitutional historian friends all had scars. Let me give a personal example. In the late 1960s, I traveled to New York City to use some old and rare books in the Columbia

Law School Library. After I turned in my call slips and cooled my heels for what seemed a long time, a librarian informed me that I could not have the books. Why not? They were in the office of Professor Julius Goebel, an elderly and eminent legal historian who had refused to hand over the books, declaring that "Katz is not a lawyer and is not competent to read these books"! My friend, Columbia law professor Joseph Smith, later retrieved the volumes from Goebel's office so that I could read them, but the story dramatizes the gap between law school and liberal arts historians at that time. To some extent such attitudes intimidated the history department–based historians and kept us from undertaking important investigations. And, I confess, we frequently retaliated by deprecating the historical skills of the law school historians when we reviewed their books in historical journals.

The gap between legal and historical scholars still exists, though in subtler forms. It was the primary subtext for Murphy's complaint and exhortation in 1963, but even then things were changing for the better. At about the same time as my adventure with Goebel, I received a call from Professor Jerome Cohen of the Harvard Law School, asking if I would accept a fellowship to study law at Harvard. "We think your work in legal history is pretty good," Cohen said, "but we think it would be a lot better if you learned a little real law." Fair enough, I thought, and so did many other young historians who were offered the opportunity to attend law school for a period of time to sharpen their legal skills. Several of the contributors to this volume had similar experiences, and a few went the whole way and earned J.D. degrees. Correspondingly, many bright, historically inclined lawyers (such as William E. Nelson) earned Ph.D. degrees in history. Indeed, today many of our history graduate students already have law degrees, and most others have some significant legal training. Many teachers of legal history in history departments have law degrees, and most law school legal historians have Ph.D.'s. The emergence of legal history as a crossover professional field is what has most profoundly transformed our field both intellectually and in terms of good relations between law and history teachers.

The overt complaint in Murphy's "Time to Reclaim" was, however, that history was being used improperly, that the historical record was being ransacked in order to find arguments to serve instrumental purposes. Many years later Morton Horwitz characterized this abuse as "looking for one's friends in history." This is what Murphy meant by "law office" history, and it cannot go away entirely, since it will always be one of the necessary techniques of legal advocacy. But the fact is that, today, judges have a far superior secondary literature in legal history to draw on, and their clerks are more likely to have had some competent training in American legal history.

I think that Murphy's more subtle concern in "Time to Reclaim" was that law needed to be situated and understood in the context of social, political, and economic change. He thought of this as creating the "cultural" history of constitutional law and urged historians, at a time when we were breaking out from the narrow bonds of purely political history, to take a broadly historical view of the development of constitutional law. He wanted us, in other words, to look beyond legal doctrine and formal legal institutions to a holistic understanding of constitutionalism in American history.

A comparable "external" view of legal history was also what was being championed at this time by Willard Hurst, especially in his *Law and the Conditions of Freedom in the Nineteenth-Century United States.* Hurst saw law as much more than the work of courts and the opinions of judges, and he especially highlighted the impact of economic factors on legal change. This external history of law as it developed in this country in the 1950s and 1960s has come to dominate the field of American legal history. It also characterizes the work of Murphy's graduate students and of the contributors to this volume.

But the external history of law has been more dominant in American legal history than in constitutional history. Constitutional historians tend to focus on the larger conceptual systems of higher law that structure the activities of politics and positive law. Thus the study of individual cases, especially "great cases," and famous judges, along with a focus on leading doctrines, has tended to remain at the center of constitutional history at a time when it has nearly disappeared in legal history more generally. In part this is because so much of the writing in constitutional history has been done by law school constitutional law teachers, few of whom have historical training or interests, and by political scientists, whose intellectual agendas are seldom historical. Furthermore, apart from the students of Murphy, Harold Hyman, Stanley Kutler, Harry Scheiber, and a few others, the focus of the mainstream Hurstian legal historians has been on private and nonconstitutional public law.

This has not been accidental. Many of the new breed of externalist legal historians (especially Morton Horwitz) specifically rejected the study of constitutional law as being epiphenomenal to the development of private law and legislation, and therefore a diversion from the main agendas of the new legal history. This is to say that the Hurstian emphasis on law's structuring of everyday life and its deprecation of appellate law have tended to disparage historical scholarship on constitutional—the ultimately abstract and appellate—law. Harry Scheiber noted and complained about this unfortunate development many years ago, and even Horwitz has recently turned to the writing of rather traditional constitutional history. But, on the whole, the impact of the emergence of Hurstian legal historical scholarship has been to shove constitutional history into a corner, where it has mainly been attended to by other than historically trained scholars.

What this volume shows is why constitutional history should not have been deprecated and ignored by the mainstream of our profession. As the introduction demonstrates, these essays illustrate the rich possibilities for an external or (as Murphy would have had it) cultural approach to constitutional law—an approach taken as comfortably in law schools as in history departments. And this reaffirmation of the importance of the new constitutional history could not be more timely, since we seem to be in the midst of a profound constitutional crisis at the beginning of the twenty-first century. I believe that constitutional history was tested and found wanting in 2000 when the debates over the constitutionality of the impeachment of President Clinton were marked by more heat than light. And the debate over *Bush v. Gore* has not been on a much higher level. The problem is in part that too few of our finest minds have been committed to the study of constitutional history, and therefore that we have too few public intellectuals to help us find our way intelligently through such crises. If the professionals and the public are to be truly and helpfully informed about such desperately immediate constitutional issues, we need to have a much richer cultural account of American constitutional history available for public discussion.

The good news is that we have begun to develop such a literature. The less good news is that not enough of us are taking up the challenge Paul Murphy put to us to do the scholarship properly, and to help both the legal profession and the public understand why history matters. The bad news is that the road is long, and we have far to go.

Note

1. Paul L. Murphy, "Time to Reclaim: The Current Challenge of American Constitutional History," *American Historical Review* 69 (1963): 64.

# Introduction

By any measure Paul L. Murphy, former Regents Professor of History and American Studies at the University of Minnesota, was a remarkable scholar of the American Constitution. Of all of the qualities that shone through his scholarship, however, none was of more lasting significance than his insistence on employing the history of constitutional law as a window on the larger American soul. His seminal essay, "Time to Reclaim: The Current Challenge of American Constitutional History," argued passionately that the study of America's constitutional past was too important to be left to lawyers and judges.[1] According to Murphy, both were notoriously bad students of history, in large measure because they approached it as advocates rather than scholars. One of the most alarming consequences of such an approach was that insight based on an understanding of the historical context took a backseat to formulating an appealing brief. The lawyer's goal was to win the case, not to win a lasting insight. The appellate judge's aim was to use those arguments to frame an opinion, thereby placing the judge in the position of actually being able to freeze the past by stating "legally" what it meant. Murphy challenged historians to "reclaim" constitutional history from lawyers and judges.

In Murphy's view, such a restoration would enrich judicial and public policy, advance a tradition of justice worthy of America's democratic aspirations, and, most important, afford Americans a clearer understanding of their rights. This emphasis on the importance of rights reflected Murphy's intellectual coming-of-age amid the anticommunist and anti-intellectual hysteria of the era of Senator Joseph McCarthy. Murphy was acutely aware of how quickly rights could be undermined by a lawyer's or judge's sloppy—but authoritative—reading of the past.

Once "law office history" had been relegated to the dustbin, Murphy insisted, policy decisions might better reflect the aspirations of the American people. Murphy reminded his readers that in coming to terms with American law, either public or private, context counted for a great deal. Students of the American constitutional past could not simply limit their inquiry to printed legal documents (e.g., statutes and judicial reports); instead, they had also to canvass the relevant archival sources. Legal documents, Murphy argued, had to be interpreted in light of the influences that shaped them and why judges had interpreted them as they did. The scholar or judge who took formal documents at face value and ignored the context from which they emerged did so at his or her scholarly peril. The essays in this volume follow in that rich tradition, seeking insights into the development of the American constitutional tradition through a wide array of primary and often nonlegal materials.

Murphy's scholarship was true to these principles. His major historical works on the twentieth-century Supreme Court and on the First Amendment stressed the value of reading constitutional developments from the outside in.[2] What stirred Murphy's scholarly interest most fully was what he liked to call the cultural history of law. Any explanation of the nation's legal past, in his view, had always to be linked to the cultural assumptions that informed that past. Murphy, for example, doubted the value of studying exclusively the original meaning of the text authored by the framers, since, even if we could know with certainty the abstract meaning of those texts (something that Murphy doubted), that did not solve the problems facing a historian: What did the text mean in the societal context in which it was written? How would its meaning change when interpreted in a new and different context and by an entirely new generation? While lawyers, judges, and constitutional theorists might argue about the wisdom of adapting old texts to new contexts, the historian had the practical problem of explaining contextual change and the related problem that developed when, as was true with the case of slavery and civil rights, change did not come as quickly as some desired. Far from living in an ivory tower of scholarship, historians had the quite practical task of accounting for why the Constitution has been adapted to succeeding waves of social, political, and economic change. Murphy was as keen as any scholar to discuss the theoretical problems associated with maintaining fidelity to the founder's ideas, but he also knew that for all of the persistence of basic constitutional values there were also notable examples of old constitutional ideas, such as substantive economic due process of law in the 1930s, yielding new constitutional understandings. Simply put, what the framers wanted often was not what a subsequent generation, confronted with a host of new issues, wanted—or needed.

Murphy, however, was not a relativist. Even as he warned of the dangers of freezing history into a series of Mount Rushmore-like "truths," he also genuinely believed in the law's goodness and in the value of its neutrality. To that extent he was a modern-day legal liberal committed to the idea that a genuinely democratic process would produce "good" legislation. He also believed that judges had a countermajoritarian responsibility to strike down "bad" legislation and that in so doing they had the obligation to inform their decisions with a sophisticated interpretation of history. The great virtue of a constitution was that it provided an ongoing limit against inevitable governmental abuse of power, and Murphy concluded that one of the most important ways to prevent such abuse was for the judiciary to test old constitutional propositions against new social and economic circumstances.

Murphy's reading of the American constitutional tradition was hopeful at best and naive at worst. Not surprisingly, the legal-liberal view with which Murphy was so associated has been subjected to a searching interrogation by several authors in this volume, which is exactly what Murphy would have wanted. Before all else, he believed in the possibility of advancing knowledge by subjecting received traditions to the acid tests of evidence and critical intelligence. If "truth" would always elude even the best historians, scholars surely could hope to be faithful to the sources and advance the cause of a democracy faithful to the public memory.

Still, what made Murphy's work so attractive and influential was its insistence upon cultural sensitivity and its illumination of the historical tensions that framed social choices. For example, his brilliant study of *Near v. Minnesota* (1931) bristled with insight into the conservative and progressive tensions of early twentieth-century Minnesota.[3] His magisterial examination of the Supreme Court from World War I through the era of Chief Justice Earl Warren was studded with insights into the ways in which disputes between progressives and liberals, on the one hand, and conservatives, including reactionary groups such as the Ku Klux Klan, on the other, routinely produced a new synthesis of constitutional ideas.[4] Murphy's reading of this cultural history was often at variance with accepted wisdom. In his study of *Near*, for example, he concluded that seemingly liberal Minnesotans were often as willing to clamp limits on freedom of expression as were their supposedly less sympathetic conservative tormentors.[5]

Professor Murphy died in 1997, in the last year of his presidency of the American Society for Legal History. His former students and many friends decided to use the occasion of his passing to reflect not so much on the man and the scholar, although these would surely have been worthy topics, but instead to reexamine the state of American constitutional history—much as Murphy himself had done in "Time to Reclaim." The essays that follow explore American constitutional development as a democratizing project in the context of the appropriateness of the legal-liberal tradition in which Murphy and other scholars of his day wrote.[6] The essays, for example, explore the ways in which some previously excluded groups have come more fully into the Constitution's orbit of rights. They also serve to remind us of one of the central themes of Murphy's writing: the contingent nature of limits on the powers of government and the often ephemeral quality of rights, especially in times of political and social upheaval. Rights tend to be brought under the greatest stress when we most need them.

In recent years the field of American constitutional history has been subjected to considerable remapping in light of findings in adjacent areas of American history, notably, legal and social history.[7] Only some of these changes can be attributed to the demand for fresh scholarship during the various bicentennials celebrated between 1976 and 1991. The rest have to do with the imperatives of new schools of thought within the academy generally (e.g., the new social history, feminist theory, critical race theory, the "cultural turn," the "linguistic turn") that stress the informal components of American constitutionalism and the countervailing pressures of a conservative, law-and-Supreme-Court-centered tradition of scholarship.[8]

Self-examination by constitutional historians has produced uncertainty and even confusion about the value of studying formal structures, such as courts and legal doctrine. Many of the essays in this volume, however, underscore the value of continuing to interrogate formal structures and doctrines, even to the point in some instances of rejecting the proposition that doctrinal history is old hat and hopelessly reactionary. Doctrine, we believe, continues to matter, although as several of the essays make clear, it does so in ways different from the traditional practice of reading it as ideas disembodied from their social context. Until scholars manage to find a third way between the Solomon's choice of "internal" and "external" vantage points, tensions between those scholars who rely solely on one or the other of these perspectives will continue to bedevil—and limit—constitutional history.

The essays that follow provide a panorama of rapidly changing subfields and methodological controversies. The essays do not, however, cover every possible perspective. We have not included an essay, for example, about the role of judicial policy in shaping American Indian-white relations (an area of interest to Murphy in the last years of his career); nor do the contributors address fully recent efforts by Barry Cushman, Robert Post, John Phillip Reid, and other scholars to develop a completely "internal" or "forensic" history of the Constitution.[9] There is only slight attention to state and territorial constitutional developments, although scholars such as Kermit Hall, Donald Lutz, G. Alan Tarr, and Robert Williams have demonstrated the central role of these developments in the American constitutional tradition.[10] The contributors, however, do remind us of a number of weaknesses in contemporary historical writing about constitutionalism and rights—among them, a resistance to the idea of writing about rights consciousness or human experience with constitutionalism; unresolved anxieties about the nature of Supreme Court history and constitutional history broadly conceived; the absence of a map of intersections between "public" and "private" law; the historians' and legal theorists' ongoing fascination with constitutional originalism and the analytic categories associated with it; and, on the other side, the social or cultural historians' general insensitivity to the power of appellate courts, judicial public policy, and constitutional norms.

Part One, "Constitutional Contexts," includes three synthetic essays that link constitutional law to society and culture. Each of these essays situates a particular constitutional development in a historical context. David Konig's essay, "Constitutional Contexts," deals explicitly with the eighteenth-century "founding"—the Philadelphia Convention of 1787—in order to address questions about the historians' responsibility in the quest for the framers' original intentions. Konig amends Jack Rakove's prize-winning monograph, *Original Meanings,* which brought the methods and insights of historical scholarship to bear upon the question of "original intent" across a broad range of topical heads.[11] Rakove concluded that, in many cases, unequivocal statements about "intentions" simply cannot be made. While praising this effort, Konig insists that scholars and public officials must confront not only the framers' ideas about the Constitution in historical context but also their theoretical assumptions about history and the uses to which it might be put. "To impute a 'founding' that stood apart from history," he writes, "corrupts their appreciation of the way that their revolution was embedded in history, and history in it."

Two additional essays carry the theme of context into later periods of American history. In "The Inverted Constitution," Robert J. Kaczorowski examines how contextual change alters the meaning of legal doctrine. He explores the ironic process by which Civil War era Americans creatively invoked doctrine originally designed to protect the preeminent right recognized in the early nineteenth century—the right to property—and in particular to enforce the right of slave owners to their peculiar property. In framing a sweeping interpretation of the Fourteenth Amendment's guarantees of citizenship rights, the Reconstruction Congress adapted fugitive slave law to secure the rights of all citizens. Kaczorowski urges constitutional historians to understand the Civil War "framing" process on its own terms, without the usual distortions from scholarly aversion to slavery. William M. Wiecek, in "The Rise and Fall of Classical Legal Thought," similarly supplies the New Deal Supreme Court's "judicial revolution of 1937" with doctrinal as well as social underpinnings. The essay is notable for its emphasis on doctrine as an important element of historical context, particularly in scholarly attempts to say how and why the events of 1937 were "revolutionary," and may well point the way to surmounting the internal-external dichotomy. Wiecek maintains that a signal achievement of the New Deal was its severance of constitutional law from its traditional moorings in classical legal theory—a source of moral and constitutional authority for all branches of government, but especially for the Supreme Court. As a result, according to Wiecek, the Court has become subject to the forces of history, with disastrous consequences for its legitimacy and authority in the years since the "court-packing" episode.

Part Two moves the New Deal story forward into recent times. Presented roughly in chronological order, these chapters emphasize civil rights and civil liberties, areas that have come to be synonymous with modern American constitutional history. In "Free Speech and the Bifurcated Review Project," G. Edward White at once complements and tacitly corrects Barry Cushman's important arguments in *Rethinking the New Deal Court*. White concludes that the Supreme Court's post-1937 "revolution" built upon foundations in First Amendment jurisprudence rather than in political economy cases (e.g., *Nebbia v. New York* [1934]), as Cushman and others contend.[12] White affirms the ongoing importance of doctrinal matters for constitutional historians without denying the influence of external sociocultural forces in the making of judicial public policy.

Three essays bring impressive archival research to bear upon a received tradition and find it wanting. In "The Roles of Lawyers in a Civil Liberties Crisis," Harry N. Scheiber and Jane L. Scheiber uncover the strange bedfellows created as Hawaiians struggled to put an end to the wholesale suspension of basic procedural rights, long after a wartime emergency had passed. The American Civil Liberties Union and kindred organizations lined up with corporate leaders and political conservatives to defend citizens' basic freedoms. Based on extensive archival research and oral histories, the Scheibers reinterpret the Japanese-American internment cases and cast serious doubt on the conventional wisdom about the behavior and motives of President Franklin D. Roosevelt's allies.

Cynthia Harrison's essay, "Constitutional Equality for Women," similarly relies on fresh evidence to correct misreadings of the "original intentions" of the framers of the Equal Rights Amendment (ERA). In her examination of recent developments in equal protection jurisprudence as they affected women, Harrison argues that the complex aspirations of the original framers of the ERA may ironically have been realized. To make the case, she leans heavily upon unconventional sources and extensive knowledge of the main players in the events of 1920–23, when the ERA first emerged. In "The Warren Court and Equality," Michal R. Belknap also interrogates a received tradition in liberal accounts of the Warren Court's accomplishments. In his view, scholars simply have not attended sufficiently to the details of Warren Court decisions. As a result, they have missed the justices' abhorrence of both civil disobedience and political radicalism. Despite a literature that praises the Court for its supposedly single-minded defense of the equality principle, Belknap finds competing values and conflicting principles. Some of these values effectively sabotaged the Court's equality-centered agenda; others drove the justices into remarkably traditional positions. Among other contributions, Belknap's essay affirms the value of primary nonlegal sources as part of any attempt to reimagine and rewrite American constitutional history.

Two other chapters in this part also use archival resources and oral histories to build case biographies that enrich the narrative of modern constitutional development. These case studies underscore the value of approaching the high court not as a fount of judicial wisdom but as the flash point of embedded social conflicts that seek resolution through constitutional adjudication. This approach means that in many ways the "external" story of a case (the way in which it made its way to the high court) is as important as what happened to it once it landed on the docket. Such an approach has particular value in opening constitutional history to the light of human drama. John W. Johnson, in "The Overlooked Litigant in *Tinker v. Des Moines Independent Community School District*," persuasively argues that this litigant, while hidden from "official" view, probably held the trump card in the case and, in later years, *lived* the human consequences of a change in judicial public policy much more completely than did the Tinkers. Johnson's essay reminds us of the value of looking beyond the formal edges of a case as defined by lawyers and judges.

In much the same way, Kermit L. Hall argues in "Cultural History and the First Amendment: *New York Times v. Sullivan* and Its Times" that some of the most arresting features of the nation's greatest political libel case occurred before the litigants ever walked into the Supreme Court. Whereas scholars typically describe *Sullivan* as a shining moment in the Supreme Court's defense of the First Amendment rooted in a bias toward the civil rights movement, Hall insists that the southern protagonists in the initial lawsuit held a view of habits and manners of civility that were altogether supportable in the context of Alabama's local culture. In Hall's view, a long-standing tradition of civility among southerners, even if tainted by racism, was sacrificed on the civil liberties altar. While the Court indeed advanced important constitutional values, it did so at considerable social and cultural costs, particularly with regard to the quality of journalistic practices.

Part Three, even more completely than the first two parts of the book, is speculative and intellectually restless; it seeks new directions. While the essays by no means exhaust the envelope-pushing possibilities in the field, they do suggest something of the range of new thinking, particularly among historians interested in expanding constitutional history's focus to include previously excluded subjects and texts. These essays borrow eclectically from adjacent disciplines such as anthropology, literary theory, political science, gender studies, and critical race theory.

The first chapter in this part underscores the importance of human agency and rights consciousness in forging constitutional and cultural change. In "'Words as Hard as Cannon-Balls,'" Sandra F. VanBurkleo explores possible intersections between constitutional and women's history. The essay focuses on nineteenth-century women's experiences of speech freedom and the partial elision of the struggle for liberty of speech with suffragism, particularly after the Civil War, when women's loss of constitutional ground led many activists to think that a metaphoric "voice" (the ballot) would be more effective than face-to-face confrontations with men in debating halls and newspaper columns. It also examines the masculine character of First Amendment freedoms, at least in practice, and the possibility of remaking the narrative of American constitutional history to take account of female and, by extension, black and working-class experiences of freedom.

Mark Tushnet's "Race, State, Market, and Civil Society in Constitutional History" also mounts a critique of conventional scholarly practice. In a sweeping study of American law practice since the founding, he finds racial "markers" in regions of law quite remote from the law of slavery and contends that such marking effectively binds seemingly disparate realms of human activity together, such as the state, the market, and civil society. To say, as historians sometimes do, that "race" happens in the law only within certain jurisprudential limits misses the pervasiveness of racism in the system and, indeed, the law's accommodation of racist values. Tushnet's essay casts doubt on formal categories of not only historical but also legal analysis, perhaps paving the way for an entire revision of the received wisdom about the role of race in the American constitutional tradition.

Finally, Norman L. Rosenberg cross-examines scholarly assumptions about primary sources. In "Constitutional History and the 'Cultural Turn,'" Rosenberg emphasizes the importance of moving beyond a received canon of "constitutional texts" to understand how law makes culture and culture makes law. Only by expanding the canon to include a broader range of texts, such as movies, he argues, will scholars begin to appreciate the power of constitutional law and institutions within the larger culture. Even more important, Rosenberg insists that by examining other texts for the meaning of constitutionalism, scholars will be forced to take culture a good deal more seriously as a part of constitutional history than they presently do. To make these points, Rosenberg appraises four Henry Fonda films and the ways in which an iconic "star" both conveyed and helped to conserve bedrock American values (among them, the sanctity of the Constitution and of republicanism). Movies and other nonlegal texts can maintain the fabric of constitutionalism much more effectively than judges or journalists might do, say, by reading an opinion in open court or by spreading sensational cases, such as *Gideon v. Wainwright* (1963) or *Roe v. Wade* (1973), over the front page of newspapers. Rosenberg thus shows how constitutional history might be enriched by embracing some of the insights and methods of "cultural studies" and postmodern critical theory.

The book commences with a foreword by one of the deans of American constitutional history, Stanley N. Katz. In an invitation to readers that is at once personal and professional, Katz briefly explores the history of the field and the place that the present volume occupies in that history. Katz concludes—and we agree—that, despite important advances in recent decades, Murphy's vision has not yet been fully realized.

This volume, we trust, offers a prospectus for the future of American constitutional history. We have made no attempt to force authors to reconcile apparently contradictory findings. These tensions—the fruits of the intellectual ferment that Paul Murphy so prized—give rise to bedrock questions: Does the study of the national Constitution, of state constitutions, of formal constitutional institutions, and of the formal actors in those institutions (judges, justices, and lawyers) have a future? The answer is surely, yes. These essays also suggest, however, that business as usual, by itself, will not reclaim the important position that constitutional history once commanded in the academy. Is there a place for doctrinal and institutional studies in a culturally responsive history of American constitutionalism? The answer is certainly, yes, since to ignore both would lead to an enormous distortion of our special form of representative democracy. Is there room for innovation in a field long regarded as one of the flagships of traditional history writing? Again, the answer is a resounding yes. Indeed, what these essays tell us most compellingly is that the best way to restore value to the scholarly study of constitutionalism is to remember the social and cultural contexts, to appreciate the continuing necessity of archival research, to seek ways to escape the "external-internal" dilemma, to credit the value of new approaches and perspectives, and to accept that, in the end, the best way to explain the history of rights is to remember the courage of the people who had sufficient conviction to put the judges through their constitutional paces.

Sandra F. VanBurkleo, Detroit, Michigan
Kermit L. Hall, Logan, Utah
Robert J. Kaczorowski, New York, New York

Notes

1. Paul L. Murphy, "Time to Reclaim: The Current Challenge of American Constitutional History," *American Historical Review* 69 (October 1963): 64–79.

2. Paul L. Murphy, *The Constitution in Crisis Times, 1918–1969* (New York: Harper and Row, 1972); Murphy, *Meaning of Freedom of Speech: First Amendment Freedoms from Wilson to FDR* (Westport, Conn.: Greenwood Press, 1972); Murphy, *World War I and the Meaning of Civil Liberties in the United States* (New York: Norton, 1979); and Murphy, "*Near v. Minnesota* in the Context of Historical Developments," *Minnesota Law Review* 66 (November 1981): 95–106.

3. Murphy, "*Near v. Minnesota*," 157.

4. Murphy, *Constitution in Crisis Times*, 458–85.

5. Murphy, "*Near v. Minnesota*," 158–60.

6. On the rise and significance of legal liberalism, see Laura Kalman, *The Strange Career of Legal Liberalism* (New Haven, Conn.: Yale University Press, 1996).

7. See, e.g., Hendrik Hartog, "The Constitution of Aspiration and the 'Rights That Belong to Us All,'" *Journal of American History* 74 (December 1987): 1013–34; and Harry N. Scheiber, "American Constitutional History and the New Legal History: Complementary Themes in Two Modes," *Journal of American History* 68 (September 1981): 337–50.

8. These developments have moved the analysis of constitutional development away from formal and toward informal structures and understandings. For a particularly helpful, as well as brilliant, introduction to the concept of informal constitutionalism, see Wayne D. Moore, *Constitutional Rights and Powers of the People* (Princeton, N.J.: Princeton University Press, 1996).

9. See, e.g., Barry Cushman, *Rethinking the New Deal Court: The Structure of a Constitutional Revolution* (New York: Oxford University Press, 1998); Robert Post, *Constitutional Domains: Democracy, Community, Management* (Cambridge, Mass.: Harvard University Press, 1995); and John P. Reid, *In Defiance of the Law: The Standing-Army Controversy, the Two Constitutions, and the Coming of the American Revolution* (Chapel Hill: University of North Carolina Press, 1981).

10. Kermit L. Hall, "Mostly Anchor and Little Sail: The Evolution of American State Constitutions," in *Toward a Usable Past: Liberty Under State Constitutions*, ed. Paul Finkelman and Stephen E. Gottlieb (Athens: University of Georgia Press, 1991), 338–418; Donald S. Lutz, *Popular Consent and Popular Control: Whig Political Theory in the Early State Constitutions* (Baton Rouge: Louisiana State University Press, 1980). G. Alan Tarr, *Understanding State Constitutions* (Princeton, N.J.: Princeton University Press, 1998); and Robert F. Williams, ed., *State Constitutional Law: Cases and Materials* (Washington, D.C.: Advisory Commission on Intergovernmental Relations, 1990).

11. Jack N. Rakove, *Original Meanings: Politics and Ideas in the Making of the Constitution* (New York: Knopf, 1996).

12. Cushman, *Rethinking the New Deal Court.*

*Part I*

# Constitutional Contexts

*Chapter One*

# Constitutional Contexts: The Theory of History and the Process of Constitutional Change in Revolutionary America

David Thomas Konig

Every student of the American Constitution is aware of the frequent references to history in the framing and ratification process between 1787 and 1791. "Publius," the collective author of *The Federalist,* explicitly cites "history" thirty-three times in a recitation of cautionary tales and laudable exempla.[1] Not least among these unhappy experiences was a recent "melancholy and monitory lesson of history" growing out of failed "experiments" by "extraordinary assemblies convened for the special purpose" of establishing a permanent structure of government. Every attempt at union had fallen prey to "constitutional vices" and to the inevitable and irresistible temptation to place unwarranted faith in a final and definitive "remedy" capable of providing structure and interpretive authority based on legitimation in a great culminating act of popular sovereignty.[2]

Invoking the authority of a "special" moment in the past had little less force in 1787 than it does today. Although the concept of coherent and conclusive historical intent is itself ahistorical,[3] a search for some type of historical "fidelity" remains persistently attractive and intellectually legitimate among scholars.[4] This support derives not only from the political motives of many "originalist" advocates but also from broader cultural sympathies among those who oppose that concept. After all, history always has played a major role in constitutional interpretation, and the framers themselves appealed to history throughout the process of drafting and ratification.[5] Indeed, James Madison conceded the undeniable value of historical legitimacy when he referred in *The Federalist* to "that veneration, which time bestows on every thing, and without which perhaps the wisest and freest governments would not possess the requisite stability."[6]

Challenges to the use of history in constitutional interpretation, however, are as old as the Republic itself. It is ironic, then, that many originalist constitutional scholars have been less faithful *to* history than they have been to their claim of being faithful to the Constitution *through* history.[7] William Nelson's treatment of the effort to recapture an originalist understanding of the Fourteenth Amendment, for example, reiterates the "sound historical insight that two inconsistent but well-documented interpretations of the past are both partially correct."[8] For the constitutional founding, the problems multiply with problems of evidentiary gaps, manifest biases in record keeping, linguistic anachronisms, varying rhetorical conventions, political and economic contingency, and intractable interpretive problems.[9]

Many opponents of originalism therefore now classify the search for definitive statements about the framers' intent with the more egregious types of "law office history" that Mark DeWolfe Howe condemned in 1965: "By superficial and purposive interpretations of the past, the [Supreme] Court has dishonored the arts of the historian and degraded the talents of the lawyer."[10] Indeed, a consensus now seems to be emerging among constitutional scholars that we have seen "the end of the originalism debate" and that it is time to drop "the baggage of an old and unhelpful debate about the relationship between original meaning and constitutional interpretation."[11] But (perhaps because of this) the problem is not over for historians, and the injunction that the historian Paul Murphy delivered in 1963 remains true at the beginning of a new century: that "what is needed from historians is the most accurate, thoroughly documented, and impeccable history we are capable of producing."[12]

Such a goal not only maintains a faithfulness *to* the past as that goal is understood today; it also respects the way the founders themselves approached the historical enterprise and acknowledged its limitations. John Adams, for example, consulted numerous "passages of law and history" in 1773 to understand the doctrine of judicial independence, but he honestly confessed that faithfulness to history did not fit his forensic purposes. Although he might be confident enough to argue what, historically, that doctrine had *not* meant, he refused to make any grander claims. As he told his readers, "I have done little more than labor in the mines of ore and the quarries of stones. The materials are at the service of the public; and I leave them to the jeweller and lapidary, to refine, fabricate, and polish them."[13]

It is the purpose of this chapter to acknowledge Adams's insight and to concentrate on what Jack Rakove has called "thinking about the original meanings, intentions, and understandings of 1787–91 as a problem of historical knowledge,"[14] rather than an exercise in the theory or methodology of constitutional interpretation. Rather than arguing what history finds in the framers, therefore, the present chapter attempts to understand what the framers found in history. This is thus a two-tiered question about historical knowledge—ours and the framers'. What can we know about how the framers themselves thought of history? To what extent can we uncover the value and purposes that they derived from their knowledge of human history?

In some respects this question has been answered many times. It is hardly a revelation to invoke the historical consciousness of the Revolutionary generation; many scholars have remarked on the value of the past to the framers. It is now a commonplace to point out the framers' conventional understanding that monarchy always degenerated into tyranny, aristocracy into faction, and democracy into anarchy. In this way the framers understood the forces leading the British to adopt a system of mixed government.[15] The past taught, too, of the inevitable menace of power to liberty, and thus of the need to be ever vigilant against usurpation by grasping princes. Perhaps the work that best conveys the way in which historical example provided an overriding sense of inevitable menace and impending crisis is Bernard Bailyn's *Ideological Origins of the American Revolution.* The tradition of English Whig polemical literature, Bailyn has shown, contained within it a "theory of politics" rooted in and demonstrated by the historically repeated threat of "power" to "liberty." Seeing themselves as part of this process, Bailyn's American colonists embraced a cautionary tradition that foreshadowed an ever-worsening decline into tyranny and demanded that they act immediately before all was lost. With independence achieved, the frightening political experiences of the 1770s and 1780s pushed them to unforeseen innovations in government and a written Constitution that "fulfilled" the Revolution.[16]

Bailyn's insight, which added a "fulfillment" to the question of Revolutionary origins he had described in the first edition of his book, opens a line of inquiry that scholars have begun but not completed: Once the sword was drawn and the tyrant slain, what came next? What did history tell them about the prospect of successful change? But here, too, our received wisdom stops short. We know that they saw the end of one regime led to the establishment of another, but a "revolution" meant only a return to a point of origination on an endlessly and grimly repeating cycle.[17] This was so because, as Douglas Adair demonstrated in a now-famous essay in 1968, human nature remained unchanged and prone to the same flaws that had led to downfall in the past. David Hume's theory of human personality held pride of place in Adair's influential essay. Wrote Hume,

> Mankind are so much the same, in all times and places, that history informs us of nothing new or strange, in this particular. Its chief use is only to discover the constant and universal principles of human nature, by showing men in all varieties of circumstances and situations, and furnishing us with materials, from which we may form our observations and become acquainted with the regular springs of human action and behavior.[18]

With its implications of timeless and unchanging human ways throughout the past, Hume's analysis has provided an implicit but powerful suggestion of the way eighteenth-century Americans viewed history and applied "constant and universal principles" to constitution making. But the comment must not be taken out of its proper contexts—not only of its time but also of its place in Hume's thinking.

To begin with, this remark appears in Hume's *Enquiry Concerning Human Understanding* (1748), a work intended to describe human psychology (which it did in a very conventional eighteenth-century manner) and not history or politics. Hume gained vastly more attention with his *History of England* (1754–62).[19] As late as 1810, a hostile Thomas Jefferson remarked that the *History* had become "the manual of every student" and "still continues to be put into the hands of all our young people." Jefferson had by then come to anathematize Hume as an "apologist" for the Stuarts' heretical denial of the principle "that the people are the origin of all just power," but he conceded its influence on him many years earlier as he "devoured it when young." Hume's appeal had rested on a compelling story—both implicit and explicit—about history and the preservation of English liberty.[20]

Hume's *History* based a drama of human ambition, deceit, and tragedy on the psychological constants of the human mind. With unquestioning faith in the truths of the *Enquiry Concerning Human Understanding*—that human nature was ever the same—his readers were captivated by the fate of the boy princes in the Tower of London or repelled by the evil subtleties of avaricious clerics, "those numerous saints of the same stamp who disgrace the Romish calendar."[21] Eighteenth-century readers could identify with the feelings of victims and nod knowingly at the impulses of villains because they recognized these human impulses as the same as those prevailing in their own day.

But although *human nature* remained constant, the customs, norms, and political institutions that humans created did not. Hume's interpretation of history provided explicit examples to support the theory that liberty drew its strength from the progress of society. "One chief advantage which resulted from the introduction and progress of the arts," he wrote of the fifteenth century, "was the introduction and progress of freedom."[22] By 1600, he wrote in volume 6, "the minds of men throughout Europe, especially in England, seem to have undergone a general, but insensible revolution." While on the Continent "this universal fermentation" had produced absolutism, the case was otherwise in England, where "the love of freedom . . . acquired new force, and was regulated by more enlarged views, suitably to that cultivated understanding, which became, every day, more common among men of birth and education."[23] Parliament men resisted overt efforts to reverse these changes when, for example, they opposed James I's attempt to expand his prerogative by appealing to "its first origin" many centuries earlier.[24] Custom, and the gradual accretions of change, had become the foundation of English liberty. Conversely, Hume defended Elizabeth's vast enlargement of royal authority. Criticizing Elizabeth's Puritan opponents for their politically motivated invocation of the past, he recalled the crimes of the reign of Richard III and warned, "Those who, from a pretended respect to antiquity, appeal at every turn to an original plan of the constitution, only cover their turbulent spirit and their private ambition under the appearance of venerable forms." Indeed, he went on, "a civilized nation, like the English . . . ought to be cautious in appealing to the practices of their ancestors, or regarding the maxims of uncultivated ages as certain rules for their present conduct."[25] Any appeal to "the ancient constitution," in fact, could always be trumped by "still a more ancient constitution," he noted. "The English constitution, like all others, has been in a state of continual fluctuation."[26] Hume, then, was not invoking the *past* so much as *history*—the process of "mutability that has attended all human institutions."[27] Star Chamber might well have suited the age of the Tudors, but it had no place "in a more advanced stage of society."[28]

Reference to the ancient constitution, of course, had been a mainstay of polemical literature in the era of the English civil war, when opponents sought to break the "Norman yoke" enforced by the Stuarts. They celebrated a counternarrative of the English legal past, one of an ancient constitution of liberty existing since time "immemorial." But even this account of the past privileged process over event. The ancient constitution, it must be emphasized, had existed without any identifiable founder or act of creation and had been embraced long before that foreign French "intrusion," as John Pocock refers to it, had been clamped upon their freeborn ancestors. That it was "traceable to no original act of foundation" was a jurisprudential truism as well as a politically useful axiom: were it to derive from any such specific historical act of creation, it would be vulnerable to contingent historical forces and thus to control by the sovereign, an idea that could not be admitted. The claim to royal authority based on the historical act of the Conquest thus prompted a strong reaction by Parliament men and Puritans who elevated the liberties of the common law to challenge England's oppressive regime of absolutism.[29]

The enduring impact of this school of thought in American colonial development cannot be overemphasized. For this reason, it is entirely incorrect to write off the pre-Revolutionary tradition of historical thinking in America as one of "static originalism" producing the "cultural domination of American fundamentalist religion [that] also stood in the way of the rise of an historical consciousness" owing to the "religious focus on timeless truths outside of history."[30] Rather, a deep-rooted secular historiography of legal change and development had motivated and supported English constitutional reform. On political matters, American colonists looked to such historically minded men as John Selden, who refused to accept the notion of an unchanging body of "immemorial" custom and instead emphasized the slow but relentless ways that "questionless the *Saxons* made a mixture of the *British* customs with their own, the *Danes* with old *British*, that *Saxon* and their own; and the *Normans* the like."[31]

In its conventional form, then, the colonists' English rights rested on immemorial principles and evolved customary procedures to implement them. This is a well-known story. But one more aspect of their historical awareness needs to be added to this account: according to the way they saw the repetitive pattern of history, these established principles and procedures had to be guaranteed by the periodic assertive intervention of "whig" lawmakers and judges who purged their constitution of defects and devised new means to halt tyranny. The path of history demonstrated that constitutional continuity was not unbroken; it was, rather, a process punctuated by episodes of reform—and, if necessary, innovative reconstitution—of their governments in order to assure their constitutional inheritance of ancient English liberties. This process pervades Sir Matthew Hale's posthumously published historical treatise on English law, a work that had far more influence on American colonial thinking about law than any Puritan religious tract.[32]

Hale noted the "great Similitude that in many Things appears between the laws of England and those of Normandy," but he demonstrated how they diverged, too. One particular fiscal "tribute," for example, had been introduced and collected; despite this temporary usage, however, it "was never admitted in England . . . but was ousted by the first Law of King Hen[ry] I. as an usurpation." All in all, Hale argued that William of Normandy did not so much impose new law as confirm those laws of Edward the Confessor that still had meaning and utility in England.[33] Hale aptly compared England's legal history to that of the fabled vessel *Argonaut:*

> So that Use and Custom, and Judicial Decisions and Resolutions, and Acts of Parliament, tho' not now extant, might introduce some *New* Laws, and alter some *Old,* which we now take to be the very Common Law itself, tho' the Times and precise Periods of such Alterations are not explicitely or clearly known: But tho' those particular Variations and Accessions have happened in the Laws, yet They are the same English laws now, that they were 600 Years since in the general. As the Argonauts Ship was the same when it returned home, as it was when it went out, tho' in that long Voyage it had successive Amendments, and scarce came back with any of its former Materials.[34]

American whigs were not starting from scratch—from a blank slate or a state of nature—nor had they done so even in founding their own colonies. Contract theory may have undergirded their legal claim to their privileges and rights, but, as John Reid observes, this "original contract" had no true historical origins, and, in any case, "it said nothing explicit about the contract's terms."[35] Widely accepted as a useful concept, the very idea of an "original contract" as an artificially created event was a reification of a process for the sake of argument.

The persistence of politics won the day at the First Continental Congress when delegates debated the basis on which to make their appeal of American rights. According to John Adams's record, Richard Henry Lee ignited a lively debate when he asserted, "Our Ancestors found here no Government." After some support was expressed for his position, the weight of the discussion fell the other way. James Duane argued that the "Law of Nature" was but "a feeble Support," to which John Rutledge added, "The first Emigrants could not be considered as in a State of nature—they had no Right to elect a king."[36] No "state of nature" had existed in 1607, nor did one in 1776, 1781, or 1789.

No less a natural rights theorist than Thomas Jefferson had to caution against this notion, which he dubbed "the Vermont doctrine" after citizens in that region had declared a state of nature in order to invalidate competing claims to sovereignty there. Waiting in Baltimore in the winter of 1783 for an icebound harbor to thaw and allow him to depart for France, he learned of how the Virginia assembly had followed Vermont's lead into state-of-nature doctrine, which he labeled "a doctrine of the most mischievous tendency."[37] In Virginia, the assembly had declared property laws abrogated under a state of nature in order to legitimize the seizure of Tory assets. This declaration horrified Jefferson, who deplored such misinformed "talk of the dissolution of the social contract on a revolution of government, and much other little stuff by which I collect their meaning to have been that on changing the form of our government all our laws were dissolved, and ourselves reduced to a state of nature." Stressing the continuity of law, he warned that "the term *social contract*" should not "be forced from theoretical into practical use." This error he called "the Vermont doctrine against which the other states and Virginia most especially has been strenuously contending."[38]

Jefferson's vehemence is illuminating for its explicit rejection of an idea assumed to have been influential at the founding. Additionally, it provides us with another clear statement of a basic assumption underlying the establishment of the American constitutional order; namely, that a "foundation" was a substructure consisting of historic principles on which to build rather than an inscription made on the blank tablets of a state of nature. Parts of the social contract may be "amended," Jefferson explained, but it must be understood "that any of these may be amended without affecting the residue. If you and I have a contract of six articles and agree to amend two of them, this does not dissolve the remaining four."[39]

Reliance on historic principles as core beliefs and practices usually remained an unspoken starting point. To be sure, in the creative period of nation building after the War for Independence, the desire to purge the new polities of the corruptions of the British constitution led Americans to emphasize the novelty of their efforts. But such statements have a way of being taken out of context, thus distorting their real meaning. Such a context might be that of the particular issues under discussion at that particular time, the context of the larger document from which it was taken, or the larger context of the writer's other remarks that shed light on his meaning, not to mention the still broader context of contemporary usage. Indeed, among the most often quoted remarks to describe the 1780s as a point of constitutional origination is that of Dr. Benjamin Rush in 1786. It merits not only full quotation but also a proper contextualization:

> There is nothing more common than to confound the terms of the American Revolution with those of the American War. The American War is over: but this is far from being the case with the American Revolution. On the contrary, nothing but the first act of the great drama is closed. It remains yet to establish and perfect our new forms of government; and to prepare the principles, morals, and manners of our citizens, for these forms of government, after they are established and brought to perfection.[40]

Rush's famous comment belongs in the context of its purpose; as his title indicates, it assailed "the defects of the confederation." A physician whose many interests typified the broad-ranging combination of disciplines among many of his era, Rush wrote on the eve of the Annapolis Convention and trotted out the obvious problems of the Confederation: its "deficiency of coercive power," its lack of exclusive jurisdiction over currency and commerce, its unicameral legislature, and its "too frequent rotation of its members." What scholars overlook in using Rush's sweeping statement cited here is that in these flaws he—like so many others about to assemble in Philadelphia—recognized the need for some recourse to proven principles of stability in government. To Rush, the problem of instability and national weakness derived from an imprudent departure from traditional forms. Rotation in office, for example, had served only to eliminate from government those men who possessed an institutional memory capable of supplying this essential knowledge.[41]

Rush based his criticism of Pennsylvania's constitution on a similar notion: "No regard is paid in it," he explained, "to the ancient habits and customs of Pennsylvania in the distribution of the supreme power of the state, nor in the forms of business, or in the style of the Constitution."[42] His insistence on the continuity of "ancient habits and customs in Pennsylvania" reflected his concern, as a physician, with the physical effects of years of tumult. Reiterating his point that "the termination of the war by the peace in 1783, did not terminate the American Revolution," Dr. Rush made a diagnosis: "The excess of the passion for liberty, inflamed by the successful issue of the war, produced, in many people, opinions and conduct which could not be removed by reason nor restrained by government." The result was "a species of insanity, which I shall take the liberty of distinguishing by the name of *Anarchia*."[43]

The portrait of Rush as sweeping aside the past and announcing the advent of a new era—an original starting point, as it were—misinterprets his own caution and obscures the historical consciousness that informed him and other leaders of the public at the "founding" (a word that Publius does not use). They were, to be sure, *founding* something very new in its shape and particulars; what, precisely, *was* new, however, was a different matter, which will be discussed later. When they used the verb to "found," they most often did so by following it with a preposition for the purpose of explaining how the act was building *on* something; that something was usually drawn from the past and continuing a tradition, a principle drawn from the lessons of history, or the process of historical development.

Hints of such meanings emerge from the general way that this word and its variations are used in *The Federalist*—as well as in some revealing exceptions to the rule.[44] Although the emperor of "the Germanic Body" had the power "to found universities,"[45] for example, both his status (an imperial sovereign) and his creation (a corporation) would not apply to the founding of the federal government. Nor would Madison's comparison to the beginning ex nihilo of the Roman polity, whose "foundation . . . was laid by Romulus."[46]

The variety of historical experience described this process in different polities throughout the past. But to the typical (one might say, *conventional*) constitutional thinker of the eighteenth century, the apposite formula was a story of gradual progress marked by crises that had called forth heroic measures and acts to secure endangered rights or to redefine them—to articulate them in new forms—for the protection of liberty. English rights, history taught them, were secured and advanced at times of crisis or in struggles to reverse usurpations. The stimuli to recovery might be the Danes, the Normans, or the Stuarts; but in every case the English people had asserted their popular sovereignty, rallied to halt the decline, and provided new ways to retain old rights. It was within this theory of history that Thomas Jefferson found good resulting from tyranny. Writing from Paris about "the oppressions of monarchy" to Madison in 1787, he penned one of his most frequently quoted remarks: "Even this evil is productive of good. It prevents the degeneracy of government, and nourishes a general attention to the public affairs. I hold it that a little rebellion now and then is a good thing."[47]

James Wilson summed up this phenomenon when he delivered his lectures on constitutions and the common law at the College of Philadelphia in 1791. Quoting Bolingbroke, he described the British constitution as "a noble fabrick . . . raised by the labour of so many centuries, repaired at the expense of so many millions, and cemented by such a profusion of blood."[48] Unfortunately, Britain still did not have a true and complete constitution because, Wilson observed, its fabric of government remained too vulnerable as "the creature and the dependent of the legislative power." Royal authority, however, had been (at least partially) restrained by constitutional limitation, at a time of historical crisis and threat to liberty—an episode such as Bolingbroke's constitution being "repaired" and "cemented." The English in 1688 had risen up and reasserted "an original contract, made at some former distant period, between the king and the people. The terms of this contract have, indeed, been the subject of frequent and doubtful disputation," Wilson pointed out. Nonetheless, in the Glorious Revolution "some of them were reduced to a certainty," and on this "foundation is the monarchical part of the British constitution supported."[49] It was through the passage of historical time—not only the past but also the present and future—that the wisdom of the law would emerge, and for that reason Wilson approvingly quoted Bacon, "Sapientissima res tempus."[50]

Embedded in Wilson's description is a deep paradox explicable only by an awareness of how his generation's theory of history guided their thinking into new and creative channels even as it styled itself as continuous with the constitutional past. Wilson's purpose in discussing the British constitution was set out in the title of his lecture: "Comparison of the Constitution of the United States, with That of Great Britain." To Wilson, "no such thing as a constitution, properly so called, is known in Great Britain," for he was using the radically new definition of "constitution" that Americans had devised by the time he offered his law lectures in 1791.[51] The notion of a "constitution" as a written framework of government, specifying principles and procedures that were "reduced to a certainty" and elevated above the power of any constituent component—the legislature, especially—had no institutionalized precedent in British constitutional law. According to conventional theory, Parliament was part of the constitution, not subordinate to it, and Sir William Blackstone could thus complacently claim that "if the parliament will positively enact a thing to be done which is unreasonable, I know of no power that can control it."[52]

From Paris, Jefferson saw this historical pattern of legislative abuse of constitutional principles repeated. But it was not happening in France. In 1786 he had received word of how Americans had found themselves once again forced to resort to violence in the effort to secure their rights. Reflecting on Shays's Rebellion in Massachusetts, Jefferson wrote of his sympathy for the rebels: "What signify a few lives lost in a century or two? The tree of liberty must be refreshed from time to time with the blood of patriots and tyrants. It is it's natural manure."[53] Moreover, the people of Virginia faced the same possibility, for they were at the mercy of elected representatives who as an "ordinary legislature may alter the constitution itself."[54]

The problem confronting the Constitution's framers, of course, was *what* type of new institutional protections might be provided to protect liberty without recourse to the violence that had been provoked repeatedly in the course of British history. How might they build upon the foundation of their constitutional tradition to refresh the tree of liberty without the need to spill their own as well as tyrants' blood? Or, were the new states simply engaging in yet another ephemeral exercise in an inevitably bloody cycle of resistance and regression? Writing in 1774, long before the political instability of the 1780s would appear to repeat English constitutional history, James Wilson had cited the recurring problem his generation faced: "The constitution was ever fluctuating from one extreme to another; now despotism—now anarchy prevailed."[55]

The purpose of the Revolution was, of course, to change this historical cycle—but not to do so merely by halting despotism and returning to a status quo ante. Jefferson's reference to blood and the tree of liberty is a remark frequently taken out of the context that produced and followed it, for it was his wish—and ultimately it became his satisfied conviction—that the creative efforts of the founding would make recourse to violence unnecessary. He had written in 1785 of the impending crisis in Virginia:

> Our situation is indeed perilous, and I hope my countrymen will be sensible of it, and will apply, at a proper season, the proper remedy; which is a convention to fix the constitution, to amend its defects, to bind up the several branches of government by certain laws, which when they transgress their acts shall become nullities; to render unnecessary an appeal to the people, or in other words a rebellion, on every infraction of their rights.[56]

Though not a framer of the federal Constitution, Jefferson immersed himself in the reform of the Virginia constitution, and his concern about the legitimate and constitutional restraint of power addressed a problem engaging the minds of thoughtful—and worried—lawmakers. More particularly, he was drawing upon the historical lessons offered by a widely read constitutional treatise to prescribe an extraparliamentary convention that could establish unbreachable barriers to governmental tyranny. James Burgh described this practice in his *Political Disquisitions,* which Bernard Bailyn identifies as "the key book" in the Revolutionary generation's quest for sources and traditions.[57]

Burgh's "Conclusion"—which was "Addressed to the independent Part of the People of Great-Britain, Ireland, and the Colonies"—typified the way American and English opposition thinkers found their place in the continuum of historical time of which their constitution was a part, and his advertisement for the three volumes described them in such terms as to resonate with this awareness: they were "Calculated to Draw the Timely Attention of Government and People to a Due Consideration of the Necessity, and the Means, of Reforming Those Errors, Defects, and Abuses; of Restoring the Constitution, and Saving the State." Burgh's work had a powerful attraction to Americans because it confirmed the facts of what they were witnessing and made sense of them. By castigating "judge *Blackstone* as one of the many among us, who endeavor to lull us to sleep in this time of danger," Burgh echoed their distrust of his sanguine optimism about Parliament's self-correcting constitutionalism. He also explicitly drew the American historical experience into this sweep of time by pointedly praising New Englanders' participation in the Glorious Revolution. Their ouster of Sir Edmund Andros in 1689, he wrote, was one such time of constitutional crisis among the many that history provided.[58]

Burgh's history, though conventional in most respects, included two items that made it especially relevant to Americans. First, transatlantic events remained epiphenomenal to standard British historiography, and Burgh's inclusion of American participation in 1689 attracted the colonists by enlisting them in the long-term sweep of British constitutional history. But just as important, Burgh had imparted to that struggle a dynamic of change by emphasizing that sovereignty resided in the people, not the government. They conferred power on government, therefore, rather than the reverse. British history had been punctuated by episodes like the present, when tyranny aroused resistance, most recently in the Glorious Revolution when the people constituted themselves in an extraordinary "convention-parliament," a body "irregular in its construction" by its inclusion of many persons beyond the ordinarily elected legislative membership. Its achievement was to "bring about the greatest thing that ever was done for this island" by reducing its government to "first principles." He explained the process by quoting Pym's historical generalization: "Those commonwealths have been most durable, which have oftenest reformed, and re-composed themselves according to their first institution: for by this means they repair the breaches, and counter-work the natural effects of time."[59] But Burgh was not invoking the elusive and irretrievable institutions of a mythic origination. His historical consciousness prevented that: given the many instances in the past of innovation to check tyranny, he warned, "Let no man, therefore, object to a salutary proposal, that is new, unusual, or unheard of." Indeed, the "irregular" nature of the convention parliament now stood as a recent and demonstrably useful tool, and its being convened stood as an example for imitation in the present as a way of recapturing endangered principles or establishing them on better foundations. The efforts of 1688–89 had been "but an imperfect redress of grievances," and it was now once again necessary for the people to state (as the English "Cato" had done), "Here is the natural limitation of the magistrate's authority."[60]

For that reason, Burgh proposed a "GRAND NATIONAL ASSOCIATION FOR RESTORING THE CONSTITUTION." Again, he turned to history ("especially in England") for supporting examples of how such "acts of the people at large" had creatively restored liberty and secured rights by reforming institutions to preserve the constitution. "A parliament cannot annul the constitution," and a convention of the people could meet to prevent it from doing so. Such an association—which must include the Americans—would take its place in the sweep of the history of rights because it would be not only obstructive of tyranny but also creative in its solutions.[61]

Burgh's Britain did not convene such a "grand association" in the 1770s, but his orthodox recitation of English constitutional history harmonized with the sense of reemerging crisis among many Americans in the 1780s. So, too, did the concepts of sovereignty in the people and their periodic convening to devise new ways to implement first principles. As a result, when Wilson addressed the Pennsylvania ratifying convention in 1787, his listeners were familiar with the idea that a time of constitutional crisis and renewal was at hand, when they could participate in the grand sweep of the history of liberty. To their generation, then, had come the opportunity to act for the ages. "To control the power and conduct of the legislature by an overruling constitution," he explained, "was an improvement in the science and practice of government reserved to the American states."[62] As radical as their enterprise might seem, it had demonstrable precedent in the history of the English constitution, which gave meaning to the swirl of events since the Stamp Act Crisis. Despite—indeed, because of—the enormous political changes that had taken place in the intervening years, the prevailing theory of an ongoing, permanent constitutional revolution retained the meaning and attraction it had had in the 1770s.

Wilson's standard historical account, now matched in 1787 against the specific demands of the constitutional crisis before him, possessed a powerful and suggestive resonance for Americans. His historical narrative was ordinary, even trite; but the timelessly recurrent factors of tyranny and rescue, the abuse of power and the need for explicit and fixed limitations, and the assumptions about the enduring foundational sources of political authority in the people had a powerful appeal to the historical consciousness of the American people.

This theory of an ever-renewing constitutionalism allowed Wilson and others to place the process of constitutional "improvement" in the context of historical developments that challenged citizens to respond to threat and to devise new ways of preserving traditional rights. The British might deride American talk of rights and accuse them of creating new ones that had never existed under the British constitution, but their attacks misunderstood what John Reid calls the American "constitutional consciousness." Reid explains, "From the beginning to the end of the revolutionary controversy, American whigs relied on the same rights: their rights as Englishmen. It was parliamentary assertions of governmental power, not shifting colonial constitutional theory or aspirations, that caused different rights to be stressed in different years." The Americans were not discovering new rights but rather coming to realize that traditional rights "could be abused in ways previously not suspected or not understood."[63] Unwilling to trust to Blackstone's complacent confidence in Parliament's ultimate self-correcting nature at some distant and unspecified point in the future, they invoked the process of historical change to justify creating the formal mechanisms needed to preserve those rights on a regular basis.

Wilson's generation thus recognized that the principles of the revolution had to be institutionalized through written guarantees. That was the great step they took, for they acknowledged—history had shown them—that the future would inevitably bring new and unimagined threats. To create a permanent and ongoing revolution, then, was their constitutional purpose. "[R]evolution principles," as Wilson called them, were not "recognized by the

English constitution";[64] they would be by the United States Constitution, whose mechanisms would institutionalize popular sovereignty as a continuous process capable of accommodating the will of the people and ending the need for periodic violent uprising. It was this confidence that led Jefferson to his hopeful abandonment of his sympathies for refreshing the tree of liberty with the blood of tyrants and patriots. Despite his desire for a bill of rights and for rotation in office for the Senate and presidency, he praised the framing of the "new federal constitution" as "having set the world an example of a government reformed by reason alone without bloodshed."[65]

But where would America's "revolution principles" come from? Where *had* they come from in the first place? It is clear that they had no origination in any act of will, whether by an individual sovereign or a sovereign people convened to establish a compact ex nihilo among themselves. The past, in fact, could not be known with the certainty required to situate rights in. Present-day historians who rightly point out the basic epistemological difficulties of obtaining sufficient knowledge of the founding are amply supported by the framers' own skepticism about the historical accessibility of origins. Bolingbroke, to whom so many looked for guidance on these matters, typified the assault on sacred texts so prevalent in the seventeenth and (especially) eighteenth centuries.[66] Few ideas were more widely agreed upon in the historical thinking of the eighteenth century, in fact, than the difficulty of historical certainty. Although Blackstone had his own reasons for eschewing the constraints of legal origins, his warning about the "uncertainty of the true origin of particular customs" had such force that James Wilson closely paraphrased it for his law lectures.[67]

Present-day debates over constitutional origins, therefore, revisit ground that the framers themselves covered, and which they agreed was as infertile as it was irrelevant to constitutional interpretation. In his debate with William Brattle over the origins of judicial independence, John Adams acknowledged the limits of what we today would call originalism:

> I would not be understood, however, to lay any great stress on the opinions of historians and compilers of antiquities, because it must be confessed that the Saxon constitution is

> involved in much obscurity, and that the monarchical and democratic factions in England, by their opposite endeavors to make the Saxon constitutions swear for their respective systems, have much increased the difficulty of determining, to the satisfaction of the world, what that constitution, in many important particulars, was.[68]

Adams, like many other historians of English constitutional law, did not write off the past as useless, however. Vital to the rhetorical strategy and structure of his argument was his explanation of how the common-law principles of the English constitution had been historically developed and solidified.

Adams was no more rejecting history than Wilson would do. Both, however, were rejecting the concept of "origins" in favor of a different fundamental historical assumption about how rights and the principles that guaranteed them had emerged out of the historic past of the British people. Their history had shown them that instruments for protecting rights might emerge out of their prolonged experience of resisting corrupt officials, as well as from their periodic experience of purging their constitution of destructive principles and procedures or devising new ones to protect liberty. This is what John Dickinson meant in 1787 in his oft-quoted comment at the Philadelphia Convention that "experience must be our only guide. Reason may mislead us." Dickinson's explanation for this position, however, is less often quoted; but within it is a fuller statement that he is specifying a particular type of experience and a theory of history:

> It was not Reason that discovered the singular & admirable mechanism of the English Constitution. It was not Reason that discovered or ever could have discovered the odd & in the eye of those who are governed by reason, the absurd mode of trial by Jury. Accidents probably produced these discoveries, and experience has given a sanction to them.[69]

"Accidents" and "experience": these were part of the ongoing historical process of constitutionalism. Of the former, "accidents," John Adams observed in his long treatise on American constitutions that the constitution of the Roman republic had benefited from such happenstance conflict and threat: it "had no Lycurgus to model its constitution at first . . . yet so many were the accidents which happened in the contests betwixt the patricians and the plebeians, that chance effected what the lawgiver had not provided for."[70]

For Adams and other Revolutionary students of historical jurisprudence, the role of the "lawgiver" was therefore problematic at best. Much has been written of the choice of "Publius" as collective pseudonym for the authors of *The Federalist*, but one interpretation, which would have been obvious to the community of historical interpretation of which they were a part, has been generally overlooked.[71] Only one scholar, Charles R. Kesler, had the good sense to go back to the source that the authors actually employed and ask why Plutarch presented the historical Publius (Valerius Publicola) in the way he did: Plutarch's history did not treat figures alone, but in pairs, and Plutarch had placed the Roman Publius alongside the Greek Solon for comparison. Kesler infers, aptly, that Solon established his government and then "deserted Athens for ten years," while "the American Publius will follow the Roman Publius in remaining in his country, always ready to counsel it and thus to extirpate tyranny's hope of return."[72]

To Kesler's contextual insight should be added other meanings that the generation of *The Federalist* would have given to the historical process of which Valerius Publicola was a participant. Publius had succeeded Rome's last king, Tarquin, and his "aversion to tyrants was stronger than that of Solon." More to the point, however, Plutarch makes the cautionary note that Solon "was an original, and followed no example." Once Solon drafted his code and established an unmixed democracy, "his laws were to continue in force for a hundred years, and were written on wooden tables." The contribution of Publius was that he, too, "caused certain laws to be enacted, which greatly augmented the power of the people." But, although he remained in Rome, he did so on the expectation that he would be needed to return to action when tyranny would attempt its inevitable revival, as part of the process of liberty's struggle against power.[73] John Adams, writing almost a decade before *The Federalist*, revealed yet another conventional image of Solon and the flaw underlying his announcement of a fixed body of law: Solon's unmixed democracy had soon collapsed and produced a tyrant whose rule had to be followed by new protections, "the necessity of which Solon had not foreseen."[74]

Ralph Lerner has aptly called the framers' undertaking a "confident invitation to all—contemporaries and successors alike—to examine their principles and acts."[75] Perhaps the most radical reexamination of principle concerned the nature of confederacies and the decision to establish a federal republic with centralized powers. This innovation, Cecilia Kenyon has demonstrated in her classic analysis of the Antifederalists, was the single greatest source of contention for opponents of the Constitution and the most vulnerable point at which they could attack the new frame of government. Quoting James Winthrop that an extended republic was "in itself an absurdity, and contrary to the whole experience of mankind," she writes, "The last part of the statement, at least, was true; history was on the side of the Anti-Federalists."[76]

But history provided support for the Federalists, too. Publius took great pains to demonstrate from history that the idea of a weak confederacy was a "mistaken principle." "This exceptionable principle," Hamilton wrote, "may as truly as emphatically be stiled the parent of anarchy," while Madison called it a "fallacious principle" within the context of republicanism.[77] Their own experience had shown them the need to "discard the fallacious scheme of quotas and requisitions" and the "absolute necessity for an entire change in the first principles of the system" of union.[78] But the most effective historical argument was the implicit understanding of those who studied history that the 1780s were another episode of constitutional crisis demanding action. It is but one of the many insightful observations of Peter S. Onuf in his account of how Americans came to accept the radical concept of a federal republic that the acceptance of federalism—which he lauds as the "Federalists' greatest achievement"—was possible only because of a "founding myth." This myth was a historical one, namely, about how bad things were in the 1780s and how they were critical enough to justify innovation in the political science of creating and invoking constitutional mechanisms appropriate to the rescue of republicanism. The Federalists, therefore, were able to "articulate new images of the union"[79] by justifying them within a theory of historically protected constitutionalism. That history, they believed, had no discernible beginning; they hoped it would have no end.

Notes

I am grateful for the helpful criticisms of Peter S. Onuf, Jack N. Rakove, Richard B. Bernstein, Barry Cushman, and Stuart Banner.

1. Statements about word usage in *The Federalist* are based on entries assembled alphabetically in Thomas S. Engerman, Edward J. Erler, and Thomas B. Hofeller, eds., *The Federalist Concordance* (Chicago, 1980). Page citations from *The Federalist* are from the edition of Jacob E. Cooke (Middletown, Conn., 1961), whose pagination is used in the *Concordance*.

2. Madison alludes to "no less than four regular experiments" of this sort in the recent past, in *The Federalist*, No. 20, 128.

3. A point ably made innumerable times; as an example, see H. Jefferson Powell, "The Original Understanding of Original Intent," *Harvard Law Review* 98 (1985): 885–948, reprinted with other significant essays for and against the idea in Jack N. Rakove, *Interpreting the Constitution* (Boston, 1990).

4. See, e.g., the special symposium issue "Fidelity in Constitutional Theory," *Fordham Law Review* 65 (1997), and especially the article by Jack N. Rakove, "Fidelity Through History (Or to It)," 1587–609.

5. See, generally, Charles A. Miller, *The Supreme Court and the Uses of History* (Cambridge, Mass., 1969).

6. *The Federalist*, No. 49, 340.

7. The formulation of this distinction is from Rakove, "Fidelity Through History (Or to It)."

8. William E. Nelson, *The Fourteenth Amendment: From Political Principle to Judicial Doctrine* (Cambridge, Mass., 1988), 7–8, citing Harold M. Hyman, *A More Perfect Union: The Impact of the Civil War on the Constitution* (New York, 1973), 435–40. Suzanna Sherry makes much the same point—that "careful historical analysis of the same evidence may yield opposite conclusions"—in "The Indeterminacy of Historical Evidence," *Harvard Journal of Law and Public Policy* 19 (1996): 440.

9. The best discussion of these problems as they affect our reading of the records of the Philadelphia Convention is James H. Hutson, "Riddles of the Federal Constitutional Convention," *William and Mary Quarterly*, 3d ser., 44 (1987): 411–23. In addition, the records of the state ratifying conventions introduce the specific contexts of local concerns and political forces, as noted by Powell, "Original Understanding."

10. Mark DeWolfe Howe, *The Garden and the Wilderness: Religion and Government in American Constitutional History* (Chicago, 1965), 4, cited by Leonard W. Levy, *Original Intent and the Framers' Constitution* (New York, 1988), 313. In addition to Howe and Levy, other powerful criticisms can be found in Nelson, *Fourteenth Amendment*. John Phillip Reid, equally critical, distinguishes between the "lawyer's law office history" used by advocates and the "forensic history" used by judges to justify their decisions. "Law and History," *Loyola of Los Angeles Law Review* 27 (1993): 193–223. See also the essays on originalism assembled by Jack N. Rakove, ed., *Interpreting the Constitution* (Boston, 1990). Sensitive to the historian's plight in this debate are Rakove's *Original Meanings: Politics and Ideas in the Making of the Constitution* (New York, 1996); and Laura Kalman, *The Strange Career of Legal Liberalism* (New Haven, Conn., 1996).

11. Eric J. Segall, "A Century Lost: The End of the Originalism Debate," *Constitutional Commentary* 15 (1998): 411–39. For a sensible final word—or,

perhaps, the opening of a new round—see Michael Klarman, "Antifidelity," *Southern California Law Review* 70 (1997): 381–415.

12. Paul L. Murphy, "Time to Reclaim: The Current Challenge of American Constitutional History," *American Historical Review* 69 (1963): 77–79.

13. John Adams, to the *Boston Gazette*, February 8, 1773, in *The Works of John Adams*, 10 vols., ed. Charles Francis Adams (Boston, 1856), 3:558.

14. Rakove, *Original Meanings*, 11.

15. These formulas are concisely described by Gordon S. Wood, *The Creation of the American Republic 1776–1787* (Chapel Hill, N.C., 1969), chap. 1, "The Whig Science of Politics."

16. Bernard Bailyn, *Ideological Origins of the American Revolution* (1967; enlarged edition, Cambridge, Mass., 1992), esp. chap. 3, "Power and Liberty: A Theory of Politics," and the postscript added for the 1992 edition, "Fulfillment: A Commentary on the Constitution."

17. On this point, see H. Trevor Colbourn, *The Lamp of Experience: Whig History and the Intellectual Origins of the American Revolution* (Chapel Hill, N.C., 1965).

18. Douglas G. Adair, "'Experience Must Be Our Only Guide': History, Democratic Theory, and the United States Constitution," in *The Reinterpretation of Early American History*, ed. Ray Allen Billington (New York, 1968), 129–50, quotation on 133. This quotation already had gained wide exposure when Adair used it in 1955 in his deservedly influential article, "'That Politics May Be Reduced to a Science': David Hume, James Madison, and the Tenth Federalist," *Huntington Library Quarterly* 20 (1957): 343–60, which was reprinted (along with the 1968 essay) in *Fame and the Founding Fathers: Essays by Douglas Adair*, ed. H. Trevor Colbourn (New York, 1974).

19. David Hume, *The History of England from the Invasion of Julius Caesar to the Revolution of 1688.* The edition cited here is that of 1796, "*a New Edition, with the Author's Last Corrections and Improvements*," published in London in eight volumes.

20. Jefferson to William Duane, August 12, 1810, in *Thomas Jefferson: Writings* (New York, 1984), 1228–29; and to Major John Cartwright, June 5, 1824, ibid., 1491.

21. Hume, *History*, 1:116–17.

22. Ibid., 3:304.

23. Ibid., 6:21.

24. Ibid., 119–20.

25. Ibid., 3:304–5.

26. Ibid., 5:452 n.

27. Ibid., 3:304.

28. Ibid., 459.

29. J. G. A. Pocock, *The Ancient Constitution and the Feudal Law* (New York, 1967), 36–127. Pocock's study provides a telling counterpoint to Robert W. Gordon's premise that legal history before the late twentieth century provided only a conservative "stabilizing" function in legal argument. "The Past as Authority and as Social Critic: Stabilizing and Destabilizing Functions in Legal Argument," in *The Historic Turn in the Human Sciences*, ed. Terrence McDonald (Ann Arbor, Mich., 1996), 339–78.

30. Morton J. Horwitz, "The Constitution of Change: Legal Fundamentality Without Fundamentalism," *Harvard Law Review* 107 (1993): 117, 42–43.

31. John Selden, "Notes on Sir John Fortescue's *De Laudibus . . . in Opera*

*omnia* (London, 1725), vol. 3, col. 1892, cited by Donald R. Kelley, *The Human Measure: Social Thought and the Western Legal Tradition* (Cambridge, Mass., 1990), 178.

32. Sir Matthew Hale, *The History of the Common Law of England,* 3d ed., ed. Charles M. Gray (1739; Chicago, 1971).

33. Ibid., 72, 74, 85.

34. Ibid., 40.

35. Reid, "Law and History," 214–17. For a fuller discussion of the "original," or political, contract, see Reid's *Constitutional History of the American Revolution,* vol. 1, *The Authority of Rights* (Madison, Wis., 1986). On the contract as it affected the creation of new governments, see David Thomas Konig, "Jurisprudence and Social Policy in the New Republic," in Konig, *Devising Liberty: Preserving and Creating Freedom in the New American Republic* (Stanford, Calif., 1995), 178–216.

36. "John Adams' Notes of Debates" [September 8, 1774], in *Letters of Delegates to Congress, 1774–1789,* 24 vols. to date, ed. Paul H. Smith et al. (Washington, D.C., 1976– ), 1:47–48.

37. Jefferson to Edmund Randolph, February 15, 1783, in *The Papers of Thomas Jefferson,* 26 vols. to date, ed. Julian P. Boyd et al. (Princeton, N.J., 1950– ), 6:246–47.

38. Ibid., 248.

39. Ibid. Jefferson's fears were probably exaggerated, for, as Peter S. Onuf has pointed out, that state's advocates preferred to rest their claims on more traditional legal arguments. *Origins of the Federal Republic: Jurisdictional Controversies in the United States, 1775–1787* (Philadelphia, 1983), 132. The subtitle of this book does not do justice to the many insights provided into the topic of the title.

40. Benjamin Rush, "On the Defects of the Confederation" (1787), in *The Selected Writings of Benjamin Rush,* ed. Dagobert D. Runes (New York, 1947), 26. Jack Rakove notes that Rush had published this essay under a pseudonym in 1786. *The Birth of National Politics: An Interpretive History of the Continental Congress* (Baltimore, 1779), 460. On "perfection" as a continuing process rather than a final state, see David Spadafora, *The Idea of Progress in Eighteenth-Century Britain* (New Haven, Conn., 1990), 246.

41. Rush, "On the Defects of the Confederation," 27, 30.

42. Benjamin Rush, "Observations on the Government of Pennsylvania" (1777), in *Selected Writings,* 55.

43. Benjamin Rush, "Influence of the American Revolution" (1788), in *Selected Writings,* 325–33.

44. The following is based on an examination of all such citations in *The Federalist Concordance.*

45. [Madison], *The Federalist,* No. 19, 119.

46. *The Federalist,* No. 39, 257.

47. Jefferson to Madison, January 30, 1787, in *Papers,* 11:93.

48. *The Works of James Wilson,* ed. Robert Green McCloskey, 2 vols., paginated consecutively (Cambridge, Mass., 1967), 309.

49. Ibid., 309, 316–17.

50. "Time is the wisest of things." *Ibid.,* 334.

51. Ibid., 309.

52. Sir William Blackstone, *Commentaries on the Laws of England,* 4 vols. (London, 1765–69; facsimile edition, Chicago, 1979), 1:91.

53. Jefferson to William Stephens Smith, November 13, 1787, in *Papers,* 12:356.

54. Thomas Jefferson, *Notes on the State of Virginia* (1785), ed. William Peden (New York, 1972), 121.

55. Wilson, "Considerations on the Nature and Extent of the Legislative Authority of the British Parliament" (1774), in *Works,* 729–32.

56. Jefferson, *Notes on the State of Virginia,* Query XIII, "Constitution," at 129.

57. Bailyn, *Ideological Origins,* 41, and, generally, chap. 2, "Sources and Traditions." James Burgh's three-volume *Political Disquisitions: An Enquiry into Public Errors, Defects, and Abuses* appeared in 1774. The edition used in the present chapter is the London edition of 1775, in facsimile (New York, 1971).

58. Burgh, *Political Disquisitions,* 3:275, 421, 295.

59. Ibid., 297–98.

60. Ibid., 298, 414. The writings of "Cato," the pseudonym for the English writers John Trenchard and Thomas Gordon in the 1720s, are described by Bailyn as ranking "with the treatises of Locke as the most authoritative statement of the nature of political liberty." *Ideological Origins,* 36.

61. Burgh, *Political Disquisitions,* 3:428–32, 441.

62. Wilson, "Speech . . . in the Convention of Pennsylvania" (1787), in *Works,* 770.

63. John Phillip Reid, *Constitutional History of the American Revolution,* vol. 1, *The Authority of Rights* (Madison, Wis., 1986), 25. The analysis of specific examples from experience and the awareness of longer trends is a distinction made by Morton White in "Reason, Long Experience, and Short Experience" in his *Philosophy, the* Federalist, *and the Constitution* (New York, 1987), 45–49.

64. Wilson, *Works,* 78–79.

65. Jefferson to Edward Rutledge, July 18, 1788, in *Papers,* 13:378. Jefferson drew the distinction that "an appeal to arms" would remain an option in France, where the issue might end in "despotism." The failures of the French Revolution provided the context for his later allusions to the need for armed violent reform.

66. Pocock, *Ancient Constitution,* 239, for Bolingbroke and other writers.

67. Cf. Blackstone, *Commentaries,* 402–3, with Wilson, *Works,* 349. Hume's skepticism led him to full agreement about the elusiveness of the "original truth" of fact. It is worth noting that in his *Enquiry Concerning Human Understanding* he observed, "Though experience be our only guide in reasoning concerning matters of fact, it must be acknowledged that this guide is not altogether infallible, but in some cases is apt to lead us into errors." David Fate Norton and Richard H. Popkin, eds., *David Hume: Philosophical Historian* (New York, 1965), 56.

68. Adams, *Works,* 3:528, 542–43.

69. Max Farrand, ed., *Records of the Federal Convention of 1787,* 4 vols. (New Haven, Conn., 1937), 2:278.

70. Adams, "Defence of the Constitutions of the United States" (1784), in *Works,* 4:419.

71. Madison wrote in 1818 only that the original name, "Citizen of N.Y.," would not be accurate once he had joined Hamilton and Jay. Madison to James Kirk Paulding, March 23, 1818, in *The Writings of James Madison,* 8 vols.,

ed. Gaillard Hunt (New York, 1908), 8:410. Martin Diamond, in *The History of Political Philosophy,* 2d ed., ed. Leo Strauss and Joseph Cropsey (Chicago, 1972), 633, contrasted "Publius" with Hamilton's earlier "Caesar": "Caesar destroyed a republic, Publius saved one." Douglas Adair, "A Note on Hamilton's Pseudonyms," *William and Mary Quarterly,* 3d ser., 12 (1955): 283–84, notes only that "Publius . . . was picked from Plutarch for obvious reasons": that he had "consummated the revolution by establishing a stable and just republican government."

72. Charles R. Kesler, "The Founders and the Classics," in *The Revival of Constitutionalism,* ed. James W. Muller (Lincoln, Neb., 1988), 59.

73. *Plutarch's Lives,* trans. and ed. John Langhorne and William Langhorne (Cincinnati, 1856), 73–93.

74. Adams, *A Defence of the Constitutions of Government of the United States of America* (1778), in *Works,* 4:419.

75. Ralph Lerner, "The Constitution of the Thinking Revolutionary," in *Beyond Confederation: Origins of the Constitution and American National Identity,* ed. Richard Beeman, Stephen Botein, and Edward C. Carter II (Chapel Hill, N.C., 1987), 68.

76. Cecilia M. Kenyon, "Men of Little Faith: The Anti-Federalists on the Nature of Representative Government," *William and Mary Quarterly,* 3d ser., 12 (1955): 6.

77. Hamilton, *The Federalist,* No. 16, 99; Madison, *The Federalist,* No. 18, 113.

78. Hamilton, *The Federalist,* No. 23, 148.

79. Onuf, *Federal Republic,* 198–209.

*Chapter Two*

# The Inverted Constitution: Enforcing Constitutional Rights in the Nineteenth Century

Robert J. Kaczorowski

In 1963, constitutional historian Paul Murphy challenged historians to "reclaim" legal and constitutional history from the practitioners of "law office history" and to study the development of law in its historical context.[1] Yet, at the dawning of the twenty-first century, scholars continue to analyze the origins and history of the Constitution, and many of its important provisions, in a partial contextual vacuum. The Fourteenth Amendment is an example. Next to the Bill of Rights, the Fourteenth Amendment is arguably the most important amendment to the Constitution, since it is the constitutional instrument that has nationalized most of the Bill of Rights and secured the implied fundamental rights and equality before the law of disadvantaged groups, such as racial minorities, aliens, women, the disabled, and gays.[2] The thousands of books and articles that have been written about the Fourteenth Amendment manifest its preeminence in constitutional law and constitutional history. Nevertheless, scholars have overlooked an important context of the framing and early implementation of the Fourteenth Amendment. In so doing, they have failed to appreciate an important dimension of nineteenth-century constitutional history: that the constitutional amendments and statutes Congress adopted to protect the fundamental rights of Americans after the Civil War were largely modeled on those adopted to enforce slaveholders' property rights at the nation's founding up to the Civil War. Read within this context, the origins of the Fourteenth Amendment demonstrate not only the centrality of slavery to United States constitutionalism but also that contemporary scholars and jurists have inadequately interpreted the radical changes its framers and original enforcers understood it to have effected on the constitutional guarantees of fundamental rights and the constitutional structure of American Federalism.

The constitutional theory of rights enforcement that its framers incorporated into the Fourteenth Amendment largely derived from a constitutional guarantee of slavery and the congressional and judicial enforcement of slaveholders' constitutionally secured property right to recapture runaway slaves. This chapter will explain this rather startling historical anomaly. One can appreciate this paradox of the nineteenth-century federal enforcement of fundamental rights if one understands the Constitution's guarantee of the slaveholder's right of recaption from the perspective of the slaveholder. The abhorrence of slavery makes this a distasteful effort. But if one understands this constitutional guarantee as a fundamental personal right of property that it was, it will then become clear that the statutes Congress enacted, and the constitutional theories the courts used to enforce this constitutional right, provided the framers of the Fourteenth Amendment with important models for the constitutional and statutory guarantees of fundamental rights, which largely influenced their legislative actions and defined the meaning they attributed to them.

The fugitive slave clause conferred on slaveholders the right to recapture slaves who fled to another state.[3] The constitutional significance of this provision and the history of its enforcement have not been fully understood. Through this provision, the founders in 1787 expanded and elevated to a constitutionally secured right the common-law property right of recaption. This obscure common-law right entitled the owner of chattels that strayed or were stolen to pursue and recover them. This was a right of self-help that did not require specific legal authorization, so long as the recovery could be made peacefully. In the patriarchal era of the founding, this proprietary common-law right authorized masters to recapture fugitive servants, fathers to retrieve runaway children, and even husbands to reclaim absconding wives. Sir William Blackstone characterized this right of recaption as a "natural right" of property. It was one of the sticks in the "bundle of sticks" that made up the right of chattel property.[4]

The right to property in slaves, however, was not a natural or common-law right. Slavery existed only by positive law.[5] Therefore, the *common-law right* of recaption did not include the right to recapture runaway slaves. This right, like the right to slaves generally, existed by statutory law, if at all. In the United States, slavery was the creation of state statutes. The laws of any particular state had no effect beyond the state's territorial jurisdiction. This meant that no state was under any obligation to recognize another state's slaveholders' rights to their slaves within their territorial jurisdiction. Consequently, no state was under any obligation to return runaway slaves to their owners in another state. Under the Articles of Confederation, the recapture of slaves who fled to another state was a matter of comity between the states. Although slavery existed in every state at the time of the American Revolution, the ideology of the Revolution stimulated a resistance to slavery, which by 1787 endangered the security of slavery in the minds of Southern slaveholders.[6] Delegates to the Constitutional Convention from the Southern slave states therefore demanded and won constitutional recognition and guarantees of slavery.[7]

State and federal courts subsequently characterized the fugitive slave clause as a critically important constitutional guarantee of slavery, without which the Union would never have been formed.[8] The significance judges attributed to the fugitive slave clause is that it conferred on slave owners a new constitutional right enforceable under the authority of the national government, independent of the states, and the states were prohibited from interfering with this right.[9] During the ratification of the Constitution, James Madison acknowledged this significance when he explained that the fugitive slave clause "secures us that property which we now possess. At present, if any slave elopes to any of those states where slaves are free, he becomes emancipated by their laws."[10] The fugitive slave clause, he concluded, "was expressly inserted, to enable owners of slaves to reclaim them."[11]

The fugitive slave clause states: "No person held to Service or Labour in one State, under the Laws thereof, escaping into another, shall, in Consequence of any Law or Regulation therein, be discharged from such Service or Labour, but shall be delivered up on Claim of the Party to whom such Service or Labour may be due."[12] The founders believed that the fugitive slave clause delegated to Congress plenary authority to enforce it, for the Second Congress, at the request of President George Washington after he consulted Secretary of State Thomas Jefferson and Attorney General Edmund Randolph, exercised plenary power in enacting a statute in 1793 to enforce it.[13] This statute also enforced the fugitive from justice clause of Article IV.[14] The act comprised four sections, the first two of which provided for the interstate extradition of fugitives from justice, and the last two for the interstate rendition of fugitive slaves.

The legislative history of the Fugitive Slave Act of 1793 began in 1791, when the governor of Pennsylvania petitioned President George Washington for help in resolving a standoff between him and the governor of Virginia over the rendition of fugitives from justice and the kidnappers of an alleged fugitive slave from Virginia to Pennsylvania.[15] After considering the matter, the Virginia-dominated Washington administration proposed that the Virginia governor comply with the Pennsylvania governor's request as a matter of comity. But the Virginia governor refused, maintaining that the procedure for seizing and delivering fugitives interstate, not being prescribed in the Constitution, must be specified by Congress.[16]

The ensuing impasse between Pennsylvania and Virginia demonstrated that the national government could not rely on the states voluntarily to enforce federal duties imposed by the U.S. Constitution. It also demonstrated that a state could not be compelled to comply with the provisions of the U.S. Constitution. It became clear that the constitutional provisions relating to the interstate rendition of fugitives, whether from justice or from slavery, could not be implemented without congressional action. President Washington therefore sent copies of all the papers to Congress with a request that Congress take appropriate action. Congress responded immediately by appointing a committee of three persons to draft a bill that would prescribe the method for extraditing fugitives from justice and the process by which slave owners could exercise their right to recapture their runaway slaves. This committee reported a bill within two weeks. However, it did not pass. At the next session of Congress, in November 1792, the Senate created a new three-person committee, which drafted and presented a bill to Congress early in 1793. Congress enacted the bill on February 8, 1793, and President Washington signed it into law on February 12, 1793.[17] No one questioned the plenary power that Congress exercised in enacting this statute, even though the constitutional provisions it enforced did not delegate legislative authority to Congress.[18]

The fugitive slave provisions of the 1793 statute are extraordinary. Historians and legal scholars have focused on the summary process it provided for the return of fugitive slaves to the states in which they were held as slaves.[19] Persons accused of being runaway slaves were usually helpless before the magistrate in these proceedings, for typically they were not permitted to defend themselves. Although claimants occasionally failed to meet the statutorily defined evidentiary burden of "proof to the satisfaction" of the judge that the person seized was a runaway slave, they usually secured the certificate of removal.[20]

As important and as tragic as this history is, even more significant to nineteenth-century constitutional history are statutory provisions that scholars have overlooked. This 1793 statute conferred on slaveholders two remarkable civil remedies against anyone who knowingly interfered with their right to recapture fugitive slaves or who assisted in slaves' escape. The first was a "penalty" of $500 recoverable in an action of debt.[21] This "penalty" was actually a private right of action in debt for a civil fine.[22] Even more remarkable was the second remedy: a tort action for damages.[23] Thus, this federal statute, enacted at the behest of President George Washington after consulting Secretary of State Thomas Jefferson and Attorney General Edmund Randolph, just four years after the ratification of the United States Constitution by many of its framers and ratifiers, conferred on private parties civil causes of action to vindicate violations of their constitutionally secured property right with civil remedies of a fine and tort damages![24] It presents important evidence not only of the founders' broad, nationalistic conception of the Constitution and constitutional rights, and of their understanding of the broad scope of implied congressional powers to enforce them, but also of the method the founders chose to vindicate violations of constitutional rights. Moreover, the 1793 statute is a significant example of constitution making by the executive and legislative branches of the government, for it constituted the exercise of a federal police power that overrode the police powers of the states.[25]

Slave owners brought civil suits pursuant to the 1793 Fugitive Slave Act in federal and state courts to enforce their constitutionally secured right of recaption. Sometimes they sued parties who assisted runaway slaves to escape for the civil penalty in actions of debt.[26] At other times they sued for compensatory damages in tort actions.[27] The frequency with which slaveholders or their agents won their cases suggests that judges and juries attempted to render judgments according to federal law, regardless of their personal views on slavery.

Antebellum judges in the states of the North apparently felt an obligation, inherent in their judicial function, to enforce the fugitive slave clause and the Fugitive Slave Act of 1793 notwithstanding their personal abhorrence of slavery.[28] Federal and state appellate judges generally asserted that the constitutional recognition of the slaveholder's right of recapture inherently delegated legislative power to Congress to enforce the right. When they did not explain this theory of delegation, judges simply assumed that the fugitive slave clause secured the slaveholder's property right, and that this recognition inherently delegated to Congress the power to enforce the right. Courts were consistently deferential to Congress's legislative action in these fugitive slave cases.[29] Judges not only recognized Congress's power to enforce the fugitive slave clause but also refused to pass judgment on the justice, fairness, and policy considerations of the legislation. For example, Chief Justice Isaac Parker of the Massachusetts Supreme Judicial Court observed that the people of his state were especially troubled that the 1793 statute gave slave owners the legal power to seize an alleged fugitive slave without judicial warrant. Nevertheless, he was constrained by his judicial role to dismiss this concern, commenting, "Whether the statute is a harsh one, is not for us to determine."[30]

Judges used the same reasoning in urging jurors faithfully to perform their legal duty under the Fugitive Slave Act even though they might find the statute morally repulsive. In 1833, United States Supreme Court Justice Henry Baldwin, as circuit justice, admonished members of a jury to set aside their personal feelings about slavery and to vindicate the "personal rights which are made inviolable under the protection" of the fugitive slave clause and the Fugitive Slave Act of 1793.[31] The jury did its duty and returned a verdict of $4,000 for the false arrest of slave catchers who sued a Pennsylvania justice of the peace, a local constable, and private citizens of Montgomery County, Pennsylvania, under the 1793 Fugitive Slave Act for detaining them under a Pennsylvania, antikidnapping statute.

Through the first half of the nineteenth century, in every case in which the constitutionality of the 1793 Fugitive Slave Act was challenged, the court upheld it. As late as 1853, Supreme Court Justice John McLean observed that not a single judge or court had held the Fugitive Slave Act unconstitutional.[32] Consequently, when litigants challenged the constitutionality of the Fugitive Slave Act of 1793, they did not ordinarily question Congress's legislative authority to implement the fugitive slave clause.[33] Rather, when they attacked the statute, they argued that it violated the alleged fugitive slave's Bill of Rights guarantees or her rights under state legal process.[34] The courts universally upheld the statute.

However, with blacks unable to defend themselves at summary fugitive slave hearings by testifying or entering evidence in their behalf, kidnapping blacks and selling them into slavery became a frequent practice.[35] Several free states responded to this practice in the early decades of the nineteenth century by enacting antikidnapping or personal liberty laws that nullified the federal right of self-help recaption and imposed higher evidentiary burdens to prove the claimant's title to the alleged fugitive slave before the magistrate was authorized to issue a certificate of removal.[36] Some statutes also required a jury trial to determine the status of an alleged fugitive slave.[37] Although the fugitive slave was not permitted to testify on her own behalf, she was nevertheless permitted to enter evidence relating to her status.[38] State appellate and federal courts refused to enforce these state statutes even though they were central to traditional state police powers, holding that the supremacy clause forced any state legislation or constitutional provisions on the subject to yield to the Fugitive Slave Act.[39]

These state antikidnapping statutes also subjected to heavy fines and prison terms anyone who illegally seized a person with the intention of holding her or selling her into slavery.[40] If a claimant exercised his federally secured right to self-help and seized an alleged runaway slave under the 1793 act, without a warrant from a local magistrate or a federal judge, he could be prosecuted as a kidnapper under state law.[41] Ostensibly designed to protect the personal liberty of free blacks, these personal liberty laws interposed state legal process between the national government and individuals claiming rights under the Constitution and laws of the United States. Thus, federal legal process, which enforced a federal constitutional and statutory right, was brought into direct conflict with essential state police powers and duties to protect the personal safety and personal liberty of its citizens and inhabitants. Moreover, with only one or two federal judges in a state, claimants were often forced to rely on local magistrates and the risk that, because of public hostility to slavery and the practice of kidnapping free blacks, local judges might either be slow to act or refuse to assist or, if they assisted, follow the more difficult state process rather than the federal summary process.[42] Recognizing that these state statutes and judges posed serious deterrents to the recapture of fugitive slaves, pro-slavery Southerners turned to the U.S. Supreme Court to resolve the resulting conflicts between state and federal law.[43]

The states of Maryland and Pennsylvania contrived a test case, cited as *Prigg v. Pennsylvania*,[44] that afforded the Court the opportunity to resolve the conflicting theories of Federalism.[45] The specific issue presented to the Court was the constitutionality of the Pennsylvania Personal Liberty Law of 1826. The Court unanimously held that the Pennsylvania statute was unconstitutional. It also unanimously held that the Fugitive Slave Act of 1793 was constitutional in every respect save one. The constitutional infirmity of the 1793 statute was the jurisdiction Congress attempted to confer on state magistrates. All but three of the justices held that Congress's power under the fugitive slave clause was exclusive and that Congress could confer jurisdiction to enforce constitutional rights and federal statutes only on federal courts.

Justice Joseph Story wrote the opinion for the Court.[46] Before he addressed the merits of the case, he asserted a deferential theory of judicial review as the approach the Court should take in deciding constitutional questions presented to it. Story defined the Court's function as interpreting the Constitution "in such a manner, as, consistently with the words, shall fully and completely effectuate the whole objects of it."[47] As a general rule of interpretation, Story opined, "No Court of justice can be authorized so to construe any clause of the Constitution as to defeat its obvious ends, when another construction, equally accordant with the words and sense thereof, will enforce and protect them."[48]

Examining the framers' intent, Story observed, "Historically, it is well known, that the object of this [fugitive slave] clause was to secure to the citizens of the slaveholding states the complete right and title of ownership in their slaves, as property in every state in the Union into which they might escape from the state where they were held in servitude."[49] Story applied his theory of original intent as an instrument of broad interpretation to "fully and completely effectuate the whole objects" of constitutional provisions and to "enforce and protect them." Guided by his understanding of the judicial function and of the framers' intent, Story broadly interpreted the fugitive slave clause as containing two fundamental guarantees.

The first constitutional guarantee prohibited the states from freeing fugitive slaves. This guarantee was expressed in the first part of the fugitive slave clause: "No person held to Service or Labour in one State under the Laws thereof, escaping into another, shall in Consequence of any Law or Regulation therein, be discharged from such Service or Labour." Story explained the obvious and literal meaning of this language: "The slave is not to be discharged from service or labour, in consequence of any state law or regulation."[50] Significantly, Story interpreted this prohibition against state action as an affirmative recognition of "a positive and absolute right."[51] "The clause manifestly contemplates the existence of a positive, unqualified right on the part of the owner of the slave, which no state law or regulation can in any way qualify, regulate, control, or restrain," Story declared.[52] Consequently, the fugitive slave clause nationalized the slave owner's right to his slave, for it "puts the right to the service or labour upon the same ground and to the same extent in every other state as in the state from which the slave escaped, and in which he was held to the service and labour. If this be so," Story concluded, "then all the incidents to that right attach also."[53]

Story identified the common-law origin of this constitutionally secured right of slave recaption:

> [T]his is no more than a mere affirmance of the principles of the common law applicable to this very subject. Mr. Justice Blackstone (3 Bl. Comm. 4) lays it down as unquestionable doctrine. "Recaption or reprisal (says he) is another species of remedy by the mere act of the party injured. This happens when any one hath deprived another of his property in goods or chattels personal, or wrongfully detains one's wife, child, or servant; in which case the owner of the goods, and the husband, parent, or master may lawfully claim and retake them, where ever he happens to find them, so it be not in a riotous manner, or attended with a breach of the peace."[54]

Story then asserted that this common-law property right was elevated to a federally enforceable constitutional right. "Upon this ground we have not the slightest hesitation in holding, that, under and in virtue of the Constitution, the owner of a slave is clothed with entire authority, in every state in the Union, to seize and recapture his slave, whenever he can do it without any breach of the peace, or any illegal violence."[55]

The fugitive slave clause contains a second provision, which requires that the fugitive slave "shall be delivered up on Claim of the Party to whom such Service or Labour may be due."[56] This language, Story observed, "contemplated some farther remedial redress than that, which might be administered at the hands of the owner himself."[57] This remedial assistance must come from the United States government, Story declared: "If, indeed, the Constitution guarantees the right, and if it requires the delivery upon the claim of the owner, (as cannot well be doubted,) the natural inference certainly is, that the national government is clothed with the appropriate authority and functions to enforce it."[58] Story then paraphrased Chief Justice John Marshall's classic statement of broad implied powers in *McCulloch v. Maryland*: "The fundamental principle, applicable to all cases of this sort, would seem to be, that where the end is required, the means are given; and where the duty is enjoined, the ability to perform it is contemplated to exist on the part of the functionaries to whom it is entrusted."[59] It is significant that the Court unanimously applied to the fugitive slave clause, which was not among Congress's enumerated powers of Article I, the same theory of implied powers that is normally associated with the expressly delegated powers of Article I. The Court evidently understood the Constitution as a delegation of powers to enforce even those provisions that do not provide for their federal enforcement and are reasonably interpreted as a reservation of state powers.[60]

Story elaborated the reason that the constitutional recognition of a right necessarily delegated to Congress, and not the states, the duty to enforce it. Congress could not compel the states to enforce constitutional rights or to perform constitutional duties. On the contrary, the Constitution required the national government, "through its own departments, legislative, judicial, or executive, as the case may require, to carry into effect all the rights and duties imposed upon it by the Constitution."[61] The power of the states to ignore the slave owner's constitutional right of recaption was an additional reason for the necessity, as well as the constitutionality, of congressional legislation to enforce it.[62] For good measure, Story quoted from Madison's *Federalist,* No. 43, as authority for the proposition that a right recognized in the Constitution implies a delegation of power to the national government to secure and enforce it.[63]

Story reinforced the Court's broad theory of constitutional delegation by applying two additional and distinct methods of constitutional interpretation that looked to contemporaneous exposition and political practice to give meaning to the Constitution. He attributed the Court's "view of the power and duty of the national government"[64] to the congressional framers of the 1793 Fugitive Slave Act. The framers of this statute were unique and had a "vast influence" on the question of its constitutionality. Story observed that many of the congressional framers of the act, as well as President George Washington, who initiated its legislative adoption and signed it into law, were also framers of the Constitution or were "intimately connected with its adoption."[65] But the fact that many of the framers of the statute were also framers and ratifiers of the Constitution was not the sole reason political practice helped to define the Constitution. Story looked to political practice "independent of the vast influence," which "a contemporaneous exposition of the provisions [of the Constitution] by those, who were its immediate framers, or intimately connected with its adoption" should have in constitutional interpretation.

Indeed, Story cited Supreme Court precedents that used political practice as a method of constitutional interpretation.[66] He declared that Congress had acted in 1793 on a "rule of interpretation" that assumed the Constitution delegated "the right as well as duty" to Congress to legislate on the subject of fugitives from justice and fugitive slaves.[67] He observed that all the provisions of the 1793 statute had been universally accepted and acted upon by state and federal governmental officials without anyone questioning its constitutionality. Also decisive was the universal acceptance of the statute's constitutionality by federal judges and state courts, which "uniformly recognised [it] as a binding and valid law."[68] Story thus invoked a "gloss on the Constitution"[69] theory of constitutional interpretation, which looked to political practice to interpret the Constitution as another justification of the Court's decision upholding the 1793 Fugitive Slave Act. He declared that "if the question were one of doubtful construction, such long acquiescence in it, such contemporaneous expositions of it, and such extensive and uniform recognition of its validity, would in our judgment entitle the question to be considered at rest; . . . Congress, the executive, and the judiciary have, upon various occasions, acted upon this as a sound and reasonable doctrine."[70] However, Story quickly added that the Court did not consider the constitutionality of the 1793 act to be a doubtful question. The Court's deference to the lawmaking decisions of the people's representatives was the judicial norm, whether the decisions were made by a constituent assembly or a legislative assembly.

The last question Story addressed was whether the power to enforce this right was exclusive in Congress or concurrent with the states. The Court held that Congress's power was exclusive for several reasons that evince the Court's view of a national sovereignty-based theory of dual Federalism. First, the constitutional right of recaption "is recognised as an absolute, positive, right and duty, pervading the whole Union with an equal and supreme force, uncontrolled and uncontrollable by state sovereignty or state legislation."[71] Second, this right was a new right created by the Constitution and beyond state jurisdiction.[72] "The natural inference deducible from this consideration," Story reasoned, "certainly is, in the absence of any positive delegation of power to the state legislatures, that it belongs to the legislative department of the national government, to which it owes its origin and establishment."[73]

The national character of this right, and the consequent need for national uniformity in enforcing it, reinforced the exclusive character of Congress's power to enforce the fugitive slave clause. Story reasoned that, if the states had the power to enforce this right, they could legislate in ways that actually undermined its effective enforcement.[74] Indeed, the Pennsylvania statute demonstrated that the free states might destroy the right. "It purports to punish as a public offence against that state, the very act of seizing and removing a slave by his master, which the Constitution of the United States was designed to justify and uphold."[75] Consequently, the Pennsylvania statute was not only unconstitutional. It demonstrated the need to exclude all state regulation over the rendition of fugitive slaves. The Court's decision voiding the Pennsylvania Personal Liberty Law and affirming the constitutionality of the Fugitive Slave Act was unanimous. However, Chief Justice Roger B. Taney, Justice Smith Thompson, and Justice Peter Daniel dissented from the Court's decision that the power to enforce the fugitive slave clause was vested exclusively in Congress.[76]

Although the Court's decision in *Prigg* affirmed the constitutionally and statutorily secured right of slave owners, the Court largely undermined the ability of slave owners to enforce their right when it restricted to federal institutions the power and duty of enforcing it.[77] Northern free states interpreted *Prigg* as a license to refuse to assist slave owners to recapture their slaves. They enacted new personal liberty laws to enforce the due process rights of alleged fugitive slaves and prohibited state officials from assisting their recapture in any way.[78] These actions added to an increasing pattern of lawlessness in which groups hostile to slavery interfered with the recapture of fugitive slaves and aided in their escape. In nullifying state authority to aid in recapturing runaway slaves, the *Prigg* decision encouraged the organization of groups to help runaways escape to freedom. *Prigg* thus contributed to growing sectional conflict between the free states of the North and the slave states of the South.[79]

Northern resistance led to Southern demands for a more effective federal statute. Congress complied in 1850. As in 1793, Congress in 1850 enacted a statute to enforce the constitutional right of slaveholders and to obviate the conflicts between the slave and free states.[80] The 1850 Fugitive Slave Act,[81] however, represented an even more remarkable exercise of national authority to enforce constitutional rights than its earlier counterpart. Congress authorized federal judges to appoint commissioners with "the powers that any justice of the peace, or other magistrate of any of the United States," had to arrest, imprison, or bail offenders of any crime against the United States,"[82] and concurrent jurisdiction with federal circuit, district, and territorial court judges to grant certificates of removal to claimants of fugitive slaves "upon satisfactory proof being made."[83] A scholar early in this century correctly analogized this federal enforcement structure to federal administrative agencies, such as the Interstate Commerce Commission and boards of immigrant inspectors.[84]

Moreover, the 1850 statute imposed upon federal legal officers the duty to enforce its provisions under penalty of a heavy fine of $1,000 payable to the slave owner.[85] Should the fugitive slave escape while in custody of federal officials, they were made liable for the full value of the slave.[86] The statute also imposed on private citizens the duty to enforce the slaveholder's constitutional and statutory rights. It authorized commissioners to call a *posse comitatus* and "commanded" "all good citizens" to assist in the execution of the statute whenever their aid was required.[87]

The 1850 statute combined the right of self-help recapture with compulsory federal summary legal process.[88] It expressly prohibited the alleged fugitive slave from entering evidence on her own behalf, and it expressly made the certificate of removal an absolute authorization to return the fugitive to the state from which she escaped. It expressly invoked the supremacy clause[89] and made the certificate an absolute bar to "any process issued by any court, judge, magistrate, or other person whomsoever."[90]

The 1850 Fugitive Slave Act superseded the civil penalty provided in the 1793 Fugitive Slave Act with criminal penalties for knowingly and willingly violating the statute. On conviction, the defendant was subject to a fine of up to $1,000 and imprisonment for up to six months.[91] Violators were also subject to "civil damages" in the amount of $1,000 for each fugitive slave lost, payable to the owner in an action of debt.[92] This provision doubled the amount of the civil penalty recoverable under the 1793 Fugitive Slave Act.[93] The statutory "civil damages" of $1,000 in the 1850 Fugitive Slave Act also should have benefited slaveholders because it was greater, on average, than the damages awarded in tort actions under the 1793 act. The courts interpreted these damages as a tort remedy that claimants might seek as an alternative to the tort action provided in the 1793 Fugitive Slave Act.[94]

The fee structure provided in the 1850 act also appeared to favor slave owners. The fees of federal marshals, deputy marshals, and court clerks in fugitive slave cases were set at $10 if a certificate of removal was issued and only $5 if the certificate was denied.[95] However, the federal officer who executed process was entitled to a fee of $5 and any other necessary costs incurred, such as food and lodging during the fugitive slave's detention, which were to be paid by the claimant. Should the return of fugitive slaves be met with local resistance in a free state, Congress provided for the removal of the fugitive by federal force and at federal expense.[96]

The 1850 Fugitive Slave Act, although part of the famous Compromise of 1850 intended by Henry Clay and Daniel Webster to ease sectional feelings over slavery, actually heightened those tensions. The summary process culminating in the certificate of removal of the alleged fugitive slave became the focus of antislavery political opposition in the North.[97] The statutory denial of the right to a jury trial, the right of the accused to testify in his own behalf, and the right to habeas corpus combined with the summary nature of the removal proceedings based exclusively on the claimant's evidence relating to the alleged fugitive's status effectively prevented the free states' presumption of freedom and other personal liberty guarantees from interfering with the slaveholder's right of recaption. Moreover, the disparity in fees appeared to abolitionists and antislavery sympathizers as a bribe to ensure that the commissioner or judge would issue the certificate of removal.[98] Abolitionists, such as Wendell Phillips, urged Northerners to resist and disobey the statute.[99] Even more moderate antislavery societies declared that moral and religious people could not obey such an immoral and irreligious law.[100]

Northerners did resist with acts of civil disobedience to

federal legal process with varying degrees of force and violence.[101] Presidents Millard Fillmore in 1851 and Franklin Pierce in 1854 personally intervened to enforce the federal Fugitive Slave Acts, the latter with federal force against mobs that attempted to rescue fugitive slaves who were held in federal custody.[102] The Kansas-Nebraska Act of 1854, the open warfare instigated by John Brown in Kansas, and the Supreme Court's *Dred Scott* decision[103] produced additional fierce Northern backlash. By the middle of the 1850s, many Northern state legislatures and judiciaries interposed their police powers to nullify the Fugitive Slave Acts.[104]

Wisconsin presented the most notorious example of Northern state interposition and nullification, for the state's executive, legislative, and judicial branches joined its citizens in strenuous efforts to nullify federal law.[105] Indeed, the Wisconsin Supreme Court rejected precedents of the U.S. Supreme Court and lower federal courts[106] and declared the Fugitive Slave Act of 1850 unconstitutional. It issued a writ of habeas corpus directing the federal marshal to release defendants arrested under the statute for leading a mob that stormed a jail and freed an alleged fugitive slave, and it refused to recognize the Supreme Court's appellate jurisdiction over its decisions in the matter.[107] The U.S. Supreme Court vehemently asserted its appellate jurisdiction,[108] but the state did not appear when the appealed cases were later argued on their merits.

The U.S. Supreme Court reversed the Wisconsin Supreme Court's decisions in an opinion written by Chief Justice Roger B. Taney, which emphatically affirmed the supremacy of national sovereignty over state sovereignty.[109] In an unequivocal rejection of Wisconsin's attempted interposition and nullification of federal law, the Court asserted its appellate jurisdiction over the Wisconsin Supreme Court under section 25 of the Judiciary Act of 1789[110] and upheld the constitutionality of the Fugitive Slave Act of 1850 "in all of its provisions."[111] The Wisconsin Supreme Court subsequently failed to decide whether to acquiesce to the Supreme Court's appellate jurisdiction, for the state's chief justice decided in favor of the Court's appellate jurisdiction; a second justice decided against it; and the third justice, having been of counsel for one of the parties, recused himself.[112]

The Civil War intervened to end the struggle between the free states' efforts to protect the personal liberties of alleged runaway slaves and federal efforts to enforce the constitutional and statutory rights of slave owners. Ironically, the forces of slavery and of civil liberty switched sides in the ensuing political debate over the nature of constitutional Federalism. The slave states of the South seceded and based their constitutional justification for secession on a state sovereignty compact theory of Federalism, which they derived from Thomas Jefferson's and James Madison's Kentucky and Virginia Resolutions.[113] Their express legal basis for withdrawing from the Union was the Northern states' refusal to enforce the fugitive slave clause and their active interference with its enforcement. For example, the "South Carolina Declaration of Causes of Secession"[114] proclaimed "that fourteen of the States have deliberately refused for years past to fulfil [*sic*] their constitutional obligations, and we refer to their own statutes for the proof." The declaration then quoted the fugitive slave clause and asserted the principle that drove so many courts, including the Supreme Court of the United States, to affirm Congress's authority to enforce it, namely, that the fugitive slave clause "was so material to the compact that without it that compact would not have been made." Naming each of the nonslaveholding states of the North, the declaration accused these states of "hav[ing] enacted laws which either nullify the [Fugitive Slave] acts of Congress, or render useless any attempt to execute them. In many of these States the fugitive is discharged from the service or labor claimed, and in none of them has the State Government complied with the stipulation made in the Constitution." The declaration recited specific examples of the North's recalcitrance, such as the antislavery feeling in New Jersey that had led the state "to enact laws which render inoperative the remedies provided by her own laws and by the laws of Congress. In the State of New York even the right of transit for a slave has been denied by her tribunals."

The close connection between the rendition of fugitive slaves and the extradition of fugitive criminals that led to the first Federal Fugitive Slave Act in 1793 persisted to the South's secession in 1860. South Carolina complained that "the States of Ohio and Iowa have refused to surrender to justice fugitives charged with murder, and with inciting servile insurrection in the State of Virginia." Having cited these examples of Northern state lawlessness, South Carolina concluded: "Thus the constitutional compact has been deliberately broken and disregarded by the non-slaveholding States; and the consequence follows that South Carolina is released from her obligation." Asserting the principle of governmental legitimacy expressed in the Declaration of Independence, this Declaration of Causes of Secession proclaimed: "These ends [to protect individual rights] for which this Government was instituted have been defeated . . . by the action of the non-slaveholding States." It specified the right

> those [Northern] States . . . have denied [is] the right of property established in fifteen of the States and recognized by the [fugitive slave clause of the] Constitution. . . . They have encouraged and assisted thousands of our slaves to leave their homes; and those who remain have been incited by emissaries, books, and pictures, to servile insurrection.

The constitutional resolution of the deal-breaking issue that enabled the formation of the Union in 1787 collapsed, and it became the deal-breaking issue that disrupted the Union in 1860.

President Abraham Lincoln, for the free states of the North, rejected secession and the constitutional theory of state sovereignty advanced to justify it as a matter of law. He countered with a ringing affirmation of the popular sovereignty theory of American Federalism that assumed the supremacy of national sovereignty.[115] The Northern states exercised the nation's sovereign power by abolishing slavery with the adoption of the Thirteenth Amendment.[116] The Thirty-ninth Congress announced the amendment's ratification in December 1865.

In organizing the Thirty-ninth Congress, Republican congressional leaders announced their intention of making the Thirteenth Amendment's promise of freedom a practical reality.[117] They fulfilled their promise with the enactment of the Civil Rights Act of 1866.[118] To justify Congress's authority to enact this statute, its framers asserted the constitutional theories of broad delegation of legislative authority to enforce constitutional rights that the Supreme Court adopted in *Prigg v. Pennsylvania* to uphold the constitutionality of the Fugitive Slave Act of 1793. Recall that Justice Story, for a unanimous Supreme Court, reasoned that the fugitive slave clause's negative prohibitions on the states from interfering with the slaveholders' property right in their slaves recognized "a positive, unqualified right on the part of the owner of the slave," which, together with the duty to deliver up the slave, "clothed [the national government] with the appropriate authority and functions to enforce it."[119] In like manner, the supporters of the Civil Rights Act of 1866 interpreted the Thirteenth Amendment's abolition of slavery as an affirmative guarantee of freedom and the fundamental rights of freemen in which freedom consists. They also interpreted this constitutional guarantee of freedom as a delegation of plenary power to Congress to secure the status and enforce the rights of all United States citizens.[120] Senator John Sherman, for example, declared that the Thirteenth Amendment's prohibition of slavery "secures to every man within the United States liberty in its broadest terms."[121] The House floor manager of the Civil Rights Bill, Congressman James Wilson, expressly cited *Prigg* and *McCulloch v. Maryland*[122] as authority for the framers' broad theory of constitutional delegation under the Thirteenth Amendment and declared that the "possession of the rights [of free men] by the citizen raises by implication the power in Congress to provide appropriate means for their protection; in other words, to supply the needed remedy."[123] But the Thirteenth Amendment was a more explicit delegation of legislative power than the fugitive slave clause because section 2 expressly delegated to Congress legislative authority to enforce it. Thus, Senator Sherman quoted this section and declared: "Here is not only a guarantee of liberty to every inhabitant of the United States but an express grant of power to Congress to secure this liberty by appropriate legislation."[124]

As Congress had exercised plenary power under the fugitive slave clause to enforce the constitutionally secured property right of slaveholders in 1793 and 1850, so Congress exercised plenary power under the Thirteenth Amendment to enforce the fundamental rights of freemen by enacting the Civil Rights Act of 1866.[125] Senator Lyman Trumbull, the principal author of the Civil Rights Act of 1866, made this point when he introduced the Civil Rights Bill to the Senate and noted that many of its provisions were copied from the Fugitive Slave Act of 1850: "Surely we have the authority to enact a law as efficient in the interest of freedom, now that freedom prevails throughout the country, as we had in the interest of slavery when it prevailed in a portion of the country."[126] Senator Trumbull echoed Justice Story's interpretation of the fugitive slave clause's prohibition against state interference with the right of recaption as an affirmative guarantee of the right that delegated to Congress the power to enforce it.[127] Trumbull asserted that the Thirteenth Amendment's prohibition of slavery was a declaration "that all persons in the United States should be free." He declared that the framers of the Civil Rights Bill "intended to give effect to that declaration and secure to all persons within the United States practical freedom," that is, to secure the rights and privileges "which are essential to freemen."[128] The purpose of this bill, he elaborated, was to secure "the liberty which a person enjoys in society. . . . [T]he liberty to which every citizen is entitled, that is the liberty which was intended to be secured by the Declaration of Independence and the Constitution of the United States originally, and more especially by the [Thirteenth] Amendment which has recently been adopted."[129]

The framers equated the status and rights of freemen secured by the Thirteenth Amendment with the status and rights of citizens. In section 1 of the Civil Rights Act, the framers conferred citizenship and certain civil rights they deemed essential to political freedom and individual autonomy.[130] Senator Trumbull insisted, "To be a citizen of the United States carries with it some rights; and what are they? They are those inherent, fundamental rights which belong to free citizens or free men in all countries, such as the rights enumerated in this bill, and they belong to them in all the states of the Union."[131] As the fugitive slave clause and the Fugitive Slave Acts of 1793 and 1850 secured the property right of slave owners independent of state law and state institutions, so did the Civil Rights Act of 1866 secure the civil rights of American citizens.

In a twist of irony, the Fugitive Slave Act of 1850 served as a model for the remedial provisions of the Civil Rights Act of 1866. Like the 1850 act, the 1866 statute criminalized certain violations of the rights[132] the statute secured to citizens,[133] and it conferred primary civil and criminal jurisdiction on the federal courts to vindicate these rights whenever the citizen was unable to enforce them through state law enforcement institutions.[134] The 1866 statute, like the 1850 act, provided federal legal process and conferred on citizens causes of action to vindicate their rights through federal institutions. Indeed, several sections of the Civil Rights Act were taken from the Fugitive Slave Act of 1850.[135] Trumbull acknowledged his bill's pedigree:

> Most of [its provisions] are copied from the late fugitive slave act, adopted in 1850 for the purpose of returning fugitives from slavery into slavery again. The act that was passed at that time for the purpose of punishing persons who should aid negroes to escape to freedom is now to be applied by the provisions of this bill to the punishment of those who shall undertake to keep them in slavery.[136]

However, unlike the fugitive slave statutes as interpreted by the Supreme Court, the framers of the Civil Rights Act of 1866 intended the states to retain concurrent jurisdiction over citizens' fundamental rights.[137]

The framers of the Civil Rights Act of 1866 also drafted the Fourteenth Amendment[138] with the understanding that it incorporated into the Constitution their interpretation of the Thirteenth Amendment and the plenary power to enforce citizens' rights that they had just exercised in enacting the Civil Rights Act under the Thirteenth Amendment.[139] Indeed, many of its supporters expressly intended to incorporate the 1866 act into the Fourteenth Amendment to ensure the statute's constitutionality.[140] Like the statute, the Fourteenth Amendment confers citizenship on all Americans, and, like the fugitive slave clause with respect to the right it secured, the Fourteenth Amendment prohibits the states from infringing the rights of United States citizens and also from denying to all persons due process and equal protection of the law. The framers' reasons for drafting the amendment as prohibitions against the states were several: to make it self-enforcing, to ensure the constitutionality of the Civil Rights Act, and to avoid the possibility that a future Congress might repeal the Civil Rights Act or refuse to enact additional legislation that might be required to secure citizens' rights more effectively.[141]

Despite the Fourteenth Amendment's wording as prohibitions against the states, the framers understood these clauses as affirmative constitutional guarantees of citizenship and the fundamental rights of citizens which delegated plenary power to Congress to enforce them.[142] In other words, they understood the Fourteenth Amendment in the same way that the congressional drafters of the Fugitive Slave Acts of 1793 and 1850 and the state and federal judges who upheld their constitutionality interpreted the fugitive slave clause. Indeed, many of the framers of the Fourteenth Amendment subsequently exercised plenary power under it and enacted more far-reaching civil rights enforcement statutes in 1870[143] and 1871.[144] These statutes, like the Civil Rights Act of 1866, borrowed provisions from the Fugitive Slave Act of 1850. In structure and substance, they followed the instruments of constitutional rights enforcement Congress established in the Fugitive Slave Acts of 1793 and 1850: they imposed federal civil liability and criminal penalties on anyone who violated the rights secured by the Thirteenth, Fourteenth, and Fifteenth Amendments.

The lower federal courts adopted this understanding of the Reconstruction amendments. They enforced these statutes and affirmed Congress's plenary power to secure citizens' rights.[145] Justice Noah Swayne, as circuit justice, upheld the Civil Rights Act of 1866 shortly after its enactment.[146] Citing *Prigg v. Pennsylvania* and *McCulloch v. Maryland,* among other authorities, he interpreted the Thirteenth Amendment as an affirmative guarantee of freedom that conferred the status and fundamental rights of citizenship on all Americans, rendering the Civil Rights Act merely declaratory in this regard.[147] U.S. Circuit Court Judge William B. Woods, a few years before his appointment to the U.S. Supreme Court, interpreted the Fourteenth Amendment as a guarantee of all the fundamental rights of citizenship, including "the right of freedom of speech, and the other rights enumerated in the first eight articles of amendment to the Constitution of the United States," which delegated to Congress "the power to protect them by appropriate legislation."[148] With the election of Ulysses S. Grant to the presidency in 1868, all three branches of the national government shared the same understanding of the national government's plenary power to enforce citizens' rights and united in protecting citizens' personal liberties from terrorists' violence.[149] The Department of Justice and the lower federal courts enforced the Reconstruction civil rights statutes so vigorously they virtually destroyed the first Ku Klux Klan.[150]

In a stunning rejection of national civil rights enforcement policy, the U.S. Supreme Court reversed the lower federal courts, rejected Congress's plenary power to enforce citizens' fundamental rights under the Thirteenth and Fourteenth Amendments, and eliminated much of the legal authority exercised by the Department of Justice to protect citizens' fundamental rights.[151] Instead of fully and completely effectuating the objects of the Constitution, particularly when legislation represented contemporaneous exposition of the Constitution, as Justice Story defined the judicial function and as antebellum judges enforced the fugitive slave clause, the Supreme Court in the 1870s and 1880s applied a textual literalism in interpreting the Thirteenth and Fourteenth Amendments and diminished their plenary guarantees of fundamental rights to the abolition of slavery and its badges and prohibitions against racially discriminatory state action.[152]

There is a tragic irony in the nineteenth-century history of constitutional liberty and federal enforcement of fundamental rights. The abnegation of liberty contained in the slave owner's property right in slaves offered the founders and antebellum governmental officials the opportunity of providing constitutional guarantees of a right that some of them considered to be fundamental and others considered to be a moral abomination. Nevertheless, they responded with broad theories of constitutional protection, which Congress and the courts vigorously applied in enforcing the constitutionally secured property right of slaveholders. When the nation changed the Constitution into a guarantee of liberty and the rights of freemen, it adopted the constitutional theories and statutory mechanisms used to enforce the property right of slaveholders to enforce the rights of freemen. All three branches of the national government followed the antebellum example of federal rights enforcement and vigorously enforced these new constitutional and statutory guarantees of liberty and fundamental rights. But the Supreme Court of the United States rejected these theories and curtailed the federal government's authority to enforce constitutional rights in decisions that permitted racism to flourish in law. Understanding the extent to which slaveholders' constitutional rights were enforced before the Civil War reveals the starkness of the Court's rejection of constitutional rights enforcement after the Civil War. We still suffer the legacy of the last century's inverted constitutionalism.[153]

Notes

1. Paul Murphy, "Time to Reclaim: The Current Challenge of American Constitutional History," *American Historical Review* 69 (1963): 64.

2. See, e.g., *Palko v. Connecticut,* 302 U.S. 319 (1937); *Planned Parenthood of Southeastern Pennsylvania v. Casey,* 505 U.S. 833 (1992); *Brown v. Board of Education,* 347 U.S. 483 (1954); *Sugarman v. Dougall,* 413 U.S. 634 (1973); *United States v. Virginia,* 518 U.S. 515 (1996); *City of Cleburne v. Cleburne Living Center,* 473 U.S. 432 (1985); *Romer v. Evans,* 517 U.S. 620 (1996).

3. U.S. Const., art. IV, sec. 2, cl. 3.

4. William Blackstone, *Commentaries on the Common Law,* 4 vols. (Oxford, 1768), 3, 4–5.

5. The leading authority on this point was *Somerset v. Stewart,* Loft (G.B.) 1 (1772); 20 Howell St. Tr. (G.B.) 1 (1772). American jurisdictions followed this precedent. See, e.g., *Commonwealth v. Aves,* 18 Pick. 193 (Mass. 1836).

6. *Jones v. VanZandt,* 46 U.S. (5 How.) 215, 229 (1847); *Jones v. VanZandt,* 13 F.Cas. 1040, 1042 (No. 7,501 C.C.Ohio 1843); Arthur Zilversmit, *The First Emancipation: The Abolition of Slavery in the North* (Chicago, 1967); Thomas Morris, *Free Men All: The Personal Liberty Laws of the North, 1780–1861* (Baltimore, 1974), 15–16.

7. Although "slavery" is never mentioned in the Constitution, three clauses were drafted with the explicit intention of recognizing and securing the institution: Article 1, section 2 (the three-fifths clause); Article 1, section 9 (the slave trade clause); and Article 4, section 2 (the fugitive slave clause). William M. Wiecek identifies seven other clauses that more indirectly recognize slavery; Wiecek, *The Sources of Antislavery Constitutionalism in America, 1760–1848* (Ithaca, N.Y., 1977), 62–63.

8. See, e.g., *Prigg v. Pennsylvania,* 41 U.S. (16 Pet.) 439, 611 (1842) ("it cannot be doubted that [the fugitive slave clause] constituted a fundamental article, without which the Union could not have been formed"); *In re Susan,* 23 F.Cas. 444, 445 (No. 13,632 C.C. Ind. 1818); *Wright v. Deacon,* 5 Sarg. & Rawl. 62, 63 (Pa. Sup. Ct. 1819); *Jack v. Martin,* 12 Wend. 311, 319–21 (N.Y. Sup. Ct. 1834). For a contrary view, see Paul Finkelman, "Story Telling on the Supreme Court: Prigg v. Pennsylvania and Justice Story's Judicial Nationalism," *Supreme Court Review* 1994 (1994): 247, 259–63.

9. See *Glen v. Hodges,* 9 Johns. 67, 69 (N.Y. Sup. Ct. 1812); *Wright v. Deacon,* 5 Serge & Rawle 62, 63 (Pa. Sup. Ct. 1819); *Kauffman v. Oliver,* 10 Barr 514, 515 (Pa. Sup. Ct. 1849); *Sims's Case,* 7 Cush. 285, 296, 298, 301, 311 (Mass. 1851); *Driskill v. Parrish,* 7 F.Cas. 1100, 1101 (No. 4,089 C.C. Ohio 1845); *Giltner v. Gorham,* 10 F.Cas. 424, 425 (No. 5,453 C.C. Mich. 1848); *Ray v. Donnell,* 20 F.Cas. 325, 326 (No. 11,590 C.C. Ind. 1849); *Oliver v. Kauffman,* 18 F.Cas. 657, 659, 661 (No. 10,497 C.C. Pa. 1850); *Charge to Grand Jury,* 30 F.Cas. 1015, 1016 (No. 18,263 D. Mass. 1851); *Miller v. McQuerry,* 17 F.Cas. 335, 339 (No. 9,583 C.C. Ohio 1853).

10. Jonathan Elliott, ed., *Debates in the Several State Conventions on the Adoption of the Federal Constitution,* 5 vols. (Philadelphia, 1836–45), 3:453, in Morris, *Free Men All,* 19.

11. Ibid.

12. U.S. Const., art. IV, sec. 2.

13. Act of Feb. 12, 1793, ch. 7, 1 Stat. 302.

14. U.S. Const., art. IV, sec. 2, para. 2. It states: "A Person charged in any

State with Treason, Felony, or other Crime, who shall flee from Justice, and be found in another State, shall on demand of the executive Authority of the State from which he fled, be delivered up, to be removed to the State having Jurisdiction of the Crime."

15. Justice Joseph Story briefly referred to these incidents in his opinion in *Prigg v. Pennsylvania,* 41 U.S. (16 Pet.) 539, 616, 620 (1842). For a fuller discussion of the historical background of the 1793 statute, see William Leslie, "A Study in the Origins of Interstate Rendition: The Big Beaver Creek Murders," *American Historical Review* 57 (October 1951): 429–45; Paul Finkelman, "The Kidnapping of John Davis and the Adoption of the Fugitive Slave Law of 1793," *Journal of Southern History* 56 (1990): 397.

16. Leslie, "A Study in the Origins of Interstate Rendition," 72; Finkelman, "The Kidnapping of John Davis," 404–5.

17. See Finkelman, "The Kidnapping of John Davis," 407–18.

18. Even Paul Finkelman, who recently fervently argued that the founders did not intend to delegate legislative authority to Congress to implement the fugitive slave clause, does not offer any evidence that any of the participants even raised a question concerning Congress's authority to enact the statute. On the contrary, in an earlier article he wrote that, after Congress enacted the bill and sent it to President Washington, "Without any hesitation, President Washington signed this bill into law." Paul Finkelman, "Sorting Out *Prigg v. Pennsylvania,*" *Rutgers Law Review* 24 (1993): 605, 621. Finkelman argues that the founders did not intend to delegate legislative power to Congress in "Story Telling on the Supreme Court," 247, 259–63.

19. The best legal histories of fugitive slave recaption and the reaction of the nonslaveholding states are Stanley Campbell, *The Slave Catchers: Enforcement of the Fugitive Slave Law,* 1850–1860 (New York, 1970); Morris, *Free Men All;* Robert Cover, *Justice Accused: Antislavery and the Judicial Process* (New Haven, Conn., 1975); and Paul Finkelman, *Imperfect Union: Slavery, Federalism, and Comity* (Chapel Hill, N.C., 1981).

20. See, e.g., *In re Susan,* 23 F.Cas. 44 (No. 13,632 C.C. Ind. 1818) (federal summary process of removal is supreme, and state process providing for a trial is superseded). However, granting the certificate of removal was not automatic. See, e.g., *Ex part Simmons,* 22 F.Cas. 151 (No. 12,863 C.C.E.D. Pa. 1823) (Fugitive Slave Act of 1793 did not apply to slaves voluntarily brought from one state to another; certificate of removal denied); *Case of Williams,* 29 F.Cas. 1334 (No. 17,709 D.C.E.D. Pa. 1839) (proof of ownership of slave "must be 'to the satisfaction of the judge.'" Certificate denied because claimant failed to carry this burden).

21. Act of Feb. 12, 1793, ch. 7, 1 Stat. 302, sec. 4.

22. *Stearns v. U.S.,* 22 F.Cas. 1188, 1192 (No. 13,341 C.C. n.d. 1827–40) (private actions for penalties are civil actions).

23. Act of Feb. 12, 1793, ch. 7, 1 Stat. 302, sec. 4.

24. In 1994, Congress again adopted this method of enforcing constitutional rights when it conferred similar civil remedies on women who are victims of violent crimes motivated by gender animus; the Violence Against Women Act, 108 Stat. 1941–1942, 42 U.S.C. 13981. On May 15, 2000, the U.S. Supreme Court struck down this civil remedy, declaring that the Constitution does not delegate to Congress the authority to confer such civil remedies to vindicate constitutional rights. *United States v. Morrison,* 120 S.Ct. 1740 (2000).

25. David Currie argues that "nearly all our constitutional law was made by Congress or the President" in the first decades of our history. Currie, "The Constitution in Congress: Substantive Issues in the First Congress, 1789–1791," *University of Chicago Law Review* 61 (1994): 775, 776. See also Currie, "The Constitution in Congress: The First Congress and the Structure of Government," *University of Chicago Law School Roundtable* 2 (1995): 161.

26. See, e.g., *Hill v. Low,* 12 F.Cas. 172 (No. 6,494 C.C.E.D. Pa. 1822) (verdict for plaintiff for $500 penalty reversed for error in jury charge and new trial ordered); *Stearns v. U.S.,* 22 F.Cas. 1188 (No. 13,341 C.C. n.d., cases reported for period 1827–40) (verdict for plaintiff for $500 penalty reversed for error in jury charge); *Jones v. VanZandt,* 13 F.Cas. (No. 7,504 C.C. Ohio 1843) (verdict for plaintiff for $500) aff'd *Jones v. VanZandt,* 46 U.S. (5 How.) 215 (1847); *Vaughn v. Williams,* 28 F.Cas. 1115 (No. 16,903 C.C. Ind. 1845) (verdict for defendant).

27. See, e.g., *Glen v. Hodges,* 9 Johns. 67 (N.Y. Sup. Ct. 1812) (action of trespass vi et armis by slave owner under 1793 Fugitive Slave Act affirmed and new trial ordered); *Worthington v. Preston,* 30 F.Cas. 645 (No. 18,055 C.C.E.D. Pa. 1824) (jailor not liable for fugitive slave's escape if he was not negligent); *Jones v. VanZandt,* 13 F.Cas. 1040 (No. 7,501 C.C. Ohio 1843) (verdict for plaintiff of $1,200), aff'd *Jones v. VanZandt,* 13 F.Cas. (No. 7,503 C.C. Ohio 1851); *Giltner v. Gorham,* 10 F.Cas. 4424 (No. 5,453 C.C. Mich. 1848) (verdict and judgment for plaintiff for $2,752); *Ray v. Donnell,* 20 F.Cas. 325 (No. 11,590 C.C. Ind. 1849) (verdict and judgment for plaintiff for $1,500); *Driskill v. Parrish,* 7 F.Cas. 1100 (No. 4089 C.C. Ohio 1845) (jury could not agree); retried as *Driskell v. Parish,* 7 F.Cas. 1095 (No. 4,088 C.C. Ohio 1849) (verdict and judgment for plaintiff for $500, the proven value slaves in question); *Dreskill v. Parish,* 7 F.Cas. 1068 (No. 4,075 C.C. Ohio 1851) (per diem and travel expense costs retaxed from defendant to plaintiff for witness who was not summoned but appeared voluntarily); *Dreskill v. Parish,* 7 F.Cas. 1069 (No. 4,076 C.C. Ohio 1851) (per diem and travel expense costs retaxed from defendant to plaintiff for two witnesses who were not summoned but appeared voluntarily); *Kauffman v. Oliver,* 10 Barr 514 (Pa. Sup. Ct. 1849) (an action at common law does not lie for harboring runaway slaves or for aiding in their escape, and state courts do not have jurisdiction under the 1793 act to try such cases); *Oliver v. Kauffman,* 18 F.Cas. 657 (No. 10,497 C.C. Pa. 1850) (action on the case for harboring and concealing fugitive slaves, jury disagreed); retried as *Oliver v. Weakley,* 18 F.Cas. 678 (No. 10,502 3d Cir. 1853) (verdict and judgment for plaintiff for $2,800); *Daggs v. Frazer,* 6 F.Cas. 1112 (No. 3,538 D. Ia. 1849) (action of trover will not lie in Iowa to recover the value of slaves. Plaintiff amended his declaration and the cause continued at the costs of the plaintiff).

28. See, e.g., *Commonwealth v. Griffith,* 2 Pick. 11, 19 (Mass. 1823); *Wright v. Deacon,* 5 Serg. & Rawle 62, 63 (Pa. Sup. Ct. 1819); *Johnson v. Tompkins,* 13 F.Cas. 851, 854, 855 (No. 7,416 C.C.E.D. Pa. 1833); *Charge to Grand Jury,* 30 F.Cas. 1015, 1016 (No. 18,263 D. Mass. 1851).

29. See, e.g., *Glen v. Hodges,* 9 Johns. 67, 69 (N.Y. Sup. Ct. 1812); *Wright v. Deacon,* 5 Serg. & Rawle 62, 63 (Pa. Sup. Ct. 1818); *Commonwealth v. Griffith,* 2 Pick. 11, 13 (Mass. 1823); *Jack v. Martin,* 12 Wend. 311, 321 (N.Y. Sup. Ct. 1834), aff'd. on other grounds, *Jack v. Martin,* 14 Wend. 507 (N.Y. Ct. Err. 1835); *In re Susan,* 23 F.Cas. 444, 445 (No. 13,632 C.C. Ind. 1818); *Johnson v. Tompkins,* 13 F.Cas. 840, 851 (No. 7,416 C.C.E.D. Pa. 1833); *In re Martin,* 16

F.Cas. 881, 883–84 (No. 9,154 S.D.N.Y. n.d., 1827–40). The U.S. Supreme Court upheld Congress's legislative authority to enforce the fugitive slave clause in the first constitutional challenge it decided. *Prigg v. Pennsylvania,* 41 U.S. (16 Pet.) 439 (1842). Justice Story acknowledged that state courts universally upheld the Fugitive Slave Act of 1793. Id. at 567.

30. *Commonwealth v. Griffith,* 2 Pick. 19.

31. *Johnson v. Tompkins,* 13 F.Cas. 851, 854, 855 (No. 7,416 C.C.E.D. Pa. 1833). See also *Charge to Grand Jury,* 30 F.Cas. 1015, 1016 (No. 18,263 D. Mass. 1851) (jurors must enforce the law even though they find it morally repugnant).

32. U.S. Supreme Court Justice John McLean, as circuit justice, asserted, "The act of 1793 has been in operation about sixty years. During that whole time it has been executed as occasion required, and it is not known that any court, judge, or other officer has held the act, in this [summary process to determine right to remove alleged fugitive slave], or in any other respect, unconstitutional"; *Miller v. McQuerry,* 17 F.Cas. 335,340 (No. 9,583 C.C. Ohio 1853).

33. Exceptions are *In re Susan,* 23 F.Cas. at 445, and cases argued by the "Attorney General for Runaway Negroes," future U.S. Supreme Court Chief Justice Salmon P. Chase, such as *Jones v. VanZandt,* 13 F.Cas. 1040 (No. 7, 501 C.C. Ohio 1843) and *Jones v. VanZandt,* 46 U.S. (5 How.) 215 (1847). Chase earned this reputation representing fugitive slaves in Cincinnati, Ohio. J. W. Schuckers, *The Life and Public Services of Salmon Portland Chase* (New York, 1874), 52; John Niven, *Salmon P. Chase: A Biography* (New York, 1995), 78.

34. See, e.g., *Wright v. Deacon,* 5 Serg. & Rawle 62, 63 (Pa. Sup. Ct. 1819) (court rejected defendant's argument that the Fugitive Slave Act is unconstitutional because it denied him of his right to jury trial guaranteed by United States and Pennsylvania constitutions); *Commonwealth v. Griffith,* 2 Pick. at 15–16 (rejected Massachusetts attorney general's argument that the Fugitive Slave Act is unconstitutional because it violated the alleged fugitive slave's Fourth Amendment right against unreasonable seizures); *In re Martin,* 16 F.Cas. 881, 883 (No. 9,154 S.D.N.Y. n.d., 1827–40) (rejected defendant's argument that the 1793 act was unconstitutional because it deprived him of his Seventh Amendment right to jury trial).

35. Henry Wilson, *History of the Rise and Fall of the Slave Power in America* (Boston, 1872), 1:70. Morris, *Free Men All,* 24–34.

36. Morris, *Free Men All,* 29.

37. Ibid., 83.

38. Ibid., 51–53.

39. See, e.g., *In re Susan,* 23 F.Cas. at 445; *Johnson v. Tompkins,* 13 F.Cas. at 852; *In re Martin,* 16 F.Cas. at 882; *Wright v. Deacon,* 5 Serg. & Rawle at 63; *Commonwealth v. Griffith,* 2 Pick. at 19; *Jack v. Martin,* 12 Wend. at 324.

40. See, e.g., the 1826 Pennsylvania antikidnapping law reprinted in *Prigg v. Pennsylvania,* 41 U.S. (16 Pet.) 439, 550–51 (1842).

41. However, Justice Baldwin affirmed the claimants' right of self-help in *Johnson v. Tompkins,* 13 F.Cas. 804 (No. 7,416 C.C.E.D. Pa. 1833).

42. Carl Swisher, *The Taney Period, 1836–64,* vol. 5 of *History of the Supreme Court of the United States,* ed. P. Freund (New York, 1974), 536.

43. Morris, *Free Men All,* 94.

44. *Prigg v. Pennsylvania,* 41 U.S. (16 Pet.) 439 (1842).

45. Morris, *Free Men All,* 95; Swisher, *Taney Period,* 536. Edward Prigg

and others, acting as agents of a Maryland slave owner, secured from a local justice of the peace in Pennsylvania a warrant for the arrest of certain runaway slaves. They seized the runaways under authority of this warrant and presented them to the justice of the peace who had issued the warrant. However, under the Pennsylvania antikidnapping law of 1826, he lacked jurisdiction to hear the case, and he refused to do so. Unable to secure a warrant of removal as required by both the federal and state statutes, the agents nevertheless returned the slaves to their owner in Maryland. The agents were subsequently indicted and charged with kidnapping by a Pennsylvania grand jury under the 1826 Pennsylvania antikidnapping statute. The Pennsylvania governor applied to the governor of Maryland to extradite the accused kidnappers, but he refused. Instead, the Maryland governor referred the matter to the state legislature, which passed resolutions declaring that the right of recaption was guaranteed by the Constitution and laws of the United States and could not be abridged by the states. After a commissioner Maryland sent to Pennsylvania failed to obtain a dismissal of the indictments and modifications in the Pennsylvania antikidnapping statute, Maryland's and Pennsylvania's legislatures voted to have an expedited hearing brought before the U.S. Supreme Court to resolve the issues in dispute. Carl Swisher reports that "the Pennsylvania legislature arranged for a trial at which by special verdict Edward Prigg, one of the captors, would be found guilty and the case, challenging the constitutionality of the 1826 statute, would be handled in such a way that it could be taken to the Supreme Court"; Swisher, *Taney Period,* 538. Justice Joseph Story, in his opinion for the Court, acknowledged the origin of this suit by agreement between the states. He stated that, before he addressed "the very important and interesting questions involved in this record, it is fit to say, that the cause has been brought here by the co-operation and sanction, both of the state of Maryland, and the state of Pennsylvania, in the most friendly and courteous spirit, with a view to have those questions finally disposed of by the adjudication of this Court; so that the agitations on this subject in both states, which have had a tendency to interrupt the harmony between them, may subside, and the conflict of opinion be put at rest." *Prigg v. Pennsylvania,* 41 U.S. (16 Pet.) 609. Justice McLean was even more explicit. Asserting that the decision of the Pennsylvania Supreme Court "was pro forma," he added: "Indeed, I suppose, the case has been made up merely to bring the question before this Court." *Prigg v. Pennsylvania,* 41 U.S. (16 Pet.) 673 (McLean, J., concurring); see also his comments at 659.

46. Six justices filed concurring and dissenting opinions. Justice James M. Wayne summarized the holding of the Court and the positions of the justices on the key points: all of the justices agreed that the Pennsylvania statute was unconstitutional; that the fugitive slave clause "was a compromise between the slaveholding, and the non-slaveholding states, to secure to the former fugitive slaves as property." Wayne concluded that there was no disagreement "among the judges as to the reversal of the judgment; none in respect to the origin and object of the provision, or the obligation to exercise it." The disagreement that did exist among the justices, Wayne explained, related "to the mode of execution." Three justices insisted that the states could "legislate upon the [fugitive slave clause], in aid of the object it was intended to secure; and that such legislation is constitutional, when it does not conflict with the remedy which Congress may enact." Justice Wayne's summary reveals the positions taken by the silent justices on critical issues.

The Court was unanimous regarding the nature of the constitutional rights guaranteed by the fugitive slave clause, and that this guarantee delegated plenary legislative authority to Congress to protect and enforce the rights thus guaranteed. *Prigg v. Pennsylvania,* 41 U.S. (16 Pet.) 636–38 (Wayne, J., concurring).

47. Ibid., 612.

48. Ibid.

49. Ibid., 611. As noted earlier, this view was widely shared by antebellum judges. See the cases cited in notes 7 and 8. But see Finkelman, "Story Telling on the Supreme Court," 259–63, which argues that this was not the founders' intent or understanding.

50. *Prigg v. Pennsylvania,* 41 U.S. (16 Pet.) 612.

51. Ibid.

52. Ibid.

53. Ibid., 613.

54. Ibid.

55. Ibid.

56. U.S. Const. art. IV, sec. 2, cl.3.

57. *Prigg v. Pennsylvania,* 41 U.S. (16 Pet.) 615.

58. Ibid., 615 (emphasis added).

59. Ibid. Justice Story was paraphrasing Chief Justice Marshall's opinion in *McCulloch v. Maryland,* 17 U.S. 316, 421 (1819).

60. The fugitive slave clause was inserted in Article IV, section 2. The texts of the three provisions of this section—the privileges and immunities clause, the extradition clause, and the fugitive slave clause—are plausibly interpreted as not delegating legislative power to Congress, particularly from a states-rights or strict construction perspective. A narrow construction is strengthened, if not made compelling, by the texts of the other three sections of Article IV, all of which contained express delegations of legislative authority to Congress for their enforcement.

61. *Prigg v. Pennsylvania,* 41 U.S. (16 Pet.) 615–16. Story's full statement is, "The clause is found in the national Constitution, and not in that of any state. It does not point out any state functionaries, or any state action to carry its provisions into effect. The states cannot, therefore, be compelled to enforce them; and it might well be deemed an unconstitutional exercise of the power of interpretation, to insist that the states are bound to provide means to carry into effect the duties of the national government, nowhere delegated or intrusted to them by the Constitution. On the contrary, the natural, if not the necessary conclusion is, that the national government, in the absence of all positive provisions to the contrary, is bound, through its own proper departments, legislative, judicial, or executive, as the case may require, to carry into effect all the rights and duties imposed upon it by the Constitution." Note that this view of constitutional delegation is just the opposite of that adopted by the current Supreme Court. See, e.g., Chief Justice William Rehnquist's theory of delegation in *United States v. Lopez,* 115 S.Ct. 1624, 1626 (1995) (the founders' First Principles limited the powers of the national government to those "few and defined" powers the Constitution delegated to it and reserved to the states the "numerous and indefinite" powers of government).

62. *Prigg v. Pennsylvania,* 41 U.S. (16 Pet.) 620.

63. "The remark of Mr. Madison, in the Federalist, (No. 43,) would seem in such cases to apply with peculiar force. 'A right (says he) implies a remedy;

and where else would the remedy be deposited, than where it is deposited by the Constitution?' meaning, as the context shows, in the government of the United States." *Prigg v. Pennsylvania,* 41 U.S. (16 Pet.) 616.

64. Ibid.

65. Ibid., 621.

66. Citing *Stuart v. Laird,* 5 U.S. (1 Cranch) 299 (1803), *Martin v. Hunter's Lessee,* 14 U.S. (1 Wheat.) 304 (1819), and *Cohen v. Virginia,* 19 U.S. (6. Wheat.) 264 (1821), Story declared: "Especially did this Court in [these cases] rely upon contemporaneous expositions of the Constitution, and long acquiescence in it, with great confidence, in the discussion of questions of a highly interesting and important nature." *Prigg v. Pennsylvania,* 41 U.S. (16 Pet.) 621.

67. *Prigg v. Pennsylvania,* 41 U.S. (16 Pet.) 620.

68. Ibid., 621.

69. This theory of constitutional interpretation is associated with Justice Felix Frankfurter, who used this term in asserting that history and political practice were essential factors in interpreting the constitutional powers of the president. *Youngstown Sheet & Tube Co. v. Sawyer,* 343 U.S. 579, 610 (1952) (Frankfurter, J., concurring). However, Frankfurter cited Chief Justice John Marshall as authority for this "spacious view" of the Constitution, for Marshall used political practice as a method of constitutional interpretation in *McCulloch v. Maryland.* See *McCulloch v. Maryland,* 17 U.S. 401–2.

70. *Prigg v. Pennsylvania,* 41 U.S. (16 Pet.) 621.

71. Ibid., 623.

72. Story explained: "It is, therefore, in a just sense a new and positive right, independent of comity, confined to no territorial limits, and bounded by no state institutions or policy." Ibid.

73. Ibid.

74. Ibid., 623–24.

75. Ibid., 626.

76. Ibid., 628 (Taney, C.J., dissenting); 634–35 (Thompson, J., dissenting); 652 (Daniel, J., dissenting).

77. See, e.g., *Kauffman v. Oliver,* 10 Barr 514 (Pa. Sup. Ct. 1849), where the Pennsylvania Supreme Court held there was no common-law action for the recaption of slaves who escaped to Pennsylvania from another state; that Pennsylvania state courts "are interdicted from assuming a voluntary jurisdiction" in such cases (id. at 519); "that an action of this kind can only be sustained under the act of Congress of 1793; that our state courts have not jurisdiction of an action under the statute; and the principles of the common law do not sustain any such action in this state," (id. at 519).

78. Morris, *Free Men All,* 114–23; Swisher, *The Taney Period,* 545.

79. Swisher, *The Taney Period,* 546–48. Indeed, Lincoln's biographer Albert J. Beveridge considered the *Prigg* case as one of the most important decided by the U.S. Supreme Court in this regard. Albert Beveridge, *Abraham Lincoln, 1809–1858,* (Boston, 1928), 2:68.

80. Morris, *Free Men All,* 130–47.

81. Act of Sept. 18, 1850, ch. LX, 9 Stat. 462.

82. Ibid., sec. 1.

83. Ibid., sec. 4.

84. Allen Johnson, "The Constitutionality of the Fugitive Slave Acts," *Yale Law Journal* 31 (1921): 161, 181–82. See also Morris, *Free Men All,* 132.

85. Act of Sept. 18, 1850, ch. LX, 9 Stat. 462, secs. 1, 5.

86. Ibid., sec. 5.

87. Ibid.

88. Ibid., sec. 6. The statute authorized slave owners and their agents to reclaim runaway slaves either by warrant issued by a federal judge or commissioner or by seizing the fugitive without legal process and bringing her before a federal judge or commissioner "whose duty it shall be to hear and determine the case of such claimant in a summary manner" and, on "satisfactory proof being made," to issue a certificate authorizing the claimant or his agent to remove the slave with "such reasonable force and restraint as may be neccessary [*sic*]" back to the state in which she owed service.

89. U.S. Const., art. VI, cl. 2.

90. Act of Sept. 18, 1850, ch. LX, 9 Stat. 462, sec. 6. The only concession to state powers Congress included in the 1850 statute was a provision specifying as conclusive evidence of the identity and service owed by the alleged fugitive "satisfactory testimony, duly taken and certified by some court, magistrate, justice of the peace, or other legal officer authorized to administer an oath and take depositions under the laws of the State or Territory, from which such person owing service or labor may have escaped," with a certificate of the authority of the officer and the seal of the proper state court or officer. The last section of the statute elaborated the state process permitted as conclusive evidence of the fact of escape and the service owed to the claimant as "satisfactory proof" recorded in a court transcript authenticated by the clerk and court seal. The claimant or his agent could present this record to a federal officer in any state or territory in which the slave had escaped, and, being conclusive evidence, the federal officer was obliged to issue the certificate of removal. Act of Sept. 18, 1850, ch. X, 9 Stat. 462, sec. 10.

91. Act of Sept. 18, 1850, ch. LX, 9 Stat. 462, sec. 7.

92. Ibid.

93. See, e.g., *Jones v. VanZandt,* 13 F.Cas. 1040 (value of escaped slave was fixed at $600); *Driskill v. Parish,* 7 F.Cas. 1095, 1100 (value of two escaped slaves fixed at $500); *Giltner v. Gorham,* 10 F.Cas. 424, 427 (value of six escaped slaves fixed at $2,752); *Ray v. Donnell,* 20 F.Cas. 325 (damages of $1,500 awarded for one adult woman slave and her four children); *Oliver v. Weakley,* 18 F.Cas. 678 (damages of $2,800 awarded for twelve escaped slaves, two husbands, two wives, and eight children, *Oliver v. Kauffman,* 18 F.Cas. 657, 658).

94. *Norris v. Crocker and Egbert,* 54 U.S. (13 How.) 429, 440 (1851); *Oliver v. Kauffman,* 18 F.Cas. 657, 660 (No. 10,497 C.C.E.D. Pa. 1850).

95. Fugitive Slave Act of 1850, sec. 8.

96. Act of Sept. 18, 1850, ch. LX, 9 Stat. 462, sec. 9. On mere affidavit by the claimant or his agent that he had reason to believe that a rescue would be attempted by force before he could return the fugitive to the state from which she fled, the federal officer who made the initial arrest was required to retain as many persons as necessary to overcome such force and to return the fugitive to the claimant in the state from which the fugitive slave escaped. The fees and costs of this process were to be paid out of the United States Treasury.

97. Morris, *Free Men All,* 137–38; Johnson, "The Constitutionality of the Fugitive Slave Acts," 171–72.

98. James McPherson, *Battle Cry of Freedom: The Civil War Era* (New York, 1988), 80.

99. Ibid, 82.

100. Ibid.

101. See, e.g., *Charge to Grand Jury—Fugitive Slave Law,* 30 F.Cas. 1015 (No. 18, 263 D.C. Mass. 1851); *Norris v. Crocker and Egbert,* 54 U.S. (13 How.) 429 (1851); *Sims's Case,* 61 Mass. (7 Cush.) 285 (1851); Leonard Levy, *The Law of the Commonwealth and Chief Justice Shaw* (New York, 1957), 89–97; Morris, *Free Men All,* 151–85; Cover, *Justice Accused,* 217–21; McPherson, *Battle Cry of Freedom,* 80–91.

102. Levy, *The Law of the Commonwealth and Chief Justice Shaw,* 89–90; Morris, *Free Men All,* 166; McPherson, *Battle Cry of Freedom,* 82–83, 119–20. McPherson recounts that federal marshals appealed to President Franklin Pierce for help in returning fugitive slave Anthony Burns from Boston to Virginia when his capture in Boston triggered riots in which a man was killed in an assault on the courthouse where Burns was being held. President Pierce sent several companies of marines, cavalry, and artillery to Boston and admonished federal officers to spare no expense to ensure that federal law was enforced. They were joined by Massachusetts militia and Boston police in an effort to keep the peace. This single incident, McPherson observes, cost the government $100,000, which is "equal to perhaps two million in 1987 dollars." McPherson, *Battle Cry of Freedom,* 120.

103. *Dred Scott v. Sandford,* 60 U.S. (19 How.) 393 (1857).

104. The New England states and the states of Ohio, Michigan, and Wisconsin enacted personal liberty laws in the years 1854 through 1861 designed to undermine the Fugitive Slave Acts. Morris, *Free Men All,* 166–68, 219–22.

105. See Swisher, *Taney Period,* 654–56; Vroman Mason, "The Fugitive Slave Law in Wisconsin, with Reference to Nullification Sentiment," *Proceedings of the State Historical Society of Wisconsin* (1896): 117.

106. The U.S. Supreme Court analyzed the Fugitive Slave Act of 1850 in *Norris v. Crocker and Egbert,* 54 U.S. (13 How.) 429 (1851). It did not formally decide its constitutionality because that question was not before it. However, its discussion assumed its constitutionality. Lower federal courts did uphold its constitutionality. See *United States v. Scott,* 27 F.Cas. 990 (No. 16,240B D. Mass. 1851); *Charge to Grand Jury—Fugitive Slave Act,* 30 F.Cas. 1007 (No. 18,261 C.C.S.D. N.Y. 1851); *Miller v. McQuerry,* 34 17 F.Cas. 335 (No. 9,583 C.C. Ohio 1853). U.S. District Court Judge Andrew G. Miller upheld the slave owner's right under the 1850 statute to seize his fugitive slave, with or without a warrant, and issued a writ of habeas corpus directed to the sheriff who held him on a charge of kidnapping and assault and battery for exercising his federal right of recapture. *United States ex rel. Garland v. Morris,* 26 F.Cas. 1318 (No. 15,811 D. Wis. 1854).

107. *In re Booth,* 3 Wis. 1 (1854), aff'd., *In re Booth,* 3 Wis. 49 (1854) (habeas granted); *Ex parte Booth,* 3 Wis. 145 (1854) (habeas denied while case is within jurisdiction of another court); *In re Booth and Rycraft,* 3 Wis. 157 (1855) (habeas granted).

108. *United States v. Booth,* 59 U.S. (18 How.) 477 (1855).

109. *Ableman v. Booth,* 62 U.S. (21 How.) 506 (1858).

110. Act of Sept. 24, 1789, ch. 20, 1 Stat. 73, sec. 25.

111. *Ableman v. Booth,* 62 U.S. (21 How.) 521–22, 526.

112. *Ableman v. Booth,* 11 Wis. 498 (1859).

113. See Mississippi Resolutions on Secession (Nov. 30, 1860), reprinted in *Documents in American History,* ed. Henry Commage (Englewood Cliffs,

N.J., 1973), 1:371; South Carolina Declaration of Causes of Secession (Dec. 24, 1860), reprinted in id., 372; Kentucky Resolutions (Nov. 16, 1798) and (Feb. 22, 1799), reprinted in id., 178, 183; Virginia Resolutions (Dec. 24, 1798), reprinted in id., 182.

114. South Carolina Declaration of Causes of Secession (Dec. 24, 1860), reprinted in *Documents in American History*, 1:372.

115. President Abraham Lincoln's "First Inaugural Address (Mar. 4, 1861)" and President Lincoln's "Message to Congress in Special Session (July 4, 1861)," reprinted in *Documents in American History*, 385, 393.

116. U.S. Const., art. XIII, declares: "Sec. 1. Neither slavery nor involuntary servitude, except as a punishment for crime whereof the party shall have been duly convicted, shall exist within the United States, or any place subject to their jurisdiction. Sec. 2. Congress shall have power to enforce this article by appropriate legislation."

117. *Cong. Globe*, 39th Cong., 1st sess. 5 (1866) (Rep. Colfax).

118. Act of April 9, 1866, ch. 31, 14 Stat. 27.

119. *Prigg v. Pennsylvania*, 41 U.S. (16 Pet.) 612, 615.

120. Robert J. Kaczorowski, "To Begin the Nation Anew: Congress, Citizenship, and Civil Rights After the Civil War," *American Historical Review* 92 (February 1987): 45, 47–49; Kaczorowski, "The Enforcement Provisions of the Civil Rights Act of 1866: A Legislative History in Light of *Runyon v. McCrary*," *Yale Law Journal* 98 (1989): 565, 567–70, 581; Kaczorowski, "Revolutionary Constitutionalism in the Era of the Civil War and Reconstruction," *New York University Law Review* 61 (1986): 863, 895–99.

121. *Cong. Globe*, 39th Cong., 1st sess. 41 (1866) (Sen. Sherman).

122. *McCulloch v. Maryland*, 17 U.S. (4 Wheat.) 316 (1819).

123. *Cong. Globe*, 39th Cong., 1st sess. 1294 (1866) (Rep. Wilson). See also, id. at 1118 (Rep. Wilson); id. at 1836 (Rep. Williams).

124. *Cong. Globe*, 39th Cong., 1st sess. 41 (1866) (Sen. Sherman).

125. Act of April 9, 1866, ch. 31, 14 Stat. 27.

126. *Cong. Globe*, 39th Cong., 1st sess. 475 (1866).

127. *Prigg v. Pennsylvania*, 41 U.S. (16 Pet.) 612–13.

128. *Cong. Globe*, 39th Cong., 1st sess. 474 (1866) (Sen. Trumbull).

129. Ibid.

130. Kaczorowski, "Enforcement Provisions of the Civil Rights Act of 1866," 570.

131. *Cong. Globe*, 39th Cong., 1st sess., 1757 (1866) (Sen. Trumbull). Section 1 enumerated the rights "to make and enforce contracts, to sue, be parties, and give evidence, to inherit, purchase, lease, sell, hold, and convey real and personal property, and to full and equal benefit of all laws and proceedings for the security of person and property," as rights that all United States citizens would enjoy under the statute. Act of April 9, 1866, ch. 31, 14 Stat. 27, sec. 1.

132. Act of April 9, 1866, ch. 31, 14 Stat. 27, sec. 2.

133. Ibid., sec. 1.

134. Ibid., sec. 3.

135. In addition to the criminal penalties and civil remedies provided in sections 2 and 3 to vindicate violations of citizens' civil rights, sections 4–9 of the Civil Rights Act closely paralleled specific provisions contained in various sections of the 1850 Fugitive Slave Act.

136. *Cong. Globe*, 39th Cong., 1st sess. 475 (1866) (Sen. Trumbull). Other

legislators, both supporters and opponents of the civil rights bill, also acknowledged that the Civil Rights Act was modeled on the Fugitive Slave Act of 1850. See id. at 500 (Sen. Stewart); id. at 601 (Sen. Hendricks); id. at 602 (Sen. Lane of Indiana); id. at 603–4 (Sen. Cowan); id. at 605, 606 (Sen. Norton); id. at 605, 606, 1757 (Sen. Trumbull); id. at 1118–19, 1295 (Rep. Wilson, House Floor Manager); id. at 1296 (Rep. Latham); id. at Appendix 158–59 (Rep. Windom).

137. Kaczorowski, "To Begin the Nation Anew," 56; Kaczorowski, "Enforcement Provisions of the Civil Rights Act of 1866," 572–73.

138. U.S. Const., art. XIV. Section 1 provides: "All persons born or naturalized in the United States and subject to the jurisdiction thereof, are citizens of the United States and of the State wherein they reside. No State shall make or enforce any law which shall abridge the privileges or immunities of citizens of the United States; nor shall any State deprive any person of life, liberty, or property, without due process of law; nor deny to any person within its jurisdiction the equal protection of the laws."

139. Kaczorowski, "Revolutionary Constitutionalism," 910–13.

140. *Cong. Globe,* 39th Cong., 1st sess. 1088 (1866) (Rep. Woodbridge); id. at 2459, 2462 (Rep. Stevens); id. at 2462 (Rep. Garfield); id. at 2464, 2465 (Rep. Thayer); id. at 2498 (Rep. Broomall); id. at 2896 (Sen. Howard); id. at 2896 (Sen. Doolittle); id. 2961 (Sen. Poland); id. at Appendix 240 (Sen. Davis). Kaczorowski, "Revolutionary Constitutionalism," 910–12.

141. Kaczorowski, "Enforcement Provisions of the Civil Rights Act of 1866," 572–73; Kaczorowski, "To Begin the Nation Anew," 56–58.

142. See note 120.

143. Act of May 31, 1870, ch. 114, 16 Stat. 140. This statute also reenacted the first two sections of the Civil Rights Act of 1866 to secure its constitutionality under the Fourteenth Amendment, which was ratified in 1868.

144. Act of April 20, 1871, ch. 22, 17 Stat. 13.

145. Robert J. Kaczorowski, *The Politics of Judicial Interpretation: The Federal Courts, Department of Justice and Civil Rights, 1866–1876* (New York, 1985), 1–25; Kaczorowski, "Revolutionary Constitutionalism," 900–903, 935–38.

146. *United States v. Rhodes,* 27 F.Cas. 785 (No. 16,151 C.C. Ky 1867).

147. Ibid.

148. *United States v. Hall,* 26 F.Cas. 79, 82, 83 (No. 15,282 C.C.S.D. Ala. 1871).

149. Kaczorowski, *Politics of Judicial Interpretation,* 49–134. For a contrary view, see Kermit L. Hall, "Political Power and Constitutional Legitimacy: The South Carolina Ku Klux Klan Trials, 1871–1872," *Emory Law Journal* 33 (1984): 921; Lou Falkner Williams, *The Constitution and the Ku Klux Klan on Trial: Federal Enforcement and Local Resistance in South Carolina, 1871–1872* (Athens, Ga., 1995). They argue that federal judges in South Carolina crippled federal efforts to enforce civil rights by rejecting broad theories of federal constitutional rights enforcement authority under the Fourteenth Amendment and affirming state action limitations on that power.

150. Kaczorowski, *Politics of Judicial Interpretation,* 93–94. But Richard Zuczek, "The Federal Government's Attack on the Ku Klux Klan: A Reassessment," *South Carolina Historical Magazine* 97 (1996): 47, disagrees and argues that government's enforcement policy was ineffective in South Carolina.

151. *Blyew v. United States,* 80 U.S. (13 Wall.) 581 (1872); *Slaughter-House Cases,* 83 U.S. (16 Wall.) 36 (1873); *United States v. Cruikshank,* 92 U.S. (2 Otto)

553 (1875); *United States v. Harris,* 106 U.S. 629 (1882); Kaczorowski, *Politics of Judicial Interpretation,* 135–229; Kaczorowski, "Enforcement Provisions of the Civil Rights Act of 1866," 590–94.

152. The Supreme Court's decisions and opinions of the 1870s and 1880s manifest an aggressively activist judicial review. The Court was no longer deferential to Congress and the framers of constitutional provisions. Rather, the Court imposed its conception of American constitutionalism, one predicated on a different conception of the founders' understanding of American constitutionalism than that adopted by the Supreme Court during the chief justiceships of John Marshall and Roger B. Taney. Contrast the decisions cited in note 151 with *McCulloch v. Maryland,* 17 U.S. (4 Wheat.) 316, and *Prigg v. Pennsylvania,* 41 U.S. (16 Pet.) 439. The Court in the cases cited in note 151 imposed a states-rights-centered conception of American constitutional federalism that enhanced the power and autonomy of the states and diminished the power of the national government to enforce the rights of all Americans. In doing so, the Court ignored Justice Story's general rule of constitutional interpretation limiting the Court's power of judicial review: "No Court of justice can be authorized so to construe any clause of the Constitution as to defeat its obvious ends, when another construction, equally accordant with the words and sense thereof, will enforce and protect them." *Prigg v. Pennsylvania,* 41 U.S. (16 Pet.) 612.

153. See, e.g., *City of Boerne v. Flores,* 117 S.Ct. 2157 (1997) (Religious Freedom Restoration Act is unconstitutional on grounds that the Fourteenth Amendment does not authorize Congress to enforce substantive rights, such as the right to the free exercise of religion); *United States v. Morrison,* 120 S.Ct. 1740 (2000) (civil remedies conferred by the Violence Against Women Act on victims of violent crimes motivated by gender animus are unconstitutional for the reason stated in Boerne).

*Chapter Three*

# The Rise and Fall of Classical Legal Thought: Preface to the Modern Constitution

William M. Wiecek

The history of the U.S. Supreme Court from 1938 through 1953 has been slighted in scholarly treatment, compared with the attention paid to the dramatic struggles of the preceding and following decades.[1] Writers seem to regard those years as an uninteresting interlude between the Court-packing contest and the activism of the Warren Court. This is regrettable, because the Roosevelt and Truman Courts did much to shape the constitutional order that will greet the twenty-first century. One of the Court's most important challenges—and one that it did not meet successfully—was to devise a new theory of adjudication that would legitimate its own role in American governance.

For the half century before 1938, the Supreme Court had carried on its work under the auspices of a powerful judicial vision that scholars have variously termed "classical legal thought," "legal classicism," "legal formalism," "legal orthodoxy," "constitutional fundamentalism," "laissez-faire constitutionalism," or cognate phrases.[2] Legal classicism comprised a coherent set of beliefs and values held by many lawyers and judges in the years 1880 through 1940. The matrix of legal doctrine in that era was a comprehensive system of assumptions about liberty, power, rights, and the values that define Americans as a people and their government as a republic. This *mentalité* was not a philosophical school and was something both more and less than a jurisprudential theory. It traced its origins to the foundation of the republic, grew in authority under the guiding hands of John Marshall and Joseph Story, and became fully articulated by the last decade of the nineteenth century. Its most important function was to define the rule of law and legitimate judicial power. Erected atop this ideological foundation was the superstructure of legal doctrine in both private and public law. This doctrinal edifice incorporated a framework of constitutional norms that gave meaning to the generalities of the documentary Constitution.

Stated in briefest compass, legal orthodoxy asserted that law derived from general principles that generated doctrine, which in turn provided specific norms that would resolve any dispute. These principles, doctrines, and norms were objective: they existed outside the will or interests of individuals and groups in society. They were immanent in the legal and constitutional order: judges discovered them and did not invent them. Principles and norms were neutral and suprapolitical; that is what made them rules of law, in contrast with political decisions. These principles were arrayed hierarchically, with human liberty at the highest level, a transcendent value that subsumed all others and could be trumped by none.

Classicist lawyers defined that liberty as security of life and person, ability to exercise individual will, and sanctity of property. They assumed an inherent tension between individual liberty and governmental power. If wielded beyond the limited extent necessary to protect individual liberty, the authority of government would threaten liberty. Contemplating the society around them in the closing decades of the nineteenth century, classicist lawyers and judges saw the likeliest threat to liberty in the redistribution of wealth, which would likely occur in the form of legislative expropriation of the property of some persons (including corporations) for the benefit of others. Such acts, in this context, included political regulation of the use of property and the rates charged for it. Both, to classical lawyers, deprived owners of the beneficial use of their property.

The potential for legislative interference with contractual relationships was just as worrisome. Classical lawyers applauded Henry Maine's insight that the progress of societies from primitive to modern law was characterized by the transition from status to contract. In American experience, that advance in civilization had been exemplified first by legal reform, then by the Married Women's Property Acts, and finally by the abolition of slavery. Protecting freedom of contract ranked as high as the security of property in classical juristic values.

Property and contract enjoyed their preeminent position in classical thought because both were explicitly protected in the documentary Constitution.[3] A classical lawyer could easily demonstrate that the framers meant to protect property and contract from legislative spoliation. They had inserted provisions in the Constitution and Bill of Rights to achieve just that. What was known of the framers' intentions confirmed the classical interpretation that placed such a high value on property and contract as preconstitutional institutions of American civilization.

One of the legal order's most important responsibilities, therefore, was policing legislatures to forestall the redistribution of wealth through interference with contractual obligations or property rights. Lawyers believed in a clear distinction between public law, always potentially redistributive, and private law, which regulated consensual relations between individuals. Where these relationships were consensual, by definition no redistribution was taking place, for the exchange was voluntary and not coerced (at least not by the power of the state).

In the classical view, a constant tension existed between courts and legislatures. Legislatures, elected by democratic processes and governed by majoritarian principles, presumably reflected popular will. Constitutional reforms of the 1820s and 1830s had largely eliminated special constitutional protections for property, such as wealth qualifications for the franchise. Thus, the political process alone could not be relied on to protect accumulated wealth from legislative spoliation. That role fell to courts by default. But orthodox lawyers denied that courts had a special responsibility to defend wealth against legislative marauding by the poor. Instead, reasoning by false symmetry, lawyers tirelessly insisted that law protected the pittance of the poor with the same vigilance that it defended the opulence of the wealthy. To classical lawyers, the working man was the juridical equal of a Rockefeller or a Carnegie. Only in that sense, however, did classical law respect equality as a value.

Courts determined law by the processes of reason, not by will, numbers, or force. Judges found law in the constitutional order established by the American Revolution, in principles inherent in republican government, in the customs of the people, in the development of the common law, and even in racialist conceptions of Anglo-Saxon national character.[4] Compared with these sources, statutory law was implicitly suspect, representing as it did majority will.

Chief Justice John Marshall laid the foundations of legal classicism. His achievement was reinforced by ideological developments of the antebellum era. The modern state that emerged after the Civil War, defined by industrialization and wrenching dislocations of society and economy, provided the matrix in which classicism emerged and flowered. Classical assumptions and methods drove much of Supreme Court adjudication throughout the forty years after its premises came to dominate the Court's thinking in the 1890s.

Legal classicism was a judicial vision of comprehensive breadth and explanatory power. The marble temple dedicated in 1935 to house its chief votaries provided a resplendent symbol of that vision's authority: classical, balanced, symmetrical, spacious, and above all awe-inspiring. Yet from the beginning, classical legal thought contained the potential for disintegration. Its authority was undermined by inherent contradictions that were piled atop assumptions divorced from social reality. In the constitutional crisis that accompanied the Great Depression, these innate flaws shattered the dogmas of classicism. On the ruins of classicism, the justices of the Supreme Court after 1938 began trying to construct a legitimating paradigm of comparable authority. They have not yet succeeded, and the ideological struggles on the Court in the 1990s suggest that we will not soon see a replacement for the classical vision.

This chapter, like the larger work of which it is a précis,[5] identifies the roots of legal classicism, recapitulates its principal ideas and their application in public law, and traces the history of its rise and fall.

## The Origins of Classical Legal Thought

The complex of beliefs, values, and assumptions about society that constituted legal classicism did not suddenly appear out of nowhere in the 1880s, nor was it a radical innovation. Rather, classicism grew out of the foundational achievements of the eighteenth-century constitutional era. From there it evolved as a natural, almost organic, development of antebellum legal culture. The story is familiar,[6] but a brief survey would be useful for understanding classicism's authority as a legitimating explanation of judicial power.

The American Revolution, the constitutive event of American national life, left a rich deposit of constitutional values. Positive law was subordinated to higher law, which served as a monitor for all governmental actions. No statute could be valid if inconsistent with this higher law. Originally Americans sought the sources of higher law in the British constitution, the common law, natural law (as defined by Scholastic philosophers), the divine ordinances found in the Bible, or universal norms of behavior somehow implanted in the human psyche. In the crucible of revolutionary and republican constitution making, Americans determined that the source of fundamental law was the constitutive act of the people in their sovereign capacity, expressed in written constitutions—first of the states, then of the national government. Higher law thereby became subsumed in the supremacy of written constitutions.

Revolutionary ideology assumed a continual tension between the power of government and the liberties of the people. The resultant struggle was a zero-sum game: any accretion of governmental power would come at least potentially at the expense of popular liberty. Therefore, government had to be hedged about with inhibitions on its powers. The written constitution was the most important of these, embodying checks and balances, divided and shared power, separated powers, limited government, and so on. The legitimacy of government derived from the consent of the people, who were the source of coercive public authority. Popular consent was a necessary but not a sufficient basis of governmental power. To be legitimate, that power had to be wielded in subordination to the higher law of the Constitution.

The liberties of the people were anterior to government, which was created to control the depravity of human nature. Left unchecked, human self-interest would lead to the rule of the strong arm, where every person's life, liberty, and property might be lost to superior and lawless force. But government had the sinister propensity of itself becoming a threat to popular liberty. The republican state constitutions and the federal Constitution of 1787, together with the Bill of Rights, contained numerous constraints on governmental authority to forestall that threat, including provisions that no one's life, liberty, or property could be taken without due process of law or except by the law of the land.

Throughout the constitutional era, courts assumed an expanding role in protecting the people's liberties. But this posed a dilemma to Americans. It was essential for republican theory that governmental action be the product of the will of the people, as expressed through representative assemblies. To permit popular will to be frustrated by nonelected judges seemed a denial of the Revolution's supreme achievement, popular sovereignty. Alexander Hamilton resolved that dilemma brilliantly in *The Federalist,* No. 78 by grounding judicial power in the sovereignty of the people. "The courts were designed to be an intermediate body between the people and the legislature . . . to keep the latter within the limits assigned to their authority."[7] Because the Constitution is itself a law, the highest law and the supreme expression of the people's will, judges interpreting it merely enforce the supremacy of the people over their representatives in the legislature.

Tensions in the republican foundational principles were revealed in the opposed positions taken by Justices Samuel Chase and James Iredell in the 1798 U.S. Supreme Court case of *Calder v. Bull* on whether nontextual higher law constrained state legislative power.[8] Chase insisted in expansive dicta that "certain vital principles in our free republican governments," identified and enforced by judges, would void state legislative acts even if there was no specific textual prohibition to be found in the state constitution. He gave some examples: ex post facto laws, laws impairing contractual obligation, and "a law that takes property from A. and gives it to B." Chase thereby injected higher-law concepts into the functioning constitutional order. The taking-from-A-and-giving-to-B formula would later condemn redistribution of wealth by the state through taxation.

Iredell, representing the opposite principle in *Calder*, rejected the idea that judges could hold statutes unconstitutional because they were "contrary to the principles of natural justice." There was "no fixed standard" to identify what those principles were; "the ablest and the purest men have differed upon the subject." Between them, Chase and Iredell defined polar positions on judicial power that shaped the contours of legal classicism and that retain their relevance today.

Chief Justice Marshall validated Hamilton's justification for judicial review in *Marbury v. Madison* (1803).[9] He affirmed Hamilton's crucial insight, that the Constitution is a law. Marshall suggested an essential distinction between law and politics, contending that law, the province of courts, was the product of "reason," while politics, the province of legislatures, was the product of "will." Marshall's law-politics distinction lay at the heart of the classicist outlook. "Law" in Marshall's sense is apolitical, neutral among competing interest groups, impartial toward all, favoring none, standing above sordid politics, majestic in its indifference to interest, revealed through the processes of disinterested reason.

Marshall also partially resolved the conflict between Chase and Iredell. At first, in the 1810 case of *Fletcher v. Peck,*[10] he seemed to endorse Chase's view, stating that the Court could strike down state legislation "either by general principles which are common to our free institutions" or by specific textual provisions of the Constitution. But nine years later, in *Dartmouth College v. Woodward,*[11] he abandoned higher-law "general principles," claiming authority for courts to void state statutes only on the basis of constitutional text. Higher law in its eighteenth-century form thereafter disappeared as an operative ground of decision in the U.S. Supreme Court, though it lingered on until the 1890s in state supreme courts.

In decisions like *Fletcher* and *Dartmouth College,* the Marshall Court established the primacy of the contracts clause as a restraint on state regulatory power.[12] In the late nineteenth century, the contracts clause ceded this role to the due process clauses, but contract endured throughout the century as the basic paradigm of law. In the realm of public law, contract as compact, resting on the consent of the citizens, explained important constitutional processes. In private law, contract enabled consensual legal-economic relationships between autonomous individuals, presumed to be freely entered into for their mutual benefit.

In the antebellum era, Justice Joseph Story and other legal

academics, including David Hoffman, Simon Greenleaf, and Theodore Dwight, popularized the idea that law was a science, a "regular system" characterized by "a scientific arrangement and harmony of principles."[13] Legal science was organized around "general rules" and "fundamental principles" of universal applicability. It was politically neutral, "founded not upon any will, but on the discovery of a right already existing."[14] It was objective, capable of identifying "the law as it is, truly and accurately."[15] The rules of the common law were "fixed, certain, and invariable."[16] Legal science was expounded in a growing body of treatise literature that systematized legal development, delivering on the promise of presenting a comprehensive synopsis of American law.

The antebellum vision of the place of law in American society was well described by one of the preeminent members of the American bar, Rufus Choate, a Massachusetts lawyer second only to Daniel Webster in both popular and professional esteem.[17] In a commencement address at the Harvard Law School in 1845, Choate identified law and its practitioners as "an Element of Conservatism in the State."[18] He extolled "the supremacy of the calm and grand reason of the law over the fitful will of the individual and the crowd." Choate denied that law could be the product of majority will. It was instead some mystical "absolute justice of the State," discovered by judges, not made by legislators. Lawyers and judges were conservators of "property and good name and life . . . the great body of the ius privatum, our civil and social order."

## The Triumph of Classical Legal Thought

Americans reconstituted their constitutional order during Reconstruction. Bruce Ackerman has described this as a "constitutional moment," "a self-conscious act of constitutional creation" of such depth that the United States emerged with its third national constitutional regime.[19] As with any such fundamental constitutional reordering, ratification of new textual foundations (the Reconstruction Amendments) was only the beginning of the constitutional process. Congress, the Supreme Court, and the American people had to breathe life into inert text.

The Court, together with the lower bench and bar, readily

assumed this role. It did so in an era of unprecedented social turmoil and economic change, which produced what might be called the "Age of Anxiety."[20] Industrialization and disruptive social change threatened a social order already shaken by the horrendous human losses of the Civil War. Factory production imposed a brutal, dehumanizing labor regimen on the men, women, and children drawn into mills and mines. Working people resisted the long hours and low pay that seemed to realize the wage slavery predicted by antebellum slavocrats.[21] Recurrent spasms of union organization and labor violence replaced the comparatively placid labor organizing experience of the prewar years. Trade unions and the National Labor Union grew in membership before the depression of 1873, and the Knights of Labor, followed by the American Federation of Labor, thereafter.

Two decades of labor turbulence ensued: the Molly Maguires, the general railroad strike of 1877, the appearance of radical European social theories (socialism, communism, anarchism, syndicalism), the Haymarket riot of 1886, the Homestead Massacre of 1892, the Coeur d'Alene silver strike (1892), and the Pullman strike of 1894 were but highlights in an era of episodic bloodshed that marked capital's violent conflicts with labor. The growth of cities spurred by industrialization, and their peopling by outlandish non-Protestant, non-English-speaking immigrants from eastern and southern Europe (plus Chinese and Mexican immigrants in the western cities), frightened old-stock Americans. Fetid slums, lack of sanitation, and conspicuous problems with alcohol and prostitution seemed to validate Thomas Jefferson's revulsion against urban growth.

The middle classes reacted to this social unrest in different ways. One was xenophobia: the anti-Catholic American Protective Association, formed in 1887, demanded that immigration be closed off. Congress, driven by racism, did in fact shut down Chinese immigration between 1882 and 1902. But the demand for raw labor and the splendid bargain that the nation got by importing able-bodied, relatively young, semiskilled Europeans, Asians, and Mexicans doomed nativist hopes to disappointment. Scientific racism and its practical application, eugenics, tried to rank racial and ethnic groups hierarchically so that the ablest "races" might propagate and the "unfit" be driven to extermination by natural processes.

The spurious application of Charles Darwin's theory of natural selection to social processes, known as "social Darwinism," provided a pseudoscientific rationalization for racist social policy.

In the South, Redeemers and Bourbon Democrats established regimes of white supremacy by 1900, driving black Americans down to a status of economic servitude and political powerlessness. Whites terrorized black communities by night riding and recurrent lynchings, sometimes accompanied by rituals of torture. The "Mississippi Plan," which spread through southern legislatures and constitutional conventions after 1890, disfranchised nearly the entire black electorate.

The Gilded Age, with its gaudy political corruption and widening extremes of wealth and poverty, drove many Americans to a desperate search for order,[22] stability, and control of a society that seemed to be spinning off into anarchy. In industry, this drive for control was achieved by managerial innovation, including the organization of command and control of information flows by private bureaucracies.[23] In the public sphere, badly underdeveloped administrative capability left municipal, state, and federal governments unprepared to satisfy unprecedented needs for governance and regulation.[24]

Anxious middle-class reformers tried to cope with the social disorder they saw about them. Social scientists offered their expertise in the service of the state, on the premise that knowledge, disinterest, and expertise might avoid some of the excesses of political corruption (much of it imputed to immigrants, especially the Irish). "The best men" organized to promote good government through civil service reform, hoping to introduce professionalism and to replace spoilsmen.

Farmers in the Plains and the South organized first into social groups, then into cooperative movements to combat falling prices and a changing world that threatened their livelihood. The Farmers' Alliances created authentic grassroots democratic movements that offered a fundamental critique of American society.[25] They formulated the Populist critique in the Ocala Demands (1890) and the Omaha Platform (1892), when the Alliances evolved into the People's Party, America's most effective third-party movement. Terrified spokesmen of the middle classes mistakenly saw in the Populists the specter that was haunting Europe. Earlier fears of wealth redistribution and legislative expropriation seemed near fulfillment.

Lawyers and judges reacted to these threatening trends in much the same way as the rest of the socioeconomic elites. But unlike, say, churchmen, who could only try to influence public opinion, the bench and bar had power to do something about the ideas and people they feared. Elite lawyers threw themselves into a desperate effort to preserve social order, individual liberty, and republican government.

Lawyers, then as now, were notoriously uninterested in sustained philosophical inquiry. Thus, the philosophical foundations of their thought may seem simplistic. They believed that truth existed objectively, independently of individual belief, and could be discovered by investigation. Their logic was a simple, uncomplicated Aristotelianism, given to antinomies: substance or procedure, public or private, fact or law, and so on. They deemed all people autonomous individuals, exclusively responsible for their prospects. Social life was a competitive struggle, in which the superior were rewarded and the inferior vanquished. Equality of opportunity might be desirable, but equality of results would be an appalling perversion of the natural order, rewarding the unfit or indolent at the expense of the competent.

Lawyers' economic thinking was no more sophisticated than their social science. They clung simplemindedly to classical liberal economics. The free market would impartially reward industry and the contributions of labor and capital alike. The beneficent operations of the market must not be distorted by monopoly, favoritism, or political influence. One of the worst things that could befall society was "class" or "partial" legislation, whereby one interest group used political advantage to bestow privilege on itself or to burden rival interests.

As the apparent crisis of American society escalated after 1886, lawyers' arguments, treatises, judicial opinions, and bar association addresses sounded more and more like late-seventeenth-century jeremiads. One of these, in its extravagant and hysterical voice, conveys their flavor:

> Socialism, Communism, and Anarchism are rampant throughout the civilized world. . . . Contemplating these extraordinary

> demands of the great army of discontents, and their apparent power, with the growth and development of universal suffrage, to enforce their views of civil policy upon the civilized world, the conservative classes stand in constant fear of the advent of an absolutism more tyrannical and more unreasoning than any before experienced by man, the absolutism of a democratic majority.[26]

Out of this mélange of beliefs and fears, judges and lawyers perfected the outlook of legal classicism. They exalted individual liberty as the highest goal of organized society. People found their fulfillment in economic activity, directing their energies to productive work.[27] Their individualist ethos led lawyers to think of all social organization in the paradigm of a contract: a binding economic relationship voluntarily entered into by parties of equal bargaining stature. Law could not recognize juristic inequality in contracting, at least among adult males, for to do so would interfere with the parties' freely bargained pursuit of economic advantage.

To late-nineteenth-century lawyers, law had to be divorced from politics, neutral among individuals, groups, and classes. As judges could not be properly swayed by class bias, neither should legislatures. To the classical judicial mind, legislation had to pursue the public welfare to be valid. If instead it benefited or burdened one class in society for private advantage, it was illegitimate. Private law could not be redistributive, taking the property of A and giving it to B. This belief reinforced judges' aversion to righting contractual inequality.

## Classical Legal Thought and the Constitution

One of the first tasks of the postwar Supreme Court was to define the scope of change wrought by the constitutional moment of Reconstruction. The opportunity presented itself in the *Slaughterhouse Cases* of 1873,[28] which raised anew the fundamental problem of governmental power versus individual liberty, but now in the context of new constitutional texts, the Reconstruction Amendments. A five-judge majority, speaking through Justice Samuel F. Miller, upheld the power of a state legislature to confer monopoly privileges on a butchers' association. "Private interests must be made subservient to the general interests of the community," he wrote. "This is called the police power."

Four years later, in *Munn v. Illinois*,[29] Chief Justice Morrison R. Waite sustained a statute regulating the fees that grain elevators could charge. Construing the old maxim "requiring each citizen to so conduct himself, and so use his own property, as not unnecessarily to injure another" as "the very essence of government," Waite upheld state regulatory power as an aspect of the police power. Thus, in the transitional period between the political end of Reconstruction (1876) and the perceived onset of social crisis a decade later (1886), the governmental power side of the power-liberty continuum seemed securely established. Appearances were deceiving, however. In both *Slaughterhouse* and *Munn*, powerful dissents by Justices Joseph P. Bradley and Stephen J. Field articulated a new doctrine of substantive due process as a limitation on the states' police powers. They defined due process in such a way as to protect an individual's right to contract and to charge for the use of property. Between 1877 and 1890, this new concept slowly secured a foothold in the Supreme Court, as some state courts embraced it wholeheartedly.

Jurists hostile to unions and frightened by the violence that marred strikes and labor demonstrations counterpoised an older ideal of individual liberty against what they considered to be labor's illegitimate collective action. The leading industrial states, including New York, Massachusetts, and Pennsylvania, as well as several nonindustrial states, slashed away at statutes regulating the conditions of labor, especially hours and modes of payment.[30] The new doctrines did not remain confined to labor cases, though. Judges who were suspicious of the emergent regulatory state readily adapted antiunion dogmas to other uses. The U.S. Supreme Court affirmed the doctrine of substantive due process for the first time in 1890, in a rate-regulation case that weakened but did not overrule *Munn*.[31]

The year 1895 was a time of apparent crisis in the eyes of orthodox jurists. The violent strikes at Homestead and Coeur d'Alene in 1892 required military force to be suppressed. Frightened Republicans confused the 1892 Populist platform with socialism. The onset of depression in 1893 triggered the Pullman strike of 1894, when labor unions seemed to have it within their power to control the nation's railroad transportation network. Against this background, three major 1895 cases defined federal and state regulatory authority in ways that judges expected would rein in democratic politics, preserve the existing distribution of wealth, and suppress organized labor.[32]

The first of the triad, *United States v. E. C. Knight Co.*,[33] temporarily deflected the Sherman Antitrust Act of 1890. Chief Justice Melville W. Fuller drew the sort of dichotomous and arid distinction dear to the classical mind between manufacturing and commerce, holding that federal commerce power could not reach the former. Invoking the Tenth Amendment, Fuller, an antebellum Democrat whose mind remained frozen in the glacier of state-power ideology, clung to the prewar constitutional status quo of federalism, much as Miller (a Republican) had done in *Slaughterhouse.*

Fuller struck again five months later, holding an 1894 federal income tax unconstitutional because it was a direct tax and not apportioned among the states.[34] Justice John M. Harlan, in one of the lonely dissents that have served his reputation so well, denounced the "gross injustice" that gave "to certain kinds of property a position of favoritism," subjecting the American people "to the dominion of aggregated wealth."[35]

The third of the climacteric 1895 cases, *In re Debs*,[36] sustained the validity of the labor injunction, a powerful weapon that federal judges had been using for two decades to break unions and strikes. The labor injunction deprived individual workers of First Amendment rights of speech and press, as well as the grand and petty jury guarantees of the Fifth, Sixth, and Seventh Amendments. In dramatic contrast to Fuller's shriveled *Knight* conception of federal commerce power, Justice David J. Brewer's *Debs* opinion extolled "the strong arm of the national government" that would protect the arteries of the nation's commerce from striking workers.

The conservatism of the Court's social vision was confirmed the next year in *Plessy v. Ferguson* (1896),[37] upholding the imposition of Jim Crow in intrastate railroad transportation. Justice Henry B. Brown explicitly rested his opinion on police-power grounds, validating a differential view of state regulatory power depending on whether its objects were profit-making enterprises or African-Americans being repressed back into racial subjection. Finally, the Court debuted the daughter doctrine of substantive due process, liberty of contract, in *Allgeyer v. Louisiana* (1897).[38]

A second surge of classical adjudication began dramatically with the case that has given its name to the era, *Lochner v. New York* (1905),[39] which marked the zenith of the Court's substantive due process paternalism.[40] Justice Rufus Peckham, like Fuller a Democratic Bourbon who never learned and never forgot, exalted liberty of contract. Peckham airily dismissed the states' police-power rationale for its maximum-hours law: "[W]e do not believe in the soundness of the views which uphold this law." Seeing legislation that regulated labor contracts as "mere meddlesome interferences with the rights of the individual," Peckham sought, and thought he found, an improper legislative motive, the desire "to regulate the hours of labor between the master and his employees."[41]

The Supreme Court flaunted its single-minded antagonism to organized labor throughout the era. *Adair v. United States* (1908)[42] struck down a federal statute prohibiting yellow-dog contracts from being imposed on railway employees. Justice Harlan relied on two grounds: lack of a "real or substantial relation" to interstate commerce, and interference with liberty of contract (now subsumed under the Fifth Amendment as well, since this was a federal statute). In the same year, in the *Danbury Hatters Case*,[43] Chief Justice Fuller subjected unions to the Sherman Act, a remarkable contrast with his performance in *Knight*. Progressives juxtaposing the two cases could only conclude that for the Fuller Court, the Sherman Act would have a differential, results-oriented application, impotent to deter the formation of trusts but a fearsome weapon to flog unions. American workers learned that law was a weapon as effective as militia bayonets and police truncheons for bludgeoning labor.

No single explanatory model or hypothesis accounts for the Supreme Court's behavior in the heyday of substantive due process. Charles Warren long ago demonstrated that the Court upheld more Progressive Era regulatory legislation than it struck down,[44] and modern scholarship concurs.[45] Yet if in quantitative terms the Court sustained most state and federal statutes, in qualitative terms its best-known cases did not. This left a residue of inconsistency, producing dual streams of incompatible precedent. That posed a threat to the rule of law, which appeared incoherent in a literal sense, unable to hang together.

In antitrust, for example, the Court discarded Fuller's formalistic commerce antinomies in a string of cases[46] to end up with the "rule of reason" enunciated by Chief Justice Edward D. White in the *Standard Oil Case*.[47] The Court upheld various exercises of the federal police power,[48] yet in the two notorious *Child Labor Cases*,[49] it reverted to abstract conceptualism to strike down federal police authority. What was an attorney to advise a client, or a member of Congress to assume in drafting legislation, given such erratic performance?

The Supreme Court temporarily resolved its incoherence in the 1920s, but unfortunately it did so in the wrong direction, toward reaffirming formalism and conceptualism, an intellectually sterile approach to appellate judging that drifted ever further from reality. Most observers of the Court after World War I agreed with the opinion of Charles Warren, the conservative legal historian, who thought that *Lochner* "is certain in the near future to be disregarded by the Court."[50] Therefore, Justice George Sutherland's opinion in *Adkins v. Children's Hospital* (1923)[51] seemed shockingly retrogressive. In voiding a minimum-wage statute for women, Sutherland extolled liberty of contract as "the general rule and restraint the exception," requiring "exceptional circumstances" to justify police-power regulation. By categorical reasoning, he identified four topics where the Court had upheld regulatory legislation, including *Munn*-type rate regulations, implying that they were exclusive. Similar reasoning enabled the Court to curtail severely what was left of *Munn*'s authority, limiting it to industries that had historically been subject to regulation.[52] Under that approach, the Taft Court struck down a variety of state regulatory statutes, covering such topics as ticket scalping, employment agencies, minimum wages, and product quality, as well as retail sales of gasoline, ice, and bread.[53]

On the other hand—such ambivalence is a necessary qualification for any generalization about the Court in the forty years after 1895—the justices sustained workers' compensation measures,[54] municipal zoning, maximum hours for both men and women, and even wage regulation (clearly redistributive).[55] An impartial observer might have reasonably concluded that public law concerning federal and state regulatory power was in disarray just at a time when a clear understanding of governmental power was most needed, at the onset of the Great Depression.

Despite this dysfunctional incoherence in results, legal classicism endured on into the 1930s, its great explanatory and legitimating power seemingly intact. Then, in 1937, it collapsed with a suddenness that surprised even its critics. By 1938, it lay in ruins. How to explain such a rapid disintegration of an ideology that had developed over a century?

## The Challenge to Classical Legal Thought

Recurrently throughout the period of classicism's ascendancy, academic, judicial, and political assaults undermined its authority. This pattern repeated itself following each surge of classical adjudication: 1895, 1908, and 1923. By 1930, critics of classical thought had made a persuasive case. Far from being objective and certain, legal rules and adjudication were indeterminate, incapable of providing a reliable and certain guide to conduct. Nor were they politically neutral. Indeed, the claim of neutrality was a mask for promoting the class biases and political preferences of a conservative judiciary. The American legal order was systematically biased in favor of wealth, power, and corporate capitalism, against the interests of American workers and their unions.

The earliest and ultimately the most effective challenge to classical legal thought came from Oliver Wendell Holmes Jr. There was an irony in this, for some of Holmes's early writings had gone further in classicist directions than had contemporary judges' opinions. Yet in *The Common Law* (1881) Holmes undermined the foundations of classicism. He skewered its pretensions to scientific certitude and its reliance on abstract logic: "The felt necessities of the time [and] . . . intuitions of public policy . . . have had a good deal more to do than the syllogism in determining the rules by which men should be governed."[56] By 1898, Holmes elaborated his systematic thought, rejecting the unattainable goals of objectivity and neutrality. "Judges are called on to exercise the sovereign prerogative of choice," he wrote.[57] Such crypto-legislative weighing of policy considerations in judging "marks the demise," in Morton Horwitz's judgment, "of the late-nineteenth-century system of legal formalism."[58]

After his appointment to the U.S. Supreme Court, Holmes continued to attack the conceptions of law fostered by classical thought. In his *Lochner* dissent, he reminded his colleagues in the majority that "the Fourteenth Amendment does not enact Mr. Herbert Spencer's Social Statics" or the economic theory of laissez-faire.[59] His positivist outlook was incompatible with classicism. In 1917, he wrote that "the common law is not a brooding omnipresence in the sky but the articulate voice of some sovereign or quasi sovereign that can be identified; although some decisions with which I have disagreed seem to me to have forgotten the fact. It always is the law of some State."[60]

Holmes was not alone on the Supreme Court in his disengagement from the orthodox view of judging. In his *Lochner* dissent, Justice Harlan had acknowledged the persuasive force of social-science studies for adjudication. A five-judge majority of the Court in *Muller v. Oregon* (1908)[61] came around to that view, accepting the Brandeis Brief, which had been composed by the social worker Josephine Goldmark and her brother-in-law Louis D. Brandeis. The brief focused judges' attention on the facts of the case before them, rather than on abstract axioms; forced them to consider the results of applying a legal rule, compared with the alternatives if the rule were to be modified or another rule selected; and threw open the windows of judicial chambers to the breezes of expertise in non-legal fields. In these ways, the subversive methodology of the Brandeis Brief eroded classicism.

In the universities, historians and political scientists, philosophers and economists were overthrowing established ways of thought. In their panoramic reinterpretations of America's past, Charles A. Beard,[62] Vernon Louis Parrington,[63] and J. Allen Smith[64] stressed class conflict, the clash of economic interests, and popular resistance to social elites. (Beard, however, defended the legitimacy of judicial review,[65] a point overlooked by his critics.) Philosophers rejected formalistic and conceptualistic ways of thought in favor of approaches that we call pragmatist or functionalist.[66] Among economists, Edwin R. A. Seligman,[67] Richard T. Ely,[68] and John R. Commons[69] demonstrated the linkages between classical (conservative) economics and its legal expressions, in the process revealing the contingency of legal rules and stripping away their supposed transcendent and suprapolitical quality.

Belief in objective causation was eroding in the hard sciences as well as in philosophy. A simple, determinate, Euclidean-Newtonian natural order governed by universal laws was giving way in scientific thought to one less tangible and certain. From the Michelson-Morley experiment of 1887 (which subverted belief in absolute motion and absolute space) to Heisenberg's uncertainty principle in 1927, the comforting certainties that had made the physical universe seem rational and comprehensible disintegrated. This left lawyers' accounts of causation to appear as naive as Ptolemaic astronomy, and as a result, their worldview was shorn of its vaunted objectivity. At the same time, the higher criticism began to challenge theological assurance. Classical lawyers found themselves bewildered and abandoned in an intellectual world defined by Charles Darwin, Karl Marx, Sigmund Freud, Nils Bohr, Max Planck, and later Albert Einstein.

Closer to home, legal scholars rejected classicist principles. In articles written between 1907 and 1912, Roscoe Pound of the Harvard Law School developed the idea of "sociological jurisprudence" as an alternative to what he called "mechanical jurisprudence."[70] He scouted the assumption that law might function like some mechanical contrivance that could provide determinate answers to legal questions derived from the inputs of facts and legal rules. Pound suggested that legal axioms and rules were frequently nothing more than the disguised politics and ideology of judges, tricked out in the language of formalism, posturing as objective and neutral. In place of such conceptual mummery, he insisted that judges be aware of the consequences of applying their doctrines and consciously strive for equitable results in particular cases.

Complementing the critique from the law schools was a powerful political attack on classicism. The Populist assault on the class biases of state and federal judges had little effect after the movement itself succumbed to the fatal lure of bimetallism in 1896. But within a decade, a new generation of muckrakers and publicists, including Lincoln Steffens, Ida Tarbell, and Louis D. Brandeis, demonstrated the impact that law had on the distribution of power and wealth in American society. Progressives of various sorts picked up Populism's political struggle against the tenets of orthodoxy. Their criticism was directed less at doctrine than at results. Angered by decisions like *Lochner* and *Adair,* Progressives came to see the federal judiciary in particular as a bastion of corporate capitalism that frustrated democratic efforts to exert some control over American economic development.

One political response was direct and blunt: the Sixteenth Amendment (ratified 1913) overturned the *Income Tax Cases.* Theodore Roosevelt's attack on the federal judiciary in his Bull Moose third-party campaign of 1912 was only a bit more nuanced. He endorsed Progressive proposals that had been circulating throughout the previous decade: recall of federal judges, "recall" of judicial decisions, and nonlifetime tenure for federal judges. His program would have enabled Congress to override a Supreme Court decision holding a federal statute unconstitutional and also would have required some sort of supermajority when the Supreme Court exercised the power of judicial review.

Supporters of classical doctrine were thrown on the defensive. When the New York Court of Appeals handed down its shocking 1911 decision in *Ives v. South Buffalo Railway,*[71] holding the New York workers' compensation statute unconstitutional on substantive due process grounds, even the conservative President William Howard Taft was taken aback, referring to the decision as an "instance" of a "hidebound and retrograde conservatism on the part of courts in decisions which turn on the individual economic or sociological views of the judges," a surprisingly radical judgment from that pillar of classicism.[72]

World War I proved to be only a brief hiatus in academic, political, and judicial challenges to orthodox legal thought. The war's impact actually accelerated the disintegration of classicism by inducing a great expansion of regulation and statist involvement in economic affairs, at both the federal and the state level. Wartime railroad regulation continued after the war and reached new dirigiste heights in the Esch-Cummings Transportation Act of 1920. Its recapture provisions, redistributing railroad profits from more to less profitable lines by statutory fiat and administrative decision, constituted an outright taking-from-A-and-giving-to-B wealth transfer. Rent control, Prohibition, and federal grants-in-aid for maternal and infant welfare under the Sheppard-Towner Act of 1921 constituted other redistributive federal measures. The states experimented with a variety of economic regulations, including wage setting in vital industries like food production. In the presidential campaign of 1924, the third-party Progressive candidate, Robert LaFollette, echoed Roosevelt's 1912 call for political curbs on the federal judiciary. Though this platform proved no more successful than his candidacy, sentiment continued to build in Congress throughout the 1920s for curbs on federal jurisdiction, to eliminate the role of federal courts as refuges of corporate wealth. In particular, Progressives wanted to rein in the equity powers of federal judges, in order to leash the labor injunction.

Again, however, the more effective challenge to classical legal thought came from the universities. Yale and Columbia were nurseries of the most successful assault on legal orthodoxy, the Legal Realist[73] movement of the 1920s.[74] Realism was heterogeneous, and this defies efforts to restate its premises succinctly. As legal classicism was a state of mind and a set of attitudes rather than a jurisprudential school, Realism was a turbid confluence of individual critiques having little coherence or unity.

Realists venerated Holmes and Pound and built on their insights. They adopted one of Pound's contributions, his call for lawyers to exploit the insights of the social sciences, and made it the centerpiece of their thought, at times going so far as to deny the autonomy of the law as an intellectual endeavor. Attention to facts and the lure of quantification dominated their approach. Realists were quite capable of working with norms: Karl Llewellyn was, after all, the father of the Uniform Commercial Code, nothing if not normative. But general principles were suspect to them, and norms had to be disciplined by a short tether to reality as discovered and described by empirical research.

Exuberantly iconoclastic, the Realists devastated the principles, axioms, and assumptions of classicist thought. Realists rudely proclaimed that the emperor was not wearing any clothes, or, more accurately, that judicial robes did not conceal the man underneath them, a human being of passions and prejudices.[75] Entire new fields of law, such as administrative law or public utility regulation, emerged in the legal academy, a recognition of reality in practice that vindicated Pound's call for integrating law in books with law in action. Realists demonstrated that the public-private distinction sacred to classicism had a permeable barrier, if indeed the distinction existed at all.

The Legal Realists recognized that revolutionary changes in thought in other fields had swept away the foundations of classical thought. Classicist judges were scarcely cognizant of these changes and could not comprehend them. Objectivism had gone the way of the ether, the existence of which had also been disproved by the Michelson-Morley experiment. Aristotelian logic, Newtonian physics, and Euclidean geometry were not so much discarded as supplemented with other systems capable of explaining more complex realities. Causation was no longer simplistically objective but probabilistic. Cardozo's majority opinion in *Palsgraf,* and even more so Judge William S. Andrews's dissent there,[76] confronted judges with changed ways of thinking about physical causation. The bizarre causal chain involved in that case could have been designed to invite reconsideration of the nature of legal causality.

This ferment in the legal academy laid the foundations for tectonic shifts that rumbled below the surface of American law in the social and economic upheavals of the Great Depression. The story of the events that brought on the crisis and sudden collapse of legal classicism is well known and may be summarized briefly. Though the stock market crashed in October 1929 and the Depression worsened significantly through 1931, the constitutional issues raised by state and federal efforts to alleviate economic distress did not come before the Supreme Court until 1934. At first, the Court moved beyond classical stasis to sustain state measures to cope with financial crisis and regulate economic activity.[77] Later, it also upheld federal monetary measures[78] and regional planning.[79]

But those permissive decisions of 1934–36 were soon overwhelmed by holdings that struck down federal and state efforts to cope with the Depression. The Court gutted two centerpieces of the New Deal, the National Industrial Recovery Act and the Agricultural Adjustment Act, which had attempted to stabilize industrial wages and farm prices.[80] The Court shocked most of the legal community by exhuming *Knight*'s constricted conception of federal commerce regulatory power and, with it, the discredited doctrine of dual federalism. To make matters worse, it did this using the vehicle of a patently collusive case.[81] Finally, the Court propped up the corpses of *Lochner* and *Adkins* to void a minimum-wage law for women workers.[82] Classicism achieved its final, sweeping, but Pyrrhic victory.

After his landslide electoral triumph in 1936, President Franklin D. Roosevelt determined to shove aside the obstructionism of a Court that seemed to many Americans out of touch with reality and suicidally committed to an ideological program that protected wealth by suppressing majoritarian democracy. The result was the court-packing struggle of 1937.[83] We need not pause over the politics of that episode. Its long-term significance lay in the disintegration of legal classicism. That dissolution and its consequences have decisively formed the modern constitution. Even today, more than a half century later, constitutional thought is struggling to come to terms with the loss of the classicist outlook.

Between 1937 and 1963, the Court dismantled the doctrinal structure of classicism. To note just the highlights: the Court first repudiated substantive due process and liberty of contract. In the case that announced the abandonment of classicism and its works, *West Coast Hotel v. Parrish* (1937), Chief Justice Charles Evans Hughes wrote, "The Constitution does not speak of freedom of contract," recognized the significance of bargaining inequality, and repolarized the Court's sympathies by stating that the Constitution does not require the community to subsidize "unconscionable employers."[84] In a similar spirit, the Court first reversed, then redundantly condemned, the Fuller Court's vision of congressional commerce regulatory power and dual federalism.[85] In 1941, Justice Harlan Fiske Stone dismissed the Tenth Amendment itself: it "states but a truism that all is retained which has not been surrendered."[86] In subsequent years, the Court seemed to go out of its way to heap scorn on economic substantive due process.[87] Superfluously, Justice Hugo Black proclaimed in 1949 that the "Allgeyer-Lochner-Adair-Coppage constitutional doctrine" was defunct.[88] He affirmed Holmes's *Lochner* dissent: "[W]hether the legislature takes for its textbook Adam Smith, Herbert Spencer, Lord Keynes, or some other is no concern of ours."[89]

## After the Fall

This repudiation of classicism left the Court free to create new doctrinal superstructures, and it set about doing that immediately. Justice Harlan Fiske Stone announced the new order in

*Carolene Products'* footnote 4 (1938),[90] and he elaborated its implications as the "preferred freedoms" doctrine,[91] or the "constitutional double standard," as it is sometimes called. From this redirected doctrinal approach, with its concern for noneconomic freedoms and rights, emerged modern Supreme Court activism, including noneconomic substantive due process,[92] substantive equal protection, as well as procedures involving persons accused of crimes and First Amendment liberties.

Yet the justices of the Supreme Court erected this new doctrinal superstructure after 1937 without formulating a judicial philosophy that could replace classical legal thought. That omission has left the Court vulnerable to charges of usurpation and illegitimacy. One explanation of why the abortion controversy simply will not go away (in addition to the obvious one of the absolute moral convictions involved in the dispute) is that critics have not been persuaded that the Court's decisions either protecting[93] or restricting[94] access to abortion are legitimate. The joint opinion in the 1992 *Casey* decision was itself proof of a crisis of legitimacy in modern constitutional doctrine.[95] A vulgarized echo of Legal Realism bruited about in the political arena insists that such decisions reflect nothing more than the political preferences of shifting 5-4 majorities of the Court.

During the dominance of legal orthodoxy, Americans enjoyed the advantage of a shared faith that provided a conventional theater of engagement for constitutional debate. Legal classicism provided Americans not just the vocabulary of legal concepts that Tocqueville had earlier noted but a sense of joint enterprise as well. Its sudden demise in 1937 created a void in our national dialogue that has not been filled yet.

The Stone and Vinson Courts were the first that had to cope with this loss. In varying ways, their members proffered replacements for the abandoned outlook. Justice Felix Frankfurter's contribution was the most consistent and coherent. Building on Justice Benjamin N. Cardozo's poetically phrased concepts in *Snyder v. Massachusetts* (1934) and *Palko v. Connecticut* (1937),[96] Frankfurter strove to identify "canons of decency and fairness which express the notions of justice of English-speaking peoples" through the judicial process, convinced that procedural safeguards inherent in the judicial process will prevent judges from acting on "the idiosyncrasies of a merely personal judgment."[97] He elaborated standards for judicial discretion[98] in a tradition carried on by Justice John M. Harlan, whose influential dissent in *Poe v. Ullman* (1961)[99] achieved its highest expression.

In contrast to Frankfurter's confidence in procedural and institutional constraints on judicial discretion, Justice Hugo M. Black promoted an absolutism in constitutional interpretation, quarreling in conference and openly with Frankfurter. Black derided Frankfurter's labored efforts as a revival of natural law concepts in the twentieth century as "an incongruous excrescence on our Constitution."[100] He insisted throughout his career that only his approach would prevent judges from acting at whim,[101] but like its theological analogue, his literalist interpretive strategy sometimes degenerated into a judicial fundamentalism that led him to results based on nothing more than his personal social standards.[102]

The contrasting approaches of Frankfurter and Black constituted the only sustained, coherent, and comprehensive efforts by members of the court between 1938 and 1954 to articulate explanations for judicial power that justified doctrinal results by founding them on a theory of judicial function. Though both attempts were heroic, neither ultimately attracted the allegiance of anyone outside a small circle of disciples.

Meanwhile, it became apparent by 1950 that the Court would soon be confronted with massive and novel issues having immeasurable consequences for American society. (It seems banal to enumerate them a half century later because they are so obvious, but that is only because we look back on the moment with the advantage of hindsight.) At midcentury, these emergent issues dominated the uncertain future. They included racial segregation, the deliberate, comprehensive, and systematic degradation of minority races by the dominant white race; First Amendment issues of speech and press, which had been pressed on the Court in the 1920s; First Amendment issues of religious freedom and establishment, which the Court began to explore in the 1940s; the allocation of political power among various groups in society; questions of human sexuality, reproduction, and family life; problems of federalism, demarcating federal and state power in areas previously shared but ill defined; and the rights of persons accused or suspected of crime. (Conspicuously missing from this list was the fundamental issue settled—for a time anyway—in 1937: federal and state power to regulate the economy.) The Court would either have to address these pressing issues on the basis of some assumptions about judicial power in a democratic society or default by leaving them unresolved or by diverting them to the political branches.

Outside the Marble Palace, several legal scholars tried to work out a theory that might have provided a substitute for classicism. The result was a cluster of attitudes called "Legal Process."[103] Legal Process advocates, who maintained close personal and intellectual ties to Frankfurter, emphasized the same procedural ends that he extolled: respect for the virtues of process; a strong and disciplined sense of judicial restraint, buttressed by awareness of the limitations of judicial power; impartiality in judging, defined as a thoroughgoing neutrality toward results; an emphasis on judicial craftsmanship, demanding opinions that were rationally persuasive and derived from precedent. Advocates of Legal Process frowned on judicial commitment to substantive principles such as equality or democratic empowerment.

Confronted with the issues that the Warren Court began to address in the 1950s, especially desegregation, Legal Process adherents quickly discovered that it was impossible to formulate a theory of adjudication that did not involve commitment to some substantive values. Because it proved incapable of generating, defining, or even recognizing those values, though, Legal Process proved to be a hothouse phenomenon, influential for a decade in legal pedagogy but of little impact elsewhere. It veered into one intellectual cul-de-sac in Herbert Wechsler's attempt[104] to rebut Judge Learned Hand's shocking attack on *Brown v. Board of Education* in the 1958 Holmes Lectures,[105] and into another in the increasingly conservative writings of Alexander Bickel.[106] Though it influenced the outlook of many of the men and women who are America's judges and law professors today, Legal Process disappeared from the landscape of American legal thought in the 1960s, leaving behind it the void created by the fall of classicism.

The lack of an overarching explanatory and legitimating ideology of judicial authority comparable to classicism accounts for much of today's dysfunctional constitutional dynamic. The recurrent challenges to the legitimacy of the Court's decision making, off the bench and on (especially from Justice Scalia); the politicization of the appointment and confirmation process for nominees to the Court; the modest success, at best, of the Court's efforts to defend the authority of its decisions;[107] the dismaying volte-faces of shifting 5-4 majorities on Tenth Amendment doctrine;[108] all these are symptoms of the lost consensus on judicial authority that characterizes the modern constitution.

Legal classicism is gone irretrievably. We can no more revive or replicate it today than we can summon back the intellectual world of the Gilded Age that was its matrix. There is no possibility of retro in legal culture. But we have lost something in the passing of orthodoxy. The lack of a legitimating ideology of judicial power today invites extremist initiatives to fill doctrinal vacuums or to innovate in radically destabilizing ways. To take the place of abandoned classicism, academics have offered specious theories of originalism,[109] which have been echoed in the political arena.[110] Others spin garish doctrinal fantasies that have a superficial plausibility only because criteria to critique them are lacking.[111] Contemplating some of the radical initiatives that have come from the current Court itself,[112] even the observer who has no sympathy for classical legal thought will recall William Butler Yeats's lines:

> Turning and turning in the widening gyre
> The falcon cannot hear the falconer;
> Things fall apart; the centre cannot hold;
> Mere anarchy is loosed upon the world; . . .
> The best lack all conviction, while the worst
> Are full of passionate intensity.[113]

Notes

1. Paul Murphy's treatment of the 1938–54 Court in his New American Nation series volume is unusual for the extensive attention he paid to it, fully a quarter of the book: *The Constitution in Crisis Times, 1918–1969* (1972), 176–309.

2. Duncan Kennedy, "Towards an Historical Understanding of Legal Consciousness: The Case of Classical Legal Thought in America, 1850–1940," *Research in Law and Sociology* 3 (1980): 3; Elizabeth Mensch, "The History of Mainstream Legal Thought," in *The Politics of Law: A Progressive Critique,* rev. ed., ed. David Kairys (1990); Thomas C. Grey, "Langdell's Orthodoxy," *U. Pitt. L. Rev.* 45 (1983): 1, 2; Herbert Hovenkamp, *Enterprise and American Law, 1836–1937* (1991), ix; Morton J. Horwitz, *The Transformation of American Law, 1780–1860* (1977), 253–68; Horwitz, *The Transformation of American Law, 1870–*

*1960: The Crisis of Legal Orthodoxy* (1992) (hereafter cited as Horwitz, *Transformation II*); Donald J. Gjerdingen, "The Future of Our Past: The Legal Mind and the Legacy of Classical Legal Thought," *Ind. L. J.* 68 (1993): 743; Arthur M. Schlesinger Jr., *The Politics of Upheaval* (1960), 458.

3. U.S. Const., art. I, sec. 10 (contracts), amends. V and XIV (property), among others.

4. On the last, cf. Brown, J.: "There are certain principles of natural justice inherent in the Anglo-Saxon character, which need no expression in constitutions or statutes to give them effect or to secure dependencies against legislation manifestly hostile to their real interests." *Downes v. Bidwell*, 182 U.S. 244, 280 (1901).

5. I am preparing an interpretive study of the U.S. Supreme Court from 1941 to 1953, for which I have written an introduction on legal classicism: *The Lost World of Classical Legal Thought: Law and Ideology in America, 1886–1937* (1998).

6. The standard secondary authorities are Bernard Bailyn, *The Ideological Origins of the American Revolution* (1967), and Gordon S. Wood, *The Creation of the American Republic, 1776–1787* (1969).

7. *The Federalist*, ed. Jacob E. Cooke (1788; rpt., 1961), 525.

8. 3 Dall. (3 U.S.) 386, 388, 399 (1798).

9. 1 Cranch (5 U.S.) 137 (1803).

10. 6 Cranch (10 U.S.) 87, 139 (1810).

11. 4 Wheat. (17 U.S.) 518 (1819).

12. U.S. Const., art. I, sec. 10.

13. Joseph Story, "Course of Legal Study," *North American Review* (1817), reprinted in *The Miscellaneous Writings of Joseph Story*, ed. William W. Story (1852), 69.

14. Anon., "Law, Legislation, and Codes," *Encyclopaedia Americana* (1829–30), 576, 579. Though usually attributed to Joseph Story (e.g., R. Kent Newmyer, *Supreme Court Justice Joseph Story: Statesman of the Old Republic* [1985], 450), the first half of this article, including the phrases quoted in the text, was written by someone else, possibly Francis Lieber, and was translated from a German encyclopedia, the *Conversations Lexicon*.

15. James Kent, *Commentaries on American Law* (1826–30), 3:88 n (emphasis in original).

16. [Joseph Story], "Law, Legislation, and Codes," *Encyclopaedia Americana*, 582 (this part of the article *was* written by Story).

17. See generally Jean V. Matthews, *Rufus Choate: The Law and Civic Virtue* (1980).

18. Rufus Choate, "The Position and Functions of the American Bar, as an Element of Conservatism in the State: An Address Delivered Before the Law School in Cambridge, July 3, 1845," in *The Works of Rufus Choate: With a Memoir of His Life*, ed. Samuel G. Brown (1862), 1:414–38.

19. Bruce Ackerman, *We the People: Foundations* (1991), 34, 130, quotations on 44, 59. The regimes were pre-Confederation and Articles of Confederation; Constitution of 1787 plus Bill of Rights; the Reconstruction Amendments.

20. Grant Gilmore used this phrase to refer to the period following the Gilded Age in "The Age of Anxiety," *Yale L. J.* 84 (1975):1022, and then in *The Ages of American Law* (1977), 68. W. H. Auden appropriated the phrase for a later era, which was then given musical expression by Leonard Bernstein in

his Second Symphony. Auden, *The Age of Anxiety* (1947). But it seems a most appropriate descriptor for what is otherwise usually referred to as "the Gilded Age."

21. Twentieth-century economists have concluded, however, that the late nineteenth century was characterized by a significant secular increase in real wages and per capita income: Stuart W. Bruchey, *Enterprise: The Dynamic Economy of a Free People* (1990), 310–11. That may be true as a matter of econometrics, but contemporary workers did not see it that way. For the purposes of this chapter, it was workers' perceptions, not academic hindsight, that stoked labor unrest and, more important, middle-class reaction to that unrest.

22. Robert H. Wiebe, *The Search for Order, 1877–1920* (1967).

23. Alfred D. Chandler, *The Visible Hand: The Managerial Revolution in American Business* (1977).

24. Harold M. Hyman, *A More Perfect Union: The Impact of the Civil War and Reconstruction on the Constitution* (1973); Morton Keller, *Affairs of State: Public Life in Late Nineteenth Century America* (1977); Stephen Skowronek, *Building a New American State: The Expansion of National Administrative Capacities, 1877–1920* (1982); Thomas K. McCraw, *Prophets of Regulation: Charles Francis Adams, Louis D. Brandeis, James M. Landis, Alfred E. Kahn* (1984).

25. Lawrence Goodwyn, *Democratic Promise: The Populist Moment in America* (1976); Michael Kazin, *The Populist Persuasion: An American History* (1995).

26. Christopher Tiedeman, *A Treatise on the Limitations of the Police Power in the United States* (1886), vi–viii.

27. James Willard Hurst, *Law and the Conditions of Freedom in the Nineteenth-Century United States* (1956), passim.

28. 16 Wall. (83 U.S.) 36, 62 (1873).

29. 94 U.S. 113, 124 (1877).

30. William E. Forbath, *Law and the Shaping of the American Labor Movement* (1991); cf. *Millett v. People,* 117 Ill. 294 (1886); *Godcharles v. Wigeman,* 113 Pa. 431 (1886); *Commonwealth v. Perry,* 155 Mass. 117 (1891); *People v. Williams,* 201 N.Y. 271 (1911); *State v. Goodwill,* 33 W.Va. 179 (1889).

31. *Chicago, Milwaukee & St. Paul Railway Co. v. Minnesota,* 134 U.S. 418 (1890).

32. For a differing treatment of these cases, see Owen M. Fiss, *Troubled Beginnings of the Modern State, 1888–1910* (1993), 53–154.

33. 156 U.S. 1 (1895).

34. As required by U.S. Const., art. I, sec. 2, cl. 3, and sec. 9, cl. 4.

35. *Pollock v. Farmers Loan and Trust Co.,* 158 U.S. 601 (1895); Harlan, J., dissenting at 685.

36. 158 U.S. 564 (1895).

37. 163 U.S. 537 (1896).

38. 165 U.S. 578 (1897).

39. 198 U.S. 45 (1905).

40. On the Court's paternalist ethos, see Aviam Soifer, "The Paradox of Paternalism and Laissez-Faire Constitutionalism: The United States Supreme Court, 1888–1921," *Law and History Review* 5 (1987): 249–79. For a differing interpretation, see Howard Gillman, *The Constitution Besieged: The Rise and Demise of Lochner Era Police Powers Jurisprudence* (1993).

41. 198 U.S. 61, 64.

42. 208 U.S. 161 (1908).

43. *Loewe v. Lawlor*, 208 U.S. 274 (1908).

44. Charles Warren, "The Progressiveness of the United States Supreme Court," *Colum. L. Rev.* 13 (1913): 294; "A Bulwark to the State Police Power: The United States Supreme Court," *Colum. L. Rev.* 13 (1913): 667.

45. Melvin I. Urofsky, "Myth and Reality: The Supreme Court and Protective Legislation During the Progressive Era," *1983 Yearbook of the Supreme Court Historical Society*, 53–72; Urofsky, "State Courts and Protective Legislation During the Progressive Era: A Reevaluation," *Journal of American History* 72 (1985): 63–91.

46. The most important of which were *United States v. Trans-Missouri Freight Association*, 166 U.S. 290 (1897); *Addyston Pipe and Steel Co. v. United States*, 175 U.S. 211 (1899); *Northern Securities Co. v. United States*, 193 U.S. 197 (1903); and *Swift & Co. v. United States*, 196 U.S. 375 (1905).

47. *Standard Oil Co. v. United States*, 221 U.S. 1 (1911).

48. *Champion v. Ames*, 188 U.S. 321 (1903); *McCray v. United States*, 195 U.S. 27 (1904).

49. *Hammer v. Dagenhart*, 247 U.S. 251 (1918); *Bailey v. Drexel Furniture Co.*, 259 U.S. 20 (1922).

50. Charles Warren, *The Supreme Court in United States History*, rev. ed. (1926), 2:741.

51. 261 U.S. 525 (1923).

52. *Wolff Packing Co. v. Kansas Court of Industrial Relations*, 262 U.S. 522 (1923).

53. *Tyson and Bros. v. Banton*, 273 U.S. 418 (1927); *Ribnik v. McBride*, 277 U.S. 350 (1928); *Williams v. Standard Oil Co.*, 278 U.S. 235 (1929); *New State Ice Co. v. Liebmann*, 285 U.S. 262 (1932); *Jay Burns Baking Co. v. Bryan*, 264 U.S. 504 (1924); *Connally v. General Construction Co.*, 269 U.S. 385 (1926); *Weaver v. Palmer Bros. Co.*, 270 U.S. 402 (1926).

54. *New York Central Railroad Co. v. White*, 243 U.S. 188 (1917).

55. *Muller v. Oregon*, 208 U.S. 412 (1908); *Bunting v. Oregon*, 243 U.S. 426 (1917); *Euclid v. Ambler Realty*, 272 U.S. 365 (1926).

56. Oliver Wendell Holmes Jr., *The Common Law* (1881), reprinted in *The Collected Works of Justice Holmes: Complete Public Writings and Selected Judicial Opinions of Oliver Wendell Holmes*, ed. Sheldon Novick (1995), 3:115.

57. Oliver Wendell Holmes, "The Path of the Law," *Harvard Law Review* (1897), in *Collected Works of Justice Holmes*, 3:391–406; Holmes, "Law in Science and Science in Law" (1899), ibid. 406–20, quotation on 418–19.

58. Horwitz, *Transformation II*, 131.

59. *Lochner v. New York*, 198 U.S. 45, 75 (1905).

60. *Southern Pacific Co. v. Jensen*, 244 U.S. 205, 222 (1917) (Holmes, J., dissenting).

61. 208 U.S. 412 (1908).

62. Charles A. Beard, *An Economic Interpretation of the Constitution of the United States* (1913); Charles A. Beard and Mary R. Beard, *The Rise of American Civilization*, new ed. (1933).

63. Vernon Louis Parrington, *Main Currents in American Thought: An Interpretation of American Literature from the Beginnings to 1920*, 3 vols. (1927–30).

64. J. Allen Smith, *The Spirit of American Government* (1907).

65. Charles A. Beard, *The Supreme Court and the Constitution* (1912).

66. See generally Morton G. White, *Social Thought in America: The Revolt Against Formalism* (1949).

67. Edwin R. A. Seligman, *The Economic Interpretation of History* (1902).

68. E.g., Richard T. Ely, *Property and Contract in Their Relations to the Distribution of Wealth* (1914).

69. John R. Commons, *A Documentary History of American Industrial Society*, 11 vols. (1910–11); Commons, *Legal Foundations of Capitalism* (1924).

70. Roscoe Pound, "The Need of a Sociological Jurisprudence," *Green Bag* 19 (1907): 607; Pound, "Mechanical Jurisprudence," *Colum. L. Rev.* 8 (1908): 605; Pound, "Liberty of Contract," *Yale L. J.* 18 (1909): 454; Pound, "Law in Books and Law in Action," *Am. L. Rev.* 44 (1910): 12; Pound, "The Scope and Purpose of Sociological Jurisprudence," *Harv. L. Rev.* 24 (1911): 591; 25 (1912): 489. On the evolution of Pound's thought, see N. E. H. Hull, *Roscoe Pound and Karl Llewellyn: Searching for an American Jurisprudence* (1998).

71. 201 N.Y. 271 (1911).

72. President William H. Taft, veto of the Arizona Enabling Bill, Aug. 22, 1911, in James D. Richardson, comp., *A Compilation of the Messages and Papers of the Presidents* (1914), 18:8023. Paul Murphy, with his coeditor James Morton Smith, was the first to disseminate this important document to a wide academic audience in his superb collection of primary sources of the American Constitution, *Liberty and Justice* (1958, 1965), now regrettably out of print. Speaking as one who has participated in the creation of a cases-and-materials type of casebook, I gladly acknowledge the magisterial role that Smith and Murphy's collection has played in shaping the way that an entire generation of constitutional historians think, write, and teach.

73. I reluctantly adopt the convention of capitals simply to avoid confusion with the generic senses of "realism." Much more than other movements designated by capitalization, Realism's heterogeneity defies capture in a cage of synopsis.

74. See generally William W. Fisher III, Morton J. Horwitz, and Thomas A. Reed, eds., *American Legal Realism* (1993); Laura Kalman, *Legal Realism at Yale, 1927–1960* (1986); William L. Twining, *Karl Llewellyn and the Realist Movement* (1973); Horwitz, *Transformation II*, 169–246; Wilfrid E. Rumble, *American Legal Realism; Skepticism, Reform, and the Judicial Process* (1968).

75. Realist judges themselves proclaimed this: Joseph C. Hutcheson Jr., "The Judgment Intuitive: The Function of the 'Hunch' in Judicial Decision," *Cornell L. Q.* 14 (1929): 274.

76. *Palsgraf v. Long Island Rail Road*, 248 N.Y. 339, 162 N.E. 99 (1928).

77. *Home Building and Loan Assn. v. Blaisdell*, 290 U.S. 398 (1934); *Nebbia v. New York*, 291 U.S. 502 (1934).

78. *Norman v. Baltimore & Ohio R.R. Co.*, 294 U.S. 240 (1935); *Nortz v. United States*, 294 U.S. 317 (1935).

79. *Ashwander v. TVA*, 297 U.S. 288 (1936).

80. *Panama Refining Co. v. Ryan*, 293 U.S. 388 (1935); *Schechter Poultry Corp. v. United States*, 295 U.S. 495 (1935); *United States v. Butler*, 297 U.S. 1 (1936). See also *Railroad Retirement Board v. Alton*, 295 U.S. 330 (1935).

81. *Carter v. Carter Coal Co.*, 298 U.S. 238 (1936).

82. *Morehead v. New York ex rel. Tipaldo*, 298 U.S. 587 (1936).

83. On which, cf. William E. Leuchtenburg, *The Supreme Court Reborn: The Constitutional Revolution in the Age of Roosevelt* (1995), 82–178, with Barry Cushman, *Rethinking the New Deal Court: The Structure of a Constitutional Revolution* (1998).

84. *West Coast Hotel Co. v. Parrish*, 300 U.S. 379 (1937), 391, 393, 399.

85. In *National Labor Relations Board v. Jones and Laughlin Steel Corp.*, 310 U.S. 1 (1937); *Steward Machine Co. v. Davis*, 301 U.S. 548 (1937); *Wickard v. Filburn*, 317 U.S. 111 (1942).

86. *United States v. Darby*, 312 U.S. 100, 124 (1941).

87. *Olsen v. Nebraska*, 313 U.S. 236 (1941); *Williamson v. Lee Optical Co.*, 348 U.S. 483 (1955).

88. *Lincoln Federal Labor Union v. Northwestern Iron & Metal Co.*, 335 U.S. 525, 535 (1949).

89. *Ferguson v. Skrupa*, 372 U.S. 726, 732 (1963).

90. *United States v. Carolene Products Co.*, 304 U.S. 144 (1938), fn. 4.

91. Beginning in *Jones v. Opelika*, 316 U.S. 584, 608 (1942): "[T]he Constitution, by virtue of the First and the Fourteenth Amendments, has put those [First Amendment] freedoms in a preferred position" (Stone, C.J., dissenting). See generally Peter Linzer, "The Carolene Products Footnote and the Preferred Position of Individual Rights: Louis Lusky and John Hart Ely vs. Harlan Fiske Stone," *Const. Commentary* 12 (1995): 277. "Double standard": Gerald Gunther, *Constitutional Law*, 12th ed. (1991), 464.

92. *Griswold v. Connecticut*, 381 U.S. 479 (1965); *Roe v. Wade*, 410 U.S. 113 (1973); *Planned Parenthood of Southeastern Pennsylvania v. Casey*, 112 S.Ct. 2791 (1992).

93. *Roe v. Wade*, 410 U.S. 113 (1973); *Planned Parenthood of Southeastern Pennsylvania v. Casey*, 112 S.Ct. 2791 (1992).

94. *Maher v. Roe*, 432 U.S. 464 (1977); *Harris v. McRae*, 448 U.S. 297 (1980). On the internal dynamics of this struggle over contested legitimacy, see Edward Lazarus, *Closed Chambers: The First Eyewitness Account of the Epic Struggles Inside the Supreme Court* (1998).

95. Morton J. Horwitz, "The Constitution of Change: Legal Fundamentality Without Fundamentalism," *Harv. L. Rev.* 107 (1993): 32, 40.

96. 302 U.S. 319, 325–27 (1937), and 291 U.S. 97, 105 (1934), respectively.

97. *Adamson v. California*, 332 U.S. 46, 67–68 (1947) (Frankfurter, J., concurring).

98. *Rochin v. California*, 342 U.S. 165, 171–72 (1952).

99. 367 U.S. 497, 522 (1961) (Harlan, J., dissenting).

100. *Adamson v. California*, 332 U.S. at 75 (Black, J., dissenting).

101. See, e.g., *Duncan v. Louisiana*, 391 U.S. 145, 168 (1968) (Black, J., concurring).

102. E.g., *Cohen v. California*, 403 U.S. 15, 27 (1971) (Black, J., joining in Justice Blackmun's dissent); *Tinker v. Des Moines School District*, 393 U.S. 503, 515 (1969) (Black, J., dissenting).

103. Henry M. Hart and Albert M. Sacks, eds., *The Legal Process: Basic Problems in the Making and Application of Law* (1958; rpt., with introductory essay by William N. Eskridge and Philip P. Frickey, 1994); G. Edward White, *Patterns of American Legal Thought* (1978), 136–62.

104. Herbert Wechsler, "Toward Neutral Principles of Constitutional Law," *Harv. L. Rev.* 73 (1959): 1 (the 1959 Holmes Lectures).

105. Published as Learned Hand, *The Bill of Rights* (1964) (the 1958 Holmes Lectures).

106. Cf. Alexander M. Bickel, *The Least Dangerous Branch: The Supreme Court at the Bar of Politics* (1962), with Bickel, *The Supreme Court and the Idea of Progress* (1978). See Edward A. Purcell Jr., "Alexander M. Bickel and the Post-Realist Constitution," *Harv. C.R.-C.L. L. Rev.* 11 (1976): 521.

107. E.g., the joint opinion in *Planned Parenthood of Southeastern Pennsylvania v. Casey*, 112 S.Ct. 2791 (1992).

108. *United States v. Darby*, 312 U.S. 100 (1941); *National League of Cities v. Usery*, 426 U.S. 833 (1976); *Garcia v. San Antonio Metropolitan Transit Authority*, 469 U.S. 528 (1985); *New York v. United States*, 505 U.S. 144 (1992); *United States v. Lopez*, 514 U.S. 549 (1995); *U.S. Term Limits v. Thornton*, 514 U.S. 779 (1995).

109. Robert H. Bork, *The Tempting of America: The Political Seduction of the Law* (1990); Bernard H. Siegan, *The Supreme Court's Constitution* (1987); Raoul Berger, *Government by Judiciary: The Transformation of the Fourteenth Amendment* (1977), and the entire corpus of his subsequent law review publications; Lino Graglia, *Disaster by Decree: The Supreme Court Decisions and the Schools* (1976); Earl Maltz, "The Prospects for a Revival of Conservative Activism in Constitutional Jurisprudence," *Ga. L. Rev.* 24 (1990): 629.

110. Edwin Meese, "Speech Before the American Bar Association, July 9, 1985," reprinted in *The Great Debate: Interpreting Our Constitution* (pamphlet published by the Federalist Society, 1986).

111. Hadley Arkes, *The Return of George Sutherland: Restoring a Jurisprudence of Natural Rights* (1994); Richard A. Epstein, *Takings: Private Property and the Power of Eminent Domain* (1985); Bernard H. Siegan, *Economic Liberties and the Constitution* (1981).

112. *Planned Parenthood of Southeastern Pennsylvania v. Casey*, 112 S.Ct. 2791, 2873 (1992) (Scalia, J., dissenting); *United States v. Lopez*, 115 S.Ct. 1624, 1642 (1995) (Thomas, J., concurring).

113. William Butler Yeats, "The Second Coming" (1920), in *The Variorum Edition of the Poems of W. B. Yeats* (1957).

*Part II*

# The Modern Constitutional Republic in Historical Perspective

*Chapter Four*

# Free Speech and the Bifurcated Review Project: The "Preferred Position" Cases

G. Edward White

## I

I want to begin with some general observations about the intellectual history of free speech in twentieth-century America. The observations have been detailed and supported at much greater length elsewhere;[1] in this chapter I am merely asserting them in attenuated form. I then want to discuss one set of early twentieth-century free speech decisions by the Supreme Court of the United States—the "preferred position" cases—that I will suggest was a core episode in this intellectual history. Finally, I want to argue that the conventional view of the origins of the "double standard" of constitutional review that has characterized much of constitutional jurisprudence in the twentieth century has significantly underestimated the importance of free speech decisions in generating that project.

First, some comments of a relatively abstract sort. The First Amendment came of age in America at a particular point in time, the years between the two world wars. That period was characterized not only by the emergence of what I have elsewhere called a modernist consciousness,[2] but also by the presence of external features in American culture that bore a generative relationship to that consciousness. Two particularly foundational features were the presence of a democratic model of politics and a capitalist model of economics. Modernity in twentieth-century America was taken to be exemplified, in important part, by both of those models, but the cultural status of the models, at the time free speech began to be taken seriously as a constitutional ideal in America, was not identical.

In the period between the world wars, the democratic model of politics, especially in the idealized versions of democratic theory, progressively expanded in influence. At the same time the capitalist model of economics, in its idealized late nineteenth-century version of a "laissez-faire" economic marketplace characterized by the absence of governmental regulation, receded in influence. As the meaning and normative significance of democracy expanded, the meaning of capitalism as unregulated economic activity became severed from democratic theory. Freedom in the political sphere became embodied by democratic theory and practices,[3] but freedom in the economic sphere was increasingly pictured as producing inequitable distributions of power and wealth, so that regulation of the economic marketplace became associated with democratic theory.

Now to a more specific line of argument. The shifting influence of the democratic model of politics and the capitalist model of economics was reflected in a fundamental development in American constitutional jurisprudence in the period between the wars. The emergence of free speech as constitutionally and culturally special was intimately tied to that development. I am calling that development the "bifurcated review project." It was an effort to fashion a double standard of constitutional review in which judges would defer to legislative regulation of the economy but scrutinize legislative regulation of noneconomic rights, including the right to free speech. The basis for that heightened scrutiny was the close connection between the freedom personified in noneconomic liberties and democratic theory. The basis for judicial deference to legislative regulation of economic rights was similar. Such deference not only alleviated fears of an undemocratic substitution, under the guise of constitutional interpretation, of judicial for legislative theories of the economy, but also left in place legislative regulations designed to alleviate the undemocratic consequences of the unregulated economic marketplace.

The bifurcated review project represented a modernist-inspired effort to give shape to two of the principal defining features of modernity. By fostering judicial deference in the area of economic regulation, the project embraced the perceived truth that unregulated economic activity actually infringed on the freedom of a significant number of actors in the economic marketplace and reinforced rational regulatory policies that were based on that truth. By fostering judicial scrutiny of legislative restrictions on speech and other noneconomic liberties, the project underscored the centrality of freedom as a modernist goal, at least when freedom could be associated with the goals of democratic theory.

Thus the evolution of free speech jurisprudence in twentieth-century America, stretching from the years before World War I to the present, can be seen as a series of episodes in which the major premises of modernism, as interpreted by courts and commentators, successively contributed to elevating the constitutional and cultural status of free speech. The episodes served to demonstrate how vital free speech jurisprudence was to the bifurcated review project and, at the same time, how that jurisprudence came to be at war with itself, ultimately threatening not only its own assumed internal coherence but also the coherence of bifurcated review as a judicial stance. As episodes in the twentieth-century intellectual history of free speech jurisprudence produced various rationales for the protection of speech—the "search for truth" in a "marketplace of ideas," self-governance, and individual autonomy or self-fulfillment—those rationales began to conflict with, as well as to reinforce, one another and eventually to threaten, as well as to implement, the juristic goals of the bifurcated review project.

In recent years, as protection for speech has begun to disengage itself from democratic political theory and to invade the realm of economic regulation, a sharp separation between the juristic realms of noneconomic and economic freedom has increasingly appeared problematic to courts and commentators. But this sharp separation had been the essence of the bifurcated review project and arguably the essence of an enlightened judicial approach to modernity. The result has been to stimulate a reconsideration of the significance of speech in America.

## II

In this chapter I will not be pursuing the intellectual history just sketched beyond the close of World War II. My interest here is in focusing on one episode in that history, one in which the close relationship of enhanced protection for free speech to the juristic goals of the bifurcated review project was first grasped by justices on the Supreme Court.

Commentators on twentieth-century constitutional history have been aware of the existence of the bifurcated review project but have tended to locate its origins in the political and economic transformations that eventually ushered in a much greater regulatory presence for the federal government after the 1932 election.[4] Most commentary identifies the origins of bifurcated review with two developments in constitutional jurisprudence in the late 1930s.

One was the appearance of First Amendment opinions suggesting that the freedoms of speech, assembly, and religion occupied a "preferred" position in constitutional jurisprudence and in American culture. That set of opinions has received surprisingly little attention from legal commentators.[5] The other was Justice Stone's footnote in *United States v. Carolene Products Co.*,[6] in which he suggested that there might be more searching judicial review of legislative activity when a statute affected rights explicitly mentioned in the text of the Constitution or when it was directed at "discrete and insular minorities" whose status adversely affected their access to the legislative forum.

The primary impact of the *Carolene Products* footnote has been in equal protection jurisprudence. But it should be understood that the first paragraph of the footnote, with its attention to textually protected rights, provided a justification for a higher level of judicial scrutiny for First Amendment claims than for legislative infringements on *Lochner*-type rights.[7] Modern commentators have tended not to concentrate on this paragraph, but at the same time to see the *Carolene Products* footnote as initiating bifurcated review.[8]

Although recognition of the existence of decisions in the 1930s endorsing bifurcated review has been commonplace, the explanations for their appearance have remained attenuated. To the extent a general explanation has been advanced, it has been at the level of an intuition: with the presence of an expanded role for government in the 1930s came a recognition of the potential of government to infringe upon noneconomic rights. The emergence around the time of the New Deal of "preferred position" cases,[9] and of the two-tiered theory of judicial review suggested in *Carolene Products,* has been seen as a natural consequence of reflections on the intrusive potential of an expanded governmental apparatus.[10]

The difficulty with seeing the "preferred position" interlude in First Amendment jurisprudence as part of a natural response to the emergence of expanded government in the twentieth century is that such an explanation supplies no intellectual basis for why a group of judges and jurists should have responded to expanded government by bifurcating constitutional review. The logic of the modernist critique of "substantive" judicial interpretation launched by Holmes's dissent in *Lochner v. New York*[11] led in the direction of less judicial activism on behalf of legislatively regulated "liberties," whatever their content. Moreover, the civil rights movement, with its enhanced consciousness of the oppressed status of minorities in America, was hardly a mainstream phenomenon in the late 1930s.[12]

Thus there does not appear to be any obvious explanation for why those justices who can be identified with the brief development of "preferred position" free speech jurisprudence should have concluded that although governmental restrictions on *Lochner*-type rights were now presumptively rational, governmental restrictions on noneconomic rights needed to be carefully scrutinized.

There is, however, an explanation for the emergence of bifurcated review that can be grounded in the language of the "preferred position" cases themselves. That explanation begins with an understanding that from Justice Louis Brandeis's 1927 concurrence in *Whitney v. California*[13] to 1942, the very time interval in which the *Lochner* majority's approach to due process cases was rejected[14] and the Court increasingly sanctioned an expansion of congressional and state power to regulate the economy,[15] every Supreme Court case exhibiting an increased level of scrutiny of a legislative regulation was a First Amendment case.[16] Moreover, many of those cases openly suggested that First Amendment rights should receive greater judicial solicitude than other rights: that was what "preferred position" meant.

Finally, the cases that did assign First Amendment rights to a "preferred position" posited an explanation for their being singled out. The explanation was not fully developed: it often consisted, in fact, of a single rhetorical assertion. But that assertion nonetheless was of real significance in the twentieth-century history of free speech. It posited an "indispensable connection" between free speech and the meaning of "democracy" in America. The "preferred position" cases decided by the Supreme Court, beginning in 1937, reveal that several justices had intuitively concluded that First Amendment rights were in a different category from other constitutional "liberties" and deserved greater constitutional protection than existing police power formulas afforded them. Moreover, those justices had intuitively concluded that the reason for this enhanced protection for First Amendment rights lay not only in the close connections between free speech and democratic theory but also in the enhanced significance of democratic theory itself, as a defining aspirational feature of American civilization.

As a doctrinal development, the "preferred position" interlude was cryptic and abortive. Between 1937 and the early 1950s, various justices on the Court declared openly, or implied, that First Amendment rights occupied a "preferred position." Their scattered remarks, although invoked by majority opinions in subsequent cases, neither clarified the precise doctrinal meaning of "preferred position" nor provided any extended justification for why freedom of speech, religion, and assembly should be given preferred status. Eventually the Court implicitly abandoned the phrase "preferred position" altogether and explored other interpretive techniques for carving out a high degree of protection for speech.

But the episode, coming at the time it did, aptly illustrated the search for a bifurcated standard of constitutional review that had come to be at the heart of the Court's jurisprudential enterprise by the late 1930s. The "preferred position" sequence of cases represented an attempt on the Court's part to enshrine the modernist premise of cognitive freedom and to associate that premise with a powerfully evocative theme that surfaced for Americans in the third and fourth decades of the twentieth century, the theme of

America as a democratic society. In an interval of time, beginning in the 1930s and stretching through the years of World War II, the idea of America as a democracy dramatically expanded its cultural meaning, signifying not only a society based on freedom but also a society opposed to tyranny and arbitrariness, an antitotalitarian society that represented the world's last best hope for rationality and truth.[17]

Free speech, in the "preferred position" episode, became democratic speech. It became closely associated with the intertwined ideas of creative self-fulfillment (freedom to express oneself) and equality (freedom from discrimination or oppression). Those ideas were taken to be at the foundation of America as a democratic society. Free democratic speech signified the power of the human actor in modernity, liberated from the dominance of external forces, free to determine his or her individual destiny, required only to respect the freedoms of others.

Modernist conceptions of freedom suggested that free democratic speech was unlike the other "liberties" in orthodox nineteenth-century jurisprudence. Such "liberties" had come to be associated with the undemocratic economic excesses that had rewarded the rich at the expense of the poor and caused the Great Depression. Free speech was not to be a source of protection for rights associated with material possessions but for rights embodied in the ideal of democracy. Its "preferred position" in constitutional jurisprudence came from its close connection to democratic processes and practices, and from the heightened significance of the democratic form of government in a world that was showing tendencies of abandoning democracy for totalitarianism and of restricting human freedoms along the way.

## III

The sequence of "preferred position" cases started in a decision in which the phrase itself was not employed, but the theme of democratic speech surfaced. That was *Palko v. Connecticut*,[18] a year before the *Carolene Products* footnote, in which Justice Cardozo, for the Court, defined free speech as "the matrix, the indispensable condition, of nearly every other form of freedom." "Liberty" in

America, he concluded, "has been enlarged . . . to include liberty of the mind as well as liberty of action."[19] It is not clear whether by those remarks Cardozo meant to suggest that free speech rights, by being a "matrix" of other rights, were to be preferred over all other constitutional guaranties. But *Palko* was a case in which he was searching for Bill of Rights freedoms that were "of the very essence of a scheme of ordered liberty," so that "neither liberty nor justice would exist if they were sacrificed."[20] "[F]reedom of thought and speech" was first on his list.

Between *Palko* and the close of World War II, the Court's free speech cases regularly involved challenges against state and municipal regulations by members of the Jehovah's Witnesses sect. Many Witnesses believed that the Old Testament's First Commandment, forbidding the worship of any graven image, prevented them from participating in flag salute ceremonies. They were thus the petitioners in one of the Court's most celebrated sequences of decisions, *Minersville School District v. Gobitis*[21] and *West Virginia v. Barnette*,[22] in which the justices reversed themselves on the constitutionality of compulsory flag salute laws, overruling an opinion that had been rendered only three years previously and had engendered only one dissent. The flag salute cases can also be shown to have been the basis for an eventual critique of the "preferred position" rationale itself by Justice Felix Frankfurter, who had initially identified himself with that rationale.

As early as 1939, Jehovah's Witnesses cases began to invoke judicial declarations that speech rights should be given special solicitude. In *Schneider v. Irvington,* Justice Roberts, for every member of the Court save McReynolds, conceptualized an antilittering ordinance directed against the distribution of Witness literature as pitting the "duty" of municipalities "to keep their streets open and available for movement of people and property" against "the guarantee of freedom of speech or of the press." In such cases the judicial task was "to weigh the circumstances and appraise the substantiality of the reasons advanced in support of the regulation of the free enjoyment of the rights."[23] Roberts made it clear what would weigh most heavily in the balancing:

> This court has characterized the freedom of speech and freedom of press as fundamental personal rights and liberties. . . .

> Legislative preferences or beliefs respecting matters of public convenience may well support regulation directed at other personal activities, but may be insufficient to justify such as diminishes the existence of rights so vital to the maintenance of democratic institutions.[24]

Not only were First Amendment freedoms "indispensable" and "fundamental"; they had been explicitly linked to the ideal of democracy.

A year after *Schneider* the first of the flag salute cases was handed down, and the idea of democratic speech greatly expanded in cultural significance and revealed itself as containing some internal ambiguities. Both Frankfurter's majority opinion, sustaining the constitutionality of a Pennsylvania school district's practice of opening each day in its public schools with a mandatory ceremony paying homage to the American flag, and Stone's dissent, finding the practice a violation of the religious freedom of Jehovah's Witness families who objected to the practice, attempted to justify their positions through invocations of the indispensable connection between "freedom" and democracy. Frankfurter asserted that "personal freedom is best maintained—so long as the remedial channels of the democratic process remain open and unobstructed—when it is . . . not enforced against popular policy by the coercion of adjudicated law."[25] Stone countered:

> The Constitution expressed more than the conviction of the people that democratic processes must be preserved at all costs. It is also an expression of faith and a command that freedom of mind and spirit must be preserved, which government must obey, if it is to adhere to that justice and moderation without which no free government can exist.[26]

The Frankfurter-Stone exchange suggested that the ideal of democracy could be translated into support for majoritarian, "popular" policies restricting speech as well as support for speech rights as the embodiment of freedom in a democratic society. As those alternative readings of the consequences for speech of the heightened awareness of America as a democracy were being set forth, the Court returned to the traditional setting of Jehovah's

Witnesses cases, municipal regulations on the distribution of leaflets. But the stakes involved in carving out special judicial protection for speech, at least within the Court, had been elevated.

In the 1942 case of *Jones v. Opelika,* a 5-4 majority of the Court upheld municipal license fees directed against Witness pamphlets, characterizing the distributions as commercial transactions, and thus not implicating speech rights, and the fees as reasonable restraints on economic activity. In his dissent Stone was not content simply to challenge the majority's characterizations of the municipal regulations. He announced:

> The First Amendment is not confined to safeguarding freedom of speech and freedom of religion against discriminatory attempts to wipe them out. On the contrary, the Constitution, by virtue of the First and the Fourteenth Amendments, has put those freedoms in a preferred position. Their commands are not restricted to cases where the protected privilege is sought out for attack. They extend to every form of taxation which, because it is a condition of the exercise of the privilege, is capable of being used to control or suppress it.[27]

Stone's dissent in *Jones v. Opelika* made it clear that the "speech dimensions" of the leaflets were what conveyed special protection on those who distributed them. By "preferred position," he meant that "every form of taxation" and other economic regulation that could be seen as infringing First Amendment rights would receive heightened judicial scrutiny. When one combines this categorization of "preferred position" rights with the original rationale for giving those rights special attention—their "indispensable" connection to the maintenance of democratic principles—it became clear that Stone was suggesting that speech rights reinforced democracy in a way that economic rights did not. This suggestion expanded the cultural significance of democracy in America during a period of totalitarian challenges and made speech rights the exemplar for bifurcated review in a post-*Lochner* constitutional universe.

This reading of Stone's dissent in *Jones v. Opelika* is supported by an unusual memorandum issued in the case by Justices Murphy, Black, and Douglas, all of whom had joined Stone's dissent.

In that memorandum the three justices stated that "the opinion of the Court sanctions a device which in our opinion suppresses or tends to suppress the free exercise of religion practiced by a minority group."[28] They then announced that they had changed their minds about the Court's decision in *Gobitis,* which they had each joined (this despite the fact that *Jones v. Opelika* had nothing to do with compulsory flag salutes). The reason they gave for changing their minds about the constitutional status of religious-based challenges to compulsory flag salute laws was that "our democratic form of government, functioning under the historic Bill of Rights, has a high responsibility to accommodate itself to the religious views of minorities, however unpopular and unorthodox those views be."[29]

A personnel change on the Court now gave additional momentum to the theory that free speech rights should occupy a "preferred position" in a democracy. Another Jehovah's Witnesses license case, *Murdock v. Pennsylvania,*[30] handed down a little over a year after *Jones v. Opelika,* overruled that case and invalidated all municipally imposed "flat taxes" on the distribution of religious literature.[31] Douglas, for the majority in *Murdock,* declared that "[f]reedom of press, freedom of speech, freedom of religion are in a preferred position." The context of his statement made it clear that he meant "preferred" to refer to a distinction between speech and commercial activity. "A license tax," he argued, "certainly does not acquire constitutional validity because it classifies the privileges protected by the First Amendment along with the wares and merchandise of hucksters and peddlers and treats them all alike."[32]

Thus by 1943 Jehovah's Witnesses cases had given the Court an opportunity to make explicit the position that religious speech was specially protected, but commercial activity, including speech proposing a commercial transaction, was not.[33] The Court now returned to the issue of compulsory flag salutes, as the national counsel for the Witnesses challenged a policy imposed by the West Virginia board of education on all state public schools.[34] After conference Stone knew that he had a clear majority to overrule *Gobitis*[35] and assigned the opinion to Jackson. Frankfurter was comparably aware that his position, which had once commanded the votes of eight justices, now, three years later, commanded the votes of only three. As the opinions in the second flag salute case unfolded, it was apparent that two themes were on the justices' minds: the "indispensable" connection between free speech and democratic theory and the jurisprudential implications of conferring a "preferred position" on speech rights.

Jackson's opinion for the Court, after noting that "[t]hose who begin coercive elimination of dissent soon find themselves exterminating dissenters," announced that "the First Amendment . . . was designed to avoid these ends by avoiding these beginnings. . . . We set up government by consent of the governed, and the Bill of Rights denies those in power any legal opportunity to coerce that consent."[36] Having identified the First Amendment as embodying an antitotalitarian ethos, he then turned to the implications of treating the Constitution as withdrawing "certain subjects," in which "fundamental rights" such as "free speech [and] freedom of worship" were implicated, "from the vicissitudes of political controversy." He had listed among "fundamental" rights "liberty" and "property."[37] Did this mean that bifurcated review was unintelligible, or that *Lochner* was revived?

Jackson's response made it clear that the "preferred position" experiment would continue and that speech rights would receive more constitutional solicitude than economic rights:

> [I]t is important to distinguish between the due process clause of the Fourteenth Amendment as an instrument for transmitting the principles of the First Amendment and those cases in which it is applied for its own sake. . . . Much of the vagueness of the due process clause disappears when the specific prohibitions of the First become its standard. The right of a State to regulate, for example, a public utility may well include, so far as the due process test is concerned, power to impose all the restrictions which a legislature may have a "rational basis" for adopting. But freedoms of speech and of press, of assembly, and of worship may not be infringed on such slender grounds. They are susceptible of restriction only to prevent grave and immediate danger to interests which the state may lawfully protect.[38]

Jackson's doctrinal conclusion was unmistakable: where First Amendment rights were involved, the "rational basis" standard for evaluating the constitutionality of legislation, now established in cases involving economic regulations, would have to yield to a version of Holmes's and Brandeis's clear and present danger test.

Perhaps stung by the invocation of Holmes and Brandeis against his majority opinion in *Gobitis,* in his dissent Frankfurter immediately took up the question of whether a "preferred position" for speech rights was necessary once one concluded that free speech bore an "indispensable" connection to democratic theory. His answer was that placing speech rights in a "preferred position" was not just unnecessary but dangerous. He began his *Barnette* dissent by noting that since he was a member of "the most vilified and persecuted minority in history," he was "not likely to be insensible to the freedoms guaranteed by our Constitution," and "were my purely personal attitude relevant I should wholeheartedly associate myself with the general libertarian views in the Court's opinion." But as a judge, he concluded, "I am not justified in writing my private notions of policy into the Constitution." "Judicial self-restraint" applied to speech cases as well as to economic due process cases. As Frankfurter put it,

> The Constitution does not give us greater veto power when dealing with one phase of "liberty" than another. . . . Judicial self-restraint is equally necessary whenever an exercise of political or legislative power is challenged. . . . Our power does not vary according to the particular provision of the Bill of Rights which is invoked. The right not to have property taken without just compensation has, so far as the scope of judicial power is concerned, the same constitutional dignity as . . . freedom of the press or freedom of speech or religious freedom.[39]

Frankfurter's dissent in *Barnette* was part of an intense and ultimately painful flirtation he had undertaken in the 1930s and 1940s with the "preferred position" experiment as it related to bifurcated review. In 1938, after reading Stone's *Carolene Products* footnote, Frankfurter wrote Stone that he had just finished a series of lectures on Holmes "in which I've tried to reconcile his latitudinarian attitude toward constitutionality in cases other than civil liberties . . . with his attitude in civil liberties cases," and that "I was extremely excited by your note 4," which "is extremely suggestive and opens up new territory."[40] In his lectures on Holmes, Frankfurter had concluded that "the liberty of man to search for truth was of a different order than some economic dogma," and "therefore Mr. Justice Holmes attributed very different legal significance to those liberties of the individual which history has attested as the indispensable conditions of a free society from that which he attached to liberties which derived merely from shifting economic arrangements."[41]

Two years later Frankfurter was on the Court, writing the majority opinion in *Gobitis,* and he wrote Stone, after the latter had circulated a draft dissent, that "I am aware of the important distinction which you so skillfully adumbrated in your footnote 4 . . . in the *Carolene Products Co.* case. I agree with that distinction; I regard it as basic."[42] And as late as 1941 he was prepared to declare, for the Court, that judges should approach efforts to restrict freedom of discussion in labor disputes "with a jealous eye," and to cite footnote 4 in *Carolene Products* for that proposition.[43]

But Frankfurter had also told Stone, in his *Gobitis* letter, about his "anxiety that, while we lean in the direction of the libertarian aspect, we do not exercise our judicial power unduly. . . . In other words, I want to avoid the mistake comparable to those whom we criticized when dealing with the control of property."[44] And after being humiliated in the flag salute sequence,[45] he signaled that any inclination he had to endorse the "preferred position" experiment had been withdrawn. Eventually, after Stone died in 1946, Frankfurter decided to mount an open attack on the "preferred position" rubric itself.

The case was *Kovacs v. Cooper,*[46] a 1949 decision in which a plurality of the Court sustained a Trenton, New Jersey, ordinance prohibiting the use of sound trucks that issued "loud and raucous noises." In the six years between *Barnette* and *Kovacs,* the "preferred position" rubric had gained momentum on the Court, reaching a high-water mark in *Thomas v. Collins*[47] and *Marsh v. Alabama.*[48] In *Thomas,* Justice Rutledge, for a plurality, had openly stated that legislative restrictions on First Amendment rights were to be subjected to a higher level of judicial scrutiny than other challenges to legislation "on due process grounds," and that "the great, the indispensable democratic freedoms secured by the First

Amendment" occupied "a preferred place in our scheme."[49] And in *Marsh,* a case where a town owned entirely by a private corporation attempted to prevent Witnesses from distributing religious literature within the town limits, Justice Black conceptualized the constitutional issue as one that required the balancing of "rights of owners of property against those of the people to enjoy freedom of press and religion" and declared that the First Amendment rights "occup[ied] a preferred position."[50] But by 1949 some additional personnel changes had occurred, which after that year resulted in three justices prominently identified with the "preferred position" rubric no longer being on the Court.[51]

In *Kovacs,* Reed, for a plurality that included Vinson and Burton, endorsed what he called "[t]he preferred position of freedom of speech in a society that cherishes liberty for all" but found that the state interest in protecting the privacy and tranquility of its citizens overrode the First Amendment claim.[52] Frankfurter and Jackson concurred in the result in *Kovacs,* with Black, Douglas, Rutledge, and Murphy dissenting.

In his concurring opinion Frankfurter launched an attack on the "preferred position" rubric. He called "preferred position" a "mischievous phrase," which had "uncritically crept into some recent opinions of this Court." He then set forth a history of "preferred position," including not only cases where the characterization was explicitly used but also those in which he concluded that the Court was adhering to a bifurcated standard of review.

The result of this historical exegesis, for Frankfurter, was that "the claim that any legislation is presumptively unconstitutional which touches the field of the First Amendment . . . has never commended itself to a majority of this Court." He then concluded with an extraordinary sentence:

> In considering what interests are so fundamental as to be enshrined in the Due Process Clause, those liberties of the individual which history has attested as the indispensable conditions of an open as against a closed society come to this Court with a momentum for respect lacking when appeal is made to liberties which derive merely from shifting economic arrangements.[53]

This was, of course, an almost verbatim paragraph of the characterization of Holmes's jurisprudence that he had made in 1938, in the course of an argument that "the liberty of man to search for truth was of a different order than some economic dogma defined as a sacred right."[54]

Frankfurter's tortured and ambivalent reaction to the "preferred position" rubric, and to the bifurcated review project itself, underscores once again the pivotal role of speech rights in launching that project. The passage quoted here from his *Kovacs* concurrence suggests that Frankfurter had internalized the central assumption of the "preferred position" cases, that speech rights could be distinguished from rights derived "merely from shifting economic arrangements" because of their "indispensable" connection to an "open," democratic society. In that passage Frankfurter signaled his tacit acceptance of the bifurcated review project while apparently protesting against it. Rutledge, dissenting in *Kovacs,* stated that Frankfurter's excursus had "demonstrate[d] the conclusion opposite to that which he draws, namely, that the First Amendment guaranties . . . occupy a preferred position not only in the Bill of Rights but also in the repeated decisions of this Court."[55]

## IV

There is no direct evidence about the reaction of any other of Frankfurter's colleagues to his attack on the "preferred position" concept in *Kovacs,* but the phrase "preferred position" virtually disappeared from the Court's free speech cases, showing up only once more, in a throwaway line by Douglas in a 1953 case.[56] The short life of the "preferred position" rubric, however, concealed its significance as an important transition phase in the twentieth-century intellectual history of First Amendment jurisprudence.

Early twentieth-century champions of extended constitutional protection for free speech, such as Zechariah Chafee and Brandeis, had hinted, but not explicitly suggested, that the "search for truth" and "self-governance" rationales were associated with the training of citizens to make informed and intelligent decisions about questions of public concern. But they had stopped short of explicitly suggesting that the speech being protected by the First Amendment was speech furthering the ideals of a democracy.

By openly identifying the basis of special constitutional protection for speech as the indispensable connection between free expression and democratic theory, and at the same time distinguishing between speech and liberties deriving from shifting economic arrangements, the "preferred position" cases had sought not only to link free speech with the idea of America as a democratic society but also to disengage protection for economic liberties from that idea. "Preferred position" meant a preference for First Amendment freedom as having a particularly close association with democratic politics, and it also meant, implicitly, that the freedoms associated with an economic model of unregulated capitalism were less democratic and hence less preferred. Liberties derived from "shifting economic arrangements" were taken to be less "indispensable" conditions of an "open" society.

There were, as the flag salute cases suggested, some difficulties with grounding a preferred position for speech rights in the expanded meaning of America as a democratic society. The difficulties centered in the tension between democratic theory as bolstering freedom of expression and democratic theory as being embodied in majoritarian policy making. If a justification for legislative regulation of economic activity was that legislatures, being representative of the majority of citizens, were appropriate institutions to make policies affecting the distribution of benefits in the economic marketplace, why were they not equally appropriate institutions to determine the forms of expression that a majority wanted to restrict as well as protect? Yet the very cases announcing that First Amendment rights were to be placed in a preferred position because of the close connection between free speech and the ideal of democracy were cases in which legislatures, on behalf of their majoritarian constituency, had restricted speech.

Thus it appeared that a further particularization of what types of speech were indispensable to a democratic society, and which were not, might be required. This was especially true if one believed that humans tended to reach subjectively and irrationally to speech issues. That belief suggested that although majoritarian policy making furthered democratic ideals, majorities were likely to suppress, perhaps even oversuppress, provocative speech. How did one determine which speech was presumptively immune from suppression? A tentative answer had been advanced in the rhetoric of the "preferred position" cases: speech that itself could be said to be "indispensable" to the functioning of a democratic model of politics.[57]

## V

We have seen that the progressive expansion of the ambit of First Amendment protection in the twentieth century was a central driving force in the development of a stance of bifurcated review toward constitutional challenges. We have also seen that the presumed efficacy of bifurcated review was at the center of the intuitive efforts of Supreme Court justices in the 1930s and 1940s to carve out a constitutionally "preferred position" for free speech rights.

But it would be erroneous to assert that the idea of speech being culturally and constitutionally special in America had become entrenched in the first three decades of the twentieth century, although that idea was growing in momentum. It would also be erroneous to claim that modernist-inspired constitutional jurisprudence had become orthodoxy in those decades. Modernist premises about law, government, and the economy were in the air between 1900 and 1930, especially among "progressive" intellectuals, but in the realm of constitutional jurisprudence they competed with premodernist premises. The majority approach to police power and due process cases in *Lochner,* after all, was revived in *Adkins v. Children's Hospital*[58] in the 1920s and remained orthodoxy until 1937.[59]

But since the early 1940s, at least, free speech has been reflexively taken by many constitutional theorists as not only furthering deliberative democracy but also as being an "indispensable" requirement of a democratic society. At the same time, however, a number of speakers who would have hardly been candidates for First Amendment protection under the original versions of bifurcated review—cable companies, multimedia enterprises, pharmacists, and political action committees—have found the Supreme Court solicitous of their claims for First Amendment protection.

Thus the paradox that current free speech theorists are confronting is as follows. If one returns to a First Amendment jurisprudence in which some expressions, by not furthering "deliberative democracy" or meeting some other inclusionary criterion, can be excluded from being candidates for protection, one threatens to revive an impressionistic apparatus for evaluating speech claims that could make the level of protection dependent on judicial intuitions.[60] On the other hand, if one reframes the sources of protection for free speech along lines consistent with the Court's recent emphasis on speech as furthering individual autonomy in a pluralistic society, one appears to invite a world in which any speaker is free to talk on any subject. When everyone can speak, and everything can be said, speech has ceased to become special and has become the equivalent of noise.

I share some of the ideological goals of those who desire a society in which the level of human discourse and the instincts and attitudes reflected in that discourse become less coarse and more respectful of others. I am also opposed to the project of channeling individual thoughts and expressions into the rubrics of "deliberative democracy," which I find either confining or not easily intelligible. I am less disturbed than some about the momentum of self-fulfillment in current First Amendment jurisprudence, but at the same time I recognize that the process of valuing some speech as deserving special protection requires an identification of speech that is not valued and consequently not protected.

But the purpose of this essay has not been to offer specific suggestions about the resolution of contemporary First Amendment issues, or to advance any overriding theoretical perspective on free speech. It has been, rather, to present a historical episode in which, as the Court considered assigning a "preferred position" to speech rights, the paradoxical status of free speech in a majoritarian democracy first surfaced. My goals have been to use that episode as a source of some enhanced understanding of the predicament in which those of us who teach and write about the First Amendment in the twenty-first century find ourselves.

Notes

An expanded version of this essay appeared as "The First Amendment Comes of Age," *Michigan Law Review* 95 (1996): 299–392. My thanks to Vincent Blasi, Mary Anne Case, Barry Cushman, Stephen J. Feldman, Jack Goldsmith, Mark Graber, Thomas Andrew Green, John Harrison, Michael Klarman, Alfred S. Konefsky, Peter Linzer, Robert Post, David Rabban, John Henry Schlegel, and Michael Seidman for their comments on earlier drafts of the expanded version. Thanks also to Cathleen Curran for research assistance.

1. White, "The First Amendment Comes of Age," 299–392.
2. Ibid., 302–8 (definitions of "modernism," "modernist consciousness," and "modernity").
3. Robert H. Wiebe, *Self-Rule: A Cultural History of American Democracy* (Chicago: University of Chicago Press, 1995), 137ff.
4. Paul Murphy, *The Constitution in Crisis Times, 1918–1969* (New York: Harper and Row, 1972), 172–75.
5. A telling example is David Currie's "The Constitution in the Supreme Court: The Preferred Position Debate, 1941–46," *Catholic University Law Review* 37 (1987): 39–71. Currie's article, which demonstrates his usual analytic acumen, devotes only fourteen of its thirty-three pages to free speech decisions. The "preferred position" free speech cases have received slightly more attention from political scientists and constitutional historians. A recent treatment is Howard Gillman, "Preferred Freedoms: The Progressive Expansion of State Power and the Rise of Modern Civil Liberties Jurisprudence," *Political Research Quarterly* 47 (1994): 623–53.
6. *United States v. Carolene Products Co.,* 304 U.S. 144, 152 n. 4 (1938).
7. The paragraph reads, "There may be narrower scope for operation of the presumption of constitutionality when legislation appears on its face to be within a specific prohibition of the Constitution, such as those of the first ten amendments, which are deemed equally specific when held to be embraced within the Fourteenth." First Amendment cases were clearly the model for this paragraph. It was followed by citations to *Stromberg v. California,* 283 U.S. 359 (1931), in which the Court struck down a California syndication statute as applied to the display of a red flag, and to *Lowell v. Griffin,* 303 U.S. 444 (1938), in which the Court invalidated a municipal ordinance prohibiting the distribution of circulars or any other literature without a permit from the city manager.
8. The following statement, from a constitutional casebook jointly authored by two political scientists and a law professor, can be taken as representative of the conventional view of the relationship of the *Carolene Products* footnote to the bifurcated review project: "The timing of the footnote is important. For much of the previous fifty years, a majority of the justices . . . had read their economic views into and out of the Constitution so as to thwart both state and federal efforts to cope with the problems of industrial and finance capitalism. The Great Depression that enveloped the country in 1929 and the Court's war against Roosevelt's New Deal had left laissez faire—and the nation—in shambles. By 1938, the Court had retreated, saying it would presume economic regulation to be constitutional. This withdrawal . . . raised fundamental questions about the future of constitutional interpretations by judges. If they were to presume economic regulation constitu-

tional, why not all regulation? On what principles could they draw lines?" See Walter Murphy, James E. Fleming, and William F. Harris II, *American Constitutional Interpretation* (Mineola, N.Y.: Foundation Press, 1986), 473. Fleming, currently on the faculty of Fordham Law School, was in private practice at the time the casebook was issued.

9. The use of the term "preferred position case" refers to any case in which an opinion of the Court used language suggesting that First Amendment rights occupied a "preferred position." As will become clear, the constitutional implications of the phrase were ambiguous, and few opinions sought to clarify exactly what "preferred position" meant.

10. See, e.g., Gillman, "Preferred Freedoms," 1645–46.

11. *Lochner v. New York,* 198 U.S. 45, 75–76 (1905).

12. See Michael J. Klarman, "Rethinking the Civil Rights and Civil Liberties Revolutions," *Virginia Law Review* 82 (1996): 1–96.

13. *Whitney v. California,* 274 U.S. 357, 374 (1927).

14. *West Coast Hotel v. Parrish,* 300 U.S. 379 (1937).

15. *Home Building and Loan Association v. Blaisdell,* 290 U.S. 398 (1934); *U.S. v. Darby,* 312 U.S. 100 (1941).

16. *Skinner v. Oklahoma,* 316 U.S. 535 (1942), marks the first instance of a majority of the Court adopting heightened scrutiny in a non–First Amendment case. It involved a compulsory sterilization law that the Court invalidated on a combination of due process and equal protection grounds.

17. Wiebe, *Self-Rule,* 202, 225–26, argues that in this period "the state," personified by the decisions of expert policy makers, decisively replaced "the People" as "democracy's last resort." He suggests that those developments, taken together, facilitated the role of institutions of the national government, including the Supreme Court, in fashioning "democratic rights" for individual citizens. I agree that the period from the early 1930s through World War II was one in which the justices on the Court increasingly came to regard themselves as guardians, and arguably creators, of free speech rights. But I think a more obvious motivation for justices to forge an explicit linkage between free speech and democracy in the 1930s and 1940s rested in their awareness that in many other nations the expansion of state power was being associated with totalitarian regimes that repressed speech. American "democracy," for them, had powerfully antitotalitarian overtones.

18. *Palko v. Connecticut,* 302 U.S. 319 (1937).

19. Ibid., 327, citing Charles Warren, "The New Liberty Under the 14th Amendment," *Harvard Law Review* 39 (1926): 431. For the Court's unanimous and unelaborated decision to incorporate the First Amendment against the states in *Gitlow,* see *Gitlow v. New York,* 268 U.S. 652 (1925).

20. *Palko v. Connecticut,* Ibid., 325–26.

21. *Minersville School District v. Gobitis,* 310 U.S. 586 (1940).

22. *West Virginia v. Barnette,* 319 U.S. 624 (1943).

23. *Schneider v. Irvington,* 308 U.S. 147, 161 (1939).

24. Ibid.

25. *Minersville School District v. Gobitis,* 310 U.S. 586, 599 (1940).

26. Ibid., 606.

27. *Jones v. Opelika,* 316 U.S. 584, 608 (1942).

28. Ibid., 623.

29. Ibid., 624. This allegedly left Roberts, Reed, Byrnes, and Jackson as continuing to adhere to Frankfurter's *Gobitis* opinion, but Byrnes and Jackson

had not been on the Court for *Gobitis,* so Frankfurter could hardly regard them as firm adherents.

30. *Murdock v. Pennsylvania,* 319 U.S. 105 (1942). Frankfurter protested against the Court's grant of certiorari in *Murdock,* which was virtually on all fours with *Jones v. Opelika.* See H. N. Hirsch, *The Enigma of Felix Frankfurter* (New York: Basic Books, 1981), 166.

31. The majority in *Murdock* consisted of the four dissenters in *Jones v. Opelika* plus newly appointed Justice Wiley Rutledge, who had replaced James Byrnes in the 1942 term. The remaining members of the majority in *Jones v. Opelika,* Frankfurter, Roberts, Reed, and Jackson, three of whom had joined the majority opinion in *Gobitis,* dissented.

32. *Murdock v. Pennsylvania,* 319 U.S. at 115.

33. The Court had specifically excluded commercial speech from First Amendment protection in *Valentine v. Chrestensen,* 316 U.S. 52 (1942). One could suggest that Jehovah's Witnesses cases had stimulated the Court to make even more fundamental distinctions about speech. In *Chaplinsky v. New Hampshire,* 315 U.S. 568 (1942), Justice Murphy, for a unanimous Court, attempted to define the content of constitutionally protected free speech rights. He excluded from First Amendment protection certain well-defined and narrowly limited classes of speech. These include the lewd and the obscene, the profane, the libelous, and the insulting or "fighting words—those which by their very utterance inflict injury or tend to incite an immediate breach of the peace. . . . [S]uch utterances are no essential part of any exposition of ideas, and are of such slight social value as a step to truth that any benefit that may be derived from them is clearly outweighed by the social interest in order and morality." Id. at 572. The petitioner in *Chaplinsky* was a Jehovah's Witness distributing sect literature on the streets of Rochester, New Hampshire, when he was accused of calling a city marshal "a God damned racketeer" and a "damned Fascist." Ibid., 569.

34. *West Virginia v. Barnette,* 319 U.S. 624 (1943).

35. The *Gobitis* majority, in addition to Frankfurter, had consisted of Chief Justice Hughes and Justices McReynolds, Roberts, Black, Reed, Douglas, and Murphy. Black, Douglas, and Murphy had signaled their desertion in *Jones v. Opelika,* Hughes's and McReynolds's seats were now occupied by Stone himself and Rutledge, and Robert Jackson had succeeded to Stone's seat. After conference discussion, Stone knew that his dissenting position in *Gobitis* was now endorsed by Rutledge and Jackson as well as the three previous defectors. He took the occasion to assign the opinion to Jackson, perhaps to avoid too pointedly signaling that his dissent had supplanted Frankfurter's majority opinion in only three years.

36. *West Virginia v. Barnette,* 319 U.S. at 641.

37. Ibid., 638.

38. Ibid., 639.

39. Ibid., 648.

40. Felix Frankfurter to Harlan Fiske Stone, April 27, 1938, Harlan Fiske Stone Papers, Library of Congress, quoted in Murphy, Fleming, and Harris, *American Constitutional Interpretation,* 490. The letter provides additional evidence that the bifurcated review project, in inchoate form, had begun with the emergence of modernist free speech jurisprudence after World War I. Frankfurter's reference to Holmes's non-"latitudinarian" attitude in "civil liberties" cases had free speech cases in mind, since Holmes was deferential to

legislatures in nearly all other cases. See G. Edward White, *Justice Oliver Wendell Holmes: Law and the Inner Self* (New York: Oxford University Press, 1993), 377–409.

41. Felix Frankfurter, *Mr. Justice Holmes and the Supreme Court* (Cambridge, Mass.: Harvard University Press, 1938), 49–51.

42. Felix Frankfurter to Harlan Fiske Stone, May 27, 1940, quoted in Murphy, Fleming, and Harris, *American Constitutional Interpretation*, 1019–20.

43. *American Federation of Labor v. Swing*, 312 U.S. 321, 325 (1941).

44. Frankfurter to Stone, May 27, 1940.

45. For evidence that the flag salute cases were a pivotal episode in Frankfurter's tenure on the Supreme Court, see Hirsch, *The Enigma of Felix Frankfurter*, 176–77, 211.

46. *Kovacs v. Cooper*, 336 U.S. 77 (1949).

47. *Thomas v. Collins*, 323 U.S. 516 (1945). In *Thomas*, Rutledge continued to assume that all First Amendment cases, whatever their setting, would be governed by a clear and present danger standard. *Thomas* was not a religious freedom case. It tested the constitutionality of a Texas statute requiring union organizers to register with the state before soliciting members. Frankfurter dissented in *Thomas*.

48. *Marsh v. Alabama*, 326 U.S. 501 (1946).

49. *Thomas v. Collins*, 323 U.S. at 530.

50. *Marsh v. Alabama*, 326 U.S. at 509. Frankfurter wrote a concurring opinion in *Marsh*, a fact that reflected his continuing ambivalence about the bifurcated review project. Justice Frank Murphy's conference notes revealed that Frankfurter was "inclined to Black's interpretation" in the Court's conference on the *Marsh* case because he felt that a company town was a "political community" even though "private." See Roger Newman, *Hugo Black: A Biography* (New York: Pantheon, 1994), 679, citing Frank Murphy Papers, University of Michigan.

51. Roberts had retired in 1945, to be succeeded by Harold Burton, and Stone had been succeeded by Fred M. Vinson in 1946. In 1949, both Murphy and Rutledge died, being replaced, respectively, by Tom C. Clark and Sherman Minton. This meant that after the 1949 term only Black, Reed, Douglas, and Jackson remained of the group of justices that had on one occasion or another joined opinions employing the "preferred position" rubric or otherwise suggesting that speech rights were to be treated as occupying a privileged constitutional position.

52. *Kovacs v. Cooper*, 336 U.S. 77, 87–88 (1949).

53. Ibid., 95.

54. Frankfurter, *Mr. Justice Holmes and the Supreme Court*, 49.

55. Ibid., 106.

56. *United States v. Rumely*, 345 U.S. 41, 56 (1953).

57. At the very time that several justices on the Court were demonstrating an enthusiasm for the preferred position rubric, they were also implicitly exploring distinctions between "protected" and "unprotected" forms of speech. *Valentine v. Chrestensen* and *Chaplinsky v. New Hampshire*, supra note 34, can be seen as the Court's first attempts to develop "higher value" and "lower value" categories of expressions.

58. *Adkins v. Children's Hospital*, 261 U.S. 525 (1923).

59. See *West Coast Hotel v. Parrish*, 300 U.S. 379 (1937). In fact, it would have not occurred to commentators in the interval between *Lochner* and *Parrish* to

call the orthodox approach to police power cases "substantive due process." That term did not even appear in a federal judicial opinion until 1942. See G. Edward White, "Revisiting Substantive Due Process and Holmes's *Lochner* Dissent," *Brooklyn Law Review* 63 (1997): 87–128.

60. For more detail, see White, "The First Amendment Comes of Age."

*Chapter Five*

# The Roles of Lawyers in a Civil Liberties Crisis: Hawaii During World War II

Harry N. Scheiber and Jane L. Scheiber

This chapter seeks to identify and analyze the varied roles of lawyers in the history of the martial law regime imposed on Hawaii during World War II. Singling out for analysis the functions and behavior of lawyers will, we hope, cast new light upon this specific episode in the history of civil liberties and the Constitution. Some useful insights can also be gained, we think, regarding the similarities and differences in the patterns of wartime repression—and the legal responses to repression—in civil liberties crises more generally in American history. Hawaii's wartime experience is also relevant to the modern scholarly discourse on the basic issues of lawyers' professional obligations and ethical standards that goes back at least to Louis Brandeis and his famous invocation in 1916 of the concept of "lawyer to the situation," or "counsel to the situation"—embracing the implicit ethical requirement for the lawyer to give attention to imperatives of the larger social good, transcending a client's immediate purposes and interests.[1]

In the case of military rule in Hawaii, some of the lawyers who influenced events acted in administrative capacities both in the army and in civilian agencies from the cabinet level on down. Others had advocacy roles in litigation; still others acted as citizens expert in law, speaking out on questions raised by the government's extended suspension of ordinary constitutional liberties.

What they had in common, however, was that all were sworn to uphold the Constitution of the United States, either as officers of the court or more specifically in the performance of duties as elective officials, administrators, or army officers. Therefore, it is especially important to recognize the differing ways in which lawyers in these varying roles interpreted their sworn obligations with respect to government policies that implicated constitutional requirements and guarantees, or with respect to the processes of legal and constitutional litigation. Of particular interest in this context is the notion that a lawyer in government service, presumably including military service, has special obligations. In elaborating this notion, a leading student of legal ethics has written that the government lawyer, in his or her ethical obligations, "is at the opposite pole of the spectrum of legal roles from the advocate, . . . [being] concerned entirely with the general welfare." The government lawyer's responsibilities "are entirely public."[2] That army lawyers are in a line of military command, even in wartime, does not relieve them of obligations to the Constitution.

Most historical and sociolegal studies of constitutional crises focus on the lawyers who have litigated the "great cases," together with the organizations (most notably the American Civil Liberties Union) that in recent times have planned the large strategies of constitutional litigation.[3] In the present chapter, we seek to broaden the scope of inquiry and to examine the activities of lawyers in a great many different roles. Fortunately, both private papers and official archival records concerning wartime Hawaii are rich in material that reveals lawyers' varied concepts of their professional obligations, their expressions of ethical standards, and their influences on the course of events in one of the most extraordinary (though seldom remembered) episodes in the history of American civil liberties.

The record of army rule in Hawaii has a unique dimension, too, in that the lawyers within the military establishment itself (whether acting as administrators or as counsel to the army and the War Department) were of central importance to the developments we treat. With the prominent exceptions of Jonathan Lurie's writings on the military courts and Peter Irons's study of the Japanese-American internments, there has been little analysis by historians of the "internal" history of military agencies as they have been advised by lawyers, both in litigation and in the formulation or implementation of policy. Moreover, nearly all the general literature on professional ethics is concerned exclusively with lawyers in various types of civil and criminal representation in normal civilian life. We hope that the discussion we provide here will encourage incorporation of the wartime and military contexts of "lawyering" into both historical and ethical frameworks of analysis.

To establish the background context for what follows, we begin with a brief summary of the military regime's character and record during the war years.

## Martial Law and Its Administration

On December 7, 1941, with the rescue work and fire fighting still going on frantically following the Japanese attack on Pearl Harbor, the governor of the Territory of Hawaii and the commanding general of the U.S. Army in Hawaii jointly announced that martial law was being imposed and the privilege of the writ of habeas corpus suspended. This action was in accord, they said, with the Organic Act of 1900, creating the territory, which provided:

> The governor shall be responsible for the faithful execution of the laws of the United States and of the Territory of Hawaii . . . and he may in case of rebellion or invasion or imminent danger thereof when the public safety requires it, suspend the privilege of the writ of habeas corpus or place the territory or any part thereof under martial law until communication can be had with the president and his decision thereon made known.[4]

The army also issued a declaration on December 7 stating that, because of "danger of invasion," it was taking complete control of government in the territory and its civilian population of over 400,000 persons, of whom some 160,000 were of Japanese birth or of Japanese-American descent.[5] The army's chief adjutant for the Hawaii command, Lieutenant Colonel Thomas H. Green, had long been preparing for such an eventuality, and he had ready for immediate promulgation a set of detailed drafts of "general orders" that closed all civilian courts; imposed a comprehensive military censorship over the mails, the press, and broadcasting; and seized control of all the agencies of civilian government and their functions.[6] Establishing total army control of governance was not explicitly authorized by the Organic Act, especially insofar as it embraced the closure of the civilian courts (including the federal district court in Hawaii).

Both the constitutionality of these actions, on the one hand, and their legality under terms of the Organic Act and other statutes, on the other, would become the subject of a series of cases challenging army rule. There were not many such cases pressed, in fact, though the first (a petition for habeas corpus by a German-American internee) came in the first weeks of the war. A brace of similar habeas cases was instituted in mid-1943, this time resulting in a notorious confrontation between federal district judge Delbert Metzger and the army's commander in Hawaii, General Robert Richardson, in which Judge Metzger found Richardson to be in contempt—leading the general, in turn, to threaten Metzger with a military trial and up to five years at hard labor! Then, in 1944, there was a set of three habeas cases of civilians held for criminal offenses after trial by the army; two of these cases finally went to the Supreme Court, as will be discussed later. It is noteworthy that all the cases in this small list involved Caucasian prisoners. At no time did any Japanese-American in Hawaii seek to obtain habeas relief while being held by the army either as an internee or after conviction by an army court of a civil or criminal offense.[7]

General Walter C. Short, who was in command at the time of Pearl Harbor, was shortly afterward removed and faced possible court-martial; but on declaring army rule he had assumed for himself the title "military governor" (one that had previously been used only in occupied areas such as those taken from Spain in the 1898 war). Short was replaced before the end of the year by General Delos Emmons, who continued to refer to himself as military governor. The first general orders also named Colonel Green, who himself would soon be promoted to general rank, justified by his expanded duties, as the "executive to the military governor." In this way, the army's chief legal officer in Hawaii was given an office that essentially became that of a czardom. As Green later recalled, his authority was "substantially unlimited." He and two junior legal officers assumed complete authority over day-to-day governance of the Hawaiian Islands and the supervision of the military courts that displaced civilian justice, in addition to formulating policy proposals for the commanding general and providing the army headquarters with legal counsel.[8]

There followed an extended period of military government, with martial law ending only in November 1944 (more than a year after a partial restoration of civilian government). Throughout that time, the army exercised authority over virtually all aspects of civilian life in the Islands. When General Robert C. Richardson replaced Emmons in 1943, he continued to rely for counsel on legal matters, and also for administration of military government, upon the army command's legal staff headed first by Green and later by Green's protégé, Major (later Lieutenant General) William Morrison, who succeeded him when Green was transferred to Washington in 1943.

The initial army general orders of December 1941—and the scores of additional orders that followed in ensuing months—acknowledged no residual or controlling powers in the territorial governor, the legislature, the municipal governments, or the courts. In fact, when the territorial courts were permitted to reopen a few months later, with limited jurisdiction in civil cases, and when various civilian agencies were permitted to resume limited operations, the army designated them "agents of the military governor," in all ways subordinate to his authority. The general orders also forbade jury trials, on grounds (stated in private correspondence with the War Department) that the multiracial character of the Island population would mean that juries could not be "impartial"![9] The army similarly assumed charge of all policies and many of the operational responsibilities of the various federal administrative agencies, reducing the Department of the Interior officers to the status of guest investigators or administrators under army supervision.[10]

Meanwhile, the FBI and the army's security branch conducted a sweep just after the Pearl Harbor attack, picking up several hundred alien residents and foreign-born citizens (the vast majority Japanese citizens or American citizens of Japanese ancestry) who were identified as possible security risks. These people initially were placed in military custody in primitive camp facilities on Sand Island, following hastily convened hearings without specification of charges or right to examine evidence, and with no access to legal counsel. From December 1941 until the war ended in 1945, some 10,000 persons would be subjected to security investigations or loyalty hearings in Hawaii; of that number, 1,569—of whom 1,466 were of Japanese descent—were interned, with many being transferred from Hawaii to the camps on the mainland and held for the entire war period.[11]

The army imposed blackout and curfew regulations in all civilian areas—understandably enough, in the immediate aftermath of an air attack—but then it kept the regulations in effect for more than three years, despite the decline in vulnerability to attack and (most galling to civilians) a relaxation of the rules as applied to the military's own bases.[12] Particularly onerous to the population under army rule was its detailed regulation of labor relations. The army's general orders made job switching and unauthorized absenteeism from work criminal offenses, with violators tried in military courts; and convictions for absenteeism were the leading reason for jail sentences. The provost courts, which enforced these labor rules and most other regulations—ranging from the most serious criminal cases to the control of prostitution and dog-leash violations—conducted some 50,000 trials of civilians during the war, with a 99 percent conviction rate in the 22,000 Oahu cases in 1942–43. The average trial lasted five minutes, and legal counsel was seldom present because it became the common wisdom that the presence of a lawyer would assure a harsh sentence.[13]

The record of military rule in wartime Hawaii was without precedent in American history in two important respects. The first was the duration of the military's control; for, as has been noted earlier, it exceeded by far any such exercise of authority over civilians in the nation's history. Second, the army's regime in Hawaii was exceptional because it entailed a full suspension of all constitutional liberties *for an entire civilian population.* By contrast, earlier periods of repression or formal wartime suspension of liberties had been aimed at specific groups identified by the government as potentially dangerous to security because of disloyalty or the intensity of their dissent. Thus, in the Civil War, President Lincoln had ordered a few civilians tried in army courts when they were accused of conspiracy against the Union; and martial law had briefly been declared in loyal states when troop movements and other military operations were threatened.[14] And in World War I, as Paul Murphy and other scholars have shown, the Wilson administration had used the Espionage Act and the Sedition Act to pursue an aggressive policy of repression of dissenting individuals and groups, including radical labor unions and left-wing or anarchist leaders who opposed the war policy.[15] Even the notorious evacuation and internment of the West Coast's entire Japanese-American population during World War II was justified on the spurious grounds that a potential threat to security in case of invasion necessitated the policy—a claim that of course is now publicly known (as was known by the FBI and the Justice Department during the war) to be entirely without evidentiary foundation of any kind.[16]

In the case of Hawaii's martial law policy, however, the army insisted that the entire population of the Islands be treated as the civilian residents of a "fortress," subject to the complete authority of the commanding general. Without such comprehensive control of civilian affairs, the army contended, the security of the Islands against attack would be compromised. It was the army's unyielding position—variously expressed by the commanding general on the ground, his legal officers in the military government, and many of the military and civilian legal officers in the War Department and army general staff—that this authority must be absolute in order to assure military readiness for Hawaii's defense.[17] The essentially racist assumption that all Japanese-Americans were potentially disloyal was central to the "fortress" argument. The army asserted that the 160,000 persons of Japanese ancestry (35,000 of them alien residents), out of a total civilian population of 465,000, constituted a manifest threat to security. The Japanese-Americans thus were subjected by the army to especially harsh treatment and some exceptional restrictions, including regulation of their religious activities and physical exclusion from certain areas of the harbor and from any fishing off the coast. However, because their labor was deemed essential to the viability of the Hawaiian economy, the Japanese-Americans were actually protected by the army from the evacuation that was approved explicitly by

President Franklin Roosevelt.[18] When confronted in 1944 with the fact that not a single act of sabotage or espionage by a Japanese-American had ever been discovered through the entire war period, the army replied that this was attributable to the security given the Islands by the selective internments and by martial law, not to loyalty of the people.[19]

The officials of the Department of the Interior, the Justice Department, and the territorial government sought as early as the spring of 1942 to obtain a restoration of at least the less sensitive duties of ordinary government to civilian authority and a reopening of all civilian courts. Not until October 1943, however, was civilian governance effectively restored, following long and difficult cabinet-level negotiations and finally a direct presidential letter of instructions. The army had resisted this change in an unstinting and sometimes unscrupulously conducted campaign of bureaucratic infighting. Even under the terms of the "restoration agreement," the army won a major point by retaining control over labor relations as well as other important aspects of civilian activity.[20] Furthermore, martial law remained in effect, and so the provost courts continued to try civilians for certain offenses until the formal termination of martial law and of the military government in November 1944. There is abundant evidence that arbitrary and humiliating treatment was given to civilians of all ethnic identities, not only the Japanese-Americans, both by the heavy-handed military administration and by the provost court system. Indeed, in a confidential investigation of the provost court operations during the war, a Justice Department counsel concluded without qualification that "they were unfair, unjudicial, and [even] unmilitary. . . . It's a very, very nasty unpleasant picture, and you just cannot justify it in any way."[21]

There is little quarreling, in retrospect, with the view of the solicitor of the Department of the Interior in December 1942, asserting: "While fighting for democracy on a dozen fronts, we have dictatorship, quite needlessly—almost by accident, in one vital part of the United States of America."[22] Similarly, a leading Hawaiian journalist, reflecting in May 1944 on the record of martial law, wrote that the Islands' civilian population "[had] experienced a greater regimentation in thirty months of war than that of any other American community in history."[23] A federal district court judge put it in blunt terms, declaring that the military regime in Hawaii was "the antithesis of Americanism."[24]

Most of the elements in the record that we have discussed here made army rule in Hawaii a unique episode in American history. In another regard, however, it manifested a familiar pattern: for in the Civil War and World War II crises, only after the war had ended did a constitutional test of the military's regime come before the U.S. Supreme Court. As noted previously, in wartime Hawaii there were several efforts by internees or prisoners convicted by the provost courts to exercise the privilege of the writ of habeas corpus in the federal district court in Honolulu. When the first case was appealed to the federal Ninth District Court in San Francisco in 1942, the army's position was upheld as the court's majority determined that "military necessity" justified the imposition of comprehensive military rule and suspension of the writ.[25] As will be discussed later, the government lawyers pursued in each instance of a habeas case, except in the 1944 cases, the strategy of releasing the appellants and thus mooting the cases; they did so explicitly to avoid what they feared would be an adverse result on appeal if the cases went to the Supreme Court.[26] This was one of several strategies pursued by lawyers associated with the army, civilian government agencies, and petitioners—litigative strategies that (as we will discuss further later) were of great influence in shaping the history that is the subject of this chapter.

Not until the fourth anniversary of the Pearl Harbor attack, in December 1945, did the Supreme Court finally hear argument in *Duncan v. Kahanamoku* and a companion case, *White v. Steer,* the first appeals to reach the highest court challenging the army's regime in the Islands. The Court's decision, which came down three months later with two justices dissenting, was a startling repudiation of the army's legal position. The majority rested its view, in an opinion written by Justice Hugo L. Black, on statutory interpretation rather than purely constitutional grounds; the Court declared the army's regime to have been manifestly illegal in terms of statutory authority, as represented by the Organic Act. But the main thrust of the opinion was cast in broad language that conveyed clearly the justices' view that the army's actions had been contrary to the fundamental traditions of liberty that had been expressed in Anglo-American political development since the seventeenth century.[27]

The *Duncan* decision came too late, of course, for the civilians whose lives had been so deeply affected by army regulation over many years, and especially for the hundreds who had been sentenced to months or years in prison without the rudiments of a fair trial. The timing was, withal, a validation of the melancholy message of John P. Frank's classic study of the development of civil liberties law in America, that the "dominant lesson of our history in the relation of the judiciary to repressions is that the courts love liberty most when it is under pressure least."[28] Relief, when it has come at all, has all too often been given by the Court well after the crisis is over. There were a few individuals who sought to obtain redress by civil indemnification suits after the war—a subject we treat briefly in the last section of this chapter—but the vast majority of those who might have had this degree of legal recourse eschewed it, and they went on with their lives in the new postwar world.

## The "Large Policy": From the Top Down

Lawyers were deeply involved in every aspect of policy making, implementation, and litigation that concerned the Hawaii regime. At every juncture when there was conflict or confrontation, whether in the courts, in public discussion, or behind doors in high government councils, the advising functions and active involvement of these lawyers were crucial to determining outcomes. Obviously, the final authority for a matter so important as whether to impose martial law rested with President Roosevelt. The president was reticent, however, about denying the army what its commanding officers wanted, especially in an outpost of American territory so exposed in the Pacific and already once so badly hurt by the Japanese air force.[29] And in fact when he came under pressure from critics of army rule from top ranks within his administration—most notably from Attorney General Francis Biddle and Secretary of the Interior Harold Ickes, both of whom were known as strong civil liberties advocates—Roosevelt relied upon a style that he had applied in the 1930s to the handling of many controversial peacetime issues: he allowed the proponents of conflicting views to hash out compromises on which he might act when he was ready, often after the passage of a significant period of time. Apart from his habitual use of this strategy for dealing with conflicts whose resolution he believed could safely be delayed, the president was determined that the goal of winning the war must prevail over all else; and in the Hawaii case, no less than in the Japanese-American internment policy, he clearly believed that the war emergency justified extraordinary measures. Indeed, he explicitly said of Hawaii that he did not worry much about constitutional constraints.[30] Also working in his mind, no doubt, was his oft-stated distrust of Japanese-Americans, citizens and aliens alike.[31] A lawyer by training, a politician by vocation, but above all a pragmatic wartime president dealing with a total mobilization and millions of lives at stake, Roosevelt was no anchor for civil liberties.

One can speculate that only if Secretary of War Henry L. Stimson had wanted to rein in the army in its martial law policies, or perhaps if there had been a strongly organized move by the president's critics in Congress on those issues, would Roosevelt have been moved to act earlier than he finally (in 1943) did to order modification and softening of the military regime. In fact, until late 1944 Stimson took the contrary position, firmly supporting the army's demands and its perception of military necessity in the Islands. Stimson and his assistant secretary, John J. McCloy—whom Stimson had brought to Washington from his Wall Street law firm, and who had principal responsibility for oversight of Hawaii as he did of the Japanese-American internments—had little sympathy for those who wanted civilian government restored. Stimson, for example, wrote in confidential correspondence with Secretary of the Interior Ickes that the army's record in governing the Philippine Islands after the Spanish-American War was "one of the brightest pages of enlightened administration in all our American history"![32] As for McCloy, it is noteworthy that in a case involving a death sentence imposed on a civilian by an army tribunal in Hawaii early in the war, McCloy responded coldly to those who demanded an administrative review of the decision by the army. "The very essence of martial law," McCloy wrote, "[is] that military courts do impose anything from a fine to a death sentence without reviewing."[33] To Ickes, who despised the regimentation of a civilian population by dictatorial military rule and demanded in cabinet meetings "the liberation of the Hawaiian

Islands"—or to Attorney General Biddle, who regarded Green as a pompous martinet who was savoring every moment of his exercise of absolutist power—Stimson's benign approach to the military's authority was incomprehensible. Indeed, in much of the correspondence among the cabinet officers there was no reconciling the premises of their opposing views of how to deal with the martial law question.[34]

Two Justice Department lawyers close to the situation contended that both Stimson and McCloy exercised their duties less like responsible civilian supervisors than like loyal hired-gun attorneys for General Emmons and for General Robert Richardson, who in mid-1943 replaced Emmons as commanding general and self-styled military governor in Hawaii.[35] McCloy was coldly dismissive of all complaints about injustices by provost courts, once saying that the only dissenting voices in Hawaii were a few lawyers wanting to protect their litigation business—a canard also voiced by pro-army editorial writers for the Islands' major conservative newspaper and by Generals Green and Richardson.[36]

McCloy was equally dismissive of constitutional considerations that were put forward by the Interior and Justice lawyers and negotiators, asserting that in wartime the commander "on the ground" must have the final word in assessing risks and deciding on priorities. Moreover, McCloy's attitude toward the Japanese-Americans' situation in particular was blatantly racist; thus, he wrote privately in September 1942 that placing the Japanese-Americans in internment camps offered "a great opportunity" to learn how to deal with "the Japanese problem in this country." Holding them in the camps, McCloy said, "afford[ed] a means of sampling their opinion and studying their customs and habits, . . . find out what they are thinking about and . . . influence their thinking in the right directions before they are again distributed into communities."[37] One disposed to see the issue in that light, even if it meant (as McCloy admitted it did) risking the charge that the internees were being "treat[ed] as guinea pigs,"[38] was not likely to be disposed to quarrel with army lawyers' premises that the very existence of the Japanese-American population in the Hawaiian Islands was a threat to the area's security.

Only in one extreme case did McCloy actually draw the line and make it clear that the army must back down. This was in the notorious episode in mid-1943 when General Richardson actually issued an order openly threatening Judge Metzger of the federal district court that if Metzger agreed to hear a habeas corpus petition, he would be subject to prosecution before a military tribunal and face a sentence of up to five years at hard labor. Even then, McCloy intervened in a rhetorical style that fell far short of a command, writing letters to Richardson that sometimes dripped with deference.[39] He also told the Justice Department that he must oppose any legal position that threatened to "impair the position and prestige of the commanding general."[40] McCloy's attitude in dealing with the army, and in defending the army position within the Roosevelt policy circle, was generally that of the advocate helping his clients to get whatever it was they wanted, almost regardless of legal or constitutional niceties, because wartime realities necessitated it. To limit the military to strictly confined jurisdiction and to restore partial civilian authority, he averred, would mean "an undesirable and dangerous inflexibility" in a situation that demanded broad discretionary power.[41] "General principles may certainly be outlined," he conceded, "but you can't draft Magna Carta for the Hawaiian Islands in time of war in the Pacific."[42] One finds in McCloy's wartime office archives almost nothing of the concern for the interest of constitutionalism and the law that is commonly regarded as the redeeming side of the patrician "best and brightest" style of government service of which McCloy is often seen as exemplar.[43] By contrast, the Department of the Interior lawyers and administrators—Ickes, his deputy secretary Abe Fortas, the department's solicitor, and staff—constantly strove, usually in vain, to frame the question in terms of the government's duty to protect constitutional norms and to recognize constitutional imperatives.[44]

The indifference to civil liberties claims and to restoration of civilian authority in Hawaii that was evident in both the White House and the War Department meant that if army rule were to be reined in, it must happen by some other process than by top-down commands. This left the field open for the lawyers in the military, the civilian agencies, and the private sector to express their differences of opinion in a variety of forums (including the federal courts) and to frame administrative, political, and litigative strategies to challenge or to defend the Hawaii regime.

## Framing the Constitutional Issues

In situations that find the government, in war or peace, suspending or attacking civil liberties, the legal and constitutional issues generally surface fairly quickly as a focus of public controversy. That is to say, lawyers, politicians, leaders of private organizations, and the individuals or groups that are the immediate target of government actions typically will step forward to articulate legal and constitutional claims that challenge what they view as repressive governmental actions. But army policy in Hawaii just after the attack on Pearl Harbor presented a very different picture, since virtually no one criticized in public the decisions to suspend civil liberties and to militarize territorial self-government. Even Secretary Ickes, a former labor lawyer deeply committed to civil liberties, and Attorney General Biddle, similarly regarded as a champion of constitutional freedoms, fully accepted the necessity of these measures. Both of them believed, however, that the military would seek to exercise its extraordinary powers only during a brief emergency period—and they had been so assured by the territorial governor on the basis of the commitments he reported the army had made to him that normal civilian functions would be restored after only a few months.[45]

One extraordinary individual did, however, step forward in Honolulu to question the army's actions from the very first days of the war. He was J. Garner Anthony, a graduate of Swarthmore College and the Harvard Law School who was a member of one of Honolulu's most prestigious corporate law firms. Anthony was a well-credentialed member of the Hawaii social elite, as he had been counsel to the Bishop Estate and some of the Islands' wealthiest corporations. When, only hours after the Pearl Harbor attack, the army command called to a meeting the members of Hawaii's territorial judiciary and some of the most prominent lawyers in Honolulu, seeking their cooperation in the implementation of martial law and provost court justice, Anthony was naturally included among the invitees. To the consternation of the military officers present, Anthony demurred when some of the other civilians present were asked to help staff the military tribunals and otherwise cooperate in administering the militarized regimes; for in his view, the legality of the army's takeover of all governing agencies and powers was questionable, with or without martial law. He further warned that there might be serious questions of civil liability after the war if persons subjected to army regulation or justice should sue any non-uniformed personnel who acted as members of the military government's bureaucracy. As a result of his intervention—which, it is important to note, occurred behind closed doors in a confidential setting—some of the judges began to weaken in their resolve to participate actively.[46] In response, General Green (now angry with Anthony, suspecting him at best of wanting to see Green's carefully constructed structure of military government collapse, and at worst being an ideologue and a crank) shortly afterward gave up much of the effort to intermix civilians officially with military personnel in administering the army's judicial regime.[47] An important exception was the composition of appointments to the loyalty review boards set up to hear internment cases, to which civilians as well as military officers were appointed.

The territorial delegate to Congress, Samuel W. King, was deeply troubled by the prolongation of martial law, and he was fully persuaded that the army's regime was going far beyond the proper bounds of even emergency powers in wartime. He became more active when Anthony wrote to him at length to lay out the reasons why, under his understanding of constitutional principles, the army should not be permitted to write its own charter of powers. Above all, Anthony told him, it was completely unacceptable to have the army close down the civilian courts and take charge of civil and criminal justice, let alone to permit the military to keep the federal district court closed so that no formal constitutional adjudication could go forward. Delegate King agreed with Anthony's position on the merits; and it seems likely that the advice given him by this respected attorney made King confident that there were indeed serious constitutional issues at stake. However, on the basis of his dismaying experience in earlier years, when he had tried in vain to recruit support in Congress for a Hawaii statehood bill, King decided it would be best to concentrate his efforts upon talks and correspondence with the cabinet officers who were involved. In this way, he hoped, he might get the War Department or, as a last resort, the White House, to force the army to pull back from its extreme position on the need for a takeover of the government.[48]

One of the most important institutional changes in patterns of constitutional debate and lawyering in the twentieth century had been the emergence of the American Civil Liberties Union (ACLU) in the World War I period as an organization specifically devoted to protection of constitutional rights and to development of litigative strategies to bring issues effectively before the courts.[49] It is not surprising, then, that the ACLU became involved only a few weeks after Pearl Harbor in the rising efforts to bring constitutional issues out into public discussion and ultimately into the federal courts; nor that both Garner Anthony and Delegate King were soon in correspondence with Roger Baldwin and other ACLU officers and lawyers in an effort to gain their objectives.[50]

Obtaining restoration of civilian authority and reopening of the courts in Hawaii remained the key objective for Anthony; it also became a consistent preoccupation of the new territorial civilian governor, Ingram Stainback, who, after his appointment in June 1942, worked closely with Ickes and Interior to bring about the necessary change in policy.[51] Meanwhile, Anthony made a major contribution toward bringing the large constitutional and legal issues to an academic forum with a learned article published in May 1942 in the *California Law Review* and reported at considerable length in the *New York Times* and in the Hawaii papers. In this study, Anthony argued vigorously that the army had acted beyond its legitimate war powers by suspending civilians' civil liberties without clear evidence that an invasion was an imminent possibility. "We must not establish by law within our own borders," he wrote, "the very tyranny that we are now pledged to destroy" on fields of battle.[52]

Anthony's article served essentially to flush out the army, forcing it to respond publicly on the constitutional issues that he had raised. In particular, his June article inspired a detailed rejoinder, in the same law review's September 1942 issue, by one of the highest-ranking officers in the judge advocate general's staff, Colonel Archibald King. The centerpiece of Colonel King's rejoinder was what had by that time become the army's mantra in defense of the Hawaii regime: invasion was always a possibility for Hawaii in a war of this kind; the commander on the ground must have complete authority in order to assure security; there was no room for civilian officials or courts to second-guess or challenge the military in such a situation; and the specific terms of legislation already on the books fully warranted the army's actions in the Islands.[53] Thus, by placing the issues out in the academic forum as he did so early in the war, Anthony assured that at least the constitutional questions would receive open debate and the army's regime in Hawaii would not proceed without scrutiny in the legal community.

Anthony's importance to the emerging dynamics of challenge to army rule was further enhanced after December 1942, when he took leave from his lucrative law practice to accept the low-paid position of territorial attorney general for Hawaii. He immediately drafted a comprehensive report for Governor Stainback on how the army had displaced civilian government. This report included a set of well-reasoned arguments as to the lack of practical or legal justification for many of the military's actions. It also reiterated Anthony's views of the legal and constitutional principles that were at stake. It was outrageous, he contended, for Hawaii's civilians to be governed as though they were aliens resident in a "conquered province." In sum, Anthony pursued in his official capacity as he had, earlier, in his private role the cause of framing the legal issues. No one could have established the intellectual groundwork better than Anthony had done, either for pressing the constitutional issues in administrative circles (as Governor Stainback did, aided by Ickes and Biddle as his powerful allies in Washington councils) or for setting out the arguments that might be advanced in litigation.[54]

Anthony did not himself pursue litigation in his term as attorney general, but he did give advice privately to ACLU officers and other litigators, and clearly he used his personal prestige in Hawaii's elite social and economic circles to maintain the respectability of principled dissent. In 1944, after leaving public office, Anthony would serve prominently as pro bono counsel to the prisoner-petitioner in the Duncan case that eventually went to the Supreme Court. In the extended trial of Duncan's habeas petition in the federal district court, and then in subsequent appeals, Anthony played a key role in framing and driving strategies.

Needless to say, Anthony's outspoken criticism of the army—especially when compounded by a courageous commencement speech at the University of Hawaii in which he condemned the

Japanese-American internments as a policy better suited to the nation's fascist enemies than to the United States—exposed him to charges of bad judgment at best and questionable loyalty at worst. And the army lawyers in the commanding general's office responded in exactly this way. It is clear that General Green came to despise Anthony, a feeling not softened by Anthony's appreciation for symbolic gestures when he successfully demanded a return of the attorney general's Iolani Palace office—then occupied by Green—to the territorial government.[55] Green's successor as the executive, General William R. C. Morrison, actually approached directors of some of the companies that were Anthony's clients, urging them to stop giving his law firm their work.[56]

At one point in the course of the 1944 Duncan trial in Honolulu, during Anthony's examination of General Richardson, the commanding general, Richardson implied that Anthony was not interested in advancing the cause of winning the war. A crucial intervention by Edward Ennis, the Justice Department lawyer representing the army, defused the courtroom confrontation: for Ennis praised Anthony for giving his client the kind of representation that reflected the American concept of constitutional justice and for raising the important constitutional issues. This dramatic courtroom statement, later reiterated in a speech to the local bar association in which he said that a legal test of army authority was "a healthy sign in a democracy," exemplified Ennis's approach to constitutional litigation: it transcended the immediate issues of advocacy and embodied a deep concern for the integrity of process and for the larger objective of keeping government within constitutional (and justiciable) channels.[57]

General Morrison's conniving against Anthony's law firm and the dramatic exchange at the Duncan trial (the proceedings of which were reported in detail by the Honolulu press) serve to remind us how a public critic, whether lawyer or layperson, of martial law ran significant personal and financial risks. In the atmosphere of the times, Ennis's support of constitutional principles while serving as counsel for the army in the trial setting was critically important in providing Anthony and others with some protection against what might have snowballed into a superpatriotic public reaction.

Another factor that gave critics of martial law some measure of protection in Hawaii was their own prior military service. Anthony, for example, was a veteran of World War I (he had run away to join the marines at sixteen years of age, then, when found out, ran away again to enlist in the army).[58] In Honolulu society, wartime or otherwise, a war record provided valuable protection for one who had negative things to say about the army. Similarly situated was Delegate Samuel King, who had a distinguished record with the navy and who requested reactivation of his commission to serve again with the navy in the Pacific during 1942–44. Federal district judge Metzger—who in the 1943 confrontation held General Richardson in contempt—had served in the Army Corps of Engineers during the Spanish-American War; and Governor Stainback had been a major in World War I.[59]

Membership in the social elite was similarly a valuable kind of armor against accusations of disloyalty, as exemplified not only by Anthony but also by King's successor as delegate in Congress, Joseph Farrington, whose father had been governor and who published one of the Islands' two leading newspapers. Farrington helped lead the sustained campaign to have civilian rights restored, but he was largely immune from charges of disloyalty at home by virtue of the standing that both lineage and accomplishment gave him.

An intriguing subtheme in the challenges that these leaders mounted against army rule in Hawaii was their shared worry that the armed services would move to have the War Department or the Navy Department replace the Department of the Interior in formal legal control of the territory, perhaps permanently. Samuel King and the others had all been champions of statehood for the Islands in the late 1930s, and they found reason for real concern that the citizenry of the territory might be lulled into an acceptance of a postwar status in which civil liberties and self-governance (what they termed "home rule") became less valued.[60] Although one could perhaps interpret this as evidence of an Island's elite concerned about retaining its power, it seems more accurate to regard it as the position of a leadership that valued—and openly defended against racists—the multicultural, multiracial character of the society and had every confidence in democratic self-government, as could be achieved through full statehood.[61]

In summary, the pace and direction of events were much influenced by Anthony's role in framing the constitutional issues from the war's very first days, and by Stainback and the congressional delegates who carried the issue of restoration to the Washington arena. Also instrumental in shaping events were Ickes and Biddle, who kept pressure for restoration of established civilian rights upon the War Department and finally the White House. But another feature of how the Hawaii leadership presented their case needs also to be recalled. This was the fact that the Hawaii political leaders attested repeatedly (and publicly) to the loyalty of their Japanese-American fellow citizens in the Islands.[62] While the army was constantly asserting that this segment of Hawaii's population was unreliable and that their very presence justified martial law, Delegates King and Farrington, Governor Stainback, Garner Anthony in his private and public roles, and several other prominent politicians in the Islands maintained their public position on this issue, even though they had not quarreled over arbitrary internments in the first weeks of the war. Indeed, the personal letters from some of these early internees asking for help from these Hawaii civilian leaders in 1942 had occasioned the early correspondence between these leaders and the cabinet departments in Washington; soon afterward they also became involved in exchanging information on the internee situation with the ACLU.[63] As a consequence, within a month after the attack on Pearl Harbor, the first legal moves were made to bring the issue of the army's wartime authority in Hawaii into the federal courts.

## Lawyering and the Process of Litigation

While the debate sparked by Anthony and others over the constitutional questions and large policy was gaining attention in academic journals, and debate was being launched in government councils, the possibility of legal action emerged. The initial action was by one of the first internees, Dr. Hans Zimmerman, an American citizen of German birth who had a prominent naturopathic practice in Honolulu. Zimmerman sought help from Farrington (who was his patient) and others to mount a formal challenge by forcing a court hearing on the legality of his confinement.[64] Coinciding with Zimmerman's initiative, an army court on Maui passed a death sentence on a young native Hawaiian, Saffrey Brown, for the shooting death of his wife, after a trial that many saw as a travesty because of procedural railroading, lack of adequate legal counsel for the defendant, and the widespread belief that the shooting had been accidental. Those concerned with civil liberties in the Islands immediately perceived the Brown case as an example of drumhead justice, an ominous portent of what future trials in army courts might produce for the local people; this, in turn, energized efforts by Hawaii civilian leaders to pressure Washington to have army rule reconsidered. While correspondence went back and forth over whether there was any legal recourse for the condemned man, ACLU officials and volunteer lawyers began to compile information about the Zimmerman internment.[65] (When the army, after review by the War Department, commuted Brown's sentence, the ACLU and civilian officials in Hawaii lost interest in the matter, focusing attention instead upon the Zimmerman case and more generally on the status of internees.)

By early May 1942, the ACLU was regularly in touch with both Delegate King and Garner Anthony. Anthony's correspondence began when the *New York Times* report on Anthony's *California Law Review* article was published, leading Roger N. Baldwin of the ACLU to write personally to Anthony to inform him of the organization's possible interest in the Zimmerman case appeal; Baldwin also requested further information on the martial law situation in the Islands.[66] In his reply to Baldwin, Anthony reiterated his view that the army had gone beyond its authority with respect to military government, and in any event that it had no proper authority to subject civilians to military trials. His eye was not on litigation at the time, for his main recommendation to Baldwin was that the ACLU "make a lasting contribution to American democracy" by pressing the Roosevelt administration and Congress to formulate and enact legislation that would define the jurisdiction of the army in Hawaii and expedite an immediate reopening of the civilian courts.[67] Such legislation would place army power on a "proper basis," and Hawaii would then be entitled to what even the Japanese-American internees on the Coast had been granted, namely, the right to have the legality or constitutionality of army decisions reviewed in the regular processes of the federal courts.

Hence Anthony took a liberal constitutionalist position, as we term it: so long as the federal courts were restored in their full power to enforce army orders (as was done in the case of the mainland internees), the requirements of the Constitution were met, even if the policy was misguided—or, as he believed, "fascist." The admirers of army rule did not make fine distinctions nor give the benefit of the doubt to liberal constitutionalists: for it became evident that Anthony was feeling the heat of reactions to him and other critics when he wrote, with regard to public opinion in March 1942:

> It is curious how some people feel that a state of war is the signal that all thinking should forthwith cease and that anyone who endeavors to analyze a problem with the view to getting it on an efficient and proper basis is doing something that verges on sedition. No one feels any more strongly than I do the necessity, if the world is to be a fit place to live, of destroying the Axis dictatorships. No reasonable sphere of power should be withheld from the military commander, but this does not require a wholesale junking of the Bill of Rights, particularly in the field of criminal law.[68]

The subsequent course of events in the ACLU indicates that the organization did not pursue the Hawaii issues without some soul-searching along the way by individuals and the board of directors. There was considerable debate over litigative strategy, and some individual lawyers felt constrained to hold back or withdraw from participation—factors that are entirely familiar to those who, like one of the present authors, have served as officers in the ACLU or participated in its litigation. In this instance, the organization had to decide upon the advisability of representing Dr. Zimmerman, specifically, or other internees who sought the organization's legal help. Several board members were uncomfortable with having the ACLU take on the case of an alleged Nazi sympathizer (which is what the army's hearing board had decided Zimmerman was, and some of the ACLU feared he might actually prove to be). When the army packed Zimmerman off to

Camp McCoy, Wisconsin, in order to avoid the possibility of Judge Metzger's declaring his federal district court open to petitions in Honolulu, the ACLU received information from its Wisconsin correspondents that it was hopeless to seek relief in the federal district court in that state because the incumbent judge was a solid bet to uphold the army—and probably, as the ACLU was warned, the judge would do so "with much free comment on the subject of treason."[69] (The army lacked similar confidence in the outcome, for Zimmerman was abruptly shipped back to internment in Honolulu as soon as the military lawyers learned that a habeas proceeding was imminent on the ACLU's initiative in the Wisconsin court!)[70]

Another familiar aspect of the ACLU's involvement was that volunteer counsel had to be recruited—and that it was not easy, especially in wartime, to obtain the services of the best-qualified lawyers. Hopeful of persuading a prominent Wisconsin attorney, W. Wade Boardman, to represent Zimmerman and two Italian-American internees from Honolulu who were also held in Camp McCoy, the ACLU was stiffly rebuffed. Internment issues were problems, Boardman wrote, that ought to be "worked out through the War Department," and there was nothing in the record that he believed warranted "a hostile challenging of the military authorities."[71]

After further correspondence with Zimmerman's private counsel in Hawaii, the ACLU board decided to take responsibility for filing a brief when the army appealed Judge Metzger's ruling in the Ninth Circuit Court in San Francisco.[72] The eminent labor lawyer A. L. Wirin of Los Angeles had by this time become involved as an adviser on legal strategy in the case, and he was asked to write the brief. Unlike Boardman in Wisconsin, Wirin had his heart and soul in this assignment; he was fully persuaded that the army was acting entirely beyond its constitutional or legal authority in Hawaii, and that redress could be won in the courts.[73]

Here again, an insight is afforded into the internal dynamics of a civil liberties organization: at first, Wirin operated only behind the scenes, preparing research on the law, acting as ghostwriter on a habeas brief, and collecting materials that could be of help in the appeal. He explained his reluctance to involve himself in a public way when, in a letter of June 1942, he revealed to the ACLU that his main labor union client was unfavorable to his associating his name with a possible Nazi sympathizer accused or suspected of disloyalty. Wirin came down very differently from the way Boardman had. He had given "deep consideration" for several months, Wirin wrote, "as to whether I can and should participate publicly in civil liberties cases which are frowned upon by the CIO, for whom I am counsel. I have finally arrived at a determination—for myself at least; and that is that I shall follow the dictates of my conscience first, and the demands of others second."[74] Accordingly, Wirin said, he not only had decided to play an active role in the Zimmerman case but also was committing himself to preparation of a test case against the government to challenge the exclusion orders against the Japanese-Americans on the West Coast.[75]

In subsequent months, Wirin, drawing heavily upon Anthony's published work as well as his own independent efforts, did in fact prepare the brief—and it was brilliantly argued—on behalf of Zimmerman before the Circuit Court. The Ninth Circuit ruled against Zimmerman, however, in a divided opinion that turned on the argument regarding whether the army command's judgment should be the last word on "military necessity" requiring martial law and military government, or whether instead the courts should retain authority to decide.[76] Immediately Wirin and the ACLU geared up to appeal to the U.S. Supreme Court—but not until the ACLU board had ordered its mediation committee to conduct an independent investigation of Zimmerman's background to be certain he was not linked to the Nazis.[77] The prospect of the Supreme Court appeal was worrisome enough to the army command's lawyers in Hawaii that they decided (apparently after the Justice Department had advised the case was weak) to moot the issue by releasing Zimmerman rather than face the possibility of an adverse outcome. Subsequently, the Supreme Court did in fact rule that the case was moot and so declined to hear the appeal.[78]

This mooting tactic—which Anthony and even some of the Justice Department lawyers regarded as a deplorable way of keeping a vitally important constitutional issue away from the Supreme Court—was pursued again by the army in the two 1943 cases of petition for habeas corpus by German-American Hawaii internees.[79] The judges of the federal district court in Honolulu ruled against the army in both cases, and an appeal to the Ninth Circuit was anticipated by the petitioners and counsel. But the military decided instead to release the two men, again on advice of the Department of Justice that there was slender factual foundation for holding them as security risks. An irony of all this maneuvering was that each side had its eye on the possibility that the Court would regard the military government's Hawaii regime as being so outrageous that it might not only result in the overturning of martial law in the Islands but also affect the Court's attitude toward petitioners' claims in the Japanese-American cases then coming through the system. For Wirin, on the mainland the Zimmerman appeal was thus important on its own terms but also as "a test precursor for the Japanese evacuation cases."[80] On the other side, the army lawyers in Hawaii had confidence that the Supreme Court would uphold their position so long as the case that finally came up for decision involved a Japanese-American internee rather than a European-American. Hence they not only mooted the Zimmerman case but later either released or moved to the mainland all internees who were not Japanese-American, believing this would set the stage for a test case that they would be entirely satisfied to see reach the highest tribunal.[81]

The army lawyers were destined to be disappointed in this regard, however, for not a single one of the hundreds of Japanese-Americans interned in Hawaii, nor any of their families in their behalf, ever sought redress in the courts. As suggested by Senator Hiram Fong (who himself, as a young lawyer in Hawaii both before and just after the attack on Pearl Harbor, was an outspoken defender of Japanese-American loyalty), this unanimity probably can be explained by the fear in the Japanese-American community that any such challenge to the army's authority might have led to even more severe measures against them, possibly even a general internment program.[82] Especially revealing on this point was a secret intelligence report in August 1942 which observed that

> conduct of this group [Japanese-Americans] has been more circumspect since Dec. 7th. Besides the operation of normal law abiding influences, the group has been constrained by the known inclusion in concentration camps in the Territory, of a considerable complement from their number, . . . [and] frequently repeated comments of recently arrived U.S. troops, concerning what they would be prepared to do to the group.[83]

When the Duncan case appeal finally went to the Supreme Court in late 1945, there was once again considerable complexity in the litigation strategies being pursued behind the scenes. A simple portrayal of "the government" against Duncan's legal claim does not begin to reflect fully the realities of how lawyers and the forces behind the legal conflict were aligned. The principal complexity resided in the fact that the Interior Department's legal staff and a key Department of Justice litigator were privately in accord that the Hawaii martial law regime was unconstitutional. The Department of the Interior lawyers went so far as to permit Garner Anthony to use their offices, giving him access to file materials as he prepared for oral argument as counsel in the Duncan appeal. Further, John P. Frank, later an eminent constitutional litigator and historian, then a young counsel who served under Abe Fortas, the deputy secretary of the interior throughout the war, worked at Anthony's side, under Fortas's tutelage, to help prepare for oral argument.[84]

While this extraordinary collaboration was going on, the Department of Justice lawyers were preparing to argue for the government—despite their own private reservations regarding the correctness of the army's cause. In fact, Edward Ennis, mentioned earlier as having come to Anthony's defense in the Duncan hearing in Honolulu, had become convinced by early 1943 that the army was entirely wrong in its legal position as to its authority in Hawaii. Martial law, Ennis thought, should be placed on a proper legal basis, together with an immediate restoration of the privilege of the writ of habeas corpus and with a cessation of the army's legal challenges to the power of the federal district court to hear habeas petitions.[85] Ennis had made it clear to the army commander and his legal staff in Hawaii that he would represent their position in court as best he could, but that he believed their course was misguided. His doubts about the army's position were heightened by his own review of the army and FBI records on the habeas petitioners who were interned. He regarded the factual foundation as deficient in each case, and he anticipated the Supreme Court would assume final discretion to examine the validity of the "military necessity" rationale, hence might take judicial notice of the weak factual foundation. When the military lawyers considered mooting the Duncan case, employing the tactic they had used in three previous habeas appeals beginning with Zimmerman's in 1942, Ennis opposed the Justice Department's permitting it. "I thought martial law was entirely wrong in Hawaii after the first year," he recalled in a 1972 interview. "I . . . took those cases to the Supreme Court and argued them and lost them, I am glad to say. I thought they [the army] were wrong at the time. I made no secret of my views."[86]

The foregoing indicates that Ennis sought to perform faithfully his function as a government lawyer, meeting the expectation that he present the best arguments he could muster on behalf of his client. At first blush he appears, then, to have taken the role of "advocate" with sole responsibility, within the law, to advance the client agencies' objectives.

A deeper look into the evidence gives a more qualified picture. First, Ennis pursued the army's interests within the framework of legal process, resisting all suggestions in 1945 that the Duncan case be mooted or that the army otherwise evade review by the federal courts. In this he was seconded by Solicitor General Fahy, who worked with Ennis as the Duncan appeal strategy was being developed, to assure that the Court would have the final word on the important legal and constitutional questions involved. Second, even more indicative of how they saw their ethical obligations, Fahy and Ennis—to the army lawyers' dismay—included in their brief to the Court an explicit invitation for the justices to rule on whether the army or the courts should be the final authority with respect to "military necessity." They made the case for the army's interest in having that authority in an emergency; but they fully conceded what the army lawyers in the Hawaii command—though not all the army's legal staff in Washington—had never been willing to recognize, namely, that the federal courts had jurisdiction to determine whether the facts of the situation warranted a suspension of civil liberties.[87]

This departure from single-minded advocacy in response to the client's interests or wishes alone indicates that the Justice Department lawyers were committed to the classic concept of the lawyer as officer of the court, with a commitment to seeing that constitutional imperatives were obeyed.[88] This was especially so with Ennis, whose behavior throughout the litigation of the several cases in the district court and on appeal was that of the classic

Brandeisian "counselor to the situation."[89] In that mode, when General Richardson issued his notorious general order in 1943 threatening Judge Metzger of the federal district court with hard labor in a military prison if he agreed to hear a habeas petition, Ennis sent off a confidential memorandum to Richardson urging that he set aside the counsel he had received from the Hawaii command's local legal staff and instead view the matter as presenting a potential constitutional crisis. To confront a federal judge in this manner, Ennis warned Richardson, was to go far beyond the scope of "a narrow technical, legal problem in which the commanding General might [be] . . . justified in relying on technical legal advice alone."[90] Ennis hinted, too, at an iron hand beneath the velvet glove of his counsel, warning the general that if his order were not rescinded, it could produce "[a] situation in which it would not be possible to represent the military authorities whom the Department of Justice wishes to represent where any defense is available."[91] Solicitor General Fahy was entirely in accord. Appealing to McCloy and others in a lawyer-to-lawyer manner, he told McCloy that "the military . . . should be led by men such as Secretary Stimson, Judge Patterson and yourself to believe that it is wise and not dangerous to permit such cases as this to take a normal course of solution by judicial processes rather than by the exercise of military power." It was absolutely imperative, if the letter and spirit of constitutional law were to prevail, that they find "some reasonable method of getting the case back in justiciable posture."[92]

While representing the army, it should be noted, Ennis also proved willing to make to the ACLU lawyers what they called "informal suggestion[s]" with regard to procedure in the course of appeals in at least one habeas case out of Hawaii. He acted, it seems fair to say, not in violation of obligations to his client but rather consistently with the ideology of the lawyer as officer of the court and as counsel to the situation—especially since he had made clear to General Richardson where his professional ethics took him on a constitutional issue of this magnitude.[93] In retrospect, Anthony would write that, in the face of the support for Richardson's stance extended both by the War Department and by Chief of Staff General George C. Marshall, it took the interventions of Fahy and Ennis "to bring General Richardson to a final acceptance that he and every other person in the land was under the law, a fundamental lesson in our polity that goes back to the historic clash between Lord Coke and James I."[94]

The "counsel to the situation" style similarly was evident in Garner Anthony's role during the confrontation between General Richardson and Judge Metzger's federal district court in 1943. Anthony, then still serving as territorial attorney general, consulted with Governor Stainback and Richardson, offering to work out a compromise in separate confidential discussions with the army commander and Judge Metzger, bringing in the U.S. attorney and other counsel as appropriate. An escalation of threat and counterthreat between the federal court and the general was the alternative, Anthony told the army. "Such a situation would be disgraceful," he wrote, proposing a set of procedural moves that would save face on both sides and permit the issues to go forward on appeal to the Ninth Circuit in an orderly manner.[95] In this sense, Anthony was operating on the same premises regarding the imperatives of the law, and in a manner complementary to what the Department of Justice lawyers Ennis and Fahy were attempting. The main immediate objective of both Anthony and the Department of Justice was to get the question into adjudicative channels; they hoped (though they could not be certain) that the longer-term objective, the restoration of the right to the habeas corpus privilege, would be upheld by proper judicial authority.

Assistant Secretary McCloy recognized full well that the War Department could not possibly long justify a commanding general in the posture of defiance that Richardson had taken toward Judge Metzger's court. Indeed, in an incident a year earlier when the Hawaii command, advised by its local legal officers, had insisted on its authority to "supervise" the federal court, the judge advocate general in Washington had given his opinion that such a claim by the army was "of doubtful legal validity" and in any event was "inconsistent with the dignity of the court and amounts to the exercise of judicial power by the [general] himself."[96] As General Richardson and Judge Metzger went on with a month-long standoff, McCloy and Secretary Stimson went through the motions of verbally defending Richardson against the flood tide of outraged criticism that came from Secretary Ickes and Attorney General Biddle; but all the while McCloy quietly (and not always forcefully) was pushing the army brass in Hawaii into compliance with the procedural compromise.[97]

The role of General Morrison, who, as chief legal officer and also the "executive" of military government, prepared the legal arguments that Richardson used to threaten Judge Metzger with hard labor, would win a stinging condemnation from a Justice Department special investigator in 1946. The investigator was Frederick Wiener, a leading scholar of martial law as well as a litigator of considerable reputation. Wiener's report concluded that Morrison in this instance "showed himself to be a poor lawyer, which is bad, but . . . he acted like a damn fool, which is much worse." Then, again, Wiener added parenthetically, Morrison had been the one who had "tried to get Garner Anthony's clients to boycott their lawyer," and so his giving bizarre legal advice to the commanding general was consistent with his record of bad judgment. Wiener's conclusion was harsh but not unwarranted. "This man," he wrote, "is perhaps the most vulnerable figure you could find [in the army officer ranks], if you searched the Pacific Ocean area, from the Farallon Rocks off the Golden Gate to Yokohama Harbor."[98]

Probably more than any other single factor, the army's intransigence and obtuseness to law in the Metzger-Richardson confrontation of 1943 confirmed the view of both civilian leaders in Hawaii and Justice Department lawyers that the principle of judicial review of wartime army actions affecting civil liberties must be pursued to the Supreme Court. This incident probably also explains the sense of urgency with which the Department of the Interior's lawyers would pursue the policy issue in cabinet circles and appeals to the White House, and with which they would later extend invaluable cooperation to Anthony in preparing the Duncan case against another department of the government.[99]

As to General Green, he was transferred from the Hawaii command at the insistence of Ickes and Biddle, but by the war's end he had been appointed to succeed Cramer as the judge advocate general of the army. He was also awarded a Distinguished Service Medal for his work as administrator of the military government in the Islands. To Green, and no doubt to his successor, Morrison, and also many of the high-ranking army and navy officers who served as lawyers or line officers in wartime Hawaii, the varied and sometimes coordinated efforts of their lawyer-critics smacked of naïveté about the realities of war. Green was a vindictive personality, prone to write off his "enemies" such as the Interior lawyers as "reds," "pinkos," or "vermin"; his constant objective was to maintain the fullest possible army control of every detail of civilian life in the Islands. Morrison vented his own views in a letter to Green two years after the war, referring to Judge Metzger and his fellow federal district judge McLaughlin (both of whom had approved habeas petitions over the army's objections) as "serfs of the machinations of [the] Governor." Morrison regarded the ACLU as "self-appointed meddlers" and said he wished in retrospect that the army had simply executed Zimmerman and his ilk and thus put the troublesome legal issues to rest.[100]

For their part, several critics of the army regime—Fortas, Anthony, Ickes, and Wiener—all remarked at one time or another that General Green and his military-lawyer colleagues, by fighting to keep control of all government functions in Hawaii, not coincidentally served the cause of their rapid rise through the officers' ranks to win generals' stars.[101] In any event, Green and the others were administrators as well as lawyers. The counsel they extended to the commanding general was unquestionably colored by the ethic of military line-of-authority discipline; the likelihood of hard self-criticism in the process of advising, or of resisting the commander's inclinations on important issues, was virtually nil. Instead, the only criticism came from outside, and the response of the Hawaii command's legal staff was invariably defensive. Of the army lawyers, only Judge Advocate General Cramer and a few other lawyer officers (serving on his staff in Washington or attached to the War Department) seem not to have played the game of always telling the army generals what they thought they wanted. At crucial junctures, they showed enough independence of mind to evaluate the long-run implications of the Hawaii command's view of constitutional law and wartime power—and to advise more self-restraint and a sense of constitutional principle and respect for rule of law, in the operation of the Hawaii regime.[102] There is no evidence that we have seen in all the archives of the army command in Hawaii that such an attitude had any influence in headquarters policy discussions there or in the daily administration of the military government.

## Aftermath: Civil Indemnification Suits

In the end, Green and the commanding officers would be forced to face their own day before the law, for the *Duncan* decision in March 1946 threw an entirely new light on their record. Actually, they had anticipated that there might be civil indemnification suits from the internees and those who had served prison terms after convictions by the provost courts; and their preparations for this eventuality were carefully designed. Men who had shown a disregard for considerations of ordinary due process and the demands of equal justice, in the face of wartime needs, were now converted to zealous champions of "fair play."

The first note of alarm, on this score, came from General Green when, in January 1943, anticipating his own transfer out to the mainland, he said that he feared that Governor Stainback might succeed in regaining control of civilian government functions. He therefore warned Morrison to avoid, in such a case, letting Stainback —who "has always despised us and particularly General Emmons and me"—get access to the army's military government records, for "we would never be able to see them once they were turned over."[103] From that time forward, Morrison and others in the Hawaii command's legal staff seem to have kept the possibility of civil liability in the forefront of discussion when technical or policy issues arose. There was similar concern in the office of the judge advocate general in 1944, when Green's reassignment gave the Hawaii issues a new perspective in that office. Thus in September 1944, a Judge Advocate General officer's memorandum to Stimson advised that if martial law were to be terminated by an executive order from the president, rather than by the Hawaii commanding general, it "might be of some value later on" because army officers would then "be able to plead *respondeat superior* and to have the proof of record" should lawsuits materialize.[104]

The most significant defensive moves against possible civil suits were taken in early 1946 when the Wiener investigation of martial law was announced, after the arguments of *Duncan* before the Supreme Court were completed but before the Court had acted. General Green, by then promoted to be the army's Judge Advocate General, collaborated with General Richardson in persuading the War Department to keep Morrison on duty in his general-rank grade in Honolulu. This, Green thought, would assure that the best possible light would be put on martial law in the course of the investigation; but this proved a vain hope, for, as noted earlier, Wiener wrote a thoroughly critical review.[105] The urgency of the army generals' efforts to erect a defense became more intense in the months immediately following the *Duncan* case decision by the Supreme Court, as the long-anticipated civil suits were in fact initiated. Again, General Richardson appealed to the War Department, asking that not only Morrison but also Colonel E. V. Slatterly (described as "the chief legal adviser" under martial law) be retained "on active duty in grade for an indefinite period or at least until the law suits initiated against [Richardson] and General Morrison have been tried and determined" in the federal district court in Hawaii. The two officers (one a defendant!) were, Richardson argued, the only ones "with a thorough knowledge of all the files," and so, "to relieve them now . . . would be calamitous and certainly would be most prejudicial to my personal interests."[106]

Green, meanwhile, used his authority as Judge Advocate General to mobilize an intensive effort by his subordinate staff to prepare for his own defense and that of the others being sued for civil damages. "It is a comfort," he wrote privately, "to know that I have 110 lawyers in my own shop whose services I would call on to the extent necessary. . . . I am taking no chances whatever."[107] Legal officers of captain's rank were assigned to work through all the relevant records of the War Department (the copies survive, in great volume, and are in the Green Papers today) and to present him with an interpretive report. Apparently well attuned to what their chief wanted from them, which was a factual statement and interpretive findings that could be cited in a legal brief or in public forums, the Judge Advocate General lawyers wrote a five-part summary of their findings.[108] First, they declared that General Green had exercised no independent responsibility as executive, but rather had operated in a chain of command in which "both Mr. McCloy and General Emmons took an active, and, by virtue of their superior rank, a more authoritative, part" than his. This chain-of-command argument was designed, of course, to help immunize Green from legal liability to the civilians who were suing —and in fact, attorneys for the military did use that argument as the centerpiece of their defenses in the ensuing cases. Second, any criticism directed against martial law during the war must be understood, they wrote, not as being objective nor indeed of any consequence except as "part of the campaign" by Stainback and other civilian officers in the territory to regain civilian control. Third, this "campaign" was in fact "opposed by public opinion" and was contrary to popular views in Hawaii of the army and its regime. Fourth, the records revealed repeated "underhanded efforts made by the interested persons to discredit the military authorities" (only one case was specified, but it was characterized as "typical"). The last—and most astonishing—contention concerned motives:

> Governor Stainback's letters to Secretary Ickes indicate that his chief objectives were not to assist in the protection of the Territory or to cooperate in the prosecution of the war, but to regain his peacetime jurisdiction and to injure, as much as possible, those men who had opposed him in this attempt—principally yourself, and to a somewhat less extent, General Emmons.[109]

Our own examination of the archival records, including the correspondence files that were referred to in the Judge Advocate General lawyers' report to Green, indicates almost the reverse conclusions on the crucial issues of style and motive: Green and the other Hawaii command lawyers, and also General Richardson at times, in correspondence with Washington made every effort to discredit their critics and, without supporting evidence, to question factual assertions. They often resorted to innuendo and in some instances displayed the kind of unscrupulous tactics and brazen disregard for fairness for which the Wiener Report would criticize them so severely. As to the notion that Stainback and the others were not interested in assisting in prosecution of the war, an evaluation of that charge depends on the definition of "assisting." Throughout the war period, Green and the two commanding generals had repeatedly made it clear that "assistance," or "cooperation," meant no less than absolute and unquestioning obedience to their orders and policies.[110]

Much publicity surrounded the Duncan case arguments, especially when the popular conservative radio commentator Fulton Lewis Jr., began to broadcast graphic reports of heavy-handed military rule in Hawaii.[111] This and other media coverage brought pressure from various members of Congress for hearings to review the army's actions and to consider legislation for compensation of the civilians who had been harmed under army justice. When Secretary of War Patterson was asked by Congress to respond to the Lewis broadcasts, General Green quickly prepared an extended defense of his position, which Patterson then signed, substantially unchanged. It was published in the *Congressional Record* on March 25, 1946. In it, Green contended that the Islands had been "exposed to dire peril" and that "the civil courts [were] ill adapted to cope with an emergency" such as confronted Hawaii in the war. He denied that there was a single person interned without a careful hearing or held in conditions that might be criticized as less than comfortable. Further, he contended that the regulations of martial law were progressively relaxed on the army's own initiative. In a line of reasoning that obviously was addressed to an audience in no way cognizant of the facts of the Hawaii record or of the *Duncan* decision, Green contended that "[t]he army did not in any sense oust or overthrow the civil government of the Territory. *The civil authorities of the Territory continued for the most part to function as before* [sic], *their authority supported and assured by martial law.*" He defended himself and the army against charges that the internments had been handled illegally or unconstitutionally, since the *Duncan* decision referred only to those who had been "sentenced to punitive confinement by the provost courts." Green thus deliberately ignored the fifty thousand trials conducted by the provost courts! Withal, he denied any intent or action that would suggest the military acted tyrannically or beyond its authority as it was properly understood prior to the *Duncan* decision.[112]

The *respondeat superior* defense thereafter became the keynote of Green's activities in his own behalf. In a memorandum for the chief of the War Department's public relations bureau, Green demanded that the government issue to the press an unambiguous statement absolving him of responsibility for the results of army policies and administration in Hawaii. He wrote:

> It is of course quite clear that I am not responsible for the proclamation of martial law which was issued by the Civilian

> Governor of the Territory, and was approved by the President of the United States. Likewise I am, of course, not responsible for the administration of martial law in Hawaii. It was a War Department activity from the start; the responsible head was [the commanding general].[113]

Understandably enough, in light of how McCloy and Stimson had conceived of their job in supervising the Hawaii situation, Green insisted that the War Department's responsibility be recognized. His argument did not stop there, however: in what surely was one of the most disingenuous assertions to be found in all the generals' arguments in their own defense, when the threatened civil liability suits began to materialize, Green attempted to implicate even his most implacable critics in Washington—Secretary Ickes and Attorney General Biddle. Green wrote: "The Secretary of War at all times maintained a close supervision of martial law in Hawaii. Broad policies were passed on not only by him but by the Secretary of the Interior, the Attorney General, and in some cases, the Navy Department. It is these policies which are really being attacked."[114]

Throughout 1946, suits were being filed in federal courts in Hawaii and in mainland locations, as former internees and prisoners of the provost courts sought indemnification. The lawyers for these claimants had the problem, as was recognized explicitly in courtroom proceedings, that a bill was before Congress for one-dollar-a-day compensation for time spent by provost court prisoners. The bill was opposed by the army, since it would concede its culpability; but it was supported, precisely for that reason, by the Hawaii territorial delegate, by Garner Anthony, and others. It potentially affected the civil litigation, however, because juries or judges might be swayed, in considering whether to award damages (and, if so, at what level), by the prospect of its passage.[115] This situation may well have discouraged potential plaintiffs, and for that reason or otherwise most of the suits had disappeared from the dockets by late 1947.

The withdrawal of all but a few suits did not mean, however, that the military officers who were named in the suits had an easy five years after the war. On the contrary, the archival records indicate that Generals Emmons and Richardson were outraged at being stranded, as they saw themselves, without the government's support and facing enormous financial liabilities. The War Department by mid-1946 had received the Wiener Report, which had condemned the military regime in Hawaii as virtually indefensible in much of its record; and the department followed the course Wiener advised by keeping a low profile. Specifically, the department refrained from asking Congress for any bill guaranteeing compensation to the officers if they were held liable for private damages in the ongoing suits. Emmons and Richardson regarded this as a gross betrayal that they did not deserve. They, too, offered the *respondeat superior* argument in calling on the War Department to back them in their plight; but they also put forward the military perspective. In future military emergencies, they contended, commanding generals such as themselves could not be expected to put their reputations and private assets on the line in ordering the measures that they believed to be necessary.[116] In the last analysis, the government did provide Department of Justice legal counsel to Emmons and Richardson in civil suits. Only one of these suits went to a full trial; it was held in 1950 and was publicized by the Honolulu press.

Unsurprisingly, the full trial involved a suit pressed by the indefatigable Dr. Zimmerman. Now apparently having revivified his lucrative naturopathic practice in Honolulu (and, it would appear, enjoying a stream of investment income), Zimmerman engaged A. L. Wirin—who had handled his appeals for the ACLU during the war—and several local attorneys, including in 1950 the young Hawaii labor lawyer Harriet Bouslog, to represent him. In a 1948 filing, he entered suit for $575,000 in damages against former governor Poindexter, the former FBI head in the territory (Robert Shivers), and the former chief of the army's intelligence operation in the Islands (Colonel George W. Bicknell), as well as General Emmons. Also named as a defendant was a civilian who had served on the loyalty review board convened to recommend whether Zimmerman should be taken into custody in December 1941. When the case finally went to trial in 1950, Emmons took the stand and reasserted the position he had taken in extended testimony during the Duncan trial hearings in 1944, namely, that the Islands were still in danger of invasion at that time, and that extraordinary measures were warranted by the facts of the situation and on the authority that had been given him under War Department and ultimately presidential authority. From the FBI and a deposition from General Richardson came ambiguous and contested testimony as to whether there had been any plausible evidence, or instead merely "gossip" about Zimmerman in 1941.[117]

The lawyering in this case took a turn that was probably unfortunate for Zimmerman's chances of prevailing when his attorneys, stating that they had become convinced that the others had acted in "good faith," dropped all those named in the suit except Emmons. In that light, the die may have been cast when the judge instructed the jury that they must find Emmons not liable unless he had acted "unnecessarily and arbitrarily," and that the internment had been "illegal." But even then, there was a major caveat, for the judge's instructions went on to say: "Even if you might find that Gen. Emmons' acts exceeded his authority, he can not be held liable in damages if his actions represented a reasonable judgment exercised in good faith under the circumstances as he saw them at the time in regard to matters under his general supervision."[118] The "good faith" defense, even more than *respondeat superior*, was a difficult one to discredit; and the jury came down against Zimmerman, despite Bouslog's plea in closing argument that "the usurping of powers by military authorities . . . does not belong in a democratic form of government," and that Zimmerman was owed restitution.[119] Moreover, reflecting many years later on the Zimmerman trial, former Senator Hiram Fong contended that no jury of civilians who remembered the atmosphere of fear that prevailed in the Islands during the war would have voted to hold Emmons or other army officers liable.[120] Although Zimmerman continued pursuing appeals until the Supreme Court finally issued an order rejecting his case, the issue of indemnification died out—as, for most constitutional lawyers and historians, the entire history of the Hawaii martial law period seemed to virtually disappear from memory or serious interest for many years.

Garner Anthony, who had been the sparkplug of action in much of the story, proved to be not interested in having a role in representing plaintiffs in the suits for indemnification: all that, he told an oral history interviewer, was *pau* (in the past) for him once the war had ended.[121] He returned to his practice and to a position as a leading figure in Island educational philanthropies and cultural support, and he was prominent in the campaign for Hawaii statehood and in writing the Hawaii state constitution in the 1950s. In 1955 Anthony did publish a book, based on his research for the Duncan appeals (some of it from files opened to him by his lawyer friends in Interior) and his personal recollections, which stood for more than four decades as the only reference of full scope on the history of the episode.[122]

Generals Richardson and Emmons went into retirement—a troubled time for them at first because of the lawsuits, but they apparently prospered. General Green, honored with two Distinguished Service Medals, retired from the position of judge advocate general and came through unscathed financially, moving smoothly into a life after the army as professor in military law at the University of Arizona. He gave numerous public addresses in which he reiterated his arguments about the legality and character of martial law, both in Hawaii and in general; but his manuscript addresses are intriguing for his progressively greater emphasis on how he had been in sole practical control of Hawaii's civilian life—a rather different emphasis than in his defenses when lawsuits threatened. He worked on a history of the martial law period that survives in manuscript but could not find a publisher; and he must have spent considerable time going over his diaries and correspondence to record his reflections. Most of his retrospective notations are pungent and condescending dismissals of the intelligence, rectitude, and even loyalty of those who were prominent wartime critics of his command.[123]

As to those who had been unjustly interned or fined, imprisoned, or otherwise caught in the web of military justice during the war, it seems that nearly all simply wanted to get on with their lives. In fact, it appears from scattered press accounts that many internees whose names had reached some public notice managed to rebuild their lives very successfully in the Islands once the war had ended.[124] The persistent defense of constitutional principles by lawyers in a variety of wartime roles, no less than the ways in which the military chose to apply and interpret the law—and in which the army lawyers pursued their litigative and policy strategies—had determined the fate of those people in the war years; their vindication before the law and chance to return to full lives after the war's end must be seen in light of the way in which "counsel to the situation" was of influence at crucial junctures. The initial articulation of the legal and constitutional questions by Anthony and the Interior Department lawyers had also been influential in setting the framework of internal debates in the government in Washington, and over the long haul had set the tone and framed the content of public debate in the media that became an important factor in finally ending the Hawaii military regime. Not least of the contributions by lawyers devoted to civil liberties principles was the successful pursuit of the issues in the Duncan case to a final determination in the Supreme Court in 1946.

Notes

1. On Brandeis's use of the "lawyer to the situation" concept, first used in his confirmation hearings for appointment to the Supreme Court (a concept often referred to as "counsel to the situation" in scholarly commentary on the codes of professional ethics), see John Frank, "The Legal Ethics of Louis D. Brandeis," *Stanford Law Review* 17 (1965): 683–709. On lawyers' roles and for a general analytic framework for assessing ethical considerations, see Robert Gordon, "The Independence of Lawyers," *Boston University Law Review* 68 (1988): 1–83. See also David Luban, "The *Noblesse Oblige* Tradition in the Practice of Law," *Vanderbilt Law Review* 41 (1988): 717–40 (discussing Brandeis's public statements well before 1916, exhorting the bar to honor a higher obligation than the narrow interests of a particular client without regard to the public good).

2. William Simon, "Ideology of Advocacy," *Wisconsin Law Review* (1968): 71.

3. An important exception is Peter Irons, *Justice at War: The Story of the Japanese-American Internment Cases* (New York, 1983), in which the activities of Department of Justice, army, and War Department lawyers are documented from archival sources and form much of the basis of interpretation.

4. 31 U.S. Stat. 153 (1900).

5. The army's general orders for Hawaii are reprinted in J. Garner Anthony, *Hawaii Under Army Rule* (Stanford, Calif., 1955), appendix. The present authors have written a monograph on the military and Hawaii government under martial law: Harry N. Scheiber and Jane L. Scheiber, "Bayonets in Paradise: A Half-Century Retrospect on Martial Law in Hawai'i, 1941–46," *University of Hawai'i Law Review* 19 (1997): 477–648. We refer readers to that work for detailed documentation of the general history, discussion of some of which is incorporated for purposes of providing context here of the issues of lawyers' roles.

6. See Anthony, *Hawaii Under Army Rule,* passim (and general orders in the appendix); and Scheiber and Scheiber, "Bayonets in Paradise," passim.

7. All these cases, as well as the absence of Japanese-American habeas appeals, will be discussed in the pages that follow.

8. In a draft manuscript study (never published) of martial law and military governance, Green later wrote: "Factually, I had authority from General Emmons to do whatever was necessary to be done in any emergency but to

keep him informed of what was going on. My authority was substantially unlimited." Draft, chapter 5, "Development of the Office of Military Governor," in the Papers of General Thomas Green, Judge Advocate General's School Library, Charlottesville, Virginia (hereafter cited as Green Papers, JAGS).

9. Given the "racial setup" in the Islands, General Emmons told the War Department, "justice, whether it be criminal or civil, is simply out of the window" once juries were empowered to decide. Emmons to McCloy, July 1, 1942, in Hawaii Military Government Records, RG 338, National Archives. The army commanders in Hawaii in fact regarded all civilian institutions as too unstable and too "political" to be reliable in a war emergency. When the issue finally came before the Supreme Court, Justice Murphy commented specifically on assertions in the testimony given by General Richardson in the Duncan trial, when he said that civilian courts were subject to "all sorts of influences, political and otherwise," thus warranting the military's having designated them as mere "agents" of the army. *Duncan v. Kahanamoku*, 327 U.S. 304, 332 (1946). Deputy Secretary of the Interior Abe Fortas and Attorney General Francis Biddle wrote formally to Assistant Secretary of War McCloy a year after the attack on Pearl Harbor, objecting to the basic concept of military superiority over civilian government and the idea that the army itself would decide when it was safe to restore civilian institutions of administration and justice, and demanded a change of policy. Letter of Dec. 19, 1942, in McCloy Files, War Department Records, RG 107, National Archives.

10. When Ickes sent a member of his top staff in Interior to Hawaii to confer with the army command there, the report came back to him that General Emmons and Colonel Green considered "the entire Territory [as] a theatre of military operations and that . . . all authority over civil, as well as military, life must reside in the Military Governor." Benjamin Thoron to Ickes, Feb. 23, 1942, Secretary of the Interior Records, RG 48, National Archives.

11. Michi Weglyn, *Years of Infamy: The Untold Story of America's Concentration Camps* (New York, 1976); Scheiber and Scheiber, "Bayonets in Paradise," 580–82. See also Gary Y. Okihiro, *Cane Fires: The Anti-Japanese Movement in Hawaii, 1865–1945* (Philadelphia, 1984), 195ff.

12. See Anthony, *Hawaii Under Army Rule*, 58–59.

13. The provost courts' operations are discussed in ibid., 38–58, and detailed data are available in Office of the Chief of Military History, "United States Army Forces: Middle Pacific and Predecessor Commands During World War II, 7 December 1941–2 September 1945: Civil Affairs and Military Government" (microfilm on file in the Hawaii War Records Depository, Hamilton Library, University of Hawaii).

14. Charles Fairman, *Reconstruction and Reunion, 1864–88, Part One*, Oliver Wendell Holmes Devise History of the Supreme Court of the United States, vol. 6 (New York, 1971); Mark E. Neely Jr., *The Fate of Liberty: Abraham Lincoln and Civil Liberties* (New York, 1991).

15. Harry N. Scheiber, *The Wilson Administration and Civil Liberties* (Ithaca, N.Y., 1960); H. C. Peterson and Gilbert C. Fite, *Opponents of War, 1917–1918* (Madison, Wis., 1957); Paul L. Murphy, *World War I and the Origin of Civil Liberties in the United States* (New York, 1979).

16. Peter Irons discovered the crucial evidence on this point, in an FBI report that the Justice Department litigators had in hand but suppressed when arguing the Japanese-American cases. See Irons, *Justice at War*, 280–92.

17. See our "Bayonets in Paradise," passim, for detailed documentation.

18. Memorandum, President Roosevelt to Secretary of the Navy, Feb. 26, 1942, Box 7, PSF confidential files, FDR Presidential Papers, Roosevelt Presidential Library, Hyde Park. See also Stetson Conn, R. Engelman, and B. Fairchild, *United States Army in World War II: The Western Hemisphere and Its Outposts,* vol. 2 (Washington, D.C., 1964), chaps 5–6; and Okihiro, *Cane Fires,* 195–252.

19. General Richardson to Asst. Secretary McCloy, Feb. 10, 1944, McCloy Files, War Department Records, RG 107, National Archives (in which Richardson stated: "The best evidence of the wisdom of this entire program for the past two years is the fact that it has worked").

20. We use the term "unscrupulous" because of the way in which General Green and the commanding generals manipulated public opinion and the press, and because they consistently portrayed the civilian officials and lawyers who were critical of martial law as cranks or worse. They also took advantage of their censorship authority to read the governor's correspondence with Interior officials in Washington while the Roosevelt administration's cabinet officers were debating a plan to restore partial authority to civilian government. See Scheiber and Scheiber, "Bayonets in Paradise," passim.

21. "Oral Report Made by Mr. Frederick B. Wiener, 11 May 1946" (manuscript, declassified June 25, 1975), copy in Papers of General Robert C. Richardson, Hoover Institution Archives, Stanford (hereinafter cited as Wiener Report).

22. W. W. Garner to Secretary of the Interior, Dec. 18, 1942, copy, Papers of Delegate Joseph R. Farrington, Hawaii State Archives.

23. Ernest May, "Military and Civil Rule," *Honolulu Star-Bulletin,* May 15, 1944.

24. Judge Delbert Metzger, quoted in *Honolulu Star-Bulletin,* May 18, 1944.

25. *Zimmerman v. Walker,* 132 F.2d 446 (9th Cir. 1942), cert. denied, 319 U.S. 744 (1943).

26. On the strategy of mooting, see text below at notes 78–79; and Anthony, *Hawaii Under Army Rule,* 64, 75.

27. *Duncan v. Kahanamoku* (1946), cited above. An account based on internal correspondence of the justices as well as published sources is offered in our "Bayonets in Paradise," 616–32.

28. John P. Frank, "Review and Basic Liberties," in *Supreme Court and Supreme Law,* ed. Edmond Cahn (New York, 1954), 114 (reprinted in *American Law and the Constitutional Order: Historical Perspectives,* ed. L. M. Friedman and H. N. Scheiber [Cambridge, Mass., 1978]).

29. For the extent of the damage done at Pearl Harbor and the reactions to the crisis in Washington and the armed forces, as well as for discussion of Japan's plans for possible invasion of the Hawaiian Islands in 1942 (until thwarted by defeat of the Japanese fleet at Midway in June of that year), see Michael Slackman, *Target—Pearl Harbor* (Honolulu, 1990).

30. In endorsing the idea of interning Hawaii's Japanese-American population, Roosevelt wrote to his secretary of the navy: "I do not worry about the constitutional question—first, because of my recent order [for evacuation and internment on the mainland], and, second, because Hawaii is under martial law. The whole matter is one of immediate and present war emergency. I

think you and Stimson can agree and then go ahead and do it as a military project." Roosevelt to Secretary of the Navy Frank Knox, quoted in Conn, Engelman, and Fairchild, *United States Army in World War II,* 209. When Nazi saboteurs were ordered to be tried, in the case that came to the Supreme Court as *Ex parte Quirin* (317 U.S. 1 [1942]), the president framed an order denying the defendants any rights of appeal; the Supreme Court sidestepped the question by pretending, in effect, that the order could not possibly have applied to itself. In one of the most extraordinary documents in the entire history of American constitutional law, Roosevelt in September 1942 threatened that if Congress failed to meet his wishes with respect to repealing a section of the price control laws, in light of the war emergency he would assume the power to nullify the law on his own authority! Congressional deference averted a constitutional confrontation on the issue. For this episode in the context of Roosevelt's pragmatic approach to constitutionalism, see Harry N. Scheiber, "The New Deal," in *Encyclopedia of the American Constitution,* ed. Leonard Levy and Kenneth Karst, supplement I (New York, 1992), 338.

31. Scheiber and Scheiber, "Bayonets in Paradise," 646. See also Kai Bird, *The Chairman: John J. McCloy and the Making of the American Establishment* (New York, 1992), 152–54.

32. Stimson to Ickes, Jan. 29, 1943, copy in McCloy Files, War Department Records, RG 107, National Archives.

33. McCloy to Secretary Harold Ickes, May 14, 1942, copy in Samuel King Delegate Papers, Hawaii State Archives. Ironically, the army's own judge advocate general did review the case, ordering the sentence to be commuted to life imprisonment. Reference is to the Saffrey Brown death sentence case, discussed below.

34. Biddle's view of Green is set forth in his notes for a journal, manuscript in the Biddle Papers, FDR Library, Hyde Park. Also, in a confidential memorandum to the president, Dec. 17, 1942, Biddle wrote that the military government in Hawaii was "autocratic, wasteful and unjust." Hawaii Files, Box 2, Biddle Papers, FDR Library. The quotation from Ickes is from his manuscript diaries, in the Ickes Papers, Library of Congress.

35. The two were Ennis and Rowe, in oral history interviews, Bancroft Library, UC Berkeley.

36. McCloy to Harry Hopkins, Oct. 19, 1942, copy in McCloy Files, War Department Records, RG 107, National Archives. In fact, some of the lawyers in Hawaii were uneasy about the question of how they would make their livings so long as the army controlled government and kept the courts closed (so recalled by Senator Hiram Fong, who himself was a young attorney in practice in Honolulu in 1941, in oral history interview with the senior author, August 1999). But to claim, as General Richardson and his army legal staff did, that these attorneys were the only persons in Hawaii who wanted martial law modified or terminated was absurd.

37. McCloy to Alexander Meiklejohn, Sept. 30, 1942, Japanese Relocation War Records, Bancroft Library, UC Berkeley.

38. Ibid.

39. See, e.g., Radio No. 6316, McCloy to Richardson, Aug. 31, 1943, in McCloy Files, War Department Records, RG 107, National Archives. A week later, Richardson was still taking the position that he "could not" revoke his general order entirely. A month later, McCloy, far from having ordered Richardson to revoke the order, told the Department of Justice that he believed

that to recognize Judge Metzger's jurisdiction would risk the court's requiring testimony from Richardson; McCloy insisted that "it does not become his [Richardson's] position and responsibilities to subject himself to cross-examination on military questions dealing with the object of his mission." McCloy to Solicitor General Charles Fahy, Sept. 24, 1943 (copy), Hawaiian Military Government Records, Box 57, RG 338, National Archives.

40. McCloy to Fahy, Sept. 30, 1943, McCloy Files, Box 57, War Department Records, RG 107, National Archives.

41. McCloy to Attorney General Francis Biddle, Dec. 23, 1942, McCloy Files, War Department Records, RG 107, National Archives.

42. Ibid.

43. Once the president had made it clear in 1944 that the White House would approve a termination or severe cutback in the scope of military government, however, McCloy did send clear signals to General Richardson that he should prepare to make that shift. Thus Richardson, and General Morrison and his legal staff too, shifted from a campaign of proposing various ways of perpetuating the military regime under new rubrics and instead began to work hard on portraying the termination policy as having originated with themselves! Richardson to McCloy, July 7, 1944 McCloy Files, War Department Records, RG 107, National Archives.

44. See generally Gordon, "Independence of Lawyers." In our "Bayonets in Paradise," passim, we deal with the important role of Abe Fortas as negotiator for Interior in Hawaii matters. It is especially noteworthy that during the early wartime period, Fortas proposed that the American Bar Association convene a committee to study martial law questions in view of the Hawaii situation—another aspect of lawyers' perception of their institutional responsibilities and opportunities. The proposal, which came to nothing, is discussed in "Memorandum from Benjamin W. Thoron (Aug. 12, 1942) (referring to Conference of Aug. 10 in Regard to Military Rule in Hawaii)," copy in the Green papers, JAGS Library. On Fortas's role in Interior, see generally, Laura Kalman, *Abe Fortas: A Biography* (New Haven, Conn., 1990).

45. Ickes to Secretary of War Henry L. Stimson, Aug. 5, 1942, Hawaii Military Government Records, RG 338, National Archives (recounting conversation with Poindexter and stating Poindexter had felt "coerced" by the commanding general on Pearl Harbor day, General Short, to turn over civilian government); Biddle and Abe Fortas to John J. McCloy, Dec. 19, 1942, Asst. Secretary of War Records (McCloy Files), Box 32, War Department Records, National Archives. Poindexter later gave a contested account of his understanding at the time of declaring martial law, namely, that the army would maintain control for only a few months and would return civilian functions as quickly as possible to the territorial government. Report of testimony in the Zimmerman civil case, "Poindexter Tells About Martial Law," *Honolulu Star-Bulletin*, Dec. 12, 1950.

46. General Green recalled later that Judge Coke of the territorial supreme court, having heard Anthony's counsel on this point, initially had made a request (later withdrawn, however) for a bond of indemnity before agreeing to serve on a special military commission for hearing the most serious crimes; but in that situation the army had decided to restructure the commission. Green to Harry Hossack, Dec. 15, 1945, Green Papers, JAGS Library; see also Anthony, *Hawaii Under Army Rule,* 11–12 (recalling that Coke's colleague on the court, Judge Steadman, also raised the question of personal liability).

47. This account of Anthony's role and how Green and Anthony regarded one another is based on the Green diaries, both original text and later marginal comments by Green; and also his marginal notes on an official army draft history of security in Hawaii, in the Green Papers, JAGS; on an oral history interview by the authors of Mrs. Garner Anthony in Honolulu, 1993; on Watumull Foundation oral history interview of J. Garner Anthony, Nov. 12, 1971, copy in Hawaii State Library; and on a great volume of archived correspondence of the army and the War Department. It should be noted that in some areas of civilian administration in the executive branch (e.g., food production coordination, morale, and civilian defense), there was intermixing of military and civilian officials appointed by the army.

48. Anthony-King correspondence, 1941–42, passim, in the Delegate Samuel W. King Papers, Hawaii State Archives.

49. Paul Murphy was, of course, a major contributor to the scholarship on this theme, especially in his *World War I*, cited earlier; and in *The Meaning of Freedom of Speech: First Amendment Freedoms from Wilson to FDR* (Westport, Conn., 1972).

50. This correspondence is found for the months of January–June 1942 in the ACLU Archives (microfilm edition), Princeton University Library; and the Delegate King Papers, Hawaii State Archives.

51. Neither Anthony nor Stainback believed that extraordinary wartime authority was unnecessary to Hawaii's security. In fact, both of them anticipated that once civilian authority was restored by Washington, or under court order, the governor would exercise at least some of the emergency powers that had been vested in his office in a territorial statute of 1941 known as the Mobilization Day (or M-Day) Act. And once partial restoration did occur, in late 1943, Governor Metzger did in fact invoke some of these wartime emergency executive powers.

52. J. Garner Anthony, "Martial Law in Hawaii," *California Law Review* 30 (1942): 371–96. The *New York Times* report on Anthony's article (clipping in ACLU Archives, Princeton) prompted Roger Baldwin of the ACLU to contact Anthony to ask for more information. Letter from Baldwin to Anthony, May 18, 1942, copy, Hawaii files, ACLU Archives.

53. Archibald King, "The Legality of Martial Law in Hawaii," *California Law Review* 30 (1942): 599. King's expansive view of army authority was modest by contrast with the position taken by the political scientist and lawyer on the Stanford University faculty, Charles Fairman, who was commissioned to serve as special counsel for the Army General Staff, in his scholarly publications of that period arguing that constitutionally the army enjoyed carte blanche both as to the internments and as to martial law. Charles Fairman, "The Law of Martial Rule and the National Emergency," *Harvard Law Review* 55 (1942): 1253–302. Earlier Fairman had written *The Law of Martial Rule* (Chicago, 1930), issued in a second edition in 1943.

54. The importance of Anthony's intellectual contributions and energetic pursuit of the issues was appreciated by his colleagues at the time. See especially a letter from Delegate Farrington asking Anthony to reconsider his resignation as territorial attorney general, stating that Anthony's role had been indispensable in framing the legal questions and leading the debate of martial law. Farrington to Anthony, Dec. 12, 1943, Farrington Delegate Files, Hawaii State Archives.

55. Green's detestation of Anthony is clear from his postwar notation in

his diaries regarding the incident when Anthony, newly appointed as attorney general, demanded the return of the office Green occupied; a contemporary office memorandum by Anthony for confidential office files (in possession of Mrs. Garner Anthony) gave a completely different, and we think much more plausible, account of the meeting.

56. Wiener Report.

57. This incident is recounted and documented in our article "Bayonets in Paradise," 582–87.

58. Authors' interview of Mrs. Anthony, 1993, cited above.

59. These summaries of war service are gathered from material in obituaries and other articles in the newspaper files collection (formerly the "morgue" of the two leading Honolulu papers) in the University of Hawaii Library.

60. This was certainly a major concern of Anthony's and was also expressed by King, Stainback, and others in their correspondence and some public statements, e.g., in letter from King to Ickes, June 17, 1942, copy in McCloy Files, War Department Records, RG 107, National Archives (in which King wrote: "For a civilian community to live for months under what is in effect a military government is detrimental to the maintenance of self-government and repugnant to every principle for which we are fighting"). An army intelligence document in mid-1942 reported on "the deeply rooted suspicion of many Island people, particularly some business and professional and political leaders, . . . that the Federal Government is using martial law as an excuse to foist a commission form of government on Hawaii [replacing the legislature and the governor's office] after the war is over." Political Report to Col. Kendall J. Fielder, G-2: The Governorship of Hawaii, dated July 31, 1942, copy in Green Papers, JAGS. In an oral history interview (August 1999) with the senior author, Senator Hiram Fong stated that the concerns about rising civilian apathy during the war on the matter of home rule were well founded because much of the population was becoming comfortable with having the army control affairs. On the other hand, the intelligence report previously cited here recognized that open criticism of the army was difficult because many "were afraid to be more open," and there was "reluctance to offend the military authorities," specifically (at that moment) with respect to discussion of Stainback's possible appointment as governor to succeed Poindexter.

61. Political leaders in Hawaii regularly referred to multiracial and multicultural society and political life as "the American Way." Hence it was especially significant that when partial restoration of civilian authority was announced in 1943, Farrington issued a press release welcoming the change as marking "reestablishment of the American way in Mid-Pacific territory." Press release, Mar. 9, 1943, titled "Radio," Farrington Delegate Papers, Hawaii State Archives. General Green noted in his diary after a luncheon debate on martial law with Farrington in a private home in 1943 that "his main worry is the form of government which Hawaii will have after the war"; but Green also appended a note afterward stating that Farrington "thoroughly believe[d] in the local Japanese" and that he was "for some reason . . . anti-military." Green Diary, Sept. 16, 1942, Green Papers, JAGS.

62. Thus King declared that he stood prepared to accept the political effects of a whispering campaign against him when he stood publicly against "racial persecution" and intolerance aimed at the Japanese-Americans—victims, as he wrote, of a "vicious and unamerican [*sic*] attitude." King to

Henry L. Hostein, May 14, 1942, copy in King Delegate Papers, Hawaii State Archives. On Farrington, see citation to Green diaries in previous note. Farrington also became a champion of citizenship for Filipinos who served in the home guard in Hawaii, and for Korean Americans in Hawaii (who were treated arbitrarily by the army as Japanese nationals during the war in Hawaii, on grounds they could not be distinguished from Japanese in physical characteristics, and that Korea was under Japanese imperial rule). See, e.g., Farrington to Secretary of War Henry L. Stimson, Nov. 8, 1944, Farrington Delegate Papers, Hawaii State Archives. In Samuel King's case, some adverse reaction to his defense of the Japanese-Americans' loyalty was perhaps one factor in leading him to resign from politics and to join the navy combat forces with a reactivated commission in 1942; in any event, he was disturbed by the criticism, as we know from his correspondence. King's correspondence with political associates, 1941–42, in King Delegate Papers, Hawaii State Archives.

63. See Delegate Samuel W. King to Roger N. Baldwin, Mar. 21, 1942, Hawaii Files, ACLU Archives (microfilm), Princeton University Library. (All further references to the ACLU Archives are to the Hawaii Files.)

64. Farrington-Zimmerman correspondence, 1942, in Delegate Farrington Papers, Hawaii State Archives.

65. Baldwin to A. L. Wirin, Feb. 20, 1942, and Clifford Forster to Wirin, Jan. 18, 1942, ACLU Archives (on information being gathered on Zimmerman); Scheiber and Scheiber, "Bayonets in Paradise," 510–11 (on responses to the Saffrey Brown death sentence).

66. Baldwin to Anthony, May 18, 1942, copy, in ACLU Archives.

67. Anthony to Baldwin, June 3, 1942, ibid.

68. Ibid.

69. W. Wade Boardman, Esq., Madison, Wisconsin, to Arthur Garfield Hays, June 16, 1942, ACLU Archives.

70. Rowe, oral history, Bancroft Library; evidence in Zimmerman civil suit, reported in Honolulu press, December 1950; Baldwin to Lloyd Garrison, Apr. 23, 1942, copy in ACLU Archives.

71. Boardman to Hays, June 16, 1942, ACLU Archives.

72. Clifford Forster to A. L. Wirin, Jan. 18, 1943, ACLU Archives (on board's decision not to proceed with the Zimmerman case until the mediation committee had checked his background).

73. See, e.g., Wirin to Clifford Forster, Sept. 30, 1942, ACLU Archives.

74. Wirin to Forster, June 26, 1942, ibid.

75. Ibid.

76. The course of the Zimmerman litigation is recounted in Anthony, *Hawaii Under Army Rule*, 61–64; and our article "Bayonets in Paradise," 564–67.

77. Forster to Wirin, Jan. 18, 1943, ACLU Archives.

78. Forster to Wirin, Mar. 19, 1943. One of the federal district court judges in Hawaii later deplored the mooting strategy, and more generally the army's "bluffing, stalling, threatening, dodging and evading" in litigation of the martial law cases. Judge J. Frank McLaughlin, address at the Social Science Association of Honolulu, Hawaii, May 6, 1946, transcript on file in the Papers of General Robert Richardson, Hoover Institution Archives. McLaughlin's speech was later published in the *Congressional Record*, Appendix, July 31, 1946, page A4931.

79. *Ex parte Seifert,* U.S. District Court (Hawaii) No. 296; *Ex parte Glockner,* U.S. District Court (Hawaii) No. 295. (Transcripts of record are in the Habeas Case Files, Hawaii Files, Department of Justice Records, Pacific and Sierra Regional Archive, National Archives, San Bruno, California.)

80. Wirin to Forster, Jan. 14, 1943, ACLU Archives.

81. Col. Hughes, Memorandum from Fort Shafter to McCloy, Oct. 14, 1943 (radio message), Oct. 14, 1943, Box 57, McCloy Files, War Department Records, RG 107, National Archives (saying: "[A] Japanese American case would clearly be best test case of internment power which could probably be won on basis of Hirabayashi case which Judge [Metzger] here agrees with"). When the Duncan case appeal was threatened, however, the chief legal officer in the Hawaii command, General Slatterly, was for his own reasons strongly in favor of permitting the case to go forward on appeal to the Supreme Court. To moot once again, he warned, would mean that the issue might be heard by the Court after the fighting had ended, and "the military will have its strongest position politically before the Court while the war is on." He also had a highly self-serving rationale for the strategy he proposed: "The failure on the part of the Army to prosecute [*sic*] these appeals," he wrote, would act as an inducement for further actions or suits against at least some military officers for acts of the military performed at different times during the administration of martial law." Memorandum to Lt. Col. E. V. Slatterly, "Mooting of Duncan, White and Spurlock Cases," Nov. 17, 1944, in "Habeas Corpus" file, Box 44, Hawaii Military Government Records, RG 338, National Archives.

82. Oral history interview with Senator Fong, August 1999.

83. Atherton Richards, Office of Strategic Services report to Colonel Donovan, Aug. 8, 1942, copy in Green Papers, JAGS. A contemporary social science study reported that the typical reaction to internments on the mainland by Hawaiian residents of Japanese ancestry was: "We will be next." Andrew W. Lind, *The Japanese in Hawaii Under War Conditions,* Institute of Pacific Relations Paper No. 5 (Honolulu, 1943). How anxiety in the community over possible army measures translated into an entire absence of initiative by even a single internee to take legal actions is a question that probably cannot be resolved definitively.

84. Authors' telephone oral history interview with John P. Frank; files of Frank's correspondence with Fortas, 1946, Department of the Interior Records, RG 48, National Archives.

85. Scheiber and Scheiber, "Bayonets in Paradise," 573–76.

86. Oral history interview of Edward Ennis, Dec. 20, 1972, transcript in Regional Oral History Collection, Bancroft Library, UC Berkeley.

87. As we have noted earlier, not all the army lawyers agreed on this crucial issue. In particular, in October 1942 and again in mid-1943, the judge advocate general of the army, Major General Myron Cramer, intervened when the army command in Honolulu made the claim of final authority over the federal courts, advising the War Department that this was not only an affront to the judiciary but plainly "a claim of doubtful legality." Cramer to Asst. Secretary of War, Oct. 23, 1942 (confidential), File 370.8, McCloy Files, War Department Records, RG 107, National Archives.

88. A caveat must be entered as to Solicitor General Fahy. As Peter Irons revealed in his research on the Japanese-American cases, Fahy was responsible for keeping from the Court the evidence of FBI reports asserting that

there was no evidence to support the army's claim of a military need (because of espionage and sabotage of shipping) for evacuation of the Japanese-Americans from the West Coast in 1942. See Irons, *Justice at War,* 280ff.

89. See text above, at note 1.

90. Ennis to General Richardson, memorandum, n.d., but September or October 1943, Robert C. Richardson Papers, Hoover Institution Archives, Stanford. Presumably the Judge Patterson referred to was Robert Patterson, then in the War Department hierarchy and later successor as secretary to Henry L. Stimson.

91. Ibid. For a full discussion of this episode, see our "Bayonets in Paradise," 570–78.

92. Charles Fahy to John J. McCloy, Oct. 9, 1943, Box 57, McCloy Files, War Department Records, RG 107, National Archives.

93. RNB [Roger N. Baldwin] to Wirin, Feb. 20, 1942, copy in ACLU Archives.

94. Anthony, *Hawaii Under Army Rule,* 122.

95. Anthony to General Richardson, Aug. 26, 1943, Hawaii Military Government Records, National Archives.

96. "Memorandum from Major General Cramer (The Judge Advocate General) to the Assistant Secretary of War, Subject; Change in General Order 135, Office of the Military Governor of Hawaii," Oct. 3, 1942, marked "Confidential," in McCloy Files, War Department Records, RG 107, National Archives.

97. Other prominent figures also became involved, with General Marshall in the loop and presumably the White House staff as well. This is clear especially from the correspondence of Richardson with General Julius Ochs Adler, August–October 1943, in the Hawaii Military Government Records, RG 338, National Archives.

98. Wiener Report.

99. See Anthony's book *Hawaii Under Army Rule,* passim, for numerous critical references to the attitude of army lawyers and the military's posture on the need for complete regimentation.

100. Morrison to Green, July 31, 1947, Green Papers, JAGS. (Morrison was then an officer of Theo. H. Davies & Co., Far East, Ltd., one of the Hawaii "Five Families" web of companies.) It is also worth noting that Green promoted the idea that the Hawaii command's techniques for administering a military regime in the Islands ought to be recognized as a model for postwar occupation regimes in Germany and other defeated nations. He pursued the idea in correspondence with top army brass and offered to bring officers out to Hawaii to be trained in occupation governance policies and administration. See, e.g., correspondence of Green with General C. W. Wickersham, Commandant, War Department School of Military Government, October 1942, in Green Papers, JAGS.

101. Anthony, *Hawaii Under Army Rule,* 98–99; Wiener Report; Ickes to John J. McCloy, Aug. 9, 1943, Hawaii File, Secretary of the Interior Records, Harold Ickes Papers, Library of Congress; Fortas to McCloy, Nov. 16, 1944, McCloy Files, War Department Records, RG 107, National Archives.

102. See note 87 on Judge Advocate General Cramer and his role.

103. Green to Morrison, Jan. 2, 1943, Box 65, Hawaii Military Government Records, RG 3338, National Archives.

104. Col. William J. Hughes Jr., JAGD, Memorandum for the Secretary of

War, Subj: "Reasons why martial law in Hawaii should be terminated by proclamation of the President, not of the Governor," Aug. 1, 1944, attached to letter from Ickes to President Roosevelt, Aug. 5, 1942, in McCloy Files, Box 57, War Department Records, RG 107, National Archives (copy also in Box 32, Hawaii Military Government Records, RG 338, National Archives).

105. See text above, at note 98, on Wiener and his report.

106. Richardson Memorandum for Secretary of War (endorsed "Approved by Secretary Robert Patterson"), May 3, 1946, copy in Papers of General Robert C. Richardson, Box 25, Hoover Institution Archives.

107. Green to Harry F. Hossock, Mar. 31, 1948, Green Papers, JAGS.

108. Memorandum for General Green, Subject: "Martial Law in Hawaii—Contents of Mr. McCloy's Files," Mar. 14, 1946, in Green Papers, JAGS.

109. Ibid.

110. See our "Bayonets in Paradise," 522, 535, 554 et passim.

111. Copies of the broadcast transcripts are in the Green Papers, JAGS.

112. *Congressional Record,* Appendix, A 1699 (Mar. 25, 1946) (emphasis added). The original draft manuscript is in the Green Papers, JAGS. Anthony would later comment that these arguments "disclose a lack of knowledge of the facts, and, what is even more remarkable for an able lawyer [Patterson], a lack of familiarity with the opinion of the Supreme Court which he quoted." Anthony, *Hawaii Under Army Rule,* 98.

113. Memorandum for Chief, Bureau of Public Relations, WD, SS, n.d., Green Papers, JAGS.

114. Ibid.

115. In 1950, the bill was still pending while the district court in Honolulu was trying a damage suit instituted by the internee Hans Zimmerman; and the judge charged the jury to disregard in its deliberations any knowledge of, or contentions in the trial regarding, the possible payment of damages to Zimmerman by action of Congress. "Testimony in Zimmerman Damage Suit Concluded," *Honolulu Star-Bulletin,* Dec. 20, 1950. Seven years later, Delegate John A. Burns would introduce a bill for payment to Zimmerman of $107,598 as compensation for his internment, and possibly Zimmerman had hopes of such a private bill being introduced in 1950; but the present authors can find no information of it. "Burns Offers Bill . . . ," *Honolulu Advertiser,* clipping marked "February 1957," in University of Hawaii Library newspaper files archive.

116. Emmons correspondence with the War Department, 1946–50, passim, Hawaii files, Emmons Papers, Hoover Institution; Richardson correspondence with friends and lawyers, and with the War Department, 1946–51, passim, Richardson Papers, Hoover Institution.

117. The trial was followed daily in the Honolulu newspapers.

118. "No Verdict Yet," *Honolulu Star-Bulletin,* Dec. 22, 1950.

119. "After 21 Hours, Jurors Still Without Zimmerman Case Verdict," *Honolulu Star-Bulletin,* Dec. 22, 1950.

120. Oral history interview with Senator Fong, August 1999.

121. Watumull Foundation oral history interview with Gardner Anthony, Nov. 12, 1971, copy in Hawaii State Library.

122. Reference is to Anthony, *Hawaii Under Army Rule,* published by the Stanford University Press.

123. Notations in diaries and other notes and memorandums, in the Green Papers, JAGS.

124. Based on a search of known former internees' names in the files of the *Honolulu Advertiser* and the *Star-Bulletin,* University of Hawaii Library microfiche collection. The memory of martial law was poorly served by historians in the years that followed. See Scheiber and Scheiber, "Bayonets in Paradise," 484–85n. Publication of Anthony's book by the Stanford University Press stirred some interest in the Hawaii newspaper press, as had the appearance earlier of Gwenfread Allen's classic historical volume, *Hawaii's War Years, 1941–1945* (Honolulu, 1950), a compendious social history derived from the vast collection of documents in the Hawaii War Records Depository, now held in the University of Hawaii Library and still an indispensable source for the subject. But until the last decade, there has been only occasional and little noticed study of any aspect of Hawaii's martial law period, and even the *Duncan Case* has rarely, if ever, been excerpted or even cited in constitutional treatises and casebooks. At least on the mainland, even scholarly audiences at lecture and seminar presentations of this chapter's research have generally been entirely unaware of any aspect of the history presented here.

*Chapter Six*

# Constitutional Equality for Women: Losing the Battle but Winning the War

Cynthia Harrison

In 1923, three years after the Suffrage Amendment had been ratified, the National Woman's Party (NWP) decided to seek an amendment to the Constitution guaranteeing full legal equality for women. The NWP believed itself impelled toward this strategy by the refusal of the U.S. Supreme Court to find that the Fourteenth Amendment extended its promise of "equal protection" to women. Some five decades later, a revitalized women's movement won both congressional support for the Equal Rights Amendment (ERA) and a pronouncement from the Supreme Court that women could indeed rely upon the Fourteenth Amendment. In 1982, the attempt to ratify the amendment failed, but the Court continued to offer succor to women plaintiffs from invidious distinctions in the law, using not the "strict scrutiny" it applied to racial categorizations but a "heightened scrutiny" that it developed to consider sex-based categories. In addition, relying upon its power to regulate commerce, Congress enacted a variety of measures that eliminated much of the bias in law that the NWP had targeted initially when it proposed a new constitutional amendment. State legislatures similarly added new provisions to their state codes, mirroring the new commitment to equal treatment on the federal level. By 1996, Associate Justice Antonin Scalia, in a lone dissent, accused his colleagues on the Supreme Court of imposing a new standard for sex-based differentiation in the law indistinguishable from the rigid scrutiny applied to racial categories. Perhaps the goal of constitutional equality for women had been reached.

This chapter argues that the jurisprudence of sex-based discrimination under the Fourteenth Amendment, along with statutory changes on the federal and state level, has largely fulfilled the expectations of the proponents of the Equal Rights Amendment. As of 2000, the Court had provided sufficient legal foundation to satisfy in many respects both its original proponents in 1923 and even those feminists who in 1972 succeeded in winning the support of Congress for the amendment. Moreover, the "intermediate scrutiny" that the Supreme Court fashioned would accommodate sex-based differences of which even many feminists approve. It is unlikely that adjudication would have differed materially even with the addition of the ERA to the Constitution. By the end of the century, in fact, even feminists had decided that history had overtaken the old amendment: in 1995, the National Organization for Women advanced a much more comprehensive—and politically daring—constitutional equality amendment, claiming rather than disclaiming coverage for gay men and women and a right to abortion. As in the past, future decisions on the nature of constitutional equality will turn more on effective political activism of women and on judicial politics than on specific constitutional text.

## Early Decisions

In 1923, the National Woman's Party had only a handful of Supreme Court decisions concerning sex to assess in determining the next suitable step toward women's full constitutional rights, but the few decisions had powerfully confined women's ambit. During congressional consideration of the Fourteenth and Fifteenth Amendments to the Constitution, women's rights activists tried hard to get a guarantee of suffrage for women included within their mandates; short of that objective, they sought at least to prevent the addition of the word "male" to the Constitution in the text of the Fourteenth Amendment. They failed on both scores. Once the amendments were part of the Constitution, women tried to insinuate themselves within the new legal protection, but the Court proved no more sympathetic than Congress had.

In 1873, Myra Bradwell, a legal publisher in Illinois, presented the court's first sex discrimination question. Legally trained, she wished to practice as a lawyer, an opportunity the Illinois Supreme Court denied her in part because, as a married woman, she could not make contracts without her husband's assent. Bradwell claimed that the "privileges and immunities" clause of the Fourteenth Amendment required the state to grant her request. The U.S. Supreme Court held that admission to a state bar was not a privilege or immunity of United States citizenship and therefore the Fourteenth Amendment protection did not apply. More discouraging, however, Justice Joseph Bradley's concurring opinion explicating the 8-1 decision did not merely cite federal impotence to overturn the Illinois decision; it went on to endorse the separation of the spheres that had motivated the Illinois judgment:

> Man is, or should be, woman's protector and defender. The natural and proper timidity and delicacy which belongs to the female sex evidently unfits it for many of the occupations of civil life. . . . The harmony, not to say identity, of interests and views which belong, or should belong to the family institution is repugnant to the idea of a woman adopting a distinct and independent career from that of her husband. So firmly fixed was this sentiment in the founders of the common law that it became a maxim of that system of jurisprudence that a woman had no legal existence separate from her husband. . . . The paramount destiny and mission of woman are to fulfil the noble and benign offices of wife and mother. This is the law of the Creator. And the rules of civil society must be adapted to the general constitution of things.[1]

Such understanding of the basis of state law did not bode well for women making egalitarian claims. The following year, Virginia Minor's argument that suffrage should be construed as a privilege of citizenship and states should not therefore deny it on the basis of sex fell easily before both the Court's narrow construction of privileges and immunities and its view of women's place under natural law.[2]

The arbitrary sexism of Bradley's reasoning in the Bradwell case and the dismissal of Minor's claim to suffrage might have easily sustained the argument that women required the protection of an equal rights amendment, but the question was complicated by the seeming benevolence of the Court's early twentieth-century opinions concerning labor legislation that protected women. After the 1905 decision in *Lochner v. New York*,[3] wherein the Court struck down a state law limiting hours and cited a due process "right to contract" that states could not restrict, reformers feared that the Court would invalidate any law regulating working conditions. Thus, progressive reformers were relieved when the Court in *Muller v. Oregon* (1908)[4] let stand an Oregon statute that prohibited employers from requiring women to work in factories or laundries for more than ten hours a day.

The outcome represented an entering wedge into state regulation of work and permitted states to protect the women whom they believed to be inherently weaker workers than men; the protection seemed more important to women's well-being than a statement of legal equality. The famous brief submitted by Louis Brandeis, then lawyer for the National Consumers' League (NCL), founded its argument on precisely the same reasoning Bradley had earlier expounded in *Bradwell*, and the Court repeated the NCL's assertions in its opinion. In sum, the Court asserted, "Differentiated . . . from the other sex, [woman] is properly placed in a class by herself, and legislation designed for her protection may be sustained, even when like legislation is not necessary for men and could not be sustained."[5] Although the Court did uphold hours laws for male workers within the decade,[6] it did not renounce its earlier holding that state law could still place woman "in a class by herself." This view engaged the support not only of the Court but also of myriad women's organizations.

## The Next Amendment

Thus, although the Nineteenth Amendment to the Constitution in 1920 explicitly guaranteed women the right to vote, it left standing a universe of state legislation that delimited women's world. Confronted by this state of affairs, the National Woman's Party, the militant wing of the suffrage movement, decided in 1921 to broach a new amendment that would sweep away legal constraints even without the cooperation of the Supreme Court. Initially, the NWP hoped to accommodate the advocates of protective labor legislation and retain those laws that benefited women workers by preventing the bitterest forms of exploitation; indeed, many NWP members had fought to achieve such statutes. But the argument for both equal rights and special treatment collapsed under the weight of its internal contradiction as a legal principle and the resulting difficulties in wording such an amendment and in implementing such a policy.

After almost two years of discussion and a sobering demonstration of a state effort to both guarantee equality and safeguard protections,[7] the NWP elected to pursue straight legal equality. It unveiled its proposed amendment at the party's national conference in July 1923. It read: "Men and women shall have equal rights throughout the United States and every place subject to its jurisdiction,"[8] and the party adopted it unanimously. To those who cited women's need for labor laws, the party responded at first that such laws should apply to both men and women and later that state interference in private labor contracts was undesirable. According to the party's counsel, Burnita Shelton Matthews (an attorney who in 1949 would become the first woman federal district court judge), "Protective legislation that includes women but exempts men handicaps women's economic advancement. It limits the woman worker's scope of activity and increases that of the man by barring her from certain occupations, by excluding her from employments at night, and by 'protecting' her to such an extent as to render her ineffective as a competitor."[9]

Ironically, a Supreme Court opinion issued April 9 of that very year adopted in one area precisely the position the NWP hoped for. Portions of the Court's opinion, written by Justice George Sutherland for a 5-3 majority in a case concerning a minimum wage law for women, could have been drafted by the legal committee of the NWP (which had in fact worked with lawyers behind the scenes.)[10] It appeared that, in the face of the Nineteenth Amendment, the Court had thrown over its nineteenth-century view of women. In *Adkins v. Children's Hospital,*[11] the justices enunciated a new view of woman:

> The [*Muller*] decision proceeded upon the theory that the difference between the sexes may justify a different rule respecting the hours of labor in the case of women than in the case of men. It is pointed out that these consist in difference of physical structure. . . . But the ancient inequality of the sexes, otherwise than physical, as suggested in the *Muller* case . . . has continued "with diminishing intensity." In view of the great—not to say revolutionary—changes which have taken place since that utterance, in the contractual, political and civil status of women, culminating in the Nineteenth Amendment, it is not unreasonable to say that these differences have now come almost, if not quite, to the vanishing point. In this aspect of the matter, while the physical differences must be recognized in appropriate cases, and legislation fixing hours or conditions of work may properly take them into account, we cannot accept the doctrine that women of mature age, *sui juris,* require or may be subjected to restrictions upon their liberty of contract which could not lawfully be imposed in the case of men under similar circumstances. To do so would be to ignore all the implications to be drawn from the present day trend of legislation, as well as that of common thought and usage, by which woman is accorded emancipation from the old doctrine that she must be given special protection or be subjected to special restraint in her contractual and civil relationships.

After discussing and dismissing the arguments in favor of a minimum wage in general, the Court noted in addition that it found the sex distinction itself spurious: "[N]or is there ground for distinction between women and men, for, certainly, if women require a minimum wage to preserve their morals men require it to preserve their honesty." The Court further placed men and women upon an equal plane with respect to the fruits of their labor: "The ethical right of every worker, man or woman, to a living wage may be conceded." Justice Taft in his dissent pointed out that, whatever the impact of the Nineteenth Amendment on the political power of women, it in no way changed the physiology upon which the decision in *Muller* rested, and Justice Holmes, also in dissent, scoffed that "[i]t will need more than the Nineteenth Amendment to convince me that there are no differences between men and women, or that legislation cannot take those differences into account."

But the holding made manifest the difficulty in considering women equal in the courtroom when they were not equal in the streets. The NWP's elation over the *Adkins* decision, in contrast to the horror of the National Consumers' League and other progressive women's groups, drew into sharp focus the division between the seekers of the ERA and the defenders of sex distinctions in the law. It was a division that was to last almost five decades longer.

Complicating the issue was the fact that the Court did not prove to be a reliable ally for proponents of legal equality. Although the Court defended a woman's right to contract with respect to her wages, it also upheld state laws that limited her ability to work at night.[12] The NWP determined to provide the explicit direction of a federal amendment, as the only efficient and permanent way to bring about the result it desired.

An extensive list of state and federal laws that discriminated arbitrarily against women served as the foundation of the party's argument in favor of an equal rights amendment to the Constitution. To create this definitive listing, the party appointed a legal team of twelve attorneys headed by Burnita Shelton Matthews. Matthews and her staff conducted an exhaustive investigation of state codes and deployed the research in support of both state-specific and national campaigns to repeal such laws and to urge the adoption of the federal amendment that would eliminate them in a single stroke. Included among the problems Matthews and her staff identified as "typical of those existing throughout the country" were Georgia rulings that the wages of a married woman belonged to her husband; laws in New Mexico and Nevada that permitted husbands but not wives who predeceased their spouses to will away half of the community property; a Texas statute that permitted husbands but not wives to divorce on the grounds of spousal adultery; a Florida law that permitted fathers but not mothers to collect damages for the negligent death of a child; a West Virginia law in which the father was the sole heir to the property of a child dying intestate and without descendants; and federal citizenship laws that nullified the citizenship only of an American woman who married an alien ineligible for American citizenship.

Other inequities in the law that concerned party members included exclusion of women from jury service in most state courts and therefore in federal courts (which followed state practices); barriers against women holding state office; domicile laws that permitted husbands to determine residence and made wives guilty of desertion if they refused to relocate; state pay scales for women teachers that paid them less than male teachers received; and state laws that limited the capacity of married women to conduct business (Miriam A. ["Ma"] Ferguson, governor of Texas, required her husband's consent to remove her disabilities as a married woman so that her actions as governor would not be called into question). The party also incorporated in its list laws that punished prostitutes but not their clients and legislation that prevented women from having "the same right to the control of their persons as men," meaning in this case access to contraception.[13] Most of the laws they targeted were state laws, since federal reach in the 1920s remained limited. One of the few federal problems they cited concerned the disparity in citizenship, particularly the loss of citizenship that obtained when an American woman married a foreign national (by virtue of a 1907 law) and the consequent inability of an American mother to convey U.S. citizenship to her children, as could a man married to a foreign national.[14] NWP members objected as well to the discriminatory practices in education and business that harmed women: exclusions from professional schools, unequal pay scales, businesses that would not hire women or that would hire them only for low-level positions. The party recognized that the ERA would not actually touch all these areas, but its members maintained that enshrining the principle in fundamental law would influence other institutions to accept equality.

Several of the women's organizations that opposed the ERA nevertheless supported many of these goals. They advocated a strategy that called for "specific bills for specific ills," which would target problems in the law but leave untouched legislation they deemed helpful to women, especially to the poorest working women. This strategy worked at least with respect to citizenship laws. In 1922,

Congress amended the worst of the provisions and then refined the legislation in the following decade.[15]

But the NWP could not accept a law-by-law battle, which its leaders believed would take too long and would in the end prove too uncertain. The party sought a federal amendment rather than federal or state legislation or court rulings because the amendment "would establish the principle of equal rights once and for all, insofar as anything can be permanently established by law." More than any other device, Burnita Matthews insisted,

> it would override the present discriminatory legislation and prevent the sustaining of such legislation in the future. On the other hand, should equal rights obtain only by virtue of statutes, then the continued existence of equal rights would be subject to the will of each Congress, and each successive legislature in 48 states. . . . To change one by one the state constitutional provisions, and the other multitude of laws, that hold women in subjection, would take a century or so of work. . . . And if equal rights were ever attained by this piece-work-plan, the result would be only an unstable equality which, for the most part, could be easily overthrown. On the contrary, if the equal rights principle were written in to the National Constitution, it would be a part of the supreme law of the land, and with the other fundamental principles of our government, would be protected from sudden or violent fluctuations in public opinion. So it is clear that a national amendment is by far the surest, quickest and most inexpensive method of securing the equality of men and women before the law.[16]

Said NWP founder Alice Paul, "We shall not be safe until the principle of equal rights is written into the framework of our Government."[17]

Between 1923 and 1970, differential treatment by sex came before the Court on very few occasions, and the Court ruled so inconsistently that egalitarians used these decisions as confirmation of the need for a clear directive. Ironically, the Court provided the possibility of a rapprochement among advocates for women in 1941, when it upheld a federal minimum wage/maximum hour law for both men and women. This decision, *Darby v.*

*U.S.*,[18] came only four years after two conflicting sex-based minimum wages cases, *Morehead v. NY ex rel. Tipaldo*[19] and *Parrish v. West Coast Hotel*,[20] the first striking down a New York law (a 5-4 decision), and the second upholding a Washington state law (also a 5-4 decision), both minimum wage laws applying only to women. After the *Darby* decision, it was no longer necessary to argue that state labor laws had of necessity to be limited to female workers in order to pass constitutional muster, but the new ruling did not change the old strategy of the proponents of laws for women only. They argued both that sex-specific laws were easier to enact and that women continued to be more vulnerable as workers. Male-dominated labor unions preferred that their workers see organization rather than legislation as the primary route for improvement of working conditions and continued to favor laws that pertained only to women. So long as the Court countenanced sex-specific laws, a position it had affirmed in the *Parrish* ruling, women's advocates would continue to divide on the question of strict legal equality.

Though the ruling in *Darby* did not drastically change the alignment of support around the ERA, the politics of World War II increased the number of its supporters, as had the widespread discrimination against married women during the Great Depression. The ERA had been introduced into Congress every year by a sympathetic member of Congress, but not until 1942, with the war under way, did a congressional committee report it favorably to the floor. Both the position of the United States as the avatar of democracy and the valor women displayed as workers and military personnel made their exclusion from protection of fundamental law seem both embarrassing and unfair. The amendment's first floor vote, in the Senate in 1946, drew a majority of the votes, although not the two-thirds needed.[21]

Had women's organizations coalesced around the amendment, its passage at least through Congress would likely have succeeded, but the increased support for the amendment spurred its opponents to new heights in defense of sex-specific labor laws. The breach over labor legislation created a peculiar alignment of pro-business Republicans and Southern Democrats in favor of the ERA (and the elimination of protective labor laws), with most liberals opposed to the equality measure. With the assistance of Senator

Carl Hayden (D-Ariz.), the opponents hit upon an effective blockade: at every floor vote, the senator would offer his proviso, that the ERA would not "impair any rights, benefits, or exemptions now or hereafter conferred by law, upon persons of the female sex." In 1950 and 1953, delighted to be able to vote for both equal treatment for women and special protection, the Senate duly added the Hayden rider to the ERA; ERA supporters then killed the bill.[22]

Meanwhile, the Supreme Court gave with one hand and took with the other. Writing for the majority in 1946, Justice William O. Douglas instructed the federal courts in California to include women as jurors in keeping with state law, rather than following the state practice that excluded women. In *Ballard v. United States,* Douglas explained:

> It is said . . . that an all male panel drawn from the various groups within the community will be as truly representative as if women were included. The thought is that factors which tend to influence the action of women are the same as those which influence the action of men—personality, background, economic status—and not sex. Yet it is not enough to say that women when sitting as jurors neither act nor tend to act as a class. Men likewise do not act as a class. But, if the shoe were on the other foot, who would claim that a jury was truly representative of the community if all men were intentionally and systematically excluded from the panel? The truth is that the two sexes are not fungible; a community made up exclusively of one is different from a community composed of both. . . . The exclusion of one may indeed make the jury less representative of the community than would be true if an economic or racial group were excluded.[23]

Then, in 1948, the Court gave aid and comfort to those who would limit women's sphere of action, supporting the NWP's view that advocates of protective labor laws for women served chiefly their own interests. In *Goesaert v. Cleary,*[24] the Court upheld a Michigan law that banned the employment of women as bartenders unless the woman was the wife or daughter of the owner. The law responded not to the notion that it was unsafe for a woman to be a bartender per se, since relatives of bar owners could perform the function. It did not speak to bars as unsavory locales for women workers, since it did not ban women waitressing in bars. It merely preserved the general occupation of bartending for men, an objective sought by unionized bartenders in Michigan. The mockery in Justice Felix Frankfurter's opinion eliminated any notion that the Court was in the least concerned about justice for women: "Beguiling as the subject is, it need not detain us long. To ask whether or not the Equal Protection of the Laws Clause of the Fourteenth Amendment barred Michigan from making the classification the state has made between wives and daughters of owners of liquor places and wives and daughters of nonowners, is one of those rare instances where to state the question is in effect to answer it." (The answer, for modern readers to whom it might not appear so obvious, was no.) Three justices (Rutledge, Douglas, and Murphy) demurred in dissent that the Fourteenth Amendment "does require lawmakers to refrain from invidious distinctions of the sort drawn by the statute challenged in this case."

Although Congress revised qualifications for federal jurors in 1957, making them sex-neutral and disconnecting them from the practice of the state courts, the Supreme Court continued to uphold state jury exclusions, *Ballard* to the contrary notwithstanding. In *Hoyt v. Florida,* a 1961 case that addressed the question of whether a woman defendant could receive a fair trial if the jury had no women, the Court let stand a Florida practice that placed women in the pool of jurors only upon their specific request. The Court decided that the process was sound, because "woman is still regarded as the center of home and family life."[25] The NWP thus continued confirmed in its belief that without explicit language in the Constitution, women could not count on the U.S. Supreme Court to protect their right to be free from arbitrary distinctions in the law.

## New Support

If the fifteen years following the end of the war introduced little in the way of constitutional change for women, their own economic decisions altered the social landscape. The opportunities provided by both the war and the explosion of jobs in the sectors employing women during the 1950s made the waged work of married mothers commonplace. Like men, though in smaller numbers, women took advantage of federally funded educational opportunities so that by the time of the election of John Kennedy, the stresses in the family-work dynamic had become visible enough to warrant national examination. Kennedy accepted the suggestion that he appoint a national commission to explore the status of women (in part to deflate support for the ERA). That commission, however, established four decades after the NWP first proposed a new amendment to guarantee constitutional equality, helped reignite a new women's movement, soon to be united in support of constitutional equality.

In its final report, the President's Commission on the Status of Women acknowledged the need for and the justice of a constitutional guarantee of equal protection under law. It favored a Supreme Court holding to this effect rather than the adoption of the Equal Rights Amendment, anticipating that the Court would know when to discard, and when to retain, laws that distinguished men from women. The commissioners hoped by this stratagem to preserve sensible laws that differentiated appropriately by sex (they had in mind certain labor laws) and to jettison the legislation that promoted invidious distinctions. This position represented a carefully drawn compromise, since the commission's creators in fact opposed the ERA. But by favoring a Constitution-based equal protection of the law and by encouraging women's organizations to develop a case crafted as deliberately as *Brown v. Board of Education* (explicitly the model), the commission redirected energy away from the divisive amendment and toward a conclusive determination of whether the Court could be won over. The NWP saw the entire operation as a dodge and announced it would continue to pursue the ERA, pointing to the recalcitrance the Court had already demonstrated. It did not, however, oppose in principle an ongoing effort to persuade the Court to bring women under the purview of the Fourteenth Amendment.[26]

The commission's work generated a new level of concern and activism focused on women's status. In gathering information to inform its wide-ranging recommendations, the commission accumulated copious documentation of the many disabilities women confronted on account of their sex. State commissions worked in tandem with the federal commission, and the federal government, having created a network of women informed about women's situation, inspired further momentum by holding annual national meetings in Washington.

The creation of a new women's movement, based on these component parts, occurred after Congress in 1964 unexpectedly yielded to pressure from National Woman's Party activists (working through Congressman Howard Smith [D-Va.], an ERA supporter) and the National Federation of Business and Professional Women's Clubs to include women in civil rights legislation barring discrimination in employment based on race.[27] In lobbying for such legislation, activists used the information the President's Commission had collected (although the President's Commission had called a legislative ban premature). A ban on sex discrimination in employment immediately threw into question the status of state labor laws that applied only to women. The Equal Employment Opportunity Commission (EEOC), the agency created by Congress to enforce Title VII of the 1964 Civil Rights Act, found itself in the middle of the long-standing battle, but within five years the issue had resolved itself. Federal courts held that the federal legislation superseded any state law, and, though employers might comply with both, they could not protect themselves against a charge of discrimination by citing a state labor law. Although some of the old guard argued futilely in favor of retaining sex-specific laws, by and large feminists agreed that labor laws should apply to both male and female workers, a contention that few now disputed. The EEOC likewise adopted this position in August 1969,[28] and the old bone of contention was finally buried. With its interment came swift unanimity among women's organizations behind a constitutional amendment.

The demands of the new women's movement overlapped with the older agenda of the National Woman's Party, thrilled to have fresh recruits. However, the NWP did not share all the enthusiasms of the new feminists. In particular, it disliked the emphasis on abortion rights, fearful that it would create a fatal association for the amendment. The new feminists, in fact, diverged from the NWP in key ways, particularly concerning the link between women and children. Although the NWP supported economic autonomy for women, it did not endorse androgyny, and it continued to view children as a woman's special responsibility, albeit one that could be acquitted in many ways.

But the burgeoning women's movement quickly outpaced the older and now positively staid NWP, inciting change in the lower federal courts, in state and federal legislatures, and in state courts at an amazing pace. In 1966, as the result of American Civil Liberties Union (ACLU) litigation, a three-judge federal district court in Alabama threw out the state's jury service law, which barred women from jury duty, citing the Fourteenth Amendment: "The plain effect of this constitutional provision is to prohibit prejudicial disparities before the law. This means prejudicial disparities for all citizens—including women."[29] The state declined to appeal. In 1968, a federal district court in Connecticut declared unconstitutional longer prison terms for women than for men convicted of the same crimes.[30] In 1970, courts in Illinois and New Jersey eliminated bans against women bartenders (virtually the same restriction upheld in *Goesaert v. Cleary*).[31] And that same year, a federal district court in Virginia endorsed the proposal to open Mr. Jefferson's university to coeducation, citing the equal protection clause of the Fourteenth Amendment.[32] It was a sign of the times that these decisions were not appealed to the Supreme Court, with the institutions instead capitulating to the changing legal standard. Even where courts upheld discriminatory practices, as did the Mississippi court in 1966 with the state's male-only jury law, legislatures acted to remove the disability; Mississippi amended its code in 1968.[33] In 1961, Wisconsin had become the first state to prohibit discrimination in employment within the state;[34] by 1973, the ACLU found only eleven states (eight of them in the South) without state fair employment practices (FEP) laws that included protection against sex discrimination. (By 1983, nine states still had no FEP law, all southern except North Dakota; only Georgia had an FEP law that did not include sex bias.)

Congressional resistance to the ERA dissolved in the face of the new consensus. Under the guidance of Representative Martha Griffiths (D-Mich.), a longtime proponent of equality for women, in 1970 the House of Representatives discharged the House Judiciary Committee from further consideration of the ERA, breaking the choke hold on the amendment of Representative Emanuel Celler

(D-N.Y.), the committee's chair. In the Senate, seventy-eight senators cosponsored, including Robert Dole (R-Kans.), James O. Eastland (D-Miss.), Strom Thurmond (D-S.C.), Barry Goldwater (R-Ariz.), and George McGovern (D-N.D.). In March 1972, ERA advocates succeeded with dispatch in winning the two-thirds vote in both houses of Congress, and without any qualifying provisions for the amendment that now read: "Equality of rights under the law shall not be denied or abridged by the United States or by any State on account of sex."[35] The state of Hawaii ratified the amendment on the first day it went to the states, March 22, 1972. The alacrity of the response justified Calvin Coolidge's remark to Alice Paul in 1923 that Congress would approve the ERA if American women really wanted it.[36]

With newly sympathetic legislatures and courts, what did modern feminists seek in the ERA? Feminist representatives described a wide array of desired legal changes. Writing in March 1970, the Citizens' Advisory Council on the Status of Women, now fully in the ERA camp, cited, among others, equal coverage of labor laws; equal access to social security for dependents of women; alimony available to men; elimination of the presumption in the law that the mother is the better parent; equalization of grounds for divorce; equal control over marital property for wives in community property states; elimination of preferences in inheritance laws that favored male heirs and administrators; removal of impediments to women regarding jury service and extension to men of grounds for excuse from serving; equal treatment in the military, including eligibility for the draft and elimination of barriers to women within the services (recognizing the right of the military to assign individual soldiers based on ability).[37]

At Senate committee hearings held in May 1970, numerous feminists expressed their goals for the amendment and pointed to many specific legal outcomes. Brenda Feigen Fasteau, a graduate of the Harvard Law School and legislative vice president of the National Organization for Women, the amendment's primary supporter, advised the committee:

> [The equal rights] amendment will have the general legal effect of forcing governmental employers who treat men and women differently to prove that such treatment has a functional

> justification. The amendment will also prohibit discrimination in all other situations involving Federal and State action.
>
> After the Constitution is amended the presumption will be that every difference in treatment between men and women is prima facie discrimination, rebuttable only by a showing that such treatment is functionally necessary. . . . At present, although a woman is theoretically guaranteed against discrimination by the equal protection clause of the Fourteenth Amendment, it is she who must prove that laws and practices, which allegedly protect her, in fact harm her and hold her back from using all her talents. . . . Less tangible, but maybe even more important for the future of our country, is the effect that the equal rights amendment will have on the general attitudes and beliefs about women that Americans hold. . . . Passage of the . . . amendment will indicate to the American people that the rampant oppression of women in this country is real, widespread, and not a subject for humor.[38]

Aileen Hernandez, NOW's president, argued that the ERA would create a "clear national policy that women should not be discriminated against" and in doing so would help in the enforcement of sex discrimination statutes in employment and would generally open to women "the kind of first class citizenship which will permit them early in life to make career choices that are not now available."[39]

The expansion of federal judicial power since the 1920s led new feminists to argue even more strongly than had the NWP about the intersection between the goals of the ERA and definitive Supreme Court pronouncement concerning the protection afforded by the Fourteenth Amendment. Noted Martha Griffiths: "All this amendment asks could easily be done without the amendment if the Supreme Court were willing to do it, but they are not."[40] Celebrated feminist author and NOW founder Betty Friedan asserted:

> I do not think that the equal rights amendment is sufficient to complete this revolution [of sexual equality], but it is necessary. It is necessary because the Constitution which is the doc-

> ument that embodies our conscience, our American conscience, our morality and governs in many ways . . . our behavior and our institutions, our Constitution has not yet been unequivocally interpreted to include women as people, to define women as people.[41]

Perhaps the definitive assessment of the impact and benefits of the Equal Rights Amendment appeared in the *Yale Law Journal* in April 1971, a collaboration between three women law students (Barbara Brown, Gail Falk, and Ann Freedman) identified as "active in the women's movement" and Yale law professor Thomas Emerson. These analysts also argued that the Court's refusal to apply the Fourteenth Amendment to sex discrimination—most recently in affirming a lower court decision permitting the state of South Carolina to maintain two public sex-segregated colleges—mandated pursuit of a constitutional amendment.[42] "There are no signs of theoretical or practical developments that would sweep the Supreme Court in a bold new direction," they observed. "[A]ny present hope for large-scale change can hardly be deemed realistic."[43] Similarly, efforts to change the laws in every state "would require a tremendously expensive, sophisticated, and sustained political organization" and "could drag on for many years."[44] Moreover, equal protection doctrine was not adequate to the task of guaranteeing equality of rights for women even if the court were to adopt it; thus, "[a]n unambiguous mandate with the prospect of permanence is needed to assure prompt compliance."[45] (They did acknowledge, however, that doctrine under the ERA would develop "only by the usual process of constitutional adjudication.")[46]

The Yale authors argued that, under the ERA, sex would be a prohibited classification, except where unique physical attributes obtained (permitting, for example, laws relating to wet nurses or sperm donors, rape, and determination of paternity). Legislation providing, for example, leave for child rearing would have to be written in a sex-neutral way; classification based on pregnancy would have to be narrowly drawn. "Current mores" would govern sex separation for privacy purposes: laws could thus require employment of same-sex police officers for strip searches and segregated toilet and sleeping facilities.[47] Single-sex schools could exist, so long as they remained private.[48] But classification for "benign quotas" or "compensatory aid" would not pass muster under the ERA except as remedies for past discrimination.[49] In other ways, the operation of the ERA would be both "obvious and direct,"[50] eliminating sex differences in jury service, qualifications to conduct business, age requirements, government benefits, and Social Security, and enhancing the existing trends toward equality in marriage and divorce law and in employment doctrine as begun under Title VII of the 1964 Civil Rights Law. The ERA would demand changes in criminal law where differences existed, most notably with respect to sexual conduct, although some differences might remain if they survived close judicial scrutiny to ensure their basis in "unique physical characteristics."[51] Brown and her coauthors noted that the Model Penal Code already incorporated such a stance.[52] With respect to the military, however, they warned that the amendment would have "a substantial and pervasive impact upon military practices and institutions," requiring "a radical restructuring of the military's view of women,"[53] including draft, enlistment, assignment, training, and veterans' benefits. But, they predicted, "[c]hanges in the law, where necessary to bring the military into compliance with the Amendment will not be difficult to effect."[54] They concluded that the ERA would "establish fully, emphatically, and unambiguously the proposition that before the law women and men are to be treated without difference."[55]

In sum, then, it could be argued that feminists were asking for clarity—a clear legal standard of equal treatment without regard to sex, with the burden on the state to demonstrate a compelling reason for making the distinction—and permanence, a standard that would not be subject to the vagaries of changing political winds or even court personnel. But before the decade was out, two things were plain: first, an amendment to the Constitution would not come easily; second, legislative actions and court decisions would make many feminist arguments anachronisms. Phyllis Schlafly, the conservative Republican leader of the Eagle Forum who led the fight against ratification, used as one of her central arguments that the constitutional amendment was simply unnecessary, a point that became harder to contest as the decade wore on. Despite the inability of feminists to wrest the final three states required for ratification (even with the deadline extended by Congress to June 1982), a dizzying array of new statutes and judicial holdings brought the goal of equality under law closer to reality.

## "Heightened Scrutiny": A New Weapon

Among the first changes was the alteration in Supreme Court doctrine that the Yale authors had deemed unrealistic only six months before. Although it did not initially acknowledge a departure, in 1971 (*Reed v. Reed*), the U.S. Supreme Court found that a state law that preferred male executors to female executors had distinguished irrationally on the basis of sex and therefore denied to women the equal protection of the law. Whether this decision would govern future cases or if, like *Ballard*, it would prove to be only a flash in the pan resolved quickly. The *Reed* decision was the first of many, and the Court in 1976 (*Craig v. Boren*)[56] owned that it had taken to subjecting laws that differentiated on the basis of sex to a "heightened scrutiny." The new standard did not pose so high a barrier as the "rigid scrutiny" applied to race-based classifications, yet it nevertheless required states to justify such laws by demonstrating that the measure was "substantially related" to an "important governmental interest," not simply a rational route to a legitimate government interest. In any case, as proponents had hoped, the burden of proof had shifted to the state. (Although four justices argued for a "strict scrutiny" standard in a 1973 case, that position never won a majority.)[57]

Using the new intermediate standard, the Court proceeded to strike many more sex-based laws than it permitted to stand; at the same time, Congress enacted federal measures to prohibit forms of discrimination either not open to constitutional challenge or found by the Court to be free of constitutional taint. In 1978, for example, Congress passed the Pregnancy Discrimination Act in response to the Court's determination that discrimination against pregnant workers violated neither the Constitution's demand for equal treatment nor the ban against sex discrimination in employment in Title VII of the 1964 Civil Rights Act.[58] Simultaneous efforts to seek amendments to state constitutions, sixteen of them successful, and to amend state laws also wiped sex-based laws from the books. The U.S. Supreme Court had imposed equal protection requirements even on members of Congress and state judges not then covered by federal discrimination statutes.[59]

Thus, despite the failure of the ERA to win ratification, by June 1982 a substantial body of antidiscrimination law now rested in court reporters and codes of both the federal and the state governments. And though a Republican victory in the 1980 election checked the feminist juggernaut, throughout the 1980s the Supreme Court did not reverse its course. By 1997, of the feminist goals that an equal rights amendment would reach, few remained unfulfilled. Distinctions in jury service had been eliminated by a combination of federal law and court decisions;[60] community property states could no longer distinguish between husbands and wives; states could not require alimony only of men nor impose sex-based age distinctions.[61] In short, in the words of the ACLU's specialists in women's rights law, "Despite the loss of the ERA, the 1970s gave [women] the legal structure for eradicating discrimination."[62]

The Court continued to uphold sex distinctions in the law in only a few instances, usually justifying the action by reference either to privacy or to a need for compensatory treatment. In a 1974 Florida case concerning a property tax exemption, the Court let stand preferential treatment for widows, explicitly on "affirmative action" grounds.[63] The Court noted that the women to whom this law applied had not had an ongoing attachment to the labor force, resulting in disparities between their economic capabilities and those of men; the Court cited the wage gap between men and women to support its contention that the economic circumstances of women trailed those of men. (Three justices—Brennan, Marshall, and White—found the classification irrational.) The Court also permitted some temporary sex distinctions in the social security pension program to permit a smooth transition to a sex-neutral system.[64] In a smaller set of cases, the Court provided rationales that recalled the paternalistic tradition one might have presumed abjured: in *Dothard v. Rawlinson*,[65] the Court splintered but upheld a prohibition on women prison guards in an Alabama maximum security prison based on the savage prison conditions obtaining in Alabama; and in *Michael M. v. Sonoma County Superior Court*, by a 5-4 vote, the Court let stand California's "statutory rape" law on the unsupported basis that only a sex-specific law could effectively protect young women from unintended pregnancy.[66]

In a 1987 case, *California Federal Savings & Loan Association v. Guerra*,[67] the Court upheld a California law that provided disability leave only for pregnancy, a distinction that appeared to contradict the explicit language of the Pregnancy Discrimination Act. The case found feminists arguing on both sides; ultimately, the Court justified the special treatment by appeal to the spirit of the act, which sought to equalize opportunities for pregnant and nonpregnant workers. The dispute found resolution eventually in the passage of sex-neutral leave legislation; the federal Family and Medical Leave Act was signed by President William Jefferson Clinton on February 5, 1993, following exactly the legal formula laid out in the *Yale Law Journal* article.

Another area in which the Court countenanced sex differences concerned unmarried parents, holding in several cases that differential treatment between unmarried fathers and unmarried mothers could be justified. In *Miller v. Albright*, 523 U.S. 420 (1998), the Court by a 6-3 vote let stand a lower court ruling upholding a federal statute that a child born out of wedlock and outside the United States to an alien mother and an American father be legitimated before age eighteen in order to acquire citizenship. But Justice O'Connor, joined in her concurring opinion by Justice Kennedy, noted that in her view the statute would fail "heightened scrutiny" if properly presented. In 2001, however, the Court revisited the issue in *Nguyen v. INS*, and a 5-4 majority let the distinction stand, provoking a blistering dissent written by O'Connor: "No one should mistake the majority's analysis for a careful application of this Court's equal protection jurisprudence concerning sex-based classifications. Today's decision instead represents a deviation from a line of cases in which we have vigilantly applied heightened scrutiny to such classifications to determine whether a constitutional violation has occurred. I trust that the depth and vitality of these precedents will ensure that today's error remains an aberration."[68]

The area in which the Court endorsed the largest number of sex distinctions involved, predictably, the military. Citing Congress's differential treatment of men and women, it refrained from imposing a single standard. Most notably, in a 1981 case brought by a man protesting an all-male draft, *Rostker v. Goldberg,* the Court declined to require Congress to equalize its treatment of men and women in the military, noting the "greater deference" the Court has always accorded to Congress in matters military. The Yale authors had predicted incorrectly that changes in the law would come easily. Congress had, the Court observed, considered drafting women and rejected a proposal to do so. Moreover, Congress rested the draft exclusion upon the bar to women from combat, a proviso the Court also declined to strike. (Brennan, Marshall, and White again dissented.) In 1975, the Court had agreed that the navy could treat men and women personnel differently with respect to career paths, and in 1979 the Court had also upheld veterans' preference programs.[69] But even the military could not operate with an entirely free hand: in 1973, the Court had insisted, by a margin of eight to one, that Congress treat married women equally with married men in the armed services with respect to benefits (in this case, a housing allowance).[70]

Still, in the years after *Rostker,* the actions of both Congress and the Pentagon continued to demonstrate the unsettled nature of the relationship between women and military service and the movement toward equal treatment. Most exclusions and exemptions obtaining in 1981 had been lifted by 1996. In 1991 and 1993, Congress explicitly revoked the restrictions on women in combat vessels and aircraft; in 1994 the Defense Department opened thousands of combat-related support jobs to women.[71] By 1996, women composed 14 percent of the army, and in December 1997 women made up 10 percent of the 8,500 U.S. troops deployed in Bosnia.[72] Complete equality remained elusive: the regulation that prohibited women's participation in ground combat barred them from 32 percent of military jobs. Jane Mansbridge has argued that the ERA lost crucial support because feminists insisted that the amendment would require equal treatment of women and men in the military,[73] and the pace of congressional change suggested that prevailing sentiment had not yet endorsed full equality in this arena. Nevertheless, the exceptions of the Court and Congress in this area represented a departure from a new general rule of equality.

In 1996, the U.S. Supreme Court reviewed the status of women under the Fourteenth Amendment in a case many feminists called "as important a Constitutional gender-discrimination case as this

Court has ever addressed."[74] On June 26, 1996, in *U.S. v. Virginia,* the U.S. Supreme Court decided that the Virginia Military Institute (VMI), a state-supported all-male college founded in 1839, had to admit women. Associate Justice Ruth Bader Ginsburg wrote for the 7-1 majority. Although twenty-five years earlier, in a brief written on behalf of the ACLU in *Reed v. Reed,* Ginsburg had urged the Court to apply "strict scrutiny" to sex-based distinctions, in *U.S. v. Virginia* she based her decision on the "intermediate scrutiny" of the law, which the Court had applied explicitly to sex-based distinctions since 1976. Presumably against Ginsburg's preferences, stated repeatedly in briefs written between 1971 and 1980 when she was directing the ACLU Women's Rights Project, the Court ignored the pleas of the United States and many amici to raise the standard of review to "strict scrutiny."[75]

In the plaintiff's brief, Drew Days, the solicitor general, had echoed Ginsburg's earlier arguments in contending that "strict scrutiny is, in fact, the correct constitutional standard for evaluating differences in official treatment based on sex." But though Days spoke generally of the need to eradicate continuing discrimination against women, he offered no sex-based governmental action that a new standard would invalidate. To the contrary, he mentioned parenthetically four sex-based classifications for the sole purpose of assuring the Court that "strict scrutiny" would leave them undisturbed: single-sex education for compensatory purposes where "members of the gender benefited by the classification actually suffer a disadvantage related to the classification"; affirmative action programs to counter discrimination; provisions to accommodate "individuals' privacy" (i.e., separate sleeping accommodations, bathing and toilet facilities); and, tellingly, the limitations placed on women in the military. In a footnote, Days averred: "Regardless of the level of judicial scrutiny, federal executive and congressional policies and programs having to do with the conduct and control of military affairs should continue to receive the judicial deference they have traditionally been accorded."[76]

The brief filed by the National Women's Law Center and the ACLU in support of the United States for a coalition of more than two dozen feminist organizations, including the National Woman's Party and the National Organization for Women, also argued for a declaration of sex as a "suspect classification." These "friends of the court" emphasized the need to "eliminate confusion in the lower courts" and to "resolve serious inconsistencies" in the Court's two recent major affirmative action cases, *Adarand v. Pena* and *Richmond v. Croson*.[77] "Strict scrutiny," these amici contended, "is not so easily susceptible to misunderstanding." But the examples that followed did not sustain the proposition that "strict scrutiny" would of necessity have resolved the issues in question (e.g., single-sex high schools and rape statutes). These feminist organizations conceded that physical differences between men and women might require accommodation in the law and that single-sex educational programs and compensatory programs that classified by sex might remain desirable. But they argued that strict scrutiny could permit such accommodations.[78] Neither these organizations nor a brief filed on behalf of a number of military women, which recounted the achievements of women in the military, mentioned the constitutional status of sex-based distinctions by the U.S. armed services.[79] Meanwhile, a coalition of women's colleges, advising the Court to rule that VMI must admit women or become private, also urged that the ruling protect the constitutional legitimacy of single-sex private women's colleges.[80]

If proponents of strict scrutiny ignored the issue of combat service, opponents (including Phyllis Schlafly's Eagle Forum) did not. They characterized the solicitor general's attempt to safeguard military prerogatives via footnote "a dodge in the first degree." Despite the footnote, they asserted, "The plain reality is that the Government's invitation to impose strict scrutiny on sex-based classifications will—indeed, philosophically, *must*—affect both the judiciary's role in military policy-making and, ultimately, military policy." Proponents, they insisted, cannot have it two ways: "*[E]ither the law brooks no differential treatment between men and women or it brooks some.*" These conservative amici argued that the Court should retain its "carefully developed" intermediate standard of review for sex-based classification because "race and sex have not been, and should not be, treated the same under the Constitution for the simple reason that race and sex are not the same."[81]

In her opinion, Justice Ginsburg now defended "intermediate scrutiny," although her interpretation of this standard was expansive:

> Without equating gender classifications, for all purposes to

classifications based on race or national origin, the Court, in post-*Reed* decisions, has carefully inspected official action that closes a door or denies opportunity to women (or to men) [citations omitted]. To summarize the Court's current directions for cases of official classification based on gender: Focusing on the differential treatment or denial of opportunity for which relief is sought, the reviewing court must determine whether the proffered justification is "exceedingly persuasive." The burden of justification is demanding and it rests entirely on the State. . . . The State must show "at least that the [challenged] classification serves 'important governmental objectives and that the discriminatory means employed' are 'substantially related to the achievement of those objectives.'" . . . The justification must be genuine, not hypothesized or invented *post hoc* in response to litigation. And it must not rely on overbroad generalizations about the different talents, capacities, or preferences of males and females.

The heightened review standard our precedent establishes does not make sex a proscribed classification. Supposed "inherent differences" are no longer accepted as a ground for race or national origin classification. . . . Physical differences between men and women, however, are enduring. . . .

"Inherent differences" between men and women, we have come to appreciate, remain cause for celebration, but not for denigration of the members of either sex or for artificial constraints on an individual's opportunity. Sex classifications may be used to compensate women "for particular economic disabilities [they have] suffered," . . . to "promot[e] equal employment opportunity," . . . to advance full development of the talent and capacities of our Nation's people. But such classifications may not be used, as they once were, . . . to create or perpetuate the legal, social, and economic inferiority of women. (15–16)

In a footnote, Justice Ginsburg appeared to reassure those concerned about the endurance of single-sex education, although her meaning is ambiguous: "We do not question the State's prerogative evenhandedly to support diverse educational opportunities. We address specifically and only an educational opportunity recognized . . . as 'unique.'" (16, n. 7)

Not at all persuaded by this demurrer, Justice Antonin Scalia in his dissent indignantly accused his colleagues of changing the decision rule: "The rationale of today's decision," he wrote, "is sweeping: for sex-based classifications, a redefinition of intermediate scrutiny that makes it indistinguishable from strict scrutiny." Justice Scalia correctly observed that this decision marked an important bellwether. The majority of seven included not only the appointees of President Clinton (Justices Breyer and Ginsburg) but also all the "swing" justices named by Presidents Reagan and Bush (Souter, Kennedy, and O'Connor), as well as Justice Stevens, a Nixon appointee (although usually a reliable liberal). Even Chief Justice Rehnquist, a frequent ally of Justices Scalia and Thomas, joined the result (but not the reasoning of the decision). With Justice Thomas not participating, presumably because his son attended VMI, Justice Scalia was alone in his dissent.

The coalition of seven justices, important in part for its numerical strength but more so for its alliance across political boundaries, suggested that the decision was a durable one and one that, as Justice Scalia lamented, sustained the contemporary reach of "intermediate scrutiny." If not identical to "strict scrutiny," it nonetheless permitted few distinctions. In fact, the advocates of strict scrutiny in the briefs described a level of review with results very much like that of intermediate scrutiny as the Court was now applying it: it permitted compensatory programs for women and separate educational facilities for women and men (so long as comparable programs are available for each), it did not touch military limitations placed on women, and it left in place separate public accommodations in the way of sanitary facilities. But such exceptions plainly distinguished the impact of this level of scrutiny from that of the "strict scrutiny" sought and won by the civil rights movement from the 1940s on, which targeted exactly racial classifications in educational institutions, in public accommodations (including public rest rooms), and in the military.

## A New Engagement?

Justice Ginsburg's opinion and Scalia's dissent notwithstanding, numbers of feminists continued to believe that the ERA remained essential to women's legal protection. On March 20, 1997, Democratic Representative Carolyn Maloney of New York reintroduced the ERA in the 105th Congress (H.J. Res. 66); Senator Edward M. Kennedy (D-Mass.) introduced the companion bill, S.J. Res. 24, in the Senate. During the course of the first session, 115 House members and 17 senators signed on. Given the history of Supreme Court adjudication, what were amendment advocates seeking in 1997? In her January letter soliciting cosponsors,[82] Maloney told her colleagues that "without the ERA, laws can still perpetuate gender classifications that keep women from achieving their full potential." She offered no specific examples, although in the newsletter of the National Woman's Party, she explained that the ERA would help "women . . . engaged in a constant struggle to maintain laws which protect equality in education and in the workplace." In the same issue, the NWP itself contended: "Passage of the ERA can help to make equal pay a reality for women."[83] Senator Kennedy justified his support by observing that women still faced discrimination in education, sports, and employment and "still earn only 76 cents for each dollar earned by men. . . . Existing laws against sex discrimination in all its ugly forms can't get the job done. The need for a constitutional guarantee of equal rights for women is compelling."[84] He did not, however, explain the nexus between the constitutional amendment and pay raises for women.

In any case, at the end of the century, the ERA stood no chance of approval. Conservatives were in the majority in Congress, and the compromise of specific bills for specific ills and a compliant Supreme Court, assessing on an individual basis which laws should fall and which remain, had undercut many of the amendment's strongest arguments.

In fact, by 1995, the ERA as then composed satisfied not even feminists. Many now argued that the simple formal equality of the 1972 amendment asked for too little. In order to win political allies, proponents had initially denied that the ERA would affect abortion law or secure for gay, lesbian, bisexual, and transgendered people the privileges accorded heterosexuals. The old ERA had had nothing to say about the needs of poor women. In 1995, one of the most stalwart of the amendment's advocates, the National Organization for Women, promulgated a new "Constitutional equality amendment" that explicitly prohibited discrimination based on sexual orientation and indigence, guaranteed a woman's right to terminate a pregnancy, endorsed affirmative action programs, and stipulated "strict scrutiny" as the standard of judicial review. The new proposal implicitly acknowledged that most of the goals attainable under the old rubric of "equal rights for women" had been achieved and that feminists required a different strategy to effect a more comprehensive (and long-term) agenda.[85]

The constitutional status of women had changed dramatically in the preceding quarter of a century. Although vestigial forms of discrimination remained in the law, the plethora of state and federal statutes that distinguished arbitrarily on the basis of sex had been nullified. (If the elimination of these laws took the better part of a century, as the NWP predicted in 1923, it nevertheless predated the success of the ERA.) Even the symbolic battle had been won. Feminists claimed in 1923 and again in the 1970s that constitutional equality would generate a commitment to equality also in those areas formally untouched by government power. Such a commitment now existed in almost all quarters of American life, at least on paper. (Among communities that resisted such a standard, e.g., fundamentalist Christian denominations that endorsed a biblically mandated subordination of women, no wording in the Constitution would change their beliefs.) Moreover, the few remaining distinctions permitted, such as single-sex colleges and compensatory programs, had substantial feminist support as well.

What of significance was still missing from the constitutional status of women that the language of the 1972 amendment would provide? We can locate two major lacunae. The first was that women continued to be treated differently from men by Congress with respect to military service. The second was that, at least in theory, both the constitutional standard requiring equal treatment and the legislative foundation for equal opportunity could unravel; that is, the right to equal protection lacked permanence. Would the ERA make a difference?

The position of women in the military had consistently been a sticking point, and it remained so, with feminist insistence on absolute equality driving away potential supporters of a constitutional amendment.[86] Ironically, feminist support for military adventures had always been conflicted, as evidenced by the historical association between women's reform efforts and peace movements throughout the twentieth century. Nevertheless, few ERA supporters would countenance an explicit exception for differences in military service. With women making up 14 percent of the military, performing more than two-thirds of all military functions, they already worked in combat areas, on occasion taking and returning fire. Women had lost their lives in the service of their country, and women soldiers argued vehemently that all roles in the military must be open to them.[87]

But one could not realistically predict that the ERA would resolve this question before it was concluded in some other way. Senior defense officials were as aware of the facts of women's military service as justices, and historically the Supreme Court has deferred to Congress and to the military on military matters. In the face of congressional and military resistance, the argument that men and women are differently situated with respect to military service might serve to justify any difference the Court chose to permit, even with the ERA. A court that could require the arrest and detention of American citizens based on race and cite wartime necessity (*Korematsu v. U.S.*, 323 U.S. 214 [1944]), explicit constitutional language to the contrary notwithstanding, could well acquiesce to the military with respect to women in combat. Indeed, neither dissent in *Rostker*,[88] a case decided after the finding of equal protection for women was already firmly fixed, challenged the exclusion of women from combat. On the other hand, at the 1996 Republican Party hearing on the platform, the respondents split evenly on lifting the combat exemption for women. Although the platform committee decided to support the exclusion, the appearance of dissent in this venue suggested that public opinion might be amenable to change.[89] If the army lifted the combat exclusion, much opposition to the ERA would disappear, as it did when Title VII eliminated single-sex labor laws. But this decision would need to be resolved in advance of ratification. With the possible exception of the civil war amendments, constitutional amendments are lagging indicators of change, not propellants.[90]

What about permanence? In 1996, seven justices of the Supreme Court affirmed that the Constitution does not abide invidious distinctions based on sex. Feminists argued nonetheless that the absence of explicit constitutional text rendered all decisions potentially unstable, vulnerable to reversal at the hands of new conservative justices. Perhaps explicit language in the Constitution enshrining sexual equality would prove a sturdier bulwark than a 7-1 decision; permanent language in the Constitution might well work to retard a backlash. On the other hand, as *Plessy v. Ferguson*[91] illustrates, the Court will not necessarily be deterred by the explicit language of the Constitution either. Given a profound enough period of conservative reaction, concepts like "equality," "rights," or "compelling interests" do not foreclose reinterpretation. And the history of resistance to the Supreme Court's 1962 ruling concerning prayer in public schools demonstrates that constitutional imperatives—textual or interpretive—do not perforce change local practice.[92]

By the end of the century, ERA advocates had not achieved their goal, but they nonetheless had good reason to declare victory in the war for constitutional equality as proposed by the 1972 amendment. Few explicit distinctions remained in the law; those that did had general support, in some cases (such as affirmative action and single-sex education) even from feminists. Permanence, meanwhile, is always illusory. Both opponents and proponents pointed to conflicting judicial rulings under state ERAs. Construction of equality under the law for men and women would likely continue to turn on understandings by judges of appropriate distinctions rather than constitutional text. Their understandings would be shaped by the political, economic, and social behavior of women and the popular responses to those behaviors. In 1971, Margaret Eastwood, an attorney and fervent supporter of the ERA, laid out the changes she and other supporters assumed an ERA would bring about. However, she noted that the words of the Constitution would have no effect if women did not mobilize: "[U]nless women play a greater role in all forms of government, there is no assurance that their lack of equal status under the law will not continue indefinitely despite new constitutional mandates."[93] Regardless of the language in the Constitution, what matters is the political mobilization of women. With it, constitutional equality is safe; without it, the inscribed words of the ERA would be only, in James Madison's words, "parchment barriers."

Notes

I would like to thank Susan Deller Ross, Philippa Strum, Sarah Wilson, Elizabeth Symonds, and Vivien Hart for their comments on earlier drafts. All responsibility for errors is, of course, my own.

1. *Bradwell v. State of Illinois*, 83 U.S. (16 Wall.) 130, at 141–42 (1872).
2. *Slaughterhouse Cases*, 83 U.S. (16 Wall.) 36 (1873); *Minor v. Happersett*, 88 U.S. (21 Wall.) 162 (1874).
3. 198 U.S. 45 (1905).
4. 208 U.S. 412 (1908).
5. 208 U.S. 422 (1908).
6. *Bunting v. Oregon*, 243 U.S. 426 (1917).
7. The state of Wisconsin had passed an equal rights law in 1921 to clarify women's status in the wake of the suffrage amendment. The law promised women equality under law but permitted to stand those laws that offered "special protection and privileges." Under this legal regime, the state's attorney general had ruled acceptable a law that banned women from working for state legislators on the grounds that the hours were too long. J. Stanley Lemons, *The Woman Citizen: Social Feminism in the 1920s* (Charlottesville: University Press of Virginia, 1990), 187–89.
8. Susan D. Becker, *The Origins of the Equal Rights Amendment: American Feminism Between the Wars* (Westport, Conn.: Greenwood Press, 1981), 19.
9. Burnita Shelton Matthews, "Women Should Have Equal Rights with Men: A Reply," *American Bar Association Journal* 12, no. 2 (February 1926): 117.
10. Joan G. Zimmerman, "The Jurisprudence of Equality: The Women's Minimum Wage, the First Equal Rights Amendment, and *Adkins v. Children's Hospital*, 1905–1923," *Journal of American History* 78 (June 1991): 220.
11. 261 U.S. 525 (1923).
12. *Morehead v. New York ex rel. Tipaldo*, 298 U.S. 587 (1936), striking down a minimum wage law; *Radice v. New York*, 264 U.S. 292 (1924), upholding a night-work limitation.
13. Becker, *Origins of the Equal Rights Amendment*, p. 53.
14. Nancy F. Cott, "Marriage and Women's Citizenship in the United States," *American Historical Review* 103 (December 1998): 1461–63.
15. Lemons, *The Woman Citizen*, 67–68; Cott, "Marriage and Women's Citizenship," 1469.
16. Matthews, "Women Should Have Equal Rights," 19–20.
17. Quoted in Becker, *Origins of the Equal Rights Amendment*, 19.
18. 312 U.S. 100 (1941).
19. 298 U.S. 587 (1936).
20. 300 U.S. 379 (1937).
21. For a fuller discussion, see Cynthia Harrison, *On Account of Sex: The Politics of Women's Issues, 1945–1968* (Berkeley: University of California Press, 1988), chap. 1.
22. See ibid., chap. 2.
23. *Ballard v. United States*, 329 U.S. 187 (1946), at 193–94.
24. *Goesaert v. Cleary, Liquor Control Commission of Michigan*, 335 U.S. 464 (1948).
25. 368 U.S. 57 (1961) at 52.
26. Harrison, *On Account of Sex*, chap. 7.
27. Much ink has been spilled over the question of Howard Smith's

motives in introducing an amendment to add "sex" to the employment title of the Civil Rights Act of 1964. He would, no doubt, have happily seen the entire act go down in flames, but if it were to succeed (and surely he knew it would), his own preference was likely to have (white) women included in its purview. He was, in fact, a long-standing supporter of the Equal Rights Amendment, his amendment was urged on him by his pro-ERA Virginia constituents, and he bragged about his role in his next election campaign. Moreover, the survival of the amendment in the Senate, where many opportunities to expunge it existed, gives lie to the propaganda that this dramatic change in the law was inadvertent. See ibid., 177–78, 295 n.

28. 29 CFR sec. 1604.1 (1970).

29. 251 F.Supp. 401 (M.D. Ala. 1966), at 408.

30. *United States ex rel. Robinson v. York,* 281 F.Supp. 8 (D. Conn. 1968).

31. *McCrimmon v. Daley,* 2 F.E.P. Cas. 971 (N.D. Ill. 1970); *Paterson Tavern & Grill Owners Ass'n, Inc. v. Borough of Hawthorne,* 57 N.J. 180, 270 A.2d 628 (1970).

32. *Kirstein v. Rector and Visitors of the University of Virginia,* 309 F.Supp. 184 (E.D. Va. 1970).

33. *State v. Hall,* 187 So. 2d 861 (Miss.); MISS. CODE ANN. sec. 1762 (Supp. 1968), cited in Mary Eastwood, "The Double Standard of Justice: Women's Rights Under the Constitution," *Valparaiso University Law Review* 5, no. 2 (symposium issue 1971): 290.

34. Sonia Pressman Fuentes, "Federal Remedial Sanctions: Focus on Title VII," *Valparaiso University Law Review* 5, no. 2 (symposium issue 1971): 395.

35. The amendment had been rewritten in the 1940s to conform to the language of the suffrage amendment. Alice Paul, the author of the first version, did the redraft. See Harrison, *On Account of Sex,* 16.

36. Becker, *Origins of the Equal Rights Amendment,* 93.

37. Citizens' Advisory Council on the Status of Women, "Memorandum on the Proposed Equal Rights Amendment to the United States Constitution," March 1970, explicated in Eastwood, "Double Standard of Justice," 300–317.

38. *Hearings on S. J. Res. 61 Before the Subcommittee on Constitutional Amendments of the Senate Committee on the Judiciary,* 90th Cong., 2d sess. (May 1970), 41–42.

39. Ibid., 43.

40. Ibid., 19.

41. Ibid., 180.

42. Barbara A. Brown et al., "The Equal Rights Amendment: A Constitutional Basis for Equal Rights for Women," *Yale Law Journal* 80, no. 5 (April 1971): 881; *Williams v. McNair,* 401 U.S. 951 (1971).

43. Brown et al., "Equal Rights Amendment," 882.

44. Ibid., 883.

45. Ibid., 883–84.

46. Ibid., 875, 888.

47. Ibid., 889–902.

48. Ibid., 907.

49. Ibid., 903–4.

50. Ibid., 920.

51. Ibid., 954.

52. Ibid., 966.
53. Ibid., 969.
54. Ibid., 978.
55. Ibid., 980.
56. 429 U.S. 190 (1976).
57. *Frontiero v. Richardson,* 411 U.S. 677 (1973). Perhaps ironically, Justice Lewis F. Powell declined to join his four colleagues in this case because the ERA was pending before the states and he thought it unwise for the Court "to pre-empt . . . the prescribed constitutional processes" (411 U.S. 677, 693).
58. *Geduldig v. Aiello,* 417 U.S. 484 (1974); *General Electric Co. v. Gilbert,* 429 U.S. 125 (1976).
59. *Davis v. Passman,* 442 U.S. 228 (1979); *Forrester v. White,* 484 U.S. 219 (1988).
60. See the Civil Rights Act of 1957, 42 U.S. sec. 1971; *Ballard v. U.S.,* 329 U.S. 187 (1946); *Taylor v. Louisiana,* 419 U.S. 522 (1975); *J.E.B. v. Alabama ex rel. T.B.,* 114 S.Ct. 1419 (1994).
61. Domicile: Herma Hill Kay, *Text, Cases and Materials on Sex-Based Discrimination,* 3d ed. (St. Paul, Minn.: West Publishing, 1988), 205, quoting R. Weinstraub, *Commentary on the Conflict of Laws,* 2d ed. (1980): Current state of the law: "a rebuttable presumption that the wife's domicile is the same as her husband's" (19).

Age at marriage: By 1987, all states had equalized (Kay, *Text, Cases and Materials,* 193).

Age of majority: *Stanton v. Stanton,* 425 U.S. 501 (1977).

Names: The Supreme Court has denied review of cases where states have required women to use marriage names for specific purposes, but fewer states do. "With few exceptions [cite omitted], American common and statutory law has now developed to the point where all adults, regardless of sex or marital status, have the right to choose what surname they will bear at any given stage of their lives" (Kay, *Text, Cases and Materials,* 203).

Property: Community property states may not grant to the husband exclusive rights to control disposition of community property (*Kirchberg v. Feenstra,* 450 U.S. 455, 1981). In 1971, husband legally designated as manager of community property in the eight community property states; by 1980, all had changed this practice (Texas, Washington, Arizona, California, Idaho, Louisiana, Nevada, and New Mexico).

Child custody: "Statutes and case law in the United States generally recognize that both parents are equally entitled to the custody of their children" with disputes settled according to the "best interests" of the child. But there is a "well-recognized judicial penchant for finding that the welfare of a child of 'tender years' is served best by awarding their custody to the mother." This presumption has survived constitutional attack from fathers, although the new rule is to favor the "primary caretaker" (Kay, *Text, Cases and Materials,* 316–26).

Divorce: "All . . . states have adopted some form of no-fault standard for the dissolution of marriage" (Kay, *Text, Cases and Materials,* 263). Property division is largely the prerogative of "judicial discretion."

Alimony: States may not limit the responsibility for alimony payments only to husbands (*Orr v. Orr,* 440 U.S. 268 [1979]).

62. Susan Deller Ross and Ann Barcher, *The Rights of Women: The Basic ACLU Guide to a Woman's Rights,* rev. ed. (New York: Bantam Books, 1983), xiv.

63. *Kahn v. Shevin,* 416 U.S. 351 (1974).

64. *Califano v. Webster,* 430 U.S. 313 (1977); *Heckler v. Mathews,* 465 U.S. 728 (1984).

65. 433 U.S. 321 (1977).

66. 450 U.S. 464 (1981).

67. 479 U.S. 272 (1987).

68. *Nguyen v. INS,* No. 99-2071, decided June 11, 2001. See also *Parham v. Hughes,* 441 U.S. 347 (1979); *Caban v. Mohammed,* 441 U.S. 380 (1979); *Lehr v. Robertson,* 463 U.S. 248 (1983); *Clark v. Jeter,* 486 U.S. 461 (1988).

69. *Schlesinger v. Ballard,* 419 U.S. 498 (1975); *Personnel Administrator of Massachusetts v. Feeney,* 442 U.S. 256 (1979).

70. *Frontiero v. Richardson,* 411 U.S. 677 (1973).

71. P.L. 102-190, December 5, 1991; *Washington Post,* December 30, 1997.

72. *New York Times,* December 29, 1996, April 1, 1997; *Washington Post,* December 30, 1997.

73. Jane J. Mansbridge, *Why We Lost the ERA* (Chicago: University of Chicago Press, 1986), 85.

74. Robert N. Weiner et al., "Brief of *Amici Curiae* National Women's Law Center, American Civil Liberties Union [and 21 additional amici] in support of the petition for a writ of certiorari to the U.S. Court of Appeals for the Fourth Circuit," *U.S. v. Virginia,* Docket No. 94-1941, filed June 26, 1995, Law Library, Library of Congress, Washington, D.C., p. 2.

75. Deborah L. Markowitz, "In Pursuit of Equality: One Woman's Work to Change the Law," *Women's Rights Law Reporter* 11 (summer 1989): 77–80.

76. Drew S. Days III, Solicitor General et al., "Brief for the Petitioner," *U.S. v. Virginia,* Docket No. 94-1941, filed November 16, 1995, Law Library, Library of Congress, Washington, D.C., pp. 33–35, 34 n., 45 n.

77. 115 S.Ct. 2097 (1995); 488 U.S. 469 (1989).

78. Robert N. Weiner et al., "Brief of *Amici Curiae* National Women's Law Center [and] American Civil Liberties Union in support of petitioner" (with 26 additional *Amici*) *U.S. v. Virginia,* Docket No. 94-1941, filed November 16, 1995, Law Library, Library of Congress, Washington, D.C., pp. 5, 8, 12–13, 30, 12 n., 34 n.

79. Allan L. Gropper et al., "Brief of *Amicus Curiae* Lieutenant Colonel Rhonda Cornum, USA; Brigadier General Evelyn P. Foote, USA (RET), et al. in support of the petition of the U.S.," Docket No. 94-1941, filed November 16, 1995, Law Library, Library of Congress, Washington, D.C.

80. Wendy S. White et al., "Brief of Twenty-Six Private Women's Colleges as *Amici Curiae* in support of Petitioner," *U.S. v. Virginia,* Docket Nos. 94-1941 and 94-2107, filed November 16, 1995, Law Library, Library of Congress, Washington, D.C., p. 26.

81. Mellissa Wells-Petry et al., "Brief *Amici Curiae* of the Center for Military Readiness, Family Research Council, . . . Eagle Forum [and 5 other *amici*] in support of respondent Commonwealth of Virginia," *U.S. v. Virginia,* Docket Nos. 94-1941 and 94-2107, filed December 15, 1995, Law Library, Library of Congress, Washington, D.C., pp. 1, 3, 11, 12–16, 21–22, 26–27, 29.

82. Maloney to "Dear Colleague," January 13, 1997, in the author's possession.

83. *Equal Rights,* 82, no. 1 (fall 1997): 1, 7.

84. "Statement of Senator Edward M. Kennedy, The Equal Rights Amendment," March 22, 1997.

85. The Constitutional Equality Amendment promulgated by the National Organization for Women, July 1995:

Section 1. Women and men shall have equal rights throughout the United States and every place and entity subject to its jurisdiction; through this article, the subordination of women to men is abolished;

Section 2. All persons shall have equal rights and privileges without discrimination on account of sex, race, sexual orientation, marital status, ethnicity, national origin, color or indigence (see also Sec. 4);

Section 3. This article prohibits pregnancy discrimination and guarantees the absolute right of a woman to make her own reproductive decisions including the termination of pregnancy;

Section 4. This article prohibits discrimination based upon characteristics unique to or stereotypes about any class protected under this article. This article also prohibits discrimination through the use of any facially neutral criteria which have a disparate impact based on membership in a class protected under this article.

Section 5. This article does not preclude any law, program or activity that would remedy the effects of discrimination and that is closely related to achieving such remedial purposes;

Section 6. This article shall be interpreted under the highest standard of judicial review;

Section 7. The United States and the several states shall guarantee the implementation and enforcement of this article.

Source: NOW Web site (www.now.org).

86. For elaboration of this argument, see Mansbridge, *Why We Lost the ERA*.

87. Lory Manning and Jennifer E. Griffith, *Women in the Military: Where They Stand,* 2d ed. (Washington, D.C.: Women's Research and Education Institute, 1998).

88. *Rostker v. Goldberg,* 453 U.S. 57 (1981).

89. Jo Freeman, "Change and Continuity for Women at the Republican and Democratic Conventions," *American Review of Politics* 18 (winter 1997): 353–67; National Public Radio, *All Things Considered,* August 8, 1996.

90. Other effects have been claimed for the ERA, but they are less plausible. Opponents of the ERA have claimed that the amendment would affect abortion decisions. See Gilbert Y. Steiner, *Constitutional Inequality: The Political Fortunes of the Equal Rights Amendment* (Washington, D.C.: Brookings Institution, 1985). Litigation concerning abortion has proceeded successfully on the "privacy" model established by *Griswold v. Connecticut* rather than referencing the equal protection clause, a strategy advocated by Ruth Bader Ginsburg. See, e.g., "On the Hill: High Court Nominee Confirmed by Senate Committee," *Reproductive Freedom News* 2, no. 15 (July 30, 1993): 2. It is possible that an equal rights amendment would affect future cases on this subject, but the Court, if it wished, could still take the position that pregnancy is sui generis. Although opponents of the ERA claimed that the amendment would legitimize homosexual liaisons, whether the Court would vote now to reverse its key decision upholding sodomy laws (*Bowers v. Hardwick* [478 U.S. 186], decided 5-4 in 1986) turns more on politics than on law. (The Georgia law in question was, however, stricken by the state supreme court in 1998: *Powell v. State,* November 23, 1998. See *National Law Journal,* December 14, 1998, B20.) In a 1996 decision, *Romer v. Colorado,* the Court suggested that

homosexuals could find some protection from the Constitution. The breadth of that protection is an unsettled question. The decision of the Hawaii Supreme Court, requiring the state, in light of its own equal rights amendment, to offer compelling reasons for limiting marriage to heterosexuals, lends support to the argument that homosexual rights could fare better with a constitutional amendment barring discrimination based on sex (*Baehr v. Lewin,* No. 15689, May 27, 1993). But the legislative history of the ERA specifically disclaims an impact on gay rights. If the Court inclines toward enhancing the legal rights of homosexuals, the equal protection clause of the Fourteenth Amendment provides the same opportunity an equal rights amendment would. If it is disinclined, even with an equal rights amendment it could wait a century, as an earlier court did, before striking down miscegenation laws under the Fourteenth Amendment (*Loving v. Virginia,* 388 U.S. 1 [1967]).

91. 163 U.S. 537 (1896).

92. *Engel v. Vitale,* 370 U.S. 421 (1962).

93. Eastwood, "Double Standard of Justice," 298.

*Chapter Seven*

# The Warren Court and Equality

Michal R. Belknap

"Equality," notes William Nelson, "has been the central issue of American constitutional law in the twentieth century." *Brown v. Board of Education* is "the central case," he contends, and the Supreme Court of Chief Justice Earl Warren the model for the rights-centered egalitarian judges who have elevated equality to its present preeminence. Nelson echoes sentiments expressed in 1970 by Philip Kurland, who, in a critical valedictory for the Warren Court, declared, "To the extent that the Warren Court has opened new frontiers, it has been in the development of the concept of equality as a constitutional standard." Kurland somewhat grudgingly credited Chief Justice Warren and his colleagues with making a major contribution to "the egalitarian ethos that is becoming dominant in our society."[1] His opinion and Nelson's are representative: most observers see the principle of equality as central to the jurisprudence of the Warren Court (1953–69).[2] This prevailing view is essentially correct. The Warren Court was committed to the promotion of formal equality, especially for African-Americans, and to shielding from legal harassment the civil rights activists who were working to promote that cause. Because of that commitment, it altered significantly numerous facets of the law. The changes were not as great as they might have been, however, for other concerns tempered the Warren Court's enthusiasm for the promotion of equality, causing it to stop well short of guaranteeing even African-Americans treatment as equals.[3]

## Promoting Equality

In fact, its approach to the equal protection clause was in many respects quite traditional. The Warren Court almost always sustained taxes and economic regulations alleged to violate that part of the Fourteenth Amendment, holding only one of each unconstitutional in sixteen years. The exceptions were a measure that taxed domesticated foreign corporations at a different rate and an Illinois law, struck down in *Morey v. Doud* (1957), which exempted from certain requirements that currency exchanges had to meet those that issued United States Post Office, American Express, and Western Union money orders. In other taxation and regulation cases, the Warren Court practiced the sort of deference to state legislatures that Justice Felix Frankfurter advocated, declining to second-guess how legislators classified economic actors.[4]

In other areas the Warren Court was more activist and more innovative. It developed the equal protection clause into a shield for a variety of disadvantaged groups and was especially vigorous in promoting equal rights for African-Americans. It altered the law in a number of areas in order to advance its egalitarian agenda. Although willing to uphold economic regulations and tax measures if the classifications which those embodied bore any rational relationship to a legitimate governmental interest, in other realms the Warren Court made increasing use of what a disapproving Justice John Marshall Harlan identified in 1969 as "an equal protection doctrine of relatively recent vintage." This was "the rule that statutory classifications which either are based upon certain 'suspect' criteria or affect 'fundamental rights' will be held to deny equal protection unless justified by a 'compelling' governmental interest." Actually, the suspect classification branch of this compelling governmental interest doctrine had originated in *Korematsu v. United States* (1944), well before Warren became chief justice. Some members of the Warren Court, however, sought to extend the list of suspect classifications it subjected to strict judicial scrutiny beyond the traditional one of race, which *Korematsu* had recognized, to include others, such as wealth.[5]

"The fundamental interests ingredient of the new equal protection" developed by the Warren Court after 1960 was, as Gerald Gunther noted, "particularly open ended." That was because "it circumscribed legislative choices in the name of newly articulated values that lacked clear support in constitutional text or history." Much like their pre-1937 predecessors, who had employed substantive due process to invalidate regulatory measures they considered unreasonable, Warren Court justices developed a body of "substantive equal protection" doctrine, which they utilized to pass judgment on the reasonableness of the way legislatures had classified people. To justify invalidating actions of legislators unsympathetic to interests they valued without repudiating the judicial self-restraint they had dogmatically endorsed in economic cases, these judges utilized a tactic one of them, William O. Douglas, had pioneered in the 1942 case of *Skinner v. Oklahoma. Skinner* had held that a statutory classification affecting procreation must pass strict judicial scrutiny because procreation was one of man's basic civil rights. The Warren Court employed similar reasoning to justify subjecting to strict scrutiny a law that treated those who had money differently from those who did not with respect to the right to vote. In *Harper v. Virginia State Board of Elections* (1966), it declared emphatically, "[W]here fundamental rights and liberties are asserted under the Equal Protection Clause, classifications which might invade or restrain them must be closely scrutinized and carefully confined." In 1969, over Harlan's strenuous objections, his colleagues added interstate travel to the list of rights protected by the equal protection clause because the Court considered them fundamental.[6]

Some of the statutes struck down in that case were federal ones. Like the rest of the Fourteenth Amendment, the equal protection clause applies only to the states. In order to hold school segregation in the District of Columbia unconstitutional, however, the Warren Court announced in *Bolling v. Sharpe* (1954) that the due process clause of the Fifth Amendment embodies the same ideal of fairness, adding that discrimination might sometimes "be so unjustifiable as to be violative of due process." In the first draft of his opinion, Chief Justice Warren argued that segregation denied black children due process because it arbitrarily deprived them of their liberty. Because this line of reasoning closely resembled that in pre-1937 economic substantive due process cases that several of his colleagues had publicly deplored, they rejected it. Warren then resorted to fiat, inventing a rule that had neither textual nor doctrinal foundation. Failing to acknowledge that since the Fourteenth Amendment contains a due process clause identical in wording to the one in the Fifth Amendment, the equal protection clause would be superfluous if due process included equal protection, he simply declared that it did.[7] Although Warren admitted that the two phrases were not interchangeable, *Bolling* came to stand for the proposition that "the fifth amendment's due process clause guarantees equal protection in the application of federal law."[8]

That the Warren Court would make up, pretty much out of whole cloth, an equal protection doctrine of such fundamental importance suggests the strength of its commitment to the promotion of equality. So do decisions that it rendered in fields as diverse as reapportionment and criminal procedure. The Warren Court handed down a series of rulings which required that state legislators, members of Congress, and even county commissioners represent districts of substantially equal population. These decisions represented, Kurland grumbled, "a sterile concept of equality for the sake of equality." All of them were based on the equal protection clause, but rulings that relied on that provision "did not begin to reveal the extent of the egalitarian influence on the Court's opinions." As Kurland pointed out, Warren and his colleagues utilized the Fifteenth Amendment to attack discrimination against black voters in the drawing of municipal boundaries. The Court's "broad egalitarianism" also found expression in decisions designed to eliminate wealth-based inequalities in the operation of the criminal justice system by requiring that states provide poor defendants with lawyers, give them stenographic transcripts for use in appeals, and remove other impediments to review of their convictions. *Miranda v. Arizona* (1966), although a Fifth Amendment case, also served to ensure that poor defendants would be treated more like rich ones. Writing in 1968, former Solicitor General Archibald Cox portrayed it as a product of "the egalitarianism that has become a dominant force in the evolution of our constitutional law."[9]

*Miranda* and other Warren Court decisions made constitutional law more protective of those who, because of race, poverty, or accident of birth, stood outside Richard Nixon's "middle America." This is hardly surprising, for as Morton Horwitz has pointed out, this was a Court composed largely of outsiders. Harlan, to be sure, was very much a part of the "Establishment." A product of prep school, Princeton, and Oxford, he had come to the bench from a lucrative corporate practice that paid for a commodious Manhattan apartment and a Connecticut country estate and enabled him to socialize with the legal and corporate elite on the golf course and at fox hunts. But Harlan was the Warren Court's great dissenter. The core of the liberal majority responsible for most of its egalitarian decisions was a group of men who, although prominent figures at the time of their appointments, had climbed to the Supreme Court from far less privileged origins along far less genteel routes. Warren was the son of a California railroad worker, Hugo Black of a rural Alabama storekeeper, and William Brennan of a New Jersey union leader. Douglas had been raised in poverty by a widowed mother and had struggled to overcome the effects of childhood polio. Black was an evangelical Baptist, and Brennan was a Catholic. Arthur Goldberg and Abe Fortas were both Jewish, while Thurgood Marshall was the first African-American justice. Goldberg had been a labor lawyer, Marshall a civil rights litigator, and Fortas a partner in a firm notorious for representing former New Dealers accused of communist connections. Warren, Black, and Douglas, who came to the Court without significant judicial experience and often failed to conform to accepted standards of judicial decision making, endured frequent ridicule by legal scholars. It is true that Black had once belonged to the Ku Klux Klan, that Warren had spearheaded the World War II drive to have Japanese-Americans removed from the West Coast, and that Douglas had joined Black in placing the Supreme Court's stamp of approval on that discriminatory action. Nevertheless, these were men who could relate to the victims of discrimination and to those who bore the burdens of inequality in ways that Harlan could not. Because of them, the Warren Court became, as Horwitz observes, "the first . . . in American history that empathized with the outsider."[10]

Its decisions reflected this empathy. Even before *Brown v. Board of Education* (1954), the Warren Court had begun to extend the benefits of the equal protection clause to other outsiders. On May 3, 1954, in *Hernandez v. Texas,* it held that for a state to try a Mexican-American before a jury from which Mexican-Americans had been excluded under an indictment issued by a grand jury from which they also had been excluded violated that constitutional guarantee. Texas had argued that the equal protection clause recognized only two classes of people: white and Negro. The Court unanimously rejected that contention, holding that to keep any otherwise eligible person off of a jury solely because of his ancestry or national origin violated the Fourteenth Amendment. A year later the Warren Court declined to rule for the widow of a Native American soldier killed in Korea, who had sued for the right to bury her husband in a plot she had purchased from an Iowa cemetery that had a whites-only policy. What is notable, though, is how close the Court came to deciding for the widow, before accepting Frankfurter's suggestion that it dispose of the case by holding that review should not have been granted in the first place. The Supreme Court had held in 1883 that only state action could violate the Fourteenth Amendment, but at least four, and perhaps five, members of the Warren Court were prepared to rule for the widow, even though all the state had done was permit the cemetery to use a clause restricting burial to members of the Caucasian race as a defense in a suit for breach of contract.[11]

Although it declined the opportunity in 1955 to insist that Native Americans be treated as equals, by 1968 the Warren Court was willing to challenge head-on centuries of social and legal discrimination against another group of outsiders: illegitimates. In *Levy v. Louisiana,* it held that a state had violated the equal protection clause by refusing to allow illegitimate children to recover for the wrongful deaths of their mothers on whom they were dependent. "We start from the premise," declared Douglas, "that illegitimate children are not 'nonpersons.'" While states possessed broad powers to classify people, they could not draw lines that affected invidious discrimination against a particular class. "Why should the illegitimate child be denied rights merely because of his birth out of wedlock?" Douglas asked rhetorically. In a companion case the Court held that denying a mother the right to recover for the wrongful death of her illegitimate child also violated the equal protection clause.[12]

Harlan thought these illegitimacy decisions pressed equal protection beyond its outer limits, and he resisted strongly the efforts of his more liberal colleagues to extend constitutional protection to the poor. Frank Michaelman, a professor at Harvard, criticized these initiatives, too, but his complaint was that the Court had failed to recognize that states had a constitutional duty to ensure that everyone was protected against certain economic hazards. Although rendering decisions that shielded the poor from the most elemental consequences of poverty, it failed to base these decisions on a right to minimum welfare, resorting instead to the rhetoric of equality. Contrary to what some expected, the Warren Court never held that wealth was a suspect basis of classification. Douglas wrote draft opinions in *Harper v. Virginia State Board of Elections* (1966), in which the Court invalidated state poll taxes, that would have done this, but he was apparently forced by other members of the majority to eliminate this basis for the decision. Although the chief justice made clear in conference that he considered poll taxes unconstitutional because of their "discrimination against [the] poor and against Negroes," the Court struck them down as burdens on the right to vote. This approach was similar to the one it had utilized earlier to justify the conclusion that states must furnish trial transcripts to indigent criminal defendants for use in their appeals. When the Court struck down durational residence requirements for receipt of welfare benefits in 1969, it did so on the ground that withholding these from new arrivals would burden a fundamental right of interstate travel. Although making somewhat dishonest use of the fundamental rights approach to avoid the socialistic implications of holding that wealth was a suspect basis of classification, the Warren Court repeatedly demonstrated its determination to scrutinize rigorously governmental policies that disadvantaged the poor because of their poverty.[13]

Although championing other outsider groups, it did little to promote the cause of equal rights for women. As Linda Kerber has observed, "[T]he members of the Warren Court generally were certain that discrimination on the basis of race was not equal treatment under the law[, but] they were not at all certain that discrimination on the basis of sex was equally questionable." Indeed, while Warren was chief justice the Court subjected laws that treated men and women differently to nothing more rigorous than the rational relationship test. It did, in *United States v. Dege* (1960), reject the common-law doctrine that a woman could not be guilty of conspiring with her husband, Frankfurter emphasizing in his opinion for the Court that vast changes in the status of women had wiped out the traditional submission of wives to their husbands. The following year, however, in *Hoyt v. Florida* (1961), a case bearing many similarities to *Hernandez v. Texas,* the Court ruled that a woman convicted of second-degree murder in the killing of her husband had not been denied equal protection by a state statute that excluded women from jury service unless they explicitly asked to serve. The Court declined to reconsider dicta in *Strauder v. West Virginia* (1879) that said a state might constitutionally confine jury duty to males. Because Gwendolyn Hoyt's husband had been abusive and was about to leave her, this case illustrated why female defendants sometimes needed female jurors, who could empathize with their situations in ways that men could not. At the urging of his clerk, Timothy Dyk, Warren argued in conference that Hoyt's conviction should be reversed for that reason. Douglas and Black supported the Chief, and Brennan apparently wavered for a time before voting with Frankfurter, Harlan, Tom Clark, Potter Stewart, and Charles Whittaker to affirm the conviction. Reluctant to waste any of his Court's limited political capital by highlighting its divisions over a type of discrimination he believed was dying anyhow, Warren did not dissent. Instead, he published a brief concurrence in which the minority disassociated itself from the majority's assertion that treating men and women differently with respect to jury service was reasonable; it supported affirming Hoyt's conviction on the narrow ground that the record failed to show Florida was not making a good-faith effort to avoid discrimination. The obscure paragraph the chief justice published failed to challenge the endorsement of traditional gender roles by Harlan's opinion for the Court, which declared, "Despite the enlightened emancipation of women from the restrictions and protections of bygone years, and their entry into many parts of community life formerly considered to be reserved to men, woman is still . . . the center of home and family life." This outlook kept the Warren Court from doing anything to advance the cause of sexual equality.[14]

It did a great deal, however, to advance the movement for equal treatment of the country's most persistently abused outsider group: African-Americans. The Warren Court contributed to the civil rights movement of the 1950s and 1960s in part by upholding legislation enacted by Congress. It turned aside constitutional challenges to key provisions of the Civil Rights Acts of 1957 and 1964 and the Voting Rights Act of 1965. So determined was the Warren Court to uphold civil rights legislation that it validated section 4(e) of the Voting Rights Act, which under one of its own precedents was obviously unconstitutional. The Court had held in 1959 that English-language literacy tests for voters did not violate the equal protection clause. Nevertheless, in section 4(e) Congress, purportedly relying on the authority to enforce that clause given it by section 5 of the Fourteenth Amendment, prohibited such tests for persons, such as Puerto Ricans, who had been educated in American-flag schools where the language of instruction was not English. To uphold section 4(e), the Court seemingly conceded to Congress a power to transform the Fourteenth Amendment while claiming to enforce it.[15]

Besides going to extreme lengths to uphold newly enacted civil rights legislation, the Warren Court greatly expanded the reach of existing laws. In *Boynton v. Virginia* (1960), for example, it interpreted a provision of the Interstate Commerce Act prohibiting interstate common carriers from unjustly discriminating as a ban on segregation of bus station restaurants, even ones not owned by common carriers. In a pair of 1966 cases the Court breathed new life into two federal criminal statutes enacted during Reconstruction, making them effective weapons against lynchers. Especially notable was *Jones v. Alfred H. Mayer Corp.* (1968), in which it interpreted an 1866 law as barring all racial discrimination, private as well as public, in the sale or rental of real estate, thereby transforming that old statute into an open housing act in some respects more sweeping than one Congress had just adopted.[16]

Besides upholding and expansively interpreting congressional legislation, the Warren Court used the equal protection clause to attack southern subordination of African-Americans. The case that more than any other defined its public image was *Brown*. There, at the very outset of Warren's chief justiceship, the Court declared that segregated public schools violated the equal protection clause. It did not repudiate the separate-but-equal doctrine of *Plessy v. Ferguson* (1896), merely holding that principle inapplicable to public education because "[s]egregated educational facilities are inherently unequal." Having distinguished *Plessy* in order to rule for the African-American plaintiffs, though, Warren and his colleagues proceeded to treat that half-century-old precedent as if it no longer existed. "The ban on discrimination," Kurland notes, "was quickly extended to all public facilities." Lower federal courts read *Brown* as a repudiation of all governmental segregation, and the Warren Court repeatedly affirmed their decisions, without ever bothering to explain how *Brown* had come to stand for a proposition far broader than the one articulated in the opinion.[17]

The Warren Court carried its support for black rights far beyond outlawing segregation. At first its members were extremely wary of this explosive issue. In 1958, they agreed to use the word "desegregated" rather than "integrated" because "there was a feeling [it] was a shade less offensive."[18] This caution extended to interracial marriage, which violated the white South's most strongly held taboo. Confronted in the 1956 case of *Naim v. Naim* with an attack on a Virginia miscegenation statute, "On entirely specious grounds the Court refused to consider the constitutional challenge."[19] By 1964, however, its caution had evaporated. In *McLaughlin v. Florida* (1964), the Court unanimously struck down a state law criminalizing cohabitation by an African-American and a Caucasian of opposite sexes. It did so although Black warned his colleagues, "If we reverse here, state marriage laws would have to go also." Brennan responded, "Our decisions over the last 10 years require us to reverse both this and the Miscegenation Act." Three years later, in *Loving v. Virginia,* the Court unanimously did what Brennan had predicted, striking down a law forbidding intermarriage between whites and blacks. It characterized Virginia's miscegenation statute as one involving "invidious racial discrimination." But in fact neither that law nor the one invalidated in *McLaughlin* discriminated. Florida prohibited both blacks and whites from cohabiting with persons of the other race, and Virginia subjected both participants in an interracial marriage to criminal prosecution. Such formal equality was not enough for the members of the Warren Court, who considered any use of race in legislative line drawing irrational, and hence constitutionally suspect. They recognized that these laws were pillars of a legal structure carefully erected for the purpose of subordinating African-Americans, and they were determined to dismantle that edifice.[20]

## Impact on Legal Doctrine

That determination affected significantly many areas of the law. "The strongest force in current constitutional development," Cox observed in 1968, "is the demand for racial justice." One reason for this was the special favoritism the Warren Court displayed for that cause. In *Reitman v. Mulkey* (1967), it invalidated on equal protection grounds a California constitutional amendment, adopted by popular referendum, that not only eliminated two statutes forbidding racial discrimination in housing but also prohibited the state and its political subdivisions from enacting any future measures restricting the absolute discretion of property owners to sell or rent to whomever they chose. The Court admitted that California did not have to have laws against housing discrimination, but it nevertheless insisted that by adopting this amendment, the state had "significantly involved itself with invidious discriminations." Two years later the Court held that opponents of open housing legislation had violated the equal protection clause when they amended the Akron, Ohio, city charter in a way that both eliminated an existing law on the subject and required any future open housing ordinance to secure the approval of the voters. The charter provision in question simply changed the rules for adopting a particular type of legislation; on its face it did not discriminate at all against African-Americans. But, as Warren pointed out to his colleagues when they discussed the case, this legislation made it "harder to promote open housing than other things." The reason that subject had been singled out for special treatment was obvious to eight members of the Court, and in their minds justified striking down the charter provision as an "invidious denial of the equal protection of the laws." As Black pointed out in a dissenting opinion, however, the result was to compel Akron to have and enforce an open housing law. The Court had exempted opponents of racial discrimination in housing from the operation of a democratic political process that governed the enactment and repeal of legislation on all other subjects.[21]

Black was not the only justice to complain that the Court was giving African-Americans favored treatment. Harlan lectured his colleagues frequently about the need to avoid creating a body of "Negro law." When he suggested that the Court had agreed to hear one case only because of its racial overtones, Black expressed regret that Harlan had raised this issue. Brennan, too, "protested John's . . . in effect accusing the court of giving Negroes preferred status as litigants." Yet Harlan had a point. Even Frankfurter, despite a long record of support for African-American causes, expressed concern shortly before his retirement in 1962 that the Court was bending the law to help civil rights activists. "I am sure that you and I are in agreement," he wrote to Black, "that it will not advance the cause of constitutional equality for Negroes for the Court to be taking short cuts, to discriminate as partisans in favor of Negroes."[22]

Despite such admonitions from within, the Warren Court displayed a persistent partiality for certain civil rights organizations, most notably the National Association for the Advancement of Colored People (NAACP). During the 1950s, southern officials, outraged because the NAACP had assumed leadership of an escalating campaign for African-American equality, set out to cripple the organization. They attacked it with laws regulating the conduct of out-of-state corporations, while southern legislatures enacted statutes designed to hamper the organization's support of civil rights litigation and to threaten NAACP lawyers with prosecution and disciplinary action. Legislative committees, allegedly looking for communist influence, delved into its affairs. The beleaguered civil rights group found a friend and protector in the Warren Court. When an attorney for the State of Mississippi implied during oral argument that NAACP leader Aaron Henry had engaged in homosexual acts, he received a tongue-lashing from the chief justice. In a series of cases the Court thwarted Alabama's attempt to oust the organization from the state for failing to register as an out-of-state corporation and also overturned a judicial order requiring it to disclose the names of its Alabama members. It went on to invalidate a Little Rock, Arkansas, ordinance and a Louisiana statute that required the NAACP to disclose its membership lists and to strike down an Arkansas law that compelled public school teachers to identify all the organizations to which they belonged. In addition (changing its mind after a change in membership), it reversed the contempt conviction of Father Theodore Gibson, who had refused to turn the Miami branch's membership records over to an investigating committee of the Florida legislature. Finally, the Court declared unconstitutional Virginia legislation regulating the practice of law, which forbade stirring up litigation, accepting referrals from nonlawyers, and advocating lawsuits against the state.[23]

These rulings were intended to save from unjustified harassment an organization whose only offense was working to secure equal rights. "We cannot blink the fact that strong local sentiment exists against the cause which petitioner espouses," Harlan proposed to write in one opinion, exhibiting a candor that Frankfurter resisted as impolitic. To protect the NAACP, the Warren Court sometimes eschewed neutral principles, rendering decisions justified mainly by the identity of the winning party. When Alabama reminded the Court that it had upheld a law that forced the Ku Klux Klan to divulge the names of its members, the state was told that the character of the Klan's activities justified doing to it what might not be done to the NAACP. As justification for interfering with otherwise permissible state regulation of the legal profession, the Court declared in *NAACP v. Button* (1962): "In the context of NAACP objectives litigation is not a technique of resolving private differences, it is a means of achieving the lawful objective of equality of treatment." Brennan was being less than candid when he declared that it was "constitutionally irrelevant to the ground of our decision" in *Button* that "the petitioner happens to be engaged in activities of expression and association on behalf of the rights of Negro children to equal opportunity."[24]

In fact, it was because the NAACP was fighting to win equality before the law for African-Americans that the Warren Court persistently ruled in its favor, and while theoretically the nature of the group's activities was not constitutionally significant, the Court's determination to protect those activities significantly affected constitutional doctrine. As Mark Tushnet points out, "The interaction between the NAACP's lawyers and the Supreme Court produced major innovations in free expression law." The

First Amendment right of freedom of political association really originated in *NAACP v. Alabama* (1958). Harlan, who was assigned to dispose of that case the way the Court had all of those since *Brown* that raised racial issues, with a brief per curiam opinion, found the task impossible. He drafted an extended opinion that held for the NAACP on the ground that Alabama had violated its right to freedom of speech. Frankfurter objected to that approach but insisted there was a right of association that was protected against state interference by the due process clause of the Fourteenth Amendment, which would justify the desired ruling. As Bernard Schwartz reports, "Harlan and the others accepted the Frankfurter approach and the *N.A.A.C.P.* case stands as the first decision holding that there is a constitutional right to organize and join an association for advancement of beliefs and ideas." Subsequent NAACP cases—*Bates v. Little Rock* (1959), *Shelton v. Tucker* (1960), and *NAACP v. Button* (1963)—furthered the development of that doctrine.[25] Its significance, as Warren pointed out, "reaches beyond [the] Negro problem."[26]

The same was true of the First Amendment over-breadth doctrine, which *Button* revived and developed. The notion that a statute is facially invalid if it is written so broadly that it punishes constitutionally protected speech, along with activity that government has a right to proscribe, lay behind such pre–Warren Court decisions as *Cantwell v. Connecticut* (1940) and *Kunz v. New York* (1951). It was in *Button,* however, that Brennan coined the term "over breadth," pointed out "the danger of tolerating in the area of First Amendment freedoms, the existence of a penal statute susceptible to sweeping and improper application," and laid down the rule that, "Because First Amendment freedoms need breathing space to survive, government may regulate in the area only with narrow specificity." To establish that "a vague and over broad statute lends itself to selective enforcement against unpopular causes," he cited NAACP cases.[27]

Brennan soon enhanced the importance of the over-breadth doctrine by expanding the jurisdiction of the federal courts in cases where it might apply. Civil rights demonstrators often risked prosecution under overbroad state criminal statutes. They demanded access to federal trial courts to seek injunctions restraining enforcement of such laws before they were actually used against them. In *Dombrowski v. Pfister* (1965), the Warren Court gave civil rights activists what they wanted. It held that someone threatened by state authorities with prosecution under an overbroad law was entitled to an injunction from a federal court forbidding the state to prosecute or continue to threaten him. The Warren Court unsettled the law of federal jurisdiction not only in *Dombrowski,* a decision whose meaning was always somewhat unclear and which the Burger Court largely repudiated in *Younger v. Harris* (1971), but also with its ruling in *Henry v. Mississippi* (1965). That case confused the rule that the Supreme Court will not review a state court's determination of a federal question if there is also an adequate and independent state ground for the decision by announcing that this precept might sometimes not apply if the state ground were a procedural default. The successful petitioner in that case was Mississippi NAACP leader Aaron Henry.[28]

His was one of scores of convictions of civil rights activists which the Warren Court overturned. The lunch counter sit-in by four black college students in Greensboro, North Carolina, on February 1, 1960, triggered a wave of direct action that included peaceful invasions of segregated facilities, street demonstrations, and various forms of civil disobedience. Southern officials countered this campaign for equality with prosecutions not only under segregation laws but also for such offenses as disturbing the peace and trespassing. "[I]n every case in which it granted review—as it did in most cases," Loren Miller observed in 1966, ". . . the Supreme Court upset convictions upheld by state courts of last resort." Not until *Adderly v. Florida* (1966) did civil rights demonstrators lose a case on the merits. Saving them from criminal sanctions required the Court to resort to a variety of legal principles and to do considerable doctrinal innovating.[29]

"Virtually the entire law of mass demonstrations came from [the Warren Court's] civil rights [decisions]," Lucus A. Powe Jr. notes. In *Feiner v. New York* (1951), decided two years before Warren became chief justice, the Court had upheld the disorderly conduct conviction of a street corner agitator, whom the police had arrested after he refused their requests to cease vitriolic denunciations of public officials and the American Legion and intemperate calls for armed struggle by blacks. Although Feiner had provoked many onlookers and one had threatened violence, *Edwards v.*

*South Carolina* (1963) seemed to present a stronger case for governmental restriction of expression. Yet in *Edwards* the Warren Court overturned on First Amendment grounds the breach-of-the-peace convictions of 187 student civil rights protesters, who had outraged two to three hundred white onlookers by invading the grounds of South Carolina's state house to sing songs, hear speeches, and display signs denouncing segregation, then ignored police orders to disperse. Although this was, according to Stewart, "a far cry from the situation in Feiner," as John Nowak and Ronald Rotunda point out, "the situation in *Edwards* might have been potentially more dangerous than that in Feiner." The Warren Court, however, "appreciated the ability of an expansive *Feiner* doctrine to suppress civil rights demonstrations." It announced that under our system of government one function of free speech is to invite dispute; hence, the prejudices of others cannot be permitted to silence a speaker with an unpopular message. The Warren Court overturned the convictions of other civil rights demonstrators on similar grounds in *Cox v. Louisiana* (1965) and *Gregory v. Chicago* (1969). These rulings established, according to Laurence Tribe, a principle that even imminent spectator violence cannot justify the suppression of protected speech if the police could prevent violence with reasonable crowd control tactics.[30]

The Warren Court's resolve to overturn convictions of civil rights demonstrators shaped criminal law as well as First Amendment doctrine. The American Law Institute had included in its new Model Penal Code an exception to the general rule that ignorance of the law is no excuse: reasonable reliance upon an erroneous explanation of the law by a public officer charged with interpreting, administering, or enforcing it is a defense. In *Cox v. Louisiana* (1965), the Court provided a constitutional basis for this principle. Cox had been convicted of violating a statute that made it a crime to picket or parade "near" a courthouse, although city police officials, in the presence of the mayor and sheriff, had said the demonstrators could meet where they did, 101 feet from the courthouse steps. Brennan and Clark insisted it was unfair to punish Cox for being where the "police had said it is o.k. to be"; even Harlan thought they had waived the statute. To save Cox from unfair punishment, the Court held that the due process clause did "not permit convictions under such circumstances."[31]

It injected into the criminal law a constitutional rule of even greater importance in *Bouie v. City of Columbia* (1964). *Bouie* involved protesters who had been convicted of criminal trespass for refusing to leave a drugstore restaurant, where they were staging a sit-in, when asked to do so by the manager. The law under which the demonstrators were prosecuted made it a misdemeanor to enter the premises of another after being prohibited to do so, but it said nothing about remaining there after being told to leave. In affirming the convictions the South Carolina Supreme Court construed it to apply to the latter situation as well. Under a well-established doctrine, any criminal statute that failed to give fair warning of what conduct it punished violated the due process clause. In previous cases applying this principle, however, the source of the uncertainty about the reach of the statute had been its vague language. In reversing *Bouie,* the Warren Court declared that a denial of the right of fair warning could also result "from an unforeseeable and retroactive judicial expansion of narrow and precise statutory language." Six years later the California Supreme Court provided a dramatic demonstration of how significant this constitutional limitation on the freedom of courts to interpret the language of criminal statutes could be; because previous decisions construing the state's murder statute had held that the "human beings" who could be victims of that crime must have been born alive, it dismissed murder charges against a man who had brutally attacked his ex-wife, killing her fetus.[32]

## Limits of the Court's Commitment

Although willing to promulgate a doctrine as consequential as the one announced in *Bouie* in order to free civil rights demonstrators, the Warren Court was not prepared to alter American constitutional law radically in order to promote equality. Indeed, many of the doctrinal innovations emerging from the "sit-in" cases are really evidence of its conservatism. They reveal reluctance to assign equality a higher priority than other values, such as liberty and order. The Warren Court littered the law with new doctrines because it was unwilling to change the law as fundamentally as civil rights advocates desired.

Rather than accept their arguments, the Court, encouraged by the Justice Department, found narrow grounds on which to reverse the convictions of black activists. In December 1961, Frankfurter expressed the hope that the first prosecution of sit-in demonstrators to reach the Court, *Garner v. Louisiana* (1961), would remain "a small case." "I share deeply the view expressed by you at our original Conference discussion on these cases," he wrote to Warren, "that they should be disposed of on the narrowest possible grounds." Frankfurter wanted the Court to rely on *Thompson v. Louisville* (1960), a case having nothing to do with African-American rights, in which it had reversed loitering and disorderly conduct convictions because there was no evidentiary support for them, announcing in the process that "it is a violation of due process to convict and punish a man without evidence of his guilt." *Thompson* was also a favorite of Warren, who often began conference discussions of cases involving civil rights demonstrators by asserting that there was "no evidence to justify the judgments of conviction." Harlan objected to this approach, and Douglas also expressed reservations about it, but others liked the "no evidence" tactic and the related one of holding the statute under which protectors had been prosecuted void for vagueness. Both techniques produced reversals without creating broadly applicable precedents.[33]

Cases such as *Taylor v. Louisiana* (1962) and *Wright v. Georgia* (1963) employed similar methodology but added other elements to confused constitutional concoctions developed to justify overturning the convictions of civil rights demonstrators. What muddled the reasoning in sit-in cases and inspired resort to the narrow "no evidence" rationale was the "state action" doctrine. Under the *Civil Rights Cases* (1883), only governmental action could violate the Fourteenth Amendment. If an African-American was punished for violating a law requiring places of public accommodation, such as restaurants, to be segregated, he was clearly a victim of state action. If a restaurant owner refused to serve him because of his color, however, there was no violation of the equal protection clause unless the state encouraged or assisted the restaurateur to discriminate. In *Peterson v. City of Greenville* (1963), the Court justified reversal by pointing to a municipal ordinance that prohibited whites and Negroes from dining together and reasoning that, because a trespass law was being used to enforce that ordinance, there had been a violation of the Fourteenth Amendment. The justices decided *Gober v. City of Birmingham* (1963) and *Avent v. North Carolina* (1963) on the same basis. *Lombard v. Louisiana* (1963) had arisen in New Orleans, which had no segregation ordinance, so the Court held that statements by the mayor and superintendent of police that sit-ins were prohibited there supplied the necessary state action. In *Robinson v. Florida* (1964), it declared that state health regulations requiring separate toilet and lavatory facilities for white and black customers discouraged serving the races together, and hence constituted state action coercing segregation. The deputizing of the amusement park security guard who made the trespassing arrests in *Griffin v. Maryland* (1964) was enough state involvement to produce reversal in that case.[34]

Twice the Supreme Court employed prestidigitation to make state action problems disappear. Confronted in *Bell v. Maryland* (1964) with a case devoid of evidence that the state had influenced the restaurant manager's decision to request the use of trespass laws against sit-in demonstrators, the Court returned it to the Maryland Court of Appeals for reconsideration in light of public accommodations laws the state and county had enacted after that court affirmed the convictions. Soon after *Bell,* Congress passed the Civil Rights Act of 1964, Title II of which forbade restaurants and other places of public accommodation to discriminate on the basis of race. In *Hamm v. City of Rock Hill* (1964), the Supreme Court held that this law had abated state trespass convictions based on attempts to obtain integrated service prior to its passage. The Civil Rights Act clearly prohibited such prosecutions in the future, but as Black pointed out in dissent, a statute that had been on the books for a century made it unlikely Congress intended Title II to operate retroactively.[35]

Such evasions would have been unnecessary had the Court simply conceded in *Bell* that there was state action whenever a state court punished someone for violation of a state trespass statute. As precedent for such a ruling, it could have cited *Shelley v. Kraemer* (1948), which had held that judicial enforcement of a racially restrictive covenant in a deed constituted state action. Douglas urged his colleagues to take this approach. "A State expresses a policy whenever it acts through a prosecutor and a court—a policy no less clear than when it acts through its legislator [*sic*]," he argued. "The question in the sit-in cases is . . . not whether there is state action but whether States, acting through their courts, can constitutionally put a racial cordon around businesses serving the public." For Douglas the answer to that question was clearly no. "When one citizen because of his race, creed, or color is denied the privilege of being treated as any other citizen in places of public accommodation," he declared in a separate opinion in *Bell,* "we have classes of citizenship, one being more degraded than the other." Goldberg agreed with Douglas about that but not about the soundness of the *Shelley* approach. As far as he was concerned, a state was "obligated under the Fourteenth Amendment to maintain a system of law in which Negroes are not denied protection in their claim to be treated as equal members of the community." If it used its criminal trespass laws against African-Americans who were seeking service in restaurants, a state would be frustrating their exercise of a "constitutionally guaranteed right," he wrote in a concurring opinion in *Bell.* This would be true even if all it were doing was "legitimating a proprietor's attempt at self-help." Although disagreeing with Goldberg about the applicability of *Shelley,* Warren agreed with him that there was a civil right of access to public places and opposed interposing principles of privacy and the protection of property rights between African-Americans and the enjoyment of that right. He signed his colleague's concurrence.[36]

Brennan agreed with the chief justice, Goldberg, and Douglas that restaurant owners could not call upon the state to assist them in excluding African-Americans, and he voted with them in conference to reverse the *Bell* convictions. They lost 5-4. Brennan and Warren, fearing that a Supreme Court ruling embodying Black's views might endanger prospects for passage of Title II, which was then being debated in Congress, sought to delay a decision by requesting the views of the solicitor general on the constitutional issue. Black managed to hold a majority for an opinion affirming the convictions, however, until Brennan discovered that Maryland had enacted a public accommodations law and, to avoid losing on the constitutional issue, proposed vacating the judgment and remanding the matter to the Maryland courts. Warren and Goldberg were willing to go along with him, but Douglas continued to insist that the Court should resolve the fundamental constitutional issue in the case. Brennan got a majority for his approach only after Clark, perhaps in a devious endeavor to promote that result, unexpectedly abandoned Black and wrote an opinion supporting reversal. At that point there should have been five votes for overturning the convictions as violations of the Fourteenth Amendment. Perhaps because Stewart had charged him with being motivated by expediency rather than principle, however, Brennan continued to push for sending the case back to the Maryland courts. Finally, Stewart agreed to join him if Clark would also. Warren, anxious to unite the Court, abandoned plans to write separately, and five justices endorsed an opinion that avoided the constitutional issue. Only Douglas and Black (now dissenting for himself, Harlan, and White) addressed it, and they disagreed.[37]

In a sense it did not matter how, or if, the Court resolved the issue posed by *Bell,* for within two weeks after the decision was announced, Lyndon Johnson signed the Civil Rights Act into law, giving African-Americans a statutory right to integrated service in most places of public accommodation. *Bell v. Maryland* and the other civil rights demonstration cases are important, however, because of what they reveal about the limits of the Warren Court's commitment to racial equality and its champions. They expose a conflict within the Court between positivist and natural law conceptions of liberalism in which the latter prevailed. Douglas, who approached these cases from a positivist perspective, was inclined to view discrimination by privately owned restaurants as public, at least if the state supported it by prosecuting those who demanded service from an unwilling owner. Like the inns and common carriers the law had long subjected to regulation, restaurants provided an essential service, and hence were affected with a public interest. Unlike Douglas, Black was a natural law liberal who viewed the state action doctrine as protecting an autonomous sphere that should remain beyond governmental interference. In his *Bell* dissent he wrote that the equal protection clause "does not of itself, standing alone, in the absence of some cooperative state action or compulsion, forbid property holders, including restaurant owners, to ban people from entering or remaining upon their premises, even if the owners act out of racial prejudice." Furthermore, a bigoted restaurateur had "the right to call the police and get help to throw the customer out," Black argued. When they arrested an unwanted patron for trespassing, officers were merely protecting the businessman's natural rights and, by eliminating the need for him to resort to self-help, preserving the peace. If such prosecutions were treated as state action, privacy would be destroyed. To this argument Douglas responded that there was no constitutional right to privacy (he had not yet invented it in *Griswold v. Connecticut*) and that the businesses where sit-ins had taken place bore "little resemblance to any institution of property which we customarily associate with privacy." Black insisted, though, that under the American system of private property a store owner had the same rights as a home owner.[38]

Harlan, Clark, and White agreed with him, as did the retired Frankfurter, who in 1963 urged Black to draft an opinion stating "that you would never consent to any decision which held that the Constitution of the United States compelled you to do business with whom you did not want." Surprisingly, Goldberg also thought business owners had a right to choose their own customers and to segregate if they wished. During conference discussions, only Warren and Brennan endorsed Douglas's contention that use of the criminal law to enforce an owner's choice would amount to unconstitutional state action. A majority of the Warren Court was unwilling to tolerate any sort of partnership or symbiotic relationship between private individuals who wished to discriminate and government agencies, holding, for example, that a restaurateur who leased the premises where he did business from a municipal parking authority had to comply with the equal protection clause. But while willing to stretch the concept of state action, and even to hint that Congress might ignore the doctrine when legislating against racially motivated violence, most members of the Court were unwilling to abandon entirely what they viewed as an essential safeguard of individual liberty.[39]

While their debates over the state action doctrine tended to focus on the prerogatives of property owners, these were not the only individual rights members of the Warren Court were unwilling to sacrifice to promote equality. Black opposed combating jury discrimination by eliminating peremptory challenges in criminal cases, because he considered them essential to a fair trial. Even Douglas believed "any organization exercising associational rights within the protection of the First Amendment—be they religious, political, or otherwise . . . can elect or reject whomever they please as members."[40]

Concern for liberty fueled a reaction by some members of the Court against the tactics of those who were demonstrating for equality. In *Brown v. Louisiana* (1966), the Court overturned on imprecisely articulated First Amendment grounds the disturbing-the-peace convictions of five men who had staged a peaceful sit-in at a segregated public library. Dissenting for himself, Harlan, Clark, and Stewart, Black denied that freedom of speech gave anyone "the right to use someone else's property, even that owned by government and dedicated to other purposes, as a stage to express dissident ideas." He was concerned that "the power of private nongovernmental groups" might deny those who wanted to go to the library to learn the opportunity to do so. The time had come, Black asserted, "to challenge the assumption . . . that groups that think they have been mistreated or that have actually been mistreated have a constitutional right to use the public's streets, buildings, and property to protest whatever, wherever, whenever they want, without regard to whom such conduct may disturb." Although not joining his dissent, neither White nor Brennan was willing to hold the demonstrators' activities were protected by the Constitution; White concurred on "no evidence" grounds, and Brennan used the over-breadth doctrine. To Douglas, *Brown* suggested that a majority of the Court was "moving toward the anti-Negro side."[41]

It arrived at that destination in *Adderly v. Florida* (1966)—its first decision affirming a conviction of civil rights demonstrators—because of concern within the Court about a breakdown of law and order. In *Cox v. Louisiana,* both Black's dissent and Goldberg's opinion for the Court emphasized that government could not be deprived of the power to preserve order. Rejecting the contention that the First Amendment afforded as much protection to marching and picketing as it did to pure speech, Goldberg declared: "The constitutional guarantee of liberty implies the existence of an organized society maintaining public order, without which liberty itself would be lost in the excesses of anarchy." By the time *Adderly* was decided, Goldberg had left the Court, but White remained. He believed that by obstructing public passageways and marching on a courthouse the *Cox* protesters had threatened the independence and integrity of the judiciary, and had written earlier that precluding states from prosecuting sit-in demonstrators for trespass would be "nothing short of an invitation to private warfare and a complete negation of the central peace-keeping function of the state." Clark, who had declared in *Cox,* "I have always been taught that this Nation was dedicated to freedom *under law* not under mobs, whether they be integrationists or white supremacists," held similar views. In *Adderly,* he, White, Harlan, and Stewart joined a Black opinion holding that trespassing convictions of Florida A&M students for demonstrating on the grounds of the Tallahassee jail did not violate the First Amendment. Stridently asserting that those who wanted to protest did not have a right to do so whenever and wherever they wanted, Black quoted Goldberg's *Cox* language to prove his point.[42]

As long as all civil rights demonstrators were doing was violating clearly unconstitutional segregation laws, the Warren Court found it easy to overturn their convictions. Like the NAACP, they were obviously victims of racism. Convictions for which there was no evidentiary support, especially for violation of vague and overbroad statutes that lent themselves to discriminatory enforcement, suggested the same thing. But when civil rights protesters insisted that their cause justified violating admittedly valid laws designed to protect privacy, property rights, and public order, many members of the Court drew back. They supported civil rights but not civil disobedience. In two 1966 cases the Court held that defendants allegedly being prosecuted for refusing to leave segregated restaurants could remove their cases from state to federal court, but that those alleging they would be unable to get a fair trial on other charges filed against them because of their civil rights activities could not. The language of the removal statutes provided grounds for distinguishing the two cases, but some of the Court's language is revealing. Noting that the Civil Rights Act of 1964 conferred an absolute right to violate laws that were being used to deny African-Americans equal service in restaurants, it added, "[N]o federal law confers an absolute right on private citizens—on civil rights advocates, on Negroes, or on anybody else—to obstruct a public street, to contribute to the delinquency of a minor, to drive an automobile without a license, or to bite a policeman."[43]

A majority of the Warren Court proved unwilling to condone such conduct, even when engaged in by persons struggling to achieve equal rights for African-Americans. The Supreme Court that Earl Warren led was strongly committed to the promotion of equality, especially racial equality. It was also committed to protecting those organizations and individuals that were working to advance this cause. Significant changes in numerous areas of the law attest to its commitment. The Warren Court was not willing, however, to alter constitutional doctrine sufficiently to give African-Americans a right to be treated as equals by whites. Nor was it willing to protect those black activists whose tactics seemed to a majority of the Court to endanger public order and individual liberty. Other values competed with equality for the allegiance of the Warren Court, and other concerns blunted its egalitarian inclinations.

## Notes

1. William E. Nelson, "The Changing Meaning of Equality in Twentieth-Century Constitutional Law," *Washington and Lee Law Review* 52 (1995): 4, 102; Philip B. Kurland, *Politics, the Constitution and the Warren Court* (Chicago: University of Chicago Press, 1970), 98, xx. The chapter in Kurland's book entitled "Egalitarianism and the Warren Court" is essentially the same as the article with that title that appears in *Michigan Law Review* 68 (March 1970): 629–82.

2. It is disputed by Ronald Kahn. See his "The Supreme Court as a (Counter) Majoritarian Institution: Misperceptions of the Warren, Burger, and Rehnquist Courts," *Detroit College Law Review* 1994 (spring 1994): 27; and Kahn, *The Supreme Court and Constitutional Theory, 1953–1993* (Lawrence: University Press of Kansas, 1994), 5.

3. As Ronald Dworkin explains, the right to "treatment as an equal" is the right to be treated with the same respect and concern as anyone else. Dworkin, *Taking Rights Seriously* (Cambridge, Mass.: Harvard University Press, 1978), 227.

4. Kurland, *Politics*, 163–64; *WHYY, Inc. v. Glassboro*, 393 U.S. 117 (1968); *Morey v. Doud*, 354 U.S. 457 (1957); ibid. at 475 (Frankfurter, J., dissenting). It was the exempting of some currency exchanges by name rather than some neutral formula that led a majority of the Court to vote to overturn the statute at issue in *Morey*. Conference notes, April 26, 1956, Box 1173, William O. Douglas Papers, Manuscript Division, Library of Congress (hereinafter cited as LC).

5. *Shapiro v. Thompson*, 394 U.S. 618, 658–59 (1969) (Harlan, J., dissenting); Gerald Gunther, "Forward: In Search of Evolving Doctrine on a Changing Court: A Model for a Newer Equal Protection," *Harvard Law Review* 86 (November 1972): 9–10; *Korematsu v. United States*, 323 U.S. 214, 216 (1944).

6. Gunther, "Newer Equal Protection," 8; Kurland, *Politics*, 167, 8–9; Mark V. Tushnet, *Making Constitutional Law: Thurgood Marshall and the Supreme Court, 1961–1991* (New York: Oxford University Press, 1997), 96; *Skinner v. Oklahoma*, 316 U.S. 535, 541 (1942); *Reynolds v. Sims*, 377 U.S. 533,

561–62 (1964); *Harper v. Virginia State Board of Elections,* 383 U.S. 1663, 1670 (1966); *Shapiro v. Thompson,* 394 U.S. 618 (1969).

7. *Bolling v. Sharpe,* 347 U.S. 497, 499 (1954); G. Edward White, *Earl Warren: A Public Life* (New York: Oxford University Press, 1982), 226–27; Mark V. Tushnet, *Making Civil Rights Law: Thurgood Marshall and the Supreme Court, 1936–1961* (New York: Oxford University Press, 1994), 214–15.

8. John E. Nowak and Ronald Rotunda, *Constitutional Law,* 6th ed. (St. Paul, Minn.: West Publishing, 2000), 791–92.

9. *Reynolds v. Sims,* 377 U.S. 533 (1964); *Wesbury v. Sanders,* 376 U.S. 1 (1964); *Avery v. Midland County,* 390 U.S. 474 (1968); Kurland, *Politics,* 161, 165–66; *Gomillion v. Lightfoot,* 364 U.S. 339 (1960); *Gideon v. Wainwright,* 372 U.S. 335 (1963); *Douglas v. California,* 372 U.S. 353 (1963); *Griffin v. Illinois,* 351 U.S. 12 (1956); Arthur J. Goldberg, "Equality and Governmental Action," *New York University Law Review* 39 (April 1964): 218; *Miranda v. Arizona,* 384 U.S. 436 (1966); Archibald Cox, *The Warren Court: Constitutional Decision as an Instrument of Reform* (Cambridge, Mass.: Harvard University Press, 1968), 86.

10. Morton J. Horwitz, "The Warren Court and the Pursuit of Justice," *Washington and Lee Law Review* 50 (winter 1993): 10–13; Tinsley E. Yarbrough, *John Marshall Harlan: Great Dissenter of the Warren Court* (New York: Oxford University Press, 1992), 51–52, 61–62. Horwitz makes the same point about this being a "Court of Outsiders" in his brief history of the Warren Court, *The Warren Court and the Pursuit of Justice* (New York: Hill and Wang, 1998).

11. *Hernandez v. Texas,* 347 U.S. 475 (1954); *Rice v. Sioux City Memorial Park,* 349 U.S. 70 (1954); [Felix Frankfurter], Memorandum for the Conference Re: No. 28, *Rice v. Sioux City Memorial Park Cemetery, Inc.,* n.d., Box 494, John M. Harlan Papers, Seeley G. Mudd Library, Princeton University, Princeton, New Jersey.

12. *Levy v. Louisiana,* 391 U.S. 68, 70, 71, 72 (1968); *Glona v. American Guarantee & Liability Insurance Company,* 391 U.S. 73 (1968).

13. Yarbrough, *John Marshall Harlan,* 304–7; Frank I. Michaelman, "Forward: On Protecting the Poor Through the Fourteenth Amendment," *Harvard Law Review* 83 (1969): 9–11; "No. 48—Harper v. Virginia State Board of Elections" file, Box 249, Harlan Papers; *Harper v. Virginia State Board of Elections,* 383 U.S. 663 (1966); *Griffin v. Illinois,* 351 U.S. 12 (1956); *Shapiro v. Thompson,* 394 U.S. 618 (1969). As Kahn notes, in *Shapiro,* "[T]he Warren Court never says the right to welfare is fundamental. It upholds a right to interstate movement, but not a right to welfare per se." Kahn, *Supreme Court and Constitutional Theory,* 51.

14. Linda K. Kerber, *No Constitutional Right to Be Ladies: Women and the Obligations of Citizenship* (New York: Oxford University Press, 1998), 172, 124–27, 177–82; Ruth Bader Ginsburg, "Sexual Equality Under the Fourteenth and Equal Rights Amendments," *Washington University Law Quarterly* 1979 (1979): 163–64; *United States v. Dege,* 364 U.S. 51, 54 (1960); *Hoyt v. Florida,* 368 U.S. 57, 60–61 (1961); Bernard Schwartz, *Super Chief: Earl Warren and His Supreme Court—A Judicial Biography* (New York: Oxford University Press, 1983), 400–401; Conference notes on *Hoyt v. Florida,* Box 408, William J. Brennan Jr. Papers, LC; 368 U.S. at 69 (Warren, J., concurring); ibid. at 61–62.

15. *United States v. Raines,* 362 U.S. 17 (1960); *Heart of Atlanta Motel v. United States,* 379 U.S. 241 (1964); *Katzenbach v. McClung,* 379 U.S. 294 (1964); *South Carolina v. Katzenbach,* 383 U.S. 301 (1966); *Lassiter v. Northampton County Board of Elections,* 360 U.S. 45 (1959); *Katzenbach v. Morgan,* 384 U.S.

641 (1966). In his opinion for the Court in *Morgan,* Justice Brennan insisted that the Court was not making it possible for Congress, under the guise of enforcing the Fourteenth Amendment, to abrogate or dilute the substantive guarantees of the equal protection and due process clauses. Ibid. at 651 n. 10.

16. *Boynton v. Virginia,* 364 U.S. 454, 457–63 (1960); *United States v. Guest,* 383 U.S. 745 (1966); *United States v. Price,* 383 U.S. 787 (1966); Michal R. Belknap, *Federal Law and Southern Order: Racial Violence and Constitutional Conflict in the Post-Brown South* (Athens: University of Georgia Press, 1987), 11–20, 159–82; *Jones v. Alfred H. Mayer Co.,* 392 U.S. 409 (1968).

17. Mark Tushnet, "The Warren Court as History," in *The Warren Court in Historical and Political Perspective,* ed. Mark Tushnet (Charlottesville: University Press of Virginia, 1993), 4; *Brown v. Board of Education,* 347 U.S. 483, 495 (1954); Kurland, *Politics,* 71, 124; *Muir v. Louisville Park Theatrical Association,* 347 U.S. 971 (1954); *Mayor and City Council of Baltimore City v. Dawson,* 350 U.S. 877 (1955); *Holmes v. City of Atlanta,* 350 U.S. 879 (1955); *Gayle v. Browder,* 352 U.S. 903 (1956); *New Orleans City Park Improvement Association v. Detiege,* 358 U.S. 54 (1958); *State Athletic Commission v. Dorsey,* 359 U.S. 533 (1959); *Turner v. City of Memphis,* 369 U.S. 350 (1962); *Johnson v. Virginia,* 373 U.S. 61 (1963); *Schiro v. Bynum,* 375 U.S. 395 (1964); *Lee v. Washington,* 390 U.S. 333 (1968).

18. William J. Brennan Jr. to Tom C. Clark, May 23, 1963, Box 493, Harlan Papers.

19. Tushnet, "Warren Court as History," 5; *Naim v. Naim,* 350 U.S. 985 (1956).

20. *McLaughlin v. Florida,* 379 U.S. 184 (1964); Conference notes on *McLaughlin v. Florida,* October 16, 1964, Box 1329, William O. Douglas Papers, LC; *Loving v. Virginia,* 388 U.S. 1 (1967); Felix Frankfurter to John Marshall Harlan, December 1, 1961, Box 154, Felix Frankfurter Papers, Harvard Law School Library; Kurland, *Politics,* 157.

21. Cox, *Warren Court,* 5; *Reitman v. Mulkey,* 387 U.S. 369, 380 (1967); *Hunter v. Erickson,* 393 U.S. 385, 393 (1969); ibid. at 396–97 (Black, J., dissenting); Conference notes on *Hunter v. Erickson,* Box 416, Brennan Papers.

22. Yarbrough, *John Marshall Harlan,* 236–37; draft dissent in *Holt v. Virginia,* May 7, 1965, Box 129, Brennan Papers; H.L.B. to John Harlan, May 10, 1965, Box 484, Harlan Papers; William J. Brennan Jr. to William O. Douglas, January 9, 1963, Box 85, Brennan Papers; Felix Frankfurter to Hugo Black, February 19, 1962, Box 366, Hugo L. Black Papers, LC.

23. Loren Miller, *The Petitioners: The Story of the Supreme Court of the United States and the Negro* (Cleveland: World Publishing, 1966), 375–91; Tushnet, *Making Civil Rights Law,* 272–300; *Washington Post,* October 14, 1964; *NAACP v. Alabama, ex rel. Paterson,* 357 U.S. 449 (1958); *NAACP v. Alabama,* 360 U.S. 240 (1959); *NAACP v. Gallion,* 368 U.S. 16 (1961); *Bates v. Little Rock,* 361 U.S. 516 (1960); *Louisiana ex rel. Gremillion v. NAACP,* 366 U.S. 293 (1961); *NAACP v. Alabama, ex rel. Flowers,* 377 U.S. 288 (1964); *Shelton v. Tucker,* 364 U.S. 479 (1960); *Gibson v. Florida Legislative Investigation Committee,* 372 U.S. 539 (1963); *NAACP v. Button,* 371 U.S. 415 (1963).

24. J.M.H., Memorandum for the Conference, May 23, 1958, Box 10, Brennan Papers; Tushnet, *Making Civil Rights Law,* 286; *NAACP v. Alabama,* 357 U.S. at 465; *NAACP v. Button,* 371 U.S. at 429; Announcement of Opinion in *National Association for the Advancement of Colored People v. Attorney General of Alabama,* Box 85, Brennan Papers.

25. Cox, *Warren Court,* 103; Tushnet, *Making Civil Rights Law,* 284;

Yarbrough, *John Marshall Harlan,* 161; J.M.H., Memorandum for the Conference Re: No. 91—*NAACP v. Alabama,* April 22, 1958, Box 46, Harlan Papers; *NAACP v. Alabama,* 357 U.S. at 460–61; Schwartz, *Super Chief,* 304–5; *Bates v. Little Rock,* 361 U.S. at 523; *Shelton v. Tucker,* 364 U.S. at 487–88; *NAACP v. Button,* 371 U.S. at 428–30.

26. Conference notes on *Shelton v. Tucker,* November 11, 1960, Box 1233, Douglas Papers.

27. Owen Fiss, "Dombrowski," *Yale Law Journal* 86 (1977): 1112; *Cantwell v. Connecticut,* 310 U.S. 296 (1940); *Kunz v. New York,* 340 U.S. 290 (1951); Robert C. Post, "William J. Brennan and the Warren Court," in *The Warren Court in Historical and Political Perspective,* ed. Mark Tushnet (Charlottesville: University Press of Virginia, 1993), 132–33; *NAACP v. Button,* 371 U.S. at 433, 435–36; Tushnet, "Warren Court as History," 9.

28. Fiss, "Dombrowski," 1103, 1112–16; *Dombrowski v. Pfister,* 380 U.S. 479 (1965); Charles Alan Wright, *Law of Federal Courts,* 5th ed. (St. Paul, Minn.: West Publishing, 1994), 792–94; *Younger v. Harris,* 401 U.S. 37 (1971); *Henry v. Mississippi,* 379 U.S. 443 (1965).

29. Cox, *The Warren Court,* 41, 110; Miller, *Petitioners,* 402–3.

30. Lucas A. Powe Jr., *The Warren Court and American Politics* (Cambridge, Mass.: Harvard University Press, 2000), 491; *Feiner v. New York,* 340 U.S. 315 (1951); *Edwards v. South Carolina,* 372 U.S. 229, 236–38 (1963); Nowak and Rotunda, *Constitutional Law,* 1195; *Cox v. Louisiana,* 379 U.S. 536, 551 (1965); *Gregory v. City of Chicago,* 394 U.S., 111, 112 (1969); Laurence H. Tribe, *American Constitutional Law,* 2d ed. (Mineola, N.Y.: Foundation Press, 1988), 854.

31. *Cox v. Louisiana,* 379 U.S. 559, 571 (1965); Model Penal Code Sec. 2.04(3)(b)(iv); Conference notes on No. 24—*Cox v. Louisiana,* October 23, 1964, Box 1329, Douglas Papers. The final draft of the Model Penal Code was approved by the ALI in 1962.

32. *Bouie v. City of Columbia,* 378 U.S. 347 (1964), 351–52; Wayne R. LaFave, *Criminal Law,* 3d ed. (St. Paul, Minn.: West Publishing, 2000), 110–11; *Keeler v. Superior Court of Amador County,* 2 Cal. 3d 619, 87 Cal. Rptr. 481, 470 P.2d 617 (1970).

33. Schwartz, *Super Chief,* 480–82, 486, 508–9; FF to the Chief Justice, December 4, 1961, Box 534, Harlan Papers; *Thompson v. Louisville,* 362 U.S. 199, 206 (1960); Conference notes on *Garner v. Louisiana,* Box 408, Brennan Papers; Conference notes on *Shuttlesworth v. Birmingham,* Box 416, Brennan Papers; Conference notes on *Shuttlesworth v. City of Birmingham,* November 9, 1962, Box 1280, Conference notes on *Abernathy v. Alabama,* October 16, 1964, Box 1328, and Conference notes on *Brown v. Louisiana,* December 10, 1965, Box 1352, all in Douglas Papers; *Garner v. Louisiana,* 368 U.S. 157, 185–86 (Harlan, J., concurring); Yarbrough, *John Marshall Harlan,* 242–45; Cox, *Warren Court,* 41; Memorandum from the Chief Justice, Re: *The Sit-In Cases,* n.d., Box 83, Brennan Papers; *Barr v. City of Columbia,* 378 U.S. 146 (1964).

34. *Taylor v. Louisiana,* 370 U.S. 154 (1962); *Wright v. Georgia,* 373 U.S. 284 (1963); *Civil Rights Cases,* 109 U.S. 3 (1883); *Peterson v. City of Greenville,* 373 U.S. 244 (1963); *Gober v. City of Birmingham,* 373 U.S. 374 (1963); *Avent v. North Carolina,* 373 U.S. 375 (1963); *Lombard v. Louisiana,* 373 U.S. 267 (1963); *Robinson v. Florida,* 378 U.S. 153 (1964); *Griffin v. Maryland,* 378 U.S. 130 (1964).

35. *Bell v. Maryland,* 378 U.S. 226 (1964); *Hamm v. City of Rock Hill,* 379 U.S. 306 (1964); ibid. at 319–20.

36. William O. Douglas, Memorandum to the Conference In Re: *The Sit-In Cases* Argued the Week of October 14, 1963, October 21, 1963, Box 1299, Douglas Papers; *Bell v. Maryland,* 378 U.S. at 252 (Douglas, J., dissenting); ibid. at 286, 311 (Goldberg, J., concurring); Conference notes, October 25, 1963, Box 1300, Douglas Papers; Conference notes, *Bell v. Maryland,* Box 410, Brennan Papers; Schwartz, *Super Chief,* 514–15.

37. William O. Douglas, Memorandum for the Files No. 12—*Bell v. Maryland,* June 20, 1964, Box 1314, Douglas Papers; Tushnet, "Warren Court as History," 10–11; Schwartz, *Super Chief,* 508–25; William O. Douglas to Tom C. Clark, June 8, 1964, Box A151, Tom C. Clark Papers, Tarlton Law Library, University of Texas, Austin; Earl Warren to William O. Douglas, Box 1280, Douglas Papers. Box 376 of the Black Papers contains a fairly complete documentary history of the 1964 sit-in cases, containing intra-Court correspondence and typed versions of conference notes, which was prepared by Black clerks A. E. Dick Howard and John G. Kester.

38. Paul Brest, "State Action and Liberal Theory: A Casenote on *Flagg Brothers v. Brooks,*" *University of Pennsylvania Law Review* 130 (June 1982): 1299–301; *Lombard v. Louisiana,* 373 U.S. at 279–81 (Douglas, J., dissenting); *Bell v. Maryland,* 378 U.S. at 326–28 (Black, J., dissenting) and 253–54 (Douglas, J., dissenting); Conference notes on *Peterson v. City of Greenville,* November 9, 1962, Box 1280, and Conference notes on *Griffin v. Maryland,* October 23, 1963, Box 1300, both in Douglas Papers; Conference notes on Sit-Ins, Box A135, Clark Papers.

39. Conference notes on *Peterson v. City of Greenville;* Conference notes on *Griffin v. Maryland;* Arthur Goldberg to Earl Warren, February 12, 1963, Box 370, Black Papers; [Felix Frankfurter] to Hugo Black, May 6, 1963, Box 484, Harlan Papers; *Burton v. Wilmington Parking Authority,* 365 U.S. 715 (1961); *Pennsylvania v. Board of Directors of City Trusts,* 353 U.S. 989 (1957); *Evans v. Newton,* 382 U.S. 296 (1966); *United States v. Guest,* 383 U.S. 745, 762 (1966) (Clark, J., concurring), ibid. at 782 (Brennan, J., concurring in part).

40. Hugo L. Black to Byron White, February 17, 1965, Box 384, Black Papers; William O. Douglas, Memorandum to the Conference, June 14, 1963, Box 84, Brennan Papers.

41. *Brown v. Louisiana,* 383 U.S. 131 (1966); ibid. at 166–67, 162 (Black, J., dissenting); ibid. at 150–51 (White, J., concurring); ibid. at 144, 147 (Brennan, J., concurring); Laura Kalman, *Abe Fortas: A Biography* (New Haven, Conn.: Yale University Press, 1990), 281.

42. *Cox v. Louisiana,* 379 U.S. at 554; William E. Nelson, "Byron R. White: A Liberal of 1960," in *The Warren Court in Historical and Political Perspective,* ed. Mark Tushnet (Charlottesville: University Press of Virginia, 1993), 152; draft dissenting opinion by Justice White in *Bell v. Maryland,* June 17, 1964, Box A151, Clark Papers; *Cox v. Louisiana,* 379 U.S. at 589 (Clark, J., concurring in No. 24 and dissenting in No. 49); *Adderly v. Florida,* 385 U.S. 39, 47–48 (1966).

43. Cox, *Warren Court,* 112; *Georgia v. Rachel,* 384 U.S. 780 (1966); *City of Greenwood v. Peacock,* 384 U.S. 808 (1966); ibid. at 826–27.

*Chapter Eight*

# The Overlooked Litigant in *Tinker v. Des Moines Independent Community School District* (1969)

John W. Johnson

## What's in a Name?

Consider the names Robert Townsend Hooe, Henry Winston, Ethel Louise Belton, and Carl Calvin Westover. If told that these individuals were primary litigants in four of the most important cases in United States constitutional history, could you associate them with their famous decisions? Give up? How about William Marbury, Eugene Dennis, Linda Brown, and Ernesto Miranda? That's easier, isn't it?

Marbury and Hooe were two of the midnight justice of the peace appointees of President John Adams who did not receive their commissions, sought a writ of mandamus from the U.S. Supreme Court, and occasioned Chief Justice John Marshall's brilliant opinion in *Marbury v. Madison.*[1] Dennis and Winston were two of the eleven leaders of the American Communist Party prosecuted by the federal government under the Smith Act[2] in the centerpiece decision of the cold war, *Dennis v. United States.*[3] Linda Brown and Ethel Belton were two of the named plaintiffs in the landmark 1954 desegregation cases grouped under the heading of the lead case, *Brown v. Board of Education of Topeka.*[4] Finally, Ernesto Miranda and Carl Calvin Westover were accused criminals not advised of their right to an attorney in a timely fashion; their cases were decided together by the Supreme Court in the famous criminal justice decision of *Miranda v. Arizona*.[5]

Much good scholarship on U.S. constitutional history blends names and personal stories with doctrinal analysis.[6] Almost exclusively, however, the litigants profiled by constitutional historians producing detailed case studies have been those fortunate enough to have had their names in the official titles of the cases in the *U.S. Reports*. Those whose names did not make it into the official titles of their cases or who were litigants in cases linked to a lead decision have been virtually ignored. For example, in *Simple Justice*—Richard Kluger's detailed "names and faces" account of *Brown v. Board of Education of Topeka*—Ethel Louise Belton (the plaintiff in the linked Delaware case of *Gebhart v. Belton*) is mentioned in passing on only two pages of an eight-hundred-page book.[7] Kansan Linda Brown and her parents figure much more prominently in the story told in *Simple Justice*.

Which litigant is named in the official title of a case, or which case is considered the "lead" case in a combined appeal, is sometimes determined by alphabetical order. But, as illustrated by the official names of three of the four "great" constitutional cases mentioned here, the criterion of alphabetical order is honored frequently in the breach. Normally the choice of a short, official title or the designation of a lead case among several linked cases is determined by the clerk of the court of first instance. There are no judicial "rules" for naming cases. Thus the ultimate designation of an official (or short) title for a case can be a matter of caprice.

## An Iowa Example

In a special issue celebrating the 1987 bicentennial of the writing of the U.S. Constitution, *U.S.A. Today* selected a "key constitutional ruling" from each of the country's fifty states.[8] The case chosen by "The Nation's Newspaper" for Iowa was *Tinker v. Des Moines Independent Community School District, Inc.*,[9] a 1960s controversy concerning the right of a group of Des Moines teenagers to express symbolically their opinions about the Vietnam War by wearing black armbands to the public schools. Similarly, when *Life* magazine published a special 1991 issue commemorating the two hundredth anniversary of the Bill of Rights to the U.S. Constitution, one of the six First Amendment decisions of the twentieth century receiving special attention—including a half-page picture—was the *Tinker* case.[10]

Although the outlines of the story of *Tinker v. Des Moines* are familiar to many attorneys, legal historians, and students of American law,[11] a brief recounting of the essential facts in the case is in order. In late 1965, shortly after the first large anti–Vietnam War march in Washington, D.C., a group of Des Moines secondary school students decided to wear black armbands to school to express their sorrow over the casualties in the war and to demonstrate support for a truce in the hostilities. When word reached school district authorities that such a "protest" was imminent, an order was issued banning black armbands from the city's secondary schools. On two days in mid-December 1965, somewhere between twenty and forty students defied the ban. Five were suspended or sent home. The school board ultimately upheld the administrative proscription of the wearing of armbands.

Three students and their parents, represented by the Iowa Civil Liberties Union (ICLU), filed an action in federal court asserting that the students' right of symbolic speech under the First Amendment had been denied by the school district. After the students lost at the federal district court and circuit court of appeals level, their case was heard by the U.S. Supreme Court. In February 1969, at the height of the Vietnam War, the nation's High Court handed down a 7-2 decision in favor of the students. At this contentious moment in the country's history, the Court's majority opinion, written by Justice Abe Fortas, extended broad protection for symbolic expression and students' political speech.

The *Tinker* decision was hailed by legal experts as one of the characteristically liberal and pathbreaking rulings of the Warren Court. Yet, just a few months after the Court's decision in the armband case, Earl Warren retired as chief justice, and Abe Fortas, in the face of an ethical and financial scandal, resigned from the Court. An era of unprecedented federal judicial support of civil liberties had ended. Supreme Court decisions of the Burger Court in the 1980s would undercut much of the ground on which the *Tinker* precedent rested.[12]

Most who have read and studied *Tinker v. Des Moines* are

aware of the Tinker family's role in the case. Residing in Des Moines in the 1960s, the Tinkers held profound religious convictions and maintained a passion for social justice. John and Mary Beth Tinker, two of the named plaintiffs in the eventual court case, were students at Des Moines secondary schools in the 1965–66 academic year. John was then fifteen and a sophomore at North High. Mary Beth was thirteen and an eighth grader at Warren Harding Junior High. Mary Beth wore an armband on the first day after the announced ban; she was suspended. John wore an armband the following day and, although not technically suspended, was sent home from school.

John and Mary Beth's parents were the Reverend Leonard Tinker, an ordained Methodist minister, and Lorena Jeanne Tinker, a social activist. At the time of the case, Reverend Tinker was on leave of absence from the Methodist Church serving as the peace education secretary for the American Friends Service Committee. John and Mary Beth had an older sister, Bonnie, then a student at Grinnell College, and two younger siblings, Hope and Paul, both in elementary school at the time. Bonnie had participated with her mother and John in the November 1965 anti–Vietnam War march on Washington. Hope and Paul had also worn black armbands to school in December 1965, but neither had been suspended because the school district's armband prohibition did not extend to the elementary schools.[13]

Besides John and Mary Beth, there was a third student named as an official plaintiff in the armband litigation. His name was (and is) Christopher Paul Eckhardt.[14] Eckhardt's part in the armband case is as important and as interesting as that of John and Mary Beth Tinker. Yet, because his name did not come first in the legal filing and because the official title of the case did not contain his name, his role has generally been ignored. Dan Johnston, the ICLU attorney who would represent the three armband-wearing students in their case against the school district, suggests that the clerk of the federal district court who assigned the title for the case may have simply placed the names of the Tinkers first because there were two Tinkers and only one Eckhardt. He also joked that it may have been because Tinker was "easier to say" than Eckhardt.[15]

So, if only because of a preponderance of surnames or ease of pronunciation, the case was officially titled *Tinker v. Des Moines*—

not *Eckhardt v. Des Moines.* Much like the four great constitutional decisions mentioned earlier, *Tinker v. Des Moines* is a case known widely by one name, which just as easily could have received an alternative title. The remainder of this chapter will focus on Christopher Eckhardt, the overlooked litigant in the *Tinker* case.[16] Spinning out the role of Eckhardt in this constitutional litigation, I believe, serves two important purposes. First, on a narrative level, adding Christopher Eckhardt to the story offers a more complete and nuanced portrait of the litigation than has been offered in the secondary sources.[17] Perhaps more important, placing Eckhardt squarely in the middle of the dispute gives the *Tinker* case more bite in the historical and legal context of the 1960s. The Iowa black armband case is not only the story of a gentle midwestern family of Quaker children politely challenging an ill-advised school policy; it is also the story of a young man who, as we shall see, faced more physical hostility for his opinions than did John or Mary Beth Tinker and who, unlike the Tinkers, was not always willing to turn the other cheek.

## A "Regular Kid"

Christopher Eckhardt[18] was fifteen and a sophomore at Des Moines's Theodore Roosevelt High School in December 1965. At the time of the armband case, Eckhardt's father was a clinical psychologist and a faculty member at the College of Osteopathic Medicine and Surgery in Des Moines. His mother was then the Des Moines chapter president of the Women's International League for Peace and Freedom. His parents were active in the 1960s in the same small Des Moines "peace community" that included the Reverend and Mrs. Tinker. Through their activities and support for liberal causes, the Eckhardt and Tinker families had become well acquainted.

As was the case with the Tinker children, Christopher Eckhardt was exposed to liberal politics throughout his formative years. His mother recalls him as a young boy attending speeches and meetings with various civil rights advocates whom she brought to Des Moines in her capacity as an officer for the Women's International League for Peace and Freedom. Included among the visitors that young Christopher met were black Georgia politician Julian Bond and John Howard Griffin, the author of *Black Like Me.* Christopher also accompanied his parents on a number of civil rights marches. At the November 1965 antiwar march on Washington he carried a sign that read "Follow the Geneva Accords of 1954." At Roosevelt, Eckhardt helped form what he describes as a "political action discussion group," which brought public figures to school to talk with interested students.

Liberal politics dovetailed with liberal religion for Christopher Eckhardt and his parents. Prior to coming to Iowa, Dr. and Mrs. Eckhardt had participated in several religious groups. For example, they had attended Quaker meetings in North Carolina. In Des Moines, in the mid-1960s, they attended the First Unitarian Church. Christopher was an active member of the Liberal Religious Youth (LRY) arm of the Unitarian Church and later vice president of the Unitarian Youth League. Des Moines LRY members included John Tinker and others who shared Christopher's antiwar sentiments and later came to don black armbands in defiance of school district admonitions.

As a high school student Christopher was a busy young man. He maintained about a B-plus academic average and was an elected representative to student government. He had previously been the president of two separate school student councils. He was a member of the track team, had won fishing and weightlifting trophies, and would later be voted "most likely to succeed" in his class. He was also selected as the student with the cleanest locker. Outside of school he was a youth leader at church and a Boy Scout, had a paper route, and made money shoveling snow and mowing lawns. His mother describes him as outgoing and friendly—and very helpful at home. Dan Johnston, the ICLU attorney who would argue the armband case, describes Christopher as a "regular kid."[19]

There was, however, a puckish side to young Eckhardt, distinguishing him from the more quiescent Tinker children. During his Roosevelt High years he was a member of what he describes as a social club of about thirty male students called the "All Center Bums." They "hung out" together after school and on weekends in an apartment they rented in downtown Des Moines. At school assemblies they had their own seating section of the auditorium where they ritually refused to cheer for the athletic teams or rise to sing the national anthem. Eckhardt whimsically characterizes the All Center Bums as Des Moines's version of Hell's Angels.

Although allied in the armband case and sharing the same general passion for liberal politics, John Tinker and Christopher Eckhardt were not especially close friends. They attended different high schools and, as Christopher later recalled, "We didn't hang in the same social group." While John was quiet and introspective; Christopher was active in student government and, as noted, frequently functioned as a gadfly to school administration. Being two years older and in a different school, Christopher barely knew Mary Beth Tinker.[20]

The decision of several Des Moines secondary school students to wear black armbands to class was made at a meeting at the Eckhardt home on Saturday, December 11, 1965. Eckhardt remembers the meeting lasting several hours, during which time he drifted in and out in order to shovel snow.[21] On the following Monday and Tuesday, word circulated around the Des Moines schools that there would be an armband protest beginning later that week. Fearing that the wearing of armbands would present a "disturbing situation," the superintendent's office and the secondary school principals decided to prohibit the bands. On Wednesday morning, December 15, a short article appeared in the *Des Moines Register* announcing the administrative ban on armbands.[22] An announcement of the ban was broadcast over the loudspeakers at Roosevelt and other Des Moines schools that day.[23]

Also on Wednesday, Eckhardt recalls that the gym teachers and coaches at Roosevelt were extremely upset by the possibility of a protest against the Vietnam War. He maintained that, instead of conducting calisthenics to the chant of "Beat East High," the gym teachers on that Wednesday encouraged students to substitute the phrase "Beat the Vietcong."[24] Eckhardt recalls that the coaches at Roosevelt also made it known that students wearing armbands to class were communist sympathizers and that they, as coaches and teachers, could not be held responsible for what might happen to students who demonstrated such a lack of patriotism. Confirmation of this indirect threat took place after gym class on Wednesday when Eckhardt and a friend were confronted by a group of angry male students. One of them screamed: "If you [wear armbands tomorrow] . . . you'll find our fists in your face and our foot up your ass."[25] That evening, Christopher's father remembered, his son justified his decision to wear an armband by posing a rhetorical question: "Eichmann only followed orders, didn't he?"[26]

## Too Young to Have Opinions?

Christopher Eckhardt and a friend were driven to Theodore Roosevelt High School on Thursday, December 16, 1965, by Christopher's father, Dr. William Eckhardt.[27] Dr. Eckhardt recalls that his son was "fearful and trembling" as he got out of the car. The reason for Christopher's trepidations was that, in defiance of an administrative decree, under his winter coat he was wearing a cocoa brown sport jacket with a black armband of about one and one-fourth inches in width pinned to one of his sleeves. After he removed his outer coat and placed it in his locker, Christopher's band became visible to others in the building. He proceeded immediately to the principal's office to turn himself in. As he saw it, he was engaging in an act of peaceful civil disobedience, that is, intentionally breaking a rule that he believed to be unjust and submitting to punishment so as to test the fairness or legality of the rule. On Eckhardt's way to the school's front lobby, a fellow student asked him if he realized that there was a rule against wearing an armband. Eckhardt replied that he was aware of the rule and explained the reason that he was breaking it. He recalls being confronted by the captain of the football team, who attempted to rip the band off his jacket. Eckhardt remembers telling this "big character . . . [who] later went on to play semi-pro football" to take his hands off him because he was on his way to the principal's office to turn himself in. The football player left Eckhardt with words to the effect that he had better take the armband off in the principal's office or he would come looking for him.

Eckhardt arrived in the school's administrative office suite and asked to see the principal, Dr. Charles Rowley, but he was told that Don Blackman, vice principal of Roosevelt, would be meeting with him instead. Eckhardt remembers waiting in the outer office for about forty-five minutes while other students walked by the glass-enclosed area and taunted him with caustic remarks such as "You're dead." Finally, Blackman ushered Eckhardt into his office. He asked which teacher had sent him to the office. Eckhardt replied that no one had ordered him to report to the office; he said he had come voluntarily to turn himself in because he knew that, by wearing a black armband, he was in violation of a recently established school district rule. Blackman asked whether any school official had ordered Eckhardt to remove the armband. Eckhardt said, "No." So Blackman said, "Oh, well, I'm asking you at this time to remove your armband." Eckhardt refused to remove it and stated that he believed he had a constitutional right to wear it to school. Eckhardt and Blackman talked for several more minutes. But, in spite of Blackman's repeated demands to remove the band, Eckhardt refused. About this time Velma Cross, the girls' adviser at Roosevelt, joined them. Blackman explained the situation to her, and she attempted to convince Eckhardt that a suspension would look bad on his school record. She told him that he was "too young to have opinions" and that "colleges didn't accept protesters so if . . . [he] planned to go to college . . . [he'd] better take it off." She also told him that, if he was suspended, he could look for another high school to attend because they did not want him back at Roosevelt.

At about this point, Eckhardt recalls that Blackman told him that the "senior boys were not going to like what he was doing" and then he asked him if he "was looking for a busted nose." In retrospect, Eckhardt believes that the "busted nose" comment could have had a double or even a triple meaning. It could have been a threat that Blackman himself would hit him; it could have been a prediction that fellow students might attack him once they found out about the armband incident; or it could have simply been that a suspension would look like a broken nose on Eckhardt's school record. Whatever the meaning of this statement, Eckhardt felt intimidated and started to cry.

Blackman talked to Eckhardt for several minutes, apparently attempting to find out his motivation for wearing the band. Ultimately, however, he told Eckhardt that the point of the protest was not important. What was important was that Eckhardt was a student breaking a school rule and would, therefore, be punished. He also agreed with Cross's assertion that failure to take off an armband when asked to do so by a teacher or administrator would lead to a suspension and place a blemish on Eckhardt's academic record. When it became clear that Eckhardt was not going to follow the order to remove the band, Blackman called his mother.

Mrs. Eckhardt was aware that Christopher had worn the armband that morning and that he intended to turn himself in before classes began. So she was expecting a call from the administration. Blackman informed her that her son was in his office wearing a black armband, that he had been advised that wearing an armband was against school district policy, and that he had refused to remove the armband when directly asked to do so. He indicated that Christopher would be suspended if he did not remove the offending piece of cloth, and he tried to convince her to persuade her son to comply with his order. She responded by saying, "I think he has every right to wear the arm band, and I will not ask him to take it off." In reply Blackman said, "In that case, we'll have to suspend him." And Mrs. Eckhardt said, "So be it."

In the following morning's *Des Moines Register*, Vice Principal Blackman was quoted as saying that Christopher Eckhardt was the only Roosevelt High School student—at least as far as he knew—who had worn a black armband on Thursday and that he was also the only high school student suspended in connection with this matter. Blackman also stated that there had been "no commotion or disturbance at the school in conjunction with the arm band wearing."[28]

Mary Beth Tinker wore her armband on Thursday and was suspended shortly after lunch. John Tinker did not wear his band until Friday. Although John was sent home from his school, he was not officially suspended. On the days that they wore their armbands, Mary Beth and John Tinker did not face the overt threats and hostility that greeted Christopher Eckhardt when he wore a piece of black cloth to school.[29]

## Community Reactions

On Thursday afternoon, December 16, 1965, in the wake of the suspensions of Christopher Eckhardt and Mary Beth Tinker, another meeting was held at the Eckhardt home to consider how to respond to the suspensions and whether other students should begin wearing armbands. One of the Roosevelt students at that meeting phoned the president of the Des Moines School Board, Ora Niffenegger, and appealed to him to summon a special school board meeting to discuss the right of students to wear armbands. Niffenegger informed his caller that the matter "wasn't important enough" to require a special board meeting, but that the issue could be presented at the next regularly scheduled board meeting, Tuesday, December 21.[30] In the few days before the board meeting, the Eckhardts received a number of anonymous telephone calls. In one, a sarcastic voice asked, "How do you join the Communist Party?" Another informed the Eckhardts, "You're looking for trouble, and you're going to get it."[31]

The Des Moines School Board held its next meeting, as scheduled, on December 21. Over two hundred parents, students, and interested city residents attended. Other business items on the agenda were pushed aside by the passion over the armband controversy. The Eckhardt and Tinker families—parents and children alike—all attended the meeting and appeared in photographs in the next day's newspapers. After much heated discussion involving board members and members of the audience, the board passed a motion to postpone until its next meeting—Monday, January 3, 1966—any decision on whether to maintain or reverse the armband prohibition.[32]

Over the Christmas holidays, the Eckhardts and the Tinkers received several threatening phone calls and a few mean-spirited notes. Nevertheless, both families report that they received more supportive calls and letters than critical ones. On Christmas Eve, Mrs. Eckhardt wrote a statement laying the blame for the armband controversy at the door of the American educational system for its emphasis on conformity and order as opposed to individuality and creativity. Dr. Eckhardt wrote a four-page letter to the *Des Moines Register* explaining his and his son's position on the Vietnam War and the right to wear bands to school. The Eckhardts celebrated New Year's Day 1966 with the Tinkers. Together they wrote a letter to the school board, which stated that a "democratic demonstration can only contribute toward a democratic educational process rather than disrupt it." The letter also strongly advised the board to formulate a policy permitting nonviolent free expression in the city's schools, in keeping with the spirit of the First and Fourteenth Amendments to the U.S. Constitution.[33]

The January 3, 1966, school board meeting was as contentious as the one in December. Among the many speakers were Dr. Eckhardt, Mrs. Eckhardt, and Christopher Eckhardt. Dr. Eckhardt stated that bowing without question to authority was a principle "so greatly admired in Nazi Germany." Mrs. Eckhardt told those assembled that she was proud that her son "had the faith to follow his convictions." In the course of his remarks, Christopher himself asserted: "The administrators put a ban on the arm bands because they believed it would cause a disturbance in the schools. Well, by now you ought to know that the arm bands caused no such disturbance in the schools, although the ban itself has caused quite a disturbance in the community." Although most people attending the January 3 meeting spoke in favor of the right of students to wear armbands to school, the board voted 5 to 2 to uphold the administrative prohibition of the offending pieces of cloth.[34]

Between mid-December 1965 and late January 1966, the action of Christopher Eckhardt and others to defy the school district ban on armbands generated substantial controversy in the Des Moines press. Numerous editorials, opinion columns, and letters to the editor addressed the controversy. The editorials and opinion columns generally supported the students' position. The letters to the editor were split about 2 to 1 in favor of the students' right to wear armbands. At some point in most of the letters favoring the students was language stressing the importance of tolerating free expression of unpopular views in a democracy. For example, a U.S. Marine, then in the process of being discharged from the military for a disability, wrote: "I am appalled at what I consider not only an infringement upon the civil liberties of U.S. citizens but also at the seeming lack of concern for my friends and fellow Marines who are fighting and dying in Viet Nam for this very cause. To me this is not just a great injustice but the height of hypocrisy. Why defend a society that cannot even allow its citizens to honor the very people who keep it free?"[35]

A common theme of letter writers critical of the right to wear armbands to school was that the suspended students such as Christopher Eckhardt were exploited by their "left-leaning parents." For example, the superintendent of schools from Carroll, Iowa, wrote: "Much has been said regarding the freedom of thought and action on the part of the [armband-wearing] students. It seems to me . . . it was not an idea sponsored by students but by parents who used these youngsters to propagate their personal beliefs."[36] A letter published a few days later conveyed this viewpoint by posing a series of rhetorical questions: "Do the writers of the arm-band letters really believe the children involved arrived at their own decision to wear the bands? Do they believe the children had access to and had the intellectual maturity to understand the significance of the complicated Viet Nam problem? Is it not more reasonable to suppose they were being used by their parents to publicize and foster the parents' opinions?" Later in this letter the writer urged adults to seek the remedy of the ballot box for weaknesses they perceived in American foreign policy rather than by "fixing arm-bands on their children's clothing to wear to school."[37]

When the school board voted at its January 1966 meeting to continue the prohibition, Christopher Eckhardt and the Tinker children were upset. But, rather than defying the school administration by reattaching their armbands, they followed the advice of the ICLU attorneys and returned to school the following day without the bands. But all three wore black articles of clothing that day and for some time afterward. Mary Beth Tinker recalls that her brother John wore only black until the end of the school year in June.[38] When asked for his reaction to the students' black attire, board president Ora Niffenegger reportedly said, "Well, I guess we'll have to let them keep their clothes on."[39]

Over the second half of the 1965–66 school year, Christopher Eckhardt and John and Mary Beth Tinker were the focus of a great deal of attention. There was some hostility expressed by classmates and members of the community, but there were also instances of grudging respect. Christopher Eckhardt's recollections of early 1966 are more detailed than those of John and Mary Beth. His memories are illustrative of the risks and rewards that accrue to someone who takes an unpopular stand. Eckhardt also kept a file of many of the letters and postcards on the armband affair that he and his family received in the late 1960s; they provide corroboration for his recollections. Finally, Eckhardt has also retained copies of the letters and accounts of the armband controversy that he himself wrote at the time.[40]

Christopher's father, Dr. William Eckhardt, remembers Christopher saying on January 4, 1966: "We went back to school, not because we believed the School Board was right, but because the School Board had the might."[41] Once back in school, Eckhardt found that his status among his classmates had actually climbed from the previous semester. He became more of a leader in his social group, the All Center Bums. Even the gym teachers, who had previously tolerated (or perhaps instigated) the "Beat the Viet Cong" chanting, treated him well. He recalls being invited by them to lead the class in calisthenics on several occasions in the spring 1966 semester. When asked to account for the reversal in the attitude of the gym teachers, Eckhardt maintains that it was because they were worried about being named in court actions that the Eckhardts and the Tinkers were contemplating.

During the early months of 1966, Eckhardt recalls a few occasions on which he was harassed for his role in the armband affair. In one instance a drunk called him a "communist," and in another a student playing in an informal football game yelled as Christopher walked by: "Hey, peace boy, why don't you come play football with us?"

Christopher Eckhardt and his family received a considerable amount of hate mail in 1966 and 1967—much of it anonymous and frequently marked by misspelled words and grammatical flaws. For example, one letter, addressed to Christopher's parents, contained a typed statement on the danger of communist subversion of America's youth allegedly perpetrated by leftist educators. At points in this letter where "educators" or "professors" were mentioned, the anonymous sender had added the phrase "& parents." In the upper right-hand corner of the letter is the message: "The shoe is becoming tighter & tighter for you Eckhardt." A postcard addressed to the Eckhardts read in part:

> It seems that someone needs to psychoanalysis you two parents for what you are putting your children thru. . . . I'd do a lot of thinking about this . . . because it looks like your going to have a Harvey Lee Oswald on your hands. . . . Also, if your wife doesn't like this country then she can always go back to England and Germany. . . . But it gauls all of us that stupes like you do this to the kids and they get the blame. . . . We think the community would be a better place for all concerned if people like you would move out.

Another postcard was addressed to "Herr Doctor Wilhelm E. Eckhardt" and "Frau Margt. Eckhardt."

Not all the mail that Christopher Eckhardt received in early 1966 was condemnatory. In March he received a kind note from the secretary of the Junior Youth Fellowship of Des Moines's First Methodist Church, thanking him for presenting "a very interesting, thought-provoking program" on "the arm band controversy and . . . the problems in Viet Nam." And in January he received a flattering letter from a Princeton, New Jersey, rabbi who identified himself as a former student in the Des Moines public schools. The rabbi's letter read in part:

> I was filled with admiration for your sensitivity. It . . . requires a great deal to identify . . . with the suffering of one's "enemies.". . . I was [also] inspired by your courage. It is not easy, in these times, to affirm basic human values in the face of that powerful combination of nation-state idolatry and increasingly mechanical, remote, non-human, and unfeeling instruments of human destruction. At any level, and especially within one's own immediate community, it takes great courage to challenge prevailing slogans and ideologies.

The letter ended, "Bravo for you, your parents, and all who have supported you!"

Christopher Eckhardt spent a great deal of time in early 1966 putting his thoughts about the armband controversy on paper. A letter that he wrote to President Lyndon Johnson on January 5, for example, captures the anger and cynicism that he was feeling in the immediate aftermath of his brush with authority. He wrote: "Dear President Johnson, How goes it with you? I'm sure you are busy with the Viet Nam war. Do you really believe all this killing is necessary to insure Democracy? You do not have to worry about this letter because I am only fifteen, and that makes me a non-voter." He then described briefly the Iowa black armband affair and his part in it. Finally, he expressed his feelings about American policy in Southeast Asia: "Escalation of the war can serve no useful purpose, besides the lose [*sic*] of all the people, it will also take away from important matters here in the U.S. We should try to practice Love and Peace not Hate and Fear. Why Don't you try harder to get this war over with so more people would learn more about Peace and Love and less about hate and fear."

A particularly poignant expression of the teenage Eckhardt's strong feelings was a piece of rhymed verse that Christopher composed in late 1966 or early 1967—well before the Supreme Court decision upholding his position. It was written to fulfill the terms of an English assignment that asked students to produce a parody of a piece of literature. Eckhardt chose "Mary Had a Little Lamb" as his literary foil and titled his parody "Harold Had a Black Arm Band." This is the poem in its entirety:

> Harold had a black arm band,
> As black as black could be.
> Everywhere that Harold went,
> That band was there to see.
> He wore it to his school one day,
> Which was against the rule.
> It made the teachers jump and shout
> To see it there at school.
> They said, "My boy, that band must go,
> But you may gladly stay."
> Harold would not take it off,
> Nor let this issue lay.
> Harold missed a week of school,
> Suspended for the sin
> Of wanting war to end at last
> And peace to usher in.
> Harold finally went to court,
> His rights were what he sought.
> That children also might be free
> Is that for which he fought.
> He lost that case, but not in vain,
> For much was brought to light.
> As Harold stuck by his beliefs,
> And still thinks he was right!

Christopher received an A for his parody.

## In the Courts

Following the disappointing January 3, 1966, school board meeting, individuals who supported the right of students to wear armbands on school property met once again at the Eckhardt home. Representatives of the Iowa Civil Liberties Union attending the meeting pledged support to students and their parents willing to lend their names to a challenge to the ban on armbands. The ICLU agreed to pay filing and photocopying expenses for the constitutional test case, and a fund-raising appeal was undertaken to help defray the expenses of the young ICLU attorney, Dan Johnston. The primary argument of the ICLU and its lead attorney would be that the school district's proscription of black bands denied the plaintiff students their right of symbolic expression under the First Amendment to the U.S. Constitution. From this point on, the case became more the property of ICLU attorney Dan Johnston than of Christopher Eckhardt or any of the other named plaintiffs.[42] Nevertheless, during the three years that it took the case to work its way through the federal courts, Christopher Eckhardt would remain an important figure in this constitutional challenge.

After depositions had been taken and briefs had been filed, the civil lawsuit of the Eckhardts and the Tinkers against the Des Moines schools reached federal district court in Des Moines. The key witness in the trial before Federal District Judge Roy L. Stephenson was Christopher Eckhardt. From the plaintiffs' point of view, Eckhardt was able to articulate the principles of symbolic expression and civil disobedience more clearly than either of the Tinker children. From the defendants' perspective, Eckhardt's experience on the day he wore the band suggested that disruptive incidents did occur as a direct result of his actions. Thus, Eckhardt's time on the witness stand was the longest and most contentious of any witness at the trial.[43]

In his direct testimony, Dan Johnston led Eckhardt slowly through the reasoning behind his decision to wear the armband to school and the events that transpired on the day he wore it. Under Johnston's prompting, Eckhardt indicated that he regularly talked about international politics and civil rights in the Liberal Religious Youth group of Des Moines's First Unitarian Church and that he had participated in a number of demonstrations for "civil rights, race, peace, and things of that sort." He stated emphatically that his parents had neither tried to persuade him to wear the band nor tried to dissuade him from wearing it. Then Johnston guided Eckhardt through a lengthy recounting of the incidents on the day he wore the black armband to Roosevelt High School. Finally Johnston asked Eckhardt if he had changed his mind since December 1965 regarding "this business about the war in Viet Nam." Eckhardt answered, "No." Nor, he added, would there likely be any changes in his views in the near future if the U.S. government continued its escalation of the war. Since his feelings about the war had not changed since December 1965, Eckhardt submitted that he would like to have the right to wear an armband upon return to school in the fall of 1966.

One strategy of the Des Moines Independent School District attorneys, Allan Herrick and Philip Lovrien, was to try to link the armband protest with an increasingly unpopular radical group, the Students for a Democratic Society (SDS). In the deposition of Reverend Tinker, taken earlier in the summer, Herrick had attempted unsuccessfully to elicit an admission that Iowa college chapters of SDS had been behind the December 1965 decision of the Des Moines students to wear armbands.[44] Lovrien adopted a similar tactic in his cross-examination of Christopher Eckhardt by demanding to know who attended the meeting at the Eckhardt home on December 16, 1965. Christopher indicated that several students from Roosevelt and other Des Moines schools attended, but he stated that he was not certain as to which, if any, of the attendees were members of SDS.

It took only a single day for the entire testimony in the *Tinker* case to be placed in the district court record. Five weeks later Judge Stephenson issued a terse, five-and-one-half-page "memorandum opinion." He found in favor of the school district, ruling that the policy banning armbands was constitutionally justified and denying the injunction and nominal damages sought by the Eckhardts and the Tinkers. The judge acknowledged that controversial subjects should not be excluded from the secondary school curriculum and that the black armbands in and of themselves were not disruptive. However, he submitted that "the reactions and comments from other students as a result of the arm bands would be likely to disturb the disciplined atmosphere required by any classroom." Employing the "balancing test" favored by a majority of the U.S. Supreme Court, Judge Stephenson concluded, "In this instance . . . it is the disciplined atmosphere of the classroom, not the plaintiffs' right to wear armbands on school premises, which is entitled to the protection of the law."[45]

Dan Johnston secured continued financial support from the ICLU in order to carry the appeal in *Tinker* to the Eighth Circuit of the U.S. Court of Appeals.[46] The appeal was argued twice before the Eighth Circuit Court in St. Louis. On the first occasion, a three-judge panel could not come to a decision. So, because of its importance, the case was argued again before the entire roster of Eighth Circuit judges. On the second occasion, the en banc panel split four to four.[47] Under federal court rules, a tie vote on appeal upholds the decision of the lower court. If the Eckhardts and the Tinkers were going to prevail in their quest for vindication of their First Amendment right of symbolic speech, it would have to be in the U.S. Supreme Court in Washington, D.C. Shortly after the Supreme Court granted Dan Johnston's certiorari petition and agreed to hear the appeal from the Eckhardts and the Tinkers, the Roosevelt High student newspaper carried a short article on the case. The article quoted Christopher Eckhardt: "As long as you are not hurting yourself or others, as long as you are not infringing on the rights of others, and as long as it is done peacefully, I see no reason for denying free student expression in the schools."[48]

In his written brief to the U.S. Supreme Court, Dan Johnston devoted most of his attention to the legal issues.[49] As a result, mention of the specific activities of John and Mary Beth Tinker and Christopher Eckhardt was minimal. And, at oral argument on November 12, 1968, Johnston made scant mention of Eckhardt's actions as part of the armband protest.[50]

Allan Herrick, the lead attorney for the school board, however, made a number of references in his Supreme Court brief to the role of Christopher Eckhardt in the case.[51] Herrick acknowledged that Eckhardt's own actions on the day he wore the black armband to school did not occasion much of a disruption. Few students even realized that Eckhardt had worn an armband on the day in question because he had proceeded to the principal's office and turned himself in shortly after arriving at school. In questioning from Justice Thurgood Marshall, Herrick conceded that the protest had been a pretty tame affair. Of the eighteen thousand students enrolled in Des Moines schools in 1965, Herrick acknowledged that only a handful wore armbands, occasioning minimal interference with school routine.[52]

Herrick took another tack, however, in trying to portray Eckhardt as a catalyst for disruption. Like his associate, Philip Lovrien, at the district court level, Herrick sought to link Christopher and his mother with the increasingly violence-prone SDS. He noted that Christopher and Mrs. Eckhardt had participated in the November 1965 antiwar march on Washington, sponsored in part, he alleged, by SDS. He also emphasized that there had been several SDS members attending the meeting at the Eckhardt home on December 11, 1965, in which the armband protest had been conceived. There may not have been much actual disruption that occurred in the Des Moines schools on the days the armbands were worn, but Herrick contended that—given the tension that gripped the country in late 1965 over the Vietnam War—the school district had a reasonable basis for fearing difficulties and acted appropriately. At the national level, Herrick pointed to the frequent violent protests and draft card burnings. Herrick mentioned that in Des Moines a former student in one of the city's public schools had been killed in the Vietnam War and that the school district feared that some of this student's friends could have reacted violently to the armband protest.[53]

Mrs. Eckhardt and son Christopher attended the oral argument. Mrs. Eckhardt's chief memory from the oral argument is that Allan Herrick kept trying to portray the December 1965 meetings at her house as "clandestine" and "hostile." She remembers being offended by this characterization because, as she recalls, those in attendance were just trying to come up with an effective way to express their disagreement with what they felt to be an immoral war.[54] Listening to the oral argument gave Christopher Eckhardt a sense of satisfaction. He called it "my own little piece of ego." He was awed that his wearing of a small piece of dark cloth for a few minutes several years earlier had led to a great constitutional contest capturing the attention of the "nine distinguished gentlemen" sitting solemnly on the high bench in front of him. He remembers, in particular, the exchange between Herrick and Justice Marshall over just how disruptive the armbands had been. When Marshall was successful in getting Herrick to concede that the handful of armband-wearing students had created barely a ripple in a district with eighteen thousand pupils, Eckhardt saw Marshall "sit back in his chair and just kind of shake his head a little bit" at the argument of the school district attorney.[55]

The Supreme Court decision was handed down on February 24, 1969. Justice Abe Fortas in the majority opinion and Justice Hugo Black in his dissent referred briefly to Christopher Eckhardt and the other armband-wearing students.[56] But, as would be expected in an appellate opinion, they stuck mainly to the legal analysis presented by the attorneys.

## The Aftermath

Christopher Eckhardt[57] learned of his victory in the case that did not bear his name while he was a student at Mankato State University in Minnesota. He remembers being called the day of the Court decision by a reporter for a Minneapolis newspaper who proceeded to congratulate him for his victory. Eckhardt responded, "Who the hell are you and what are you congratulating me for?" The reporter explained and asked Eckhardt for a reaction. In the vernacular of the late sixties, Eckhardt declared: "I'm overjoyed, far out." He also remembers talking further with the reporter about the implications of the Supreme Court opinion in the context of the more radical forms of student protest that had developed since the midsixties. Eckhardt emphasized that the 1965 armband protest had been peaceful and that the Supreme Court decision was a victory for nonviolent civil disobedience, not an endorsement of the antiwar violence then sweeping the country. That night Eckhardt and several friends "went out and celebrated hearty."

Christopher Eckhardt has led a varied and interesting life since he wore his armband to school in December 1965. He was elected to the Roosevelt High student council during his junior year in school, but he also persisted as a member of the school's frowned-upon social group, the All Center Bums. During the remainder of his high school years he had occasional disagreements with authorities. He was also arrested on a Des Moines sidewalk in March 1968 for throwing a snowball at a policeman. When Eckhardt gave his name to the arresting officer, the reaction was: "Oh yeah, we know about you. We talk about you down at the office sometimes. You're that armband kid, you're that troublemaker."

When his parents left the United States for Canada in 1967, Christopher Eckhardt stayed behind to complete his senior year at Roosevelt. Although he sought and received "landed immigrant" status in Canada following graduation, he wanted to remain in the United States for his college education. This posed a problem that many other young men of his age faced in the late sixties: what to do about one's military obligation? Given the pacifism that ran in his family and his own strong antagonism to the conduct of the Vietnam War, it is not surprising that Eckhardt did not want to serve in Southeast Asia. Initially, his draft classification was 1-A, but on appeal he received conscientious objector (1-0) status.

Eckhardt took his first college courses at Mankato State in 1968. For the next twenty-five years he attended several other colleges and held a variety of jobs: he sold life insurance, produced cable television programs, published a peace-oriented newspaper, served as a federal mediator, and worked for state governments in corrections and social services. In 1978, he ran unsuccessfully for the Des Moines School Board—the same body that had upheld his school suspension thirteen years earlier. In 1994, after attending various colleges on and off for more than two decades, he received a baccalaureate degree in political science from the University of South Florida.

As central as Christopher Eckhardt had been to the 1965 Iowa armband protest, until recently all recognition for taking a principled stand in the dispute accrued to Dan Johnston or to John and Mary Beth Tinker. When Roosevelt High wanted a commencement speaker in the early 1970s to mark the significance of the protest in the course of student rights, they selected Dan Johnston.[58] When an Iowa education professor wanted a living artifact of the sixties to speak to his class, the person he called upon was John Tinker.[59] When legal historian Peter Irons wanted to include a chapter on the *Tinker* case in his collection of narrative essays on civil liberties, it was Mary Beth Tinker whom he featured.[60] And when *Life* magazine wanted to focus attention on the armband case as one of the great civil liberties decisions of the century, it was Mrs. Tinker and Mary Beth who were interviewed and pictured in full color. [61]

Only in the 1990s did Christopher Eckhardt receive a proportionate share of attention for his role in the case. In 1990, when neither John nor Mary Beth Tinker wanted to accept an invitation from the American Civil Liberties Union to speak to a large audience in Boston, they passed the honor on to Eckhardt. In May 1992, Eckhardt came back to Roosevelt High in Des Moines to participate, along with John and Mary Beth Tinker and Dan Johnston, in a "visiting scholars" forum. Eckhardt, the Tinkers, and Johnston were treated like returning heroes.[62] The Roosevelt High student newspaper featured their visit and included many statements from Eckhardt in a lead story titled "Free Speech Rebels Return Home Tonight."[63] Following their visit, the editorial page editor of the *Des Moines Register* wrote that the act of civil disobedience of Christopher Eckhardt and the Tinkers in 1965 "did more to extend free speech rights to students than anybody else of their or any previous generation."[64] In December 1993, Eckhardt flew to San Francisco and accepted, on behalf of John and Mary Beth Tinker and himself, the annual Earl Warren Civil Liberties Award. Previous recipients of this award had included Rosa Parks, Joan Baez, and Thurgood Marshall.[65]

In the thirty-five years since they achieved notoriety for wearing black armbands to their Des Moines schools, the three named litigants in the *Tinker* case have been separated by geography and varied life experiences. John Tinker, when he is not traveling, pursues a variety of independent enterprises in rural Iowa. Mary Beth Tinker lives in a St. Louis brownstone and works as a nurse in one of that city's children's hospitals.[66] And Christopher Eckhardt, the former student protester, has recently been working as a financial adviser and retirement planning specialist in Clearwater, Florida.[67] The three former Des Moines, Iowa, secondary school students, now well into middle age, talk occasionally by phone. Accolades and invitations that once came primarily to the Tinkers are now being shared by all three. When interviewed recently about the dispute that will forever associate their surname with American civil liberties, members of the Tinker family emphasized the importance of obtaining Christopher Eckhardt's perspective as well as their own in striving to capture the full flavor of the landmark 1960s battle for student rights and free expression in the nation's heartland.[68]

Notes

An earlier version of this chapter was presented in the Iowa Legal History Workshop at the College of Law, University of Iowa, in April 1996. I wish to thank the members of the workshop for their constructive criticisms. Especially helpful were the comments of Bill Buss, Mary Dudziak, Linda Kerber, and Catherine Rymph. In addition, portions of this essay appeared in John W. Johnson, *The Struggle for Student Rights: Tinker v. Des Moines and the 1960s* (Lawrence: University Press of Kansas, 1997). I thank the University Press of Kansas for permission to use portions of the book in this essay.

1. Cranch 137 (1803).
2. 54 Stat. 670 (1940).
3. 341 U.S. 494 (1951).
4. 347 U.S. 483 (1954). Linda Brown was an African-American student in the Topeka school system. Belton was the mother of a black child in the Delaware desegregation case, *Gebhart, et al. v. Belton et al.*, decided the same day as *Brown v. Board of Education*.
5. 384 U.S. 436 (1966). Westover's case was titled *Westover v. U.S.*
6. See, e.g., Anthony Lewis, *Gideon's Trumpet* (New York: Knopf, 1964); C. Peter Magrath, *Yazoo, Law and Politics in the New Republic: The Case of Fletcher v. Peck* (New York: Norton, 1967); Richard Kluger, *Simple Justice: The History of Brown v. Board of Education and Black America's Struggle for Equality* (New York: Knopf, 1976); Maeva Marcus, *Truman and the Steel Seizure Case: The Limits of Presidential Power* (New York: Columbia University Press, 1977); Don Fehrenbacher, *The Dred Scott Case: Its Significance in American Law and Politics* (New York: Oxford University Press, 1978); Stanley Kutler, *Privilege and Creative Destruction: The Charles River Bridge Case* (New York: Norton, 1978); Joel Dreyfuss and Charles Lawrence III, *The Bakke Case: The Politics of Inequality* (New York: Harcourt Brace Jovanovich, 1979); Bernard Schwartz, *Swann's Way: The School Busing Case and the Supreme Court* (New York: Oxford University Press, 1986); John W. Johnson, *Insuring Against Disaster: The Nuclear Industry on Trial* (Macon, Ga.: Mercer University Press, 1986); and Anthony Lewis, *Make No Law: The Sullivan Case and the First Amendment* (New York: Random House, 1992). My own impetus for constructing detailed case studies of leading court cases came from the University of Minnesota graduate seminars in legal history conducted by Paul Murphy.
7. Kluger, *Simple Justice*, 434, 449.
8. Wayne Beissert and Tony Mauro, "Cases Across USA Help Shape Law," *U.S.A. Today*, May 22, 1987, 9F.
9. The complete, official title and citation of the case is *John F. Tinker and Mary Beth Tinker, Minors, etc., et al. v. Des Moines Independent Community School District, et al.*, 393 U.S. 503 (1969).
10. Temma Ehrenfeld and Todd Brewster, "First & Foremost," *Life* 14 (fall special 1991): 60–66.

11. As the dispute unfolded, the black armband case received extensive coverage in the Iowa press. The *Des Moines Register* and *Des Moines Tribune* carried stories on the clash between students and the school district almost daily during the winter of 1965–66 and then episodically as the case worked its way through the courts. Around the time of the Supreme Court decision, *Tinker* benefited from analysis in many law journals. See, e.g., Theodore F. Denno, "Mary Beth Tinker Takes the Constitution to School," *Fordham Law Review* 38 (October 1969): 35–62; Carl L. Aspelund, "Constitutional Law: Free Speech and Rights of School Children," *Loyola Law Review* 16 (1969–70): 165–76; Sheldon H. Nahmod, "Beyond *Tinker*: The High School as an Educational Public Forum," *Harvard Civil Rights and Civil Liberties Law Review* 5 (April 1970): 278–300; and Paul G. Haskell, "Student Expression in the Public Schools: *Tinker* Distinguished," *Georgetown Law Journal* 59 (October 1970): 37–58. Since the 1960s, the case has become a staple entry in constitutional law and school law texts. The *Tinker* case is also one of the civil liberties cases featured in Peter Irons, *The Courage of Their Convictions* (New York: Free Press, 1988), 233–52; and in Nat Hentoff, *The First Freedom: The Tumultuous History of Free Speech in America* (New York: Delacorte Press, 1980). In addition, there is a book for young readers on *Tinker*: Doreen Rappaport, *Be the Judge Be the Jury: Tinker v. Des Moines* (New York: HarperCollins, 1993). Also, see generally my *Struggle for Student Rights.*

12. See, e.g., *New Jersey v. T.L.O.*, 469 U.S. 325 (1985); *Bethel School District Number 403 v. Fraser*, 478 U.S. 675 (1986); and esp. *Hazelwood School District v. Kuhlmeier*, 484 U.S. 260 (1988).

13. Besides drawing upon public legal documents and newspaper accounts, I have gleaned information on the Tinker family from interviews with Lorena Jeanne Tinker, Fayette, Missouri, February 17, 1994; John Tinker, Cedar Falls, Iowa, February 4, 1994; and Mary Beth Tinker, St. Louis, Missouri, February 17, 1994. In addition, the Tinkers have kindly allowed me to examine and excerpt from the various files of materials they have kept on the case.

14. In the 1960s young Eckhardt was generally referred to as Chris. However, in stories about him today, he prefers the use of his full first name.

15. Interview with Dan Johnston, Des Moines, Iowa, May 17, 1994.

16. Some of what follows is drawn from telephone interviews conducted with Christopher Eckhardt and his mother, Mrs. Margaret Eckhardt, on May 4, 1994. In addition, as was the case with the members of the Tinker family, Christopher Eckhardt and Mrs. Eckhardt kindly shared and allowed me to quote from the files they have kept on the armband dispute.

17. Until recently, the best-known account of the *Tinker* case to U.S. constitutional historians was Irons, *The Courage of Their Convictions*, 233–52. Irons barely mentions the role of Christopher Eckhardt in his treatment of this test of courage and conscience.

18. Unless otherwise noted, the biographical information on Christopher Eckhardt presented in this section is drawn from the telephone interviews conducted with Christopher Eckhardt and Mrs. Margaret Eckhardt, May 4, 1994.

19. Dan Johnston interview.

20. Lorena Jeanne Tinker interview; John Tinker interview; and Mary Beth Tinker interview.

21. Christopher Eckhardt interview.

22. Jack Magarrell, "D.M. Schools Ban Wearing of Viet Truce Armbands," *Des Moines Register,* December 15, 1965, 1.

23. Christopher Eckhardt interview.

24. Christopher Eckhardt interview. The Roosevelt High football coach, Donald Pryor, stated that the change to "Beat the Viet Cong" sprang from the students themselves as a form of "spontaneous combustion." Pryor indicated, however, that he saw no reason to stop the chanting because the boys were just "proving their Americanism." Stephen Seplow, "Dispute over High School Chant of 'Beat Viet Cong,'" *Des Moines Register,* December 20, 1965, 1.

25. Christopher Eckhardt interview.

26. William Eckhardt, "The Black Arm Band Story: A Community Case Study of Conflicting Ideologies and Values," *Journal of Human Relations* 17 (1969): 496.

27. Unless otherwise indicated, the events of December 16, 1965, related here were drawn either from the telephone interviews with Christopher Eckhardt and Margaret Eckhardt or from the federal district court testimony of Christopher Eckhardt in the transcript of *Tinker v. Des Moines Independent Community School District, Inc.* (Southern District of Iowa, Civil No. 7-1810-C-1), July 25, 1966: 68–105, located in the office of the Clerk of Court of the Southern District of Iowa, Des Moines, Iowa (hereafter cited as "*Tinker* transcript").

28. Jack Magarrell, "Wear Black Arm Bands, Two Students Sent Home," *Des Moines Register,* December 17, 1965, 1.

29. John Tinker interview; Mary Beth Tinker interview.

30. Christopher Eckhardt interview.

31. Ibid.

32. The Des Moines School Board meetings on December 21, 1965, received extensive coverage by the *Des Moines Register* and the now-defunct *Des Moines Tribune.* See, e.g., Jack Magarrell, "200 Attend Ban on Arm Bands," *Des Moines Register,* December 22, 1965, 1+.

33. Christopher Eckhardt interview; Margaret Eckhardt interview. Neither of the letters mentioned in this paragraph was published in the Des Moines papers, but both are in the files kept by the Eckhardts and the Tinkers.

34. Like the December 21, 1965, school board meeting, the January 3, 1966, meeting received substantial attention in the Iowa press. See, e.g., Jack Magarrell, "Ban on Arm Bands Upheld," *Des Moines Register,* January 4, 1966, 1+. Christopher Eckhardt interview; Margaret Eckhardt interview; unpublished materials provided by Christopher Eckhardt.

35. Harry M. Cory (letter to the editor), "A Marine Opposes Arm Band Ban," *Des Moines Register,* December 27, 1965, 14.

36. Allen N. Stroh (letter to the editor), "School Man Hits Editorial on Arm Band," *Des Moines Register,* January 9, 1966, 19G.

37. Rolf M. Heiberg (letter to the editor), "Putting Arm Bands on Children," *Des Moines Register,* January 15, 1966, 4.

38. Christopher Eckhardt interview; John Tinker interview; Mary Beth Tinker interview; Lorena Jeanne Tinker interview.

39. Mary Beth Tinker interview.

40. Unless otherwise noted, the materials mentioned in the remainder of this section are in the file of correspondence, unpublished writings, and miscellaneous documents that Christopher Eckhardt has kindly shared with me.

41. Eckhardt, "The Black Arm Band Story," 507.

42. Iowa Civil Liberties Union Papers, Boxes 87 and 100, Special Collections, Rod Library, University of Northern Iowa. I thank Cryss Farley, former executive director of the ICLU, and the ICLU Board for permission to examine and quote from the ICLU papers on the *Tinker* case.

43. Unless otherwise indicated, the account of Christopher Eckhardt's federal district court testimony described below is drawn from the "Tinker Transcript," 68–105, *District Court Files.*

44. Deposition of William Eckhardt, *District Court Files.*

45. *Tinker v. Des Moines Independent Community School District* (U.S. District Court, Southern District of Iowa), 258 F. Supp. 971 (1966).

46. Iowa Civil Liberties Union Papers, Box 100.

47. *Tinker v. Des Moines Independent Community School District* (U.S. Court of Appeals, Eighth Circuit), 383 F.2d 988 (1967).

48. "Student Arm Band Case Goes to Supreme Court," *Roundup* [Roosevelt High School, Des Moines, Iowa], March 20, 1968, 1.

49. Briefs submitted to the U.S. Supreme Court in *Tinker v. Des Moines Independent Community School District,* No. 1034, October Term 1967.

50. Oral argument of Dan Johnston, *Tinker v. Des Moines Independent Community School District,* No. 21 (November 12, 1968), 3–21, 42–45.

51. Unless otherwise noted, the contentions presented by the school district discussed in this section are drawn from oral argument of Allen Herrick, *Tinker v. Des Moines Independent Community School District,* No. 21 (November 12, 1968), 22–41.

52. Ibid., 23–24.

53. Ibid., 36.

54. Margaret Eckhardt interview.

55. Christopher Eckhardt interview; oral argument of Allen Herrick, 23–24.

56. *Tinker v. Des Moines Independent Community School District,* 393 U.S. 503, 504, 516 (1969).

57. Unless otherwise indicated, the discussion of Christopher Eckhardt's activities since 1965 in this section are drawn from the Christopher Eckhardt interview and materials provided by Christopher Eckhardt.

58. Dan Johnston interview.

59. Franklin D. Stone to John Tinker, February 11, 1983, John Tinker papers.

60. Irons, *The Courage of Their Convictions,* 233–52.

61. Temma Ehrenfeld and Todd Brewster, "First and Foremost," *Life* 14 (fall special 1991): 65.

62. Christopher Eckhardt interview; Dan Johnston interview.

63. Anne Willits, "Free Speech Rebels Return Home Tonight," *Roundup* [Theodore Roosevelt High School, Des Moines, Iowa], May 7, 1992, 1.

64. Dennis Ryerson, "Reflecting on the Tinker Case," *Des Moines Register,* May 10, 1992, 3C.

65. John Stebbins, "Dunedin Man's Antiwar Protest Honored by Civil Liberties Award," *Tampa (Fla.) Tribune,* November 26, 1993, 1.

66. John Tinker interview; Mary Beth Tinker interview.

67. Christopher Eckhardt interview and business card sent to author.

68. John Tinker interview; Mary Beth Tinker interview; Lorena Jeanne Tinker interview.

*Chapter Nine*

# Cultural History and the First Amendment: *New York Times v. Sullivan* and Its Times

Kermit L. Hall

## The First Amendment, Civility, and the Importance of *Sullivan*

*New York Times v. Sullivan* (1964) was the greatest political libel case ever decided by the Supreme Court.[1] This quality alone would make it worthy of our attention. It stands, after all, as a monument to the proposition that robust and open political discourse is the best guarantee of democratic self-governance. Yet the case, as is often true of Supreme Court litigation, had a dramatic history all its own, and how one reads that history shapes the meaning attached to the case. As Anthony Lewis has wisely observed, the history of *Sullivan* sheds light on the civil rights movement in the 1960s and the ultimately failed efforts made in the South to deal it a fatal legal blow.[2] Yet other scholars, most notably Robert Post, have observed that *Sullivan* also had a negative impact on the civility of public discourse.[3] While the underlying racial motives associated with the white southerners who brought the *Sullivan* case are, as Lewis so ably notes, clear enough, an important part of the story remains to be told. That chapter centers on the legitimate assertions made by some moderate segregationists that the path to racial progress was strewn in *Sullivan* with the wreckage of broken civil discourse. From the perspective of those who lost this landmark case, the resulting new libel doctrine had real costs associated with redefining the meaning of community, the conduct of public affairs, the nature of reputation, and of civility. Viewed from their perspective, the cultural and social history of the *Sullivan* case has a meaning integral to yet removed from the civil rights struggle of which it was such an important part.

Justice William J. Brennan's opinion for a unanimous Supreme Court in *New York Times v. Sullivan* (1964) was a major constitutional achievement. It was, as well, Brennan's most important contribution to constitutional law up to that time, and, of the Court's work during the 1963 term, only the *Reapportionment Cases* matched *Sullivan*'s significance.[4] Brennan rested his opinion on a simple proposition: that the nature of public discourse shaped the character of democratic self-governance.[5] According to Brennan, the accountability of public officials rose in direct proportion to the extent to which citizens could challenge the actions of those officials. In the hope of fostering a rich political discourse and an open marketplace for ideas, Brennan established in federal constitutional law the doctrine of *actual malice.* It prohibited "a public official from recovering damages for a defamatory falsehood relating to his official conduct unless he proves that the statement was made with . . . knowledge that it was false or with reckless disregard of whether it was false or not."[6] Traditionally, truth had been a complete defense of libelous statements made about public figures. If the statements were true, then there was no libel and certainly no damages. If the statements were false, then there was a libel and a jury could award damages.[7]

*Sullivan* was revolutionary in its constitutional approach. It brought civil libels against public officials under the protection of the First Amendment through the due process clause of the Fourteenth Amendment. The justices simultaneously "constitutionalized" and "federalized" the law of political libel. Neither Brennan nor his brethren worried over the prospect of introducing the actual malice test into federal constitutional law, since it was already entrenched in the states.[8] Historically, malice had meant ill will, but in the nineteenth century judges added the concept of improper motive. Brennan put these elements together, along with knowledge of falsity or reckless disregard for the truth, to form the Court's definition of "actual malice." That definition was not a quantum leap from the common law, but it did take the most stringent elements in the common law and constitutionalize them.[9] The result was a qualified privilege for political criticisms of public officials. At this point, Justices Hugo Black, William O. Douglas, and Arthur Goldberg, each of whom urged an absolute privilege, entered concurring opinions.[10] Nonetheless, Brennan's *Sullivan* ruling had far-reaching consequences, since it held that freedom of political expression formed the central meaning of the First Amendment.[11]

The Court's decision to nationalize the law of political libel and announce a First Amendment standard for such suits faithfully mirrored the theories of then prevailing liberal legal culture.[12] *Sullivan* presented the Warren Court with a textbook example of illiberal "blockages" in the political and intellectual marketplace. Through the use of libel suits, a minority of entrenched public officials could disrupt the flow of information and undermine the public welfare. By removing these blockages, Brennan concluded, people of good will were far more likely to discover solutions to political controversies.

Brennan's actual malice test minimized the chill on political speech and gave new protection to previously repugnant forms of discourse. Even false and defamatory speech uttered "from personal spite, ill will or a desire to injure" did not amount to constitutional malice.[13] Brennan also broadened the scope of appellate review in political libel cases.[14] *Sullivan* permitted appellate judges to conduct their own independent review of the facts to make certain that a jury had not committed "a forbidden intrusion on the field of free expression."[15]

Equally important, Brennan's reasoning subjected the traditional cultural assumptions about libel law to new pressures.[16] Historically, the sense of American community drew strength from measured public discourse and deference to public officials. Political libel law had protected the so-called best men—elected and appointed officials—from slanderous attacks.[17] Brennan's opinion disrupted this traditional basis for civil discourse by eroding the concept of civic republicanism, in which virtuous persons conducted public affairs in a disinterested manner and almost always at considerable sacrifice to themselves.[18]

Many of these same southern critics also complained that the *Sullivan* decision was sectionally biased, extolling northern values while debasing those associated with the South.[19] *Sullivan* was the product of a place in time, and the place was Montgomery, Alabama, the first capital of the Confederacy, and the time was the great epic of the civil rights movement of the 1960s. Yet some of the bitterest complaints against the decision came not from rabid segregationists but from moderate southerners, who charged that Brennan's opinion was another example of an overbearing and hypocritical North foisting its egalitarian individualism on a region that relied on shared community values to structure its race relations.

Anthony Lewis has called our attention to the civil rights dimension of the *Sullivan* case in his book *Make No Law*.[20] Lewis applauds Brennan's ruling and quite properly connects it to the civil rights movement, to Martin Luther King Jr., and to significant advances in freedom of the press and of speech. While one can certainly acknowledge that these developments were important, the social history of *Sullivan* is far richer, a good deal more complicated, and ultimately more instructive about the relationship of individual to community rights and the conduct of public life than Lewis reports. The case takes on a quite different set of implications when viewed from the perspective of moderate white southerners, a perspective largely lost on students of the civil rights movement.

Moreover, Lewis is not alone in urging that we remember *Sullivan* based on its civil rights implications and the lessons about racism that it teaches.[21] *Sullivan,* in this view, was a necessary step in the legal confirmation of the movement, one that shielded its leadership from exposure to the constraining effects of state-administered common-law rules of political libel. The white public officials of the South who brought *Sullivan* and other libel actions, according to this literature, were provincial racists who hypocritically complemented the force and violence they used against the movement with a cynical invocation of the law's sweet reason. From this perspective, Justice Brennan wisely collapsed traditional lines of constitutional understanding in the face of massive, pent-up demands for racial equality.[22]

Scholars writing from this orthodox perspective of liberal legalism have taught us much. Yet they have done so by giving a remarkably one-sided reading to the events that generated the case in the first place and by ignoring the commitment of southern public officials to habits and manners of civility in public discourse.[23] Southern courts, far more than their northern counterparts, had historically protected these values through common-law rules of political libel. Justice Brennan erased this tradition. The liberal interpretation of *Sullivan* and the events surrounding it incorrectly dismisses the possibility that, quite apart from the substantive issues of racial equality, the southern white vision of civil discourse had intrinsic worth.

Many thoughtful commentators viewed this result as yet another example in the Age of Aquarius of a too powerful federal judiciary sustaining individual autonomy at the expense of community cohesion. In sum, the critics believed that Brennan's opinion eroded the core values of civic republicanism, in which virtuous persons conducted public affairs in a disinterested manner but almost always at considerable sacrifice to themselves.[24]

## "Heed Their Rising Voices"

The *Sullivan* case gained constitutional traction in an unusual way. The issue it presented was not about the veracity of news reporting or even commentary, but instead the accuracy of a full-page advertisement, titled "Heed Their Rising Voices," that appeared in the March 29, 1960 issue of the *New York Times*.[25] John Murray, a tall, thin white man, a writer by trade, and a descendant of ancestors who opposed slavery, wrote the ad, doing so under the watchful eye of Bayard Rustin, the leader of the Committee to Defend Martin Luther King Jr. and the Struggle for Freedom in the South. The ad directly solicited funds for King's legal defense against pending charges of perjury and tax evasion in Alabama. The ad listed the names of the committee members, which included such prominent figures as Harry Belafonte, Marlon Brando, Jackie Robinson, and Eleanor Roosevelt, as well as four black Alabama ministers—Ralph David Abernathy, S. S. Seay, Fred Shuttlesworth, and Joseph Lowery. Murray's original copy for the ad did not contain the ministers' names; indeed, Rustin ordered them inserted at the last moment and without their knowledge to "rev-up the appeal" for funds. Rustin assumed that doing so was acceptable because the ministers were veteran supporters of King and founders along with him of the Southern Christian Leadership Conference (SCLC).[26] Because the advertisement was placed by a responsible person, was signed by well-known persons, and appeared to be accurate, the staff of the *Times* ignored their own internal policies and published it without first confirming its accuracy. A quick check of the newspaper's own files, however, would have revealed certain small inaccuracies.[27]

The ad portrayed the desperate straits facing the civil rights movement in Alabama. The text drew particularly on the confrontation in February 1960 between Montgomery police and sit-in demonstrators at the cafeteria of the state capitol in Montgomery and at Alabama State University.[28] The ad also had a small clip-out section to be filled in by contributors.

The ad named no specific public officials in Alabama but instead called attention in somewhat hyperbolic fashion to "shotgun toting" police, to a "reign of terror," and to "Southern violators" who had "ringed the Alabama State College Campus" and "padlocked" the dining hall in "an attempt to starve them [the student protesters] into submission."[29] The ad portrayed the civil rights movement in general, and Martin Luther King Jr. in particular, in a sympathetic and heroic manner. It left little doubt in readers' minds that unnamed southern public officials were bent on King's and the movement's destruction.[30]

The ad was an emotional appeal intended to tap the wallets of northern liberals. It was also filled with certain inaccuracies. The "police," for example, had never ringed the Alabama State campus; the expulsion of student leaders had been for their part in the lunch counter sit-ins and not for singing "My Country 'Tis of Thee" on the capitol steps; and less than the full student body had protested by not reregistering for classes. Furthermore, the ad had charged that Dr. King had been arrested six times, when he had actually been arrested only four, and that "Southern violators of the Constitution" were responsible for the assaults and bombings against Dr. King, when there was no evidence indicating who had committed these crimes.[31] The inaccuracies, in short, presented southern critics of King and the liberal northern press with an opportunity to attack.

These inaccuracies prompted L. B. Sullivan, the elected Commissioner for Public Safety responsible for overseeing the police and public safety, to charge that the *Times* had defamed him. He was joined by the two other elected commissioners, Mayor Earl James and Frank Parks. The errors were minor, but they were nonetheless errors, a fact that had substantial legal ramifications in Alabama where truth was the only defense to a charge of libel.[32] The inaccuracies, in short, presented segregationist public officials, such as Sullivan, with a way of attacking the *Times*'s appeal.[33]

But why the attack? The simple (and correct) answer, when viewed from the perspective of the civil rights movement, is that humiliated southern whites were bent on its destruction. Yet there is another way of examining the events leading to *Sullivan*, one that emphasizes the class, political, and personal tensions within the white community of Montgomery and that stresses that community's often competing visions of public discourse. The emerging notion of the public marketplace of ideas associated with northern liberal intellectuals and embodied in Brennan's opinion stood in sharp contrast to the persistent belief on the part of many southern whites in the concepts of local control, manners and habits of civility, and honor and dignity in public affairs. What lay behind the case were powerful cultural assumptions on the part of whites about the nature of community, of personal autonomy, and of democratic self-governance that southern civil rights leaders and the northern liberal press threatened. What was at stake was not just traditional patterns of race relations, although they certainly were involved, but the way in which southern whites explained their public affairs to one another and the outside world.

## The Political Culture of Montgomery, Alabama

Montgomery in the 1950s divided along geographic and class, as well as racial, lines. It was also, as the historian J. Mills Thornton has written, a city whose municipal politics underwent a profound transformation.[34] From the end of World War I to the outbreak of World War II, William A. Gunter Jr. had ruled Montgomery. As mayor during most of this period, Gunter built a political machine that drew its support from the city's white upper class and its morning newspaper, the *Montgomery Advertiser*, edited by Grover C.

Hall Sr. Gunter epitomized traditions of aristocratic paternalism, political deference, honor, and gentility that stretched back to the Civil War.[35] The Gunter machine was nonetheless a machine, albeit one with a *Gone With the Wind* quality. It doled out city jobs to supporters; it kept constituents happy during the dark days of the Great Depression by running up a huge debt; it opposed Prohibition; and it denounced the Ku Klux Klan. The last of these, with strong lower-class and fundamentalist religious ties, had made Gunter and his followers special objects of hatred, but Klan attacks only served to reinforce Gunter's hold over city politics. Throughout most of this period the city's population remained racially balanced, with 55 percent white and 45 percent black.[36]

Following Gunter's death in 1940, changes in the political and demographic patterns of Montgomery gradually eroded the machine's strength and so, too, its dominant social and cultural values. Many blacks during World War II left Montgomery for the North's large industrial cities while rural white Alabamians moved into the state's capital. By 1955, Montgomery's population of 120,000 was about 64 percent white and 36 percent black. The new white lower-class residential developments on the city's east side brought the Gunter machine under increasing pressure, especially when its upper-class rivals, the Hill family, whose prominence dated only to the late nineteenth century, made increasing political appeals to them. The political calculus was further complicated by the growing power of black voters. While the percentage of blacks in the city declined, their political influence actually increased, thanks to the Supreme Court's decision in *Smith v. Allwright* (1944), which invalidated the all-white primary.[37] By 1955, more than 7 percent of the black population was registered to vote, twice as many as five years earlier. In short, with the machine losing control and the white vote increasingly split along class lines, blacks held the balance of power.[38]

For a brief period in the 1950s, control of the black vote became one of the chief objects of Montgomery politics. In 1953, David Birmingham successfully ran a populist campaign that combined black voters and east siders resentful of the longtime domination of the white business and professional classes from the south side. Once in office, Birmingham set about rewarding blacks, calling for the integration of the city's police force and public parks, something that the two other commissioners, both machine supporters, reluctantly agreed to. Only two weeks before the Supreme Court handed down its decision in *Brown v. Board of Education* (1954), the Montgomery City Council voted to hire its first black policeman.[39] This policy stirred a backlash among east side segregationists, who felt betrayed—by Birmingham and by the machine. At the same time, black leaders boldly pressed their new political advantage. High on the list of black demands was the adoption by the city council of the so-called Mobile Plan for seating on public buses.[40]

Birmingham's political strategy collapsed under the weight of demographic and economic pressures and a white population simply unprepared for significant black political participation. Montgomery was ripe for political confrontation and white backlash, especially from the east side.[41] The initial result was the election in 1955 of Clyde Sellers, a termite exterminator and ardent segregationist, to replace Birmingham as police commissioner. It was Sellers's victory that forced black leaders to use Rosa Park's defiance to seek change outside the city commission. A citywide bus boycott in 1955–56 ultimately produced a federal court order to integrate Montgomery's transportation facilities. These same events also thrust Martin Luther King Jr. into the spotlight.[42]

The bus boycott thoroughly polarized Montgomery. The largest organization in Montgomery by early 1958 was the White Citizen's Council, which demanded absolute subservience by whites to the segregationist line and which had its strength on the city's east side.[43] When, for example, a group of white women in 1958 organized a series of weekly interracial prayer meetings at a black Roman Catholic hospital, the council singled them out for public ridicule. In November, under threats that their husbands' business would be destroyed, most of the white women publicly recanted their racially moderate beliefs, although one of them, librarian Juliette Morgan, committed suicide rather than do so.[44]

These events further undermined the old Gunter machine, and with its collapse went the traditional vehicle for distributing political power, conducting public debate, and adjusting race relations. This institutional dislocation fueled tensions in the white community and between lower-class whites and blacks. The bus boycott was especially embarrassing for the white elite of the fading Gunter machine. The boycott eroded some of the machine's most cherished assumptions about the nature of the social order at the same time that political influence slipped into the hands of persons it had historically disdained—white, populist, race-baiting, lower-class, religious fundamentalists and their upper-class allies, the Hills.

The presence of an aggressive northern news media during the boycott made developments all the more galling. What the northern press reported about was not the paternalism and civility that upper-class white Montgomerians had embraced in their relations with the black community, but the ugly violence of the Klan and the lower-class segregationists. The increasing attention paid by the northern press to the boycott spurred the segregationists to press for victory over black agitators, while white moderates from the city's south side searched for a compromise, all the while damning the interference of the northern liberal press.[45] On the eve of *Sullivan,* therefore, a regime of total segregation seemed within the grasp of east side political forces at the same time that upper-class whites from the machine, who profoundly disdained this new political force, wanted to set the public record straight—they and not the Klan embodied the South's real traditions. The demagogic exploitation of race, they asserted, violated the machine's tradition of political deference based on class, paternalism toward blacks, and habits and manners of civility in public discourse.[46]

By 1960, the segregationist forces had scored impressive political and legal victories, both in the state and in Montgomery. Former attorney general John Patterson in 1958 won election to the Alabama governor's mansion by conducting a political campaign of unalloyed racism that handed George C. Wallace a surprising defeat. Patterson also won an order from Circuit Judge Walter Burwyn Jones, who would later preside over the trial phase of *Sullivan,* that outlawed the National Association for the Advancement of Colored People (NAACP) in Alabama.[47] Finally, in January 1959, Montgomery city officials made clear that they were not going to retreat from their hard segregationist line, ordering that all thirteen city parks and the city zoo be sold as a way of evading a federal court order mandating their integration.[48]

In March 1959, the power of east side segregationists surfaced again in the municipal elections. Earl James, another east side leader, had won the mayor's post over incumbent William A. Gayle, a machine supporter and son of a distinguished Alabama family. James had successfully charged Gayle with being soft on the segregation issue because he had lost the bus boycott. An even more portentous political event for segregationists was the election of Lester B. (L. B.) Sullivan over incumbent *segregationist* police commissioner Clyde Sellers.[49]

Sullivan was a former director of public safety for Alabama, a position that put him in control of the Alabama State Police.[50] In 1954, he had made his reputation, as had John Patterson and Walter B. Jones, cleaning up Phoenix City, Alabama. Phoenix City, which was close to Fort Benning military reservation, was known in the 1950s as the most corrupt city in America. Events reached a climax with the assassination of Governor Albert Patterson, the father of John Patterson. The junior Patterson, along with Sullivan and Jones, then swept through Phoenix City, freeing the city from much of the corruption into which it had sunk. This experience forged a bond among the three men, one that carried over into Montgomery. There Sullivan became involved in police and public affairs as well as with the Ku Klux Klan. Sullivan is described by those who knew him as "smooth, polished, relatively sophisticated for Montgomery. He had read a few books."[51]

Sullivan's biggest political opportunity in Montgomery came as a result of events in the city's black community during the summer of 1958. At that time, Martin Luther King Jr.'s closest associate and friend, the Reverend Ralph D. Abernathy, had an affair with one of his female parishioners. On August 29, the woman's husband, Edward Davis, who had been away studying at Indiana University, attacked Abernathy in the basement of his church office, first with a hatchet and then with a gun. The minister fled to the street, where two Montgomery police officers took Davis into custody.[52] When King arrived at the courthouse to aid Abernathy, Montgomery police, already ruffled by the bizarre behavior of both Davis and Abernathy, arrested him for loitering. He was convicted and fined ten dollars. Police Commissioner Clyde Sellers, however, decided to pay King's fine rather than have him jailed as a martyr. In the 1959 commission race, Sullivan effectively exploited this incident, charging incumbent police commissioner Sellers with using "kid gloves to handle social agitators."[53]

Sullivan and state officials crassly manipulated the legal process to their advantage.[54] In February 1960, Governor Patterson and Sullivan decided to break the sit-in movement through officially sanctioned force and intimidation. While state and Montgomery police stood idly by, baseball-bat-wielding Klansmen waded into a group of some eight hundred black students from Alabama State supporting a sit-in at the restaurant in the state capitol. It was these events that formed the basis for the charge in the *Times* ad that a "reign of terror" existed in Montgomery. On May 20, 1960, the first wave of Freedom Riders reached Montgomery with a guarantee that local law enforcement would protect them. When the Freedom Riders arrived, however, Montgomery police were nowhere to be found, and for ten minutes a white mob attacked them with chains and clubs.[55] A subsequent investigation disclosed that "Police Commissioner L. B. Sullivan had conspired with mob leader Claude Henley to allot the mob ten minutes to do with the Freedom Riders as they saw fit."[56]

These events formed the immediate background of the *Sullivan* case. Segregationists controlled the White Citizens Council and the police force, and they used both to cow white moderates and black civil rights protesters. The traditional political culture of Montgomery, with its values of paternalism, deference, and civility, was in disarray. The once powerful leaders of the Gunter machine suffered the ironic fate of political attack from east siders and a northern liberal press barrage that equated their values with those of their east side opponents. Taken together, lower-class segregationists and northern journalists threatened to rob the once powerful leaders of the Gunter machine of not just their political fortunes but their sacred honor as well.

## The Montgomery Press and the *New York Times*

The social tensions that divided Montgomery's white community, not just the black civil rights movement, surfaced in *Sullivan.* What all commentators, including Lewis, have missed is that *Sullivan* was also a case in which the moderate editor of one newspaper (the *Montgomery Advertiser*) decided to make war on another newspaper (the *New York Times*) and in which a modern but ambitious lawyer, Roland Nachman, attempted to use libel law to sustain the tradition of habits and manners of civility he so closely tied to the racially moderate, upper-class white community he aspired to join.

There is no doubt that L. B. Sullivan and two other city commissioners sued the *Times.* Moreover, by late 1960 they had considerable company, since millions of dollars in libel suits were outstanding against not only the *Times* but also CBS for its coverage of the civil rights movement in the state.

The Montgomery portion of these suits had the backing of and was actually encouraged by Grover Hall Jr., the editor of the *Montgomery Advertiser.* Hall was not a knee-jerk segregationist; to the contrary, he had earned a reputation for professional reporting on civil rights matters, and he had once served on the national board of the American Civil Liberties Union (ACLU). But Hall was also an Alabamian as well as a smart newspaper person. He felt strongly that northerners simply did not grasp the way the community of moderate white southerners had traditionally confronted the race problem. While he respected the *Times* as a model of modern newspaper reporting, he believed that it had affronted his and his paper's honor where he could least protect it—in the North.[57]

Hall was a bona fide moderate. His *Advertiser,* for example, had taken a generally moderate position during the bus boycott. He also believed that the courage of his convictions had cost him dearly, in revenue from advertisers and subscribers, and that the northern liberal press had failed to properly credit his and his paper's role. Hence, Hall had decided to recoup some of his paper's losses by sending *Advertiser* reporters to investigate race relations in the heart of liberalism. The series revealed racial injustices, discrimination, and de jure segregation in the big cities of the North. Hall was so proud of his efforts that he believed he would win the Pulitzer Prize for investigative journalism in 1957. When he did not, and the award went instead to the *New York Times,* he concluded that liberal northerners did not understand the South.[58]

It was against this background that early in the week of April 3, 1960, William H. MacDonald, the assistant editor in charge of the editorial page of the *Montgomery Advertiser,* was rummaging through the "exchanges" on his desk. Exchanges were other newspapers; MacDonald read them to find out what these papers considered newsworthy. The *New York Times* was one of the most important of these exchange papers because of its coverage of international events and foreign affairs. The editorial staff of the *Advertiser,* and its sister afternoon paper, the *Alabama Journal,* also read the *Times* for other matters, most especially the reporting and editorial commentary by the New York paper on what was then the most important issue in the region—the growing civil rights movement.[59]

Southern newspaper persons, such as MacDonald, viewed the *Times* with a mixture of awe and contempt. It was at once the epitome of the modern newspaper and the mouthpiece for the northeastern liberal establishment. What MacDonald was doing as he read through the *Times* that day was what he had been doing for the previous twelve years, when he had come to work on the paper as a summer job between his law studies at the University of Alabama. What began as a summer's job turned into a career; MacDonald never returned to law school.

As MacDonald scanned the March 29 issue of the *Times,* his eye stopped on page 25, which contained an impressive full-page ad headlined "Heed Their Rising Voices." He read the ad and "kind of chuckled," thinking to himself that "it had some foundation in fact," but that he "was not greatly distressed by it." He was sufficiently impressed by the ad to show it to his immediate superior, Grover Hall Jr. Hall gave it slight attention; he "sort of umphed" and walked on by.[60]

A short time later, MacDonald broke from his duties and walked to the Capitol Book Company, a distance of about six blocks. The ad was still on his mind when, in the course of browsing through the book and magazine racks, he came upon Calvin Whitesell, the new city attorney for Montgomery. Whitesell was a youthful thirty-one-year-old graduate of the University of Alabama Law School and an aspiring political figure who had aligned himself with the new, strongly segregationist regime in City Hall, headed by L. B. Sullivan. MacDonald, in an offhanded fashion ("The same way you would ask: 'What did you think of the football game?'"), asked Whitesell if he had read the ad. Whitesell, who never read the *Times,* had not, but his political antenna immediately perked up. He asked MacDonald to look at the ad; both men then walked the six or so blocks back to the *Advertiser* offices. There, Whitesell quickly scanned the ad and took the paper back to his office, where he shared it with Sullivan and the two other city commissioners, Earl James and Franklin "Frank" Parks. A day later, Whitesell returned the paper to MacDonald, who then sent it on to other members of the editorial staff.[61]

On April 4, Ray Jenkins, the city editor of the *Journal,* came across the ad as he worked his way through the March 29 issue of the *Times.* Jenkins was born and raised on a farm in south Georgia and graduated from the journalism school at the University of Alabama. His first job in 1954 was as a reporter for the *Columbus Ledger* in Columbus, Georgia. Jenkins was assigned to cover Phenix City, a city with which he established a "unique relationship . . . in that I participated in the vice by night and exposed it by day."[62] Jenkins covered both the assassination of Attorney General Albert Patterson and the sensational trials that followed. The *Ledger* won the Pulitzer Prize in 1955; Jenkins subsequently basked in the glow of his paper's success.

Four years later Jenkins moved his career forward another notch, this time joining the staff of the larger and more prestigious *Alabama Journal* at the behest of Grover Hall Jr. His first assignment as city editor on January 15, 1959, was to cover the inauguration of Governor John Patterson, the son of the martyred attorney general.

Jenkins immediately grasped the newsworthiness of the ad.[63] He understood that King was a figure at once revered and hated in Montgomery. The ad, among both blacks and whites, was bound to be of interest with King's tax evasion and perjury trial set to begin in only a few weeks.

Jenkins set about checking as many of the ad's assertions as possible and then composed a seven-paragraph story on his typewriter. That story listed some of the signers of the advertisement and quoted parts of the text that dealt with assertions that the civil rights movement had been subjected to "an unprecedented wave of terror." Jenkins then noted certain discrepancies in the ad and suggested that there might be others, although he was unable to confirm them in the time available. The one error he noted was a statement that "Negro student leaders from Alabama State College were expelled 'after students sang "My Country 'Tis of Thee" on the State Capitol steps.'" "Actually," Jenkins's story continued, "the students were expelled for leading a sit down strike at the courthouse grill."[64]

Jenkins also reported that the ad had erred in another way. Its authors had claimed, "When the entire student body protested [the expulsion] to state authorities by refusing to re-register, their dining hall was padlocked in an attempt to starve them into submission." Jenkins informed his readers that officials at all-black Alabama State had said that "there is not a modicum of truth in the statement." These same officials assured him that "our registration for the spring quarter was only slightly below normal," and they "deny that the dining hall was padlocked." When Jenkins finished the story, he threw the newspaper in the wastebasket, since he was the last of the editorial staff to review the exchanges. Jenkins thought the advertisement more newsworthy than did MacDonald, but both journalists concluded that it was little more than another round in the sparring between King's civil rights followers and segregationists.[65]

Neither Jenkins nor MacDonald played a decisive role in the events that followed.[66] Instead, that honor clearly belongs to Roland Nachman Jr., the attorney who eventually argued the case before the Supreme Court.

Nachman was thirty-seven years old in 1960. After graduating from Harvard College and then Harvard Law School, he returned to his home state of Alabama, serving as assistant attorney general from 1949 to 1954. Almost immediately, Nachman established himself as a successful advocate. He argued for the state in the landmark case of *Alabama Public Service Commission v. Southern Railway,* in which the U.S. Supreme Court held that federal courts should ordinarily abstain from deciding constitutional claims when a state administrative proceeding has begun on the issue and it can be reviewed by state courts. Nachman's first victory came at age twenty-seven and with less than the three years required for admission to the Supreme Court bar. The Court waived the rule, although Justice Felix Frankfurter complained, "I don't know why we have these rules if we aren't going to enforce them."[67] In 1954, Nachman entered private practice in Montgomery with Walter Knabe, a future city attorney for Montgomery, remaining there until 1959, when he joined the firm of Steiner, Crum & Baker. The Steiner firm included among its clients the city's two newspapers, the *Advertiser* and the *Journal.*

In politics, Nachman was a moderate southern Democrat who

sought to distance himself from the excesses of the states' rights wing of the Democratic Party. He supported Harry Truman in 1948 against the insurgency of Senator Strom Thurmond and the Dixiecrats; in 1956, he worked for several weeks in the Washington office of presidential candidate Adlai Stevenson. When Stevenson lost the election, Nachman returned to private practice.

Perhaps nowhere was Nachman's sense of toleration more evident than in his decision in 1958 to represent Edward Davis, the assailant of Ralph David Abernathy, in a civil suit for libel against Johnson Publishing Company. A criminal jury had acquitted Davis of charges of assault and attempted murder, but *Jet* magazine on September 18, 1958, published a patently false exposé of Davis. The magazine reported that the stories about the sexual liaison between Davis's wife and Abernathy were false, and that Davis "was the pawn of persons seeking to embarrass Reverends Abernathy and King." The story went on to explain that Davis had been discharged from his teaching position in Greenville, Alabama, a small town just south of Montgomery, because he had sexual relations with his grade school students. "It was an outrageous falsehood," Nachman complained, one that called out for help.[68] Nachman took the case, along with Truman Hobbs, a future federal district court judge who played a critical role in desegregating public facilities in Alabama. They secured a judgment in Judge Walter B. Jones's circuit court in Montgomery of $67,000 in damages, which the Alabama Supreme Court subsequently reduced to $45,000 on appeal.

The year before Nachman had also represented three city commissioners in a $750,000 libel suit against *Ken* magazine, a pulp publication based in New York City. The magazine had run a feature story entitled "Kimono Girls Check in Again" that purported to expose rampant prostitution and gambling in Montgomery. During the Gunter era the after-hours life of the city had been tawdry, but following World War II city authorities had mounted an extensive anti-vice campaign. Such actions appealed to the fundamentalists among the east siders, and it also presented to northern businesses thinking of investing in the city a sense of moral order and progressive efficiency, qualities that were particularly important in attracting business in the wake of the bus boycott. Nachman made quick work of the case in federal district court in Montgomery. He showed that the author of the essay had never visited Montgomery, that he had fabricated his lurid tales about the city's moral bankruptcy, and that the magazine had published them knowing that they were false. *Ken* settled the suit, paying $15,000 in damages to the commissioners and issuing a public apology.[69]

By the spring of 1960, Nachman had established himself as the preeminent libel lawyer in Montgomery and one of the best in the state. He had fashioned political moderation, a keen intellect, and impressive lawyering skills into an increasingly successful law practice. Perhaps as a result of his years at Harvard, Nachman held a more cosmopolitan vision of the world than did most of Montgomery's public officials. For Nachman one window on that world came from his daily reading of the *New York Times,* to which he subscribed.

Nachman discovered "Heed Their Rising Voices" at about the same time that MacDonald and Jenkins were reading their exchanges. Because of his experience as a libel lawyer, however, Nachman saw something far different than did the two journalists. He immediately recognized that the falsity of the statements in the ad might make them libelous per se under Alabama law. His success against *Ken* magazine was only the most recent manifestation of the common-law rule that persons making libelous statements about public officials that were false were subject to damages. "Heed Their Rising Voices," at least in Alabama, was no ordinary newspaper ad; it was an actionable insult.[70]

More than the lawyer's mind was at work, however. Like many moderates, Nachman was frustrated by the excesses of the burgeoning civil rights movement and its white segregationist tormentors. The ad was not just wrong, it was mean-spirited, at least in the eyes of Nachman, and it promised to contribute to an already high level of misunderstanding and distrust. When Nachman opened the page to the ad, he was, in his own words, "outraged by it and knew that some of the things were absolutely false and some of the charges were grossly exaggerated to the point of bullshit."[71] At that point, Nachman became the moving force in what would become the lawsuit brought against the *Times.*

Nachman clipped the page from the newspaper and delivered it to the three city commissioners. He indicated to Police Commissioner Sullivan that, even though he was not directly named in the ad, there could be little doubt that he could bring an action against the *Times*. The ad cast aspersions on Sullivan because it attributed to the police force he supervised complicity in bombing the home of Martin Luther King Jr., and more generally in fomenting police state terrorism. Nachman pointed out to Sullivan that the ad discredited his administration because it essentially concluded that his efforts to make the police force more progressive, better trained, more efficient, and more responsive to citizens had failed. Calvin Whitesell also reinforced these views with the commissioners. Nachman and Whitesell told the commissioners that, based on existing Alabama law, they could sue the *Times* for libel, and in doing so they were almost certain to win.[72]

They received help from an unusual source, the city's newspaper. When MacDonald had originally shown Grover Hall Jr. the advertisement, the editor had expressed little interest in it. When the copy of Jenkins's story crossed his desk the afternoon of April 5, Hall reacted entirely differently. "Grover Hall read the story," Ray Jenkins reported years later, "and came running out there and wanted to see that ad. So I fished the thing out of the trash can and gave it to him."[73] Hall had apparently not paid sufficient attention earlier to MacDonald when he first showed him the ad. Jenkins's story, however, left little doubt in Hall's mind that something was amiss.

On April 7, 1960, Hall reacted directly to the ad. In a blistering editorial, written in the space of about forty minutes, he denounced the *Times* and the author of the ad, John Murray. Hall observed that "[t]he Republic paid a dear price once for the hysteria and mendacity of abolitionist agitators. The author of this ad is a lineal descendant of those abolitionists and the breed runs true." Hall took particular exception to those portions of the ad describing the behavior of the student protesters, the supposed response of Alabama state officials in, among other things, attempting to starve the students into submission, and the role of the police in dealing with the disturbances. "Lies, Lies, Lies," Hall stridently proclaimed, "and possibly willful ones on the part of the fund-raising novelist who wrote those lines to prey on the credulity, self-righteousness and misinformation of northern citizens."[74]

A newspaper editor as egocentric and energetic as Hall might have been expected to enhance the right of the press to comment critically on public figures. Hall took the opposite position; he complained that the *Times* ad fostered a climate of disrespect for authority by holding the South up to national ridicule. Lingering below the surface of Hall's slashing editorial was a sense of inferiority that had long plagued the region. Hence, an Alabama newspaper editor, and a moderate one at that, cast his journalistic fate with segregationists that he neither liked nor respected in an attempt to protect the honor of his section and his class.

Two days after Hall's editorial appeared, Nachman instructed Sullivan, James, and Parks to write identical letters not only to the *Times* but also to each of the four Alabama preachers demanding that they prepare a full retraction.[75] The latter were joined as parties in order to keep the litigation in the Alabama courts and to block removal to the potentially more sympathetic federal courts.

The events in Montgomery were given additional momentum by developments in Birmingham to the north. Turner Catledge, the managing executive editor of the *Times* and a native of Prospect, Mississippi, had dispatched Harrison Salisbury, who had previously served in the prestigious post of Moscow correspondent, to investigate racial conditions in the South. Salisbury left on April 1, two days after "Heed Their Rising Voices" had appeared. His first stop was Birmingham, where the sit-in movement was about to begin. Salisbury interviewed blacks and whites, and he concluded that something approaching a reign of terror existed. In a two-part story that appeared on April 8 and 9, Salisbury described Birmingham as a city where telephones were tapped, mail was intercepted and opened, and the "eavesdropper, the informer, the spy have become a fact of life."[76] Salisbury dubbed Birmingham the "Johannesburg of America," words that particularly insulted the white leadership of the self-proclaimed "Magic City" of the South.[77] Chief of Police Eugene "Bull" Conner took exception to Salisbury's story, since it equated the behavior of the police there with the same state terror tactics that had characterized Hitler's Germany and that the "Heed Their Rising Voices" ad had attributed to law enforcement officials in Montgomery. As was true in Montgomery, the Birmingham press immediately attacked the *Times*. John Temple Graves, the editorial columnist for the *Birmingham News*, described Salisbury as a "tooth-and-claw hate . . . purveyor of prejudgment, malice and hate" and the *Times* as engaged in fomenting "[h]atred of the South, engendered by racial emotions" that amounted to "almost a total lie."[78]

Grover Hall in an April 17 editorial joined the Birmingham and Montgomery events. He denounced the *Times* as "abolitionist hellmouths" who propagated "the big lie" about the city's racial conditions and in doing so was "misleading the United States and much of the civilized world." Hall charged the *Times* with "dereliction and emotionalism" and observed that "[i]t seems incredible that men of honor could be challenged by a famous Southern newspaper to check the facts and ignore that challenge."[79]

Although there is no evidence to suggest any direct connection, there was nonetheless an almost simultaneous movement in the two cities to bring lawsuits against the *Times*. At Nachman's direction, on April 19, Sullivan along with commissioners Earl James and Frank Parks individually filed suits in the Montgomery County Circuit Court against the *Times* and the four ministers, seeking damages of $500,000 against each of the defendants. On May 6, the three city commissioners of Birmingham, Connor, James Morgan, and J. T. Waggoner, filed suit for libel against the *Times* and against Harrison Salisbury. In each case damages of $500,000 were asked, a total of $1.5 million in each city and a total of $3 million from the commissioners alone. On May 31, the three city commissioners of the town of Bessemer, an industrial enclave where Birmingham's steel mills were located, filed identical libel suits, seeking another $1.5 million. On July 20, 1960, a Birmingham city detective named Joe Lindsey brought a similar action asking for $150,000.

To this total must be added two other suits. The first was brought on May 30 by Governor Patterson for $1 million. The previous day an all-white jury had found King not guilty of violating Alabama income tax laws. On May 9, Patterson had written to the *Times* demanding, as had Sullivan, Parks, and James, that the newspaper retract the ad. Patterson claimed that he had been specifically maligned because in his capacity as governor he also served as "ex-officio chairman of the State Board of Education." Attorney General MacDonald Gallion urged this course of action on the governor, as did the members of the board of education. A week later the *Times* retracted the ad, noting that since it was an advertisement, it did not reflect "the judgment or the opinion of the editors of The Times." Orvil Dryfoos, the president of the *Times*, wrote to Governor Patterson on the same day and apologized.[80]

Patterson did nothing for two weeks, waiting until King's trial ended. When the all-white jury acquitted the civil rights leader, Patterson filed his own suit, not only against the *Times* and the four ministers but also against King.

Finally, Clyde Sellers, a former commissioner who had overseen the police, also brought suit against the *Times* and the four ministers. Together, therefore, by early June 1960, the *New York Times* and the four ministers faced suits amounting to $3 million in Montgomery. In addition, the *Times* faced the potential of another $3,150,000 in damages in Birmingham, and Salisbury, $1.5 million in Birmingham.

Those who remain alive in Montgomery today insist that all these actions occurred independently. Perhaps, but Montgomery in the 1960s was still a small community, one in which ties of family, friends, neighborhoods, and clubs bound persons together. Lawsuits, moreover, often make for strange bedfellows. Hall and Nachman held Sullivan and the other city commissioners in some contempt for their race demagoguery and their connections to lower-class whites on the east side. Yet they all shared a common disdain for an implacable northern press and an active black civil rights movement.

The stakes were high for all concerned. The plaintiffs saw not only their own honor and dignity impugned, but that of the region as a whole. The suit, Grover Hall proclaimed in an *Advertiser* editorial of May 22, 1960, promised that "the recent checkmating of the *Times* in Alabama will impose a restraint upon other publications."[81] For the management of the *Times*, the lawsuits represented a threat to the paper's balance sheet and, even more important, a chilling of its coverage of the civil rights movement.[82] Only an infinitesimal portion of the Alabama public would have ever read the ad had not Ray Jenkins and Grover Hall decided to report it. Nachman and others, however, were not worried about the *Times* changing minds in Alabama; they worried, instead, about the fate of their reputations in the North. Besides, Nachman was certain that, as had been the case with *Ken* magazine, the law was on his side and that he would make short work of the *Times* in the trial to follow.

Sullivan and the other plaintiffs were not worried about their reputations at home; they were concerned about how they looked elsewhere. The total Alabama circulation of the *Times* was about 350 copies a day, with about double that number sold on Sunday. The *Times* had no corporate offices in the state, and its total advertising revenues over the previous five years had amounted to only about $40,000. The paper had no resident reporter assigned to the state, relying instead on local stringers and the occasional visit by Claude Sitton, who was based in Atlanta. All of these numbers really did not matter, except as they related to the odds that someone in Alabama might actually see the ad. After all, the ad was written for northern consumption.[83]

## Judge Walter Burwyn Jones "Off the Bench"

Equally telling about the cultural assumptions upon which the suit rested was the role of the Montgomery circuit judge, Walter Burwyn Jones, who tried the case. Judge Jones was the son of former governor Thomas Goode Jones, an intellectually powerful, even intimidating man who dominated his son. Walter B. Jones was the youngest person ever elected to the circuit court bench in Alabama. By 1960, he had served almost forty years and had written the state's leading text on trial practice.[84]

Jones also wrote a weekly column for Hall's *Advertiser* entitled "Off the Bench," in which he pushed several often discordant themes. First, he urged greater economic development in Montgomery, principally through federal expansion of Maxwell Air Force Base. Second, he also urged on his readers a simultaneous commitment to state sovereignty, which after *Brown v. Board of Education* included constant harangues against the Supreme Court and the unconstitutionality of the Fourteenth Amendment. Third, he frequently and openly proclaimed belief in the inferiority of African-Americans, and he called explicitly for segregation to prevent race mixing.[85]

Jones, like Hall, took particular umbrage at the "unjust" assault by "radical newspapers and magazines, communists and the federal judiciary."[86] Jones did not worry about what the people of the South felt; he fretted, instead, over the destruction of the region's reputation in the North. "Columnists and photographers," he wrote, "have been sent to the South to take back to the people of the North untrue and slanted tales about the South. Truly a massive campaign of super-brainwashing propaganda is now being directed against the white race, particularly those who envy its glory and greatness."[87] The themes of damaged reputation and honor were deeply rooted in his racial beliefs. "Because our people have pride of race," Jones continued, "we are denounced as bigoted, prejudiced, racial propagandists and hatemongers by those who wish an impure mixed breed that would destroy the white race by mongrelization."[88]

Judge Jones was a friend and political confidant of both Hall and Governor Patterson. Jones and Hall were bachelors, both fancied themselves raconteurs in Montgomery society, both belonged to the 13 Club (the city's most prestigious intellectual group), and both of them had grown up in families dominated by strong fathers. Both men kept life-size busts of their fathers in their respective offices.[89]

Judge Jones, however, had other interests. Not the least of these was his fondness for boys. Embedded in the judge's gavel was a miniature picture of a young boy as an angel, and the walls of his home in Montgomery were festooned with pictures of male children in bathing suits. The judge had for several years run a camp for wayward and lower-class boys, mostly from the east side of Montgomery, called "Jonesboro," which he regularly visited during the summer months. Rumors about Judge Jones's interests constantly circulated just below the level of polite society in Montgomery.[90]

## The Trial

The trial of the *Times* and the four ministers in Jones's courtroom began November 1 and ended November 3, coinciding with the final week of the presidential campaign between Richard Nixon and John F. Kennedy. The then existing law of political libel in Alabama was squarely on the plaintiff's side, reflecting the greater emphasis in the South than the North on protection of reputation in public discourse. A minority of states actually protected false statements, if those statements were made in good faith and were part of privileged communications. The majority rule, on the other hand, left all false statements unprotected; truth was the only defense to a charge of libel.[91] Alabama in 1913 had adopted this latter position in *Parsons v. Age Herald Publishing Co.*, and it echoed through the state courts of the Deep South.[92] Of the sixteen states that adhered to this rule in 1960, seven were southern.[93] The southern press, at least where political libels were concerned, operated on a shorter leash than its northern counterparts.

The beginning of the trial was delayed in part because of the *Times*'s furtive efforts to remove Sullivan's suit to the federal courts, but intentional foot-dragging by local authorities also slowed the process. Governor Patterson, who had hooked his political star to Kennedy's presidential quest, nonetheless understood that too strong a connection to the Massachusetts senator might hurt him in Alabama. The timing of the trial, therefore, offered Patterson a symbol that reaffirmed for Alabama Democrats that they could vote for a liberal, Catholic Democrat at the head of the national ticket and still follow traditional party policies in their own state.[94]

Jones consistently supported the plaintiffs at every turn. Initially, the *Times*'s attorney, Thomas Eric Embry, a labor lawyer from Birmingham, sought to remove the case to the federal district court for the Middle District of Alabama.[95] Embry made a special appearance before Jones seeking to quash the service of process on the grounds that the Montgomery Circuit Court lacked both personal and subject matter jurisdiction.[96] Embry believed such an appearance would permit him to raise the jurisdictional question without conceding that the court in fact had jurisdiction. Judge Jones, however, took the position that the *Times* had not argued the matter of personal jurisdiction, as was then provided under Alabama law, but had instead argued the subject matter jurisdiction. This argument, according to Jones, could only be made by a general appearance, which in turn meant that the *Times* accepted that his court had jurisdiction. Jones also concluded that the *Times* was doing business in Alabama and that due process did not require that the cause of action arise out of business done in Alabama.[97]

The trial itself displayed Judge Jones as arbitrary, capricious, and paternalistic. He refused to stop the plaintiff's counsel and witnesses from describing blacks in derogatory terms; he refused to allow the black defense counsel for the ministers to sit with the white lawyers; he used the word "lawyer" before the name of the black attorneys and "Mister" before that of the white counsel; he refused white defense counsel Thomas Eric Embry's request to ask jurors during the voir dire process whether, since Sullivan was not mentioned by name, they would return a verdict for the *Times;* he countenanced the rigging of the voir dire process; and he ordered all the parties in the case not to speak with Embry outside the courtroom, placing a special burden on Embry's preparation of his defense.[98]

As a writer for Hall's *Montgomery Advertiser* noted, "State and City authorities have found a formidable legal bludgeon to swing at out-of-state newspapers whose reporters cover racial incidents in Alabama."[99] The courtroom atmosphere was so tainted by racial prejudice that the four ministers subsequently used it as a basis to appeal the decision to the Supreme Court.[100] Hall's *Advertiser* focused attention on the all-white jury, printing the names and photographs of the jurors in the paper.[101] Hall himself testified that the advertisement, which listed no names, had raised in his mind without a doubt that its authors intended it to apply to Sullivan.[102]

Throughout the three-day trial, Embry fenced unsuccessfully with Judge Jones and Sullivan's witnesses. In addition to Hall, five other witnesses, although never testifying that they actually believed the advertisement, insisted that persons reading it could conclude that it libeled the commissioner of public safety. Embry argued that since no one was named in the advertisement, it was impossible to reach such a conclusion. Even if a connection could be established between the events described in the ad and Sullivan, the *Times* had not published the advertisement maliciously.[103] The ministers, for their part, sought to disassociate themselves entirely from the *Times* by arguing that they knew nothing of the advertisement and had never given their consent to having their names listed.[104]

Finally, at the end of the trial Judge Jones left the jury little to do other than decide on the amount of damages. As a matter of law, he deemed the ad libelous per se, meaning that it was false and malicious. The only question left was the amount and kind of damages. The jury returned after a forty-minute deliberation to award Sullivan and the other plaintiffs $500,000 each in punitive damages against the *Times* and each of the four ministers.[105]

In retrospect, these damages seem at once enormous and tactically stupid. Roland Nachman, Sullivan's attorney, was staggered by his own success and perplexed by the swiftness with which Alabama authorities seized the ministers' meager holdings.[106] Some commentators have speculated that if the judgments had been $5,000 or even $50,000, the *Times* and the ministers would probably have paid up. Yet the strategy behind Sullivan's suit and the others involved something more than winning a legal argument. The law, we should remember, was on Sullivan's side; that is why the Supreme Court's subsequent reversal of it was so stunning. The purpose of the litigation was much more profound. It aimed at nothing less than the destruction of the civil rights movement and the silencing of what was perceived in Alabama as a hostile, alien, and implacable liberal, northern press.

Moreover, Alabama officials were determined to rid the state of agitators, and one way of doing so was to break the financial backs of the black ministers. To the public at large, Seay, Shuttlesworth, Abernathy, and Lowery appeared to be poor ministers fighting a battle against segregation at the expense of their own economic well-being.

Such a view, however, is not altogether correct. The ministers were the most influential members of the black community; each of them had property interests in Alabama. Joseph Lowery, for example, complained bitterly to Bayard Rustin and the Committee to Defend Martin Luther King that the judgment against him would wipe out the assets that he had accumulated through his ministry.

The large damage judgments, therefore, were not the product of lunatic segregationists out of touch with reality. Instead, they rested on a well-informed analysis about what it would take to punish the *Times* and to drive the Southern Christian Leadership Conference out of Alabama just as the Alabama branch of the NAACP had already been forced to scale back its activities in the state.

## The Supreme Court and the Sectional Bases of Political Libel and Reputation

When framed against this background, Justice William J. Brennan's opinion dripped with irony for the supporters of the old Gunter machine. Figures such as Hall and Jones liked to think of themselves as models for and agents of manners and habits of civility—as moderating influences on the racism of lower-class southern whites and a brake on the overbearing and hypocritical egalitarianism of the North. These self-perceptions contained some of the most profound tensions in American public life in the post–World War II era, and not the least of these, as Grover Hall's behavior so aptly illustrated, was an overweening sense of southern inferiority tied to the region's tangled history of race relations.

Upper-class southerners, who championed ideas of local control and state sovereignty, set in motion forces of constitutional nationalization that opened the South to greater outside influence and further eroded their position of social dominance in Montgomery. Justice Brennan's opinion gave the Supreme Court that they so despised new powers of review and blasted "habits and manners of civility" as an appropriate guide to public discourse.[107] One of the virtues of protecting public officials was that doing so created a climate of respect for governmental authority and encouraged the best men to enter public life. That vision of public affairs, of course, was always something of a will-o'-the-wisp, as the struggle between the Gunter machine and its opponents during the 1950s makes clear.

The *Sullivan* decision has reinforced and contributed to the prevailing ideology of liberal legalism, with its emphasis on rights consciousness and total justice, and under such circumstances, notions of deference to political authority seem antique. In the minds of some, of course, Brennan's opinion in *Sullivan* degraded public life and invited second-rate political figures to govern. The most talented persons supposedly refused to risk their political careers in a climate in which accountability was valued above independence, in which criticism was valued above truth, and in which public officials were distrusted.[108]

In this sense, *Times v. Sullivan* contributed to the decay of community values associated with First Amendment law since the

1930s. The decision helped to push American public life, at least where criticism of officials was involved, away from the idea of a New England town meeting, in which the quality of what was said was more important than the quantity.[109]

Some would argue as well that *Sullivan* has debased the news media that so eagerly embraced it. Initially, it brought a burst of enthusiasm and an expansion of investigative and regular news reporting. The news business created a milieu in which fundamental social problems became subjects of intensive media—and ultimately public—concern. The chances of reporters stepping on the reputations of important people grew accordingly and with it charges of sleazy journalism.[110]

Brennan's opinion embodied an ideal of professional journalism at odds with that in the South in general and Montgomery in particular. The real question was not whether there should be accurate reporting, since both Grover Hall and the editorial staff of the *Times* accepted as much. The important differences emerged in their contending views of reputation. As Robert Post has argued, reputation has historically been defined as property, as honor, and as dignity.[111] Each of these concepts of reputation "presupposes an image of how people are tied together, or should be tied together, in a social setting. As this image varies, so [does] the nature of the reputation that the law of defamation seeks to protect."[112]

Northern courts had historically defined reputation as a species of property in which individuals were connected to one another through the institution of the market.[113] A merchant depends on his reputation to sustain himself in the market, meaning that his reputation may vary with his or her worth in that marketplace. In short, northern courts appear to have been far less likely to treat reputation as an absolute; judges there approached it as a variable condition that the individual, through his or her own initiative, might control. This idea of reputation as property presupposed a degree of equality among all persons in the marketplace, meaning that reputation was earned through equal competition, with some individuals faring better than others. The judicial view of reputation as property complemented the entrepreneurial and industrial ethos of the free, northern states and helps to explain why judges there were more likely to grant a qualified privilege toward political libels.[114]

In the South, reputation turned more on concepts of honor and dignity than property.[115] The South's historic social stratification and racial inequality anchored the notion of reputation as honor and set the section apart from the North. Reputation as honor offered individual southerners a social order with a fixed base that did not fluctuate with the marketplace. Under such circumstances, individual reputation was unalterably linked to individual identity, so much so that a person's social behavior became conditioned by it, and deference was expected (and often given) by those below to the honorific roles filled by those above.[116] The preservation of honor in the South's deferential society was not a matter of individual well-being; instead, as Robert Bellah has observed, it was "a public good, not merely a private possession."[117]

Northerners and southerners did agree that reputation was connected to dignity, although until recently (and, in part due to the *Sullivan* decision, one might speculate) they gave different stress to it. Once again, race and market relations help to explain these approaches. The idea of reputation as dignity means that since an individual's identity is constantly being constituted through social action, what he feels about himself and how he is treated by those around him can vary. If an individual is slandered, it is not just that others will view him or her negatively but that the individual may do so as well. Under the concept of reputation as dignity, individuals can claim protection against trauma to their own sense of worth.[118]

Originally, honor and dignity were closely linked, but in this century they have separated, more quickly in the North than in the South, where ascribed social status persisted much longer. As Post has argued, the modern image of society is made possible by just such a split between honor and dignity, because without it civilization as we know it would not be possible.[119] A modern, egalitarian scheme of social relations developed much more slowly in the South than in the North, and the South's social system derived from its history of slavery and racial segregation. The white community of Montgomery, like most of the South, struggled among itself as much as it did with blacks. Upper-class whites from the south side sought to tie their identity to habits and manners of civility; lower-class whites from the east side turned to violence, intimidation, and the security of the Klan. In the North, however, the race issue did not interfere with the idea that there were universal rules that encompassed all social classes and roles. The market-based societies of the North made individual reputation a public as well as a private good, a development that reinforced ideas of individualism and equalitarianism.[120]

When we approach reputation as an incident of social organization, therefore, the *Sullivan* case speaks to us with equal if not greater force than when we recount it solely as an episode in the civil rights movement. The South, of which Montgomery, the former capital of the Confederacy, was the heart, had a long tradition of treating reputation more as honor and dignity than as property. The South not only was considerably more hierarchical than the North but also was far more suspicious of social relations created in the marketplace. Southern political leaders cut from the mold of the Gunter machine conducted public affairs that relied on hierarchy, deference, and paternalism, and that invoked race to structure interpersonal relations. Under these circumstances, the elite of Montgomery in 1960 felt confronted with a dual threat: from competing white segregationists on the east side, who dismissed as pretentious the traditional notion of reputation as honor, and from a northern press schooled to understand political reputation as a species of property, the value of which was determined in a marketplace of ideas. Hence, the reaction of Montgomery's leaders to the *New York Times* ad specifically and the civil rights movement in general can be explained as more than mean-spirited racism. It entailed an understanding that certain benefits of order and harmony would flow from a system of libel law that protected the best men. What was distinctive about events in Montgomery was not that its leaders (from either the old Gunter machine or the east side) were merely racists but that they departed from their northern counterparts in the ways they made sense of political discourse, the social bases of politics, and the purposes of the press.

The *Sullivan* case, therefore, is notable not just for the legal change that it promoted but also for the sectionally bound cultural assumptions that those who litigated it embraced. The justices adopted a modern, northern conception of libel law designed to encourage a robust exchange of ideas, but this formulation rejected a competing vision of libel law, the notion that habits and manners of civility should govern public discourse. That has been, for better or worse, the most lasting legacy of the litigation that formed *New York Times v. Sullivan.*

Notes

1. 376 U.S. 254 (1964).

2. Anthony Lewis, *Make No Law: The Sullivan Case and the First Amendment* (New York: Random House, 1991).

3. Robert Post, "Review Essay: Defaming Public Officials: On Doctrine and Legal History," *American Bar Foundation Research Journal* (1987): 539–67; Post, "The Social Foundations of Defamation Law: Reputation and the Constitution," *California Law Review* 74 (May 1986): 691–742; and, more generally, Post, *Constitutional Domains: Democracy, Community, Management* (Cambridge, Mass.: Harvard University Press, 1995).

4. On Brennan's impact on libel law during the Warren Court, see Bernard Schwartz, *Super Chief: Earl Warren and His Supreme Court—A Judicial Biography* (New York: Oxford University Press, 1983), 531–41, 566–68, 612–17, 650–52; and Lewis, *Make No Law,* 148–49, 166–67, 172–73, 177. For the Reapportionment Cases, see *Reynolds v. Sims,* 377 U.S. 533 (1964). The Court also handed down major rulings in *Malloy v. Hogan,* 378 U.S. 1 (1964); *Bell v. Maryland,* 378 U.S. 226 (1964); and *Escobedo v. Illinois,* 378 U.S. 478 (1964).

5. Robert Post, "The Concept of Public Discourse: Outrageous Speech, Opinion, and *Hustler Magazine v. Falwell*" (paper delivered at the annual meeting of the Law and Society Association, June 10, 1989).

6. 376 U.S. at 279–80. For a discussion of the concept of actual malice, see W. Wat Hopkins, *Actual Malice: Twenty-five Years After Times v. Sullivan* (New York: Praeger, 1989).

7. Although appointed by President Dwight D. Eisenhower, a Republican, eight years earlier, Brennan in *Sullivan* and several other cases departed from the president's views. Eisenhower ranked his decision to appoint Brennan one of his two greatest political mistakes—the other being the appointment of Brennan's closest ally on the bench, Chief Justice Earl Warren. Brennan's opinion in Sullivan gave the former president little reason to alter his opinion.

8. The traditional literature stresses that only a minority of states accepted the actual malice test, yet the evidence suggests that a majority of states may well have adopted it. See Hopkins, *Actual Malice,* 80–83.

9. Ibid., 110.

10. *New York Times v. Sullivan,* 376 U.S. 254, at 716, 718. The considerable wrangling within the Court that led to Brennan's opinion is discussed in Schwartz, *Super Chief,* 531–41, and Lewis, *Make No Law,* 164–82.

11. Harry Kalven, "The New York Times Case: A Note on 'The Central Meaning of the First Amendment,'" *Supreme Court Review* (1964): 191.

12. See Kermit L. Hall, *The Magic Mirror: Law in American History* (New York: Oxford University Press, 1989), 284–85; and Laura Kalman, *The Strange Career of Legal Liberalism* (New Haven, Conn.: Yale University Press, 1986). For some notable examples of liberal jurisprudence, see *Roe v. Wade,* 410 U.S.

113 (1973); *Cohen v. California*, 403 U.S. 15 (1971); and *Wooley v. Maynard*, 430 U.S. 705 (1977).

13. *Beckley Newspapers v. Hanks Corp.*, 389 U.S. 81, 82 (1987).

14. Indeed, much of the internal debate in the Court over how to dispose of the case centered on whether appellate judges should exercise such a sweeping power. Justice John Marshall Harlan was predictably the most outspoken critic of doing so, believing that the case should be sent back to the Alabama courts for retrial. Brennan objected to Harlan's strategy, since another Alabama jury would almost certainly find in favor of the public officials once again. Harlan became sufficiently agitated that he threatened to dissent from a portion of Brennan's opinion, and it took all of Brennan's and Chief Justice Earl Warren's negotiating and drafting skills to persuade Harlan to join fully in the opinion at the last moment. See Lewis, *Make No Law*, 64–182.

15. 376 U.S. at 285.

16. Norman L. Rosenberg, *Protecting the Best Men: An Interpretive History of the Law of Libel* (Chapel Hill: University of North Carolina Press, 1986), 7–9.

17. Ibid.

18. Ibid.

19. The southern press reported extensively on the High Court's decision. See, e.g., *Atlanta Constitution*, May 10, 1964; *Miami Herald*, May 11, 1946; *Richmond Dispatch*, May 10, 11, 1964. The commentary was uniformly negative and hostile to the Court.

20. Lewis, *Make No Law*, 5–6.

21. The continuing analysis of the relationship between the press and public figures has generated a huge bibliography, and most of that published since 1964 takes account of *Sullivan*. The best historical introduction to the subject of political libel law is Rosenberg, *Protecting the Best Men*. The law review literature is very full and it is ably summarized in Rodney A. Smolla, *Law of Defamation* (St. Paul, Minn.: West Publishing, 1999); and Smolla, *Suing the Press* (New York: Oxford University Press, 1986).

22. On *Sullivan* and the civil rights movement, see, e.g., Lewis, *Make No Law*, 5–6; Taylor Branch, *Parting the Waters: America in the King Years, 1954–63* (New York: Simon and Schuster, 1988), 289; and David Garrow, *Bearing the Cross: Martin Luther King, Jr., and the Southern Christian Leadership Conference* (New York: Morrow, 1986), 131, 135, 155, 310.

23. Let me be clear that my point is not that muzzling the leadership of the civil rights movement through libel law was either a *good* or a *wise* strategy on the part of southern segregationists. Nor do I intend this chapter as a paean either to southern racism or to the section's alleged gentility. Such an argument would stand the region's history so completely on its head as to beggar reality. Nonetheless, I do believe that viewing *Sullivan* from the perspective of the southern, white elite can help to cast in sharper relief the implications of Brennan's opinion, not just for the civil rights movement (as important as that was) but for our understanding of the competing vision of public discourse that informed the moderate segregationist position in the first place. In short, by dismissing the moderate segregationists, we miss an opportunity to better understand their time, the civil rights movement, and the meaning of public discourse for our own time.

24. Rosenberg, *Protecting the Best Men*, 212–24.

25. *New York Times,* March 29, 1960, 25, reprinted in 376 U.S. at 292–93. The briefs and petitions in the case are included in Philip Kurland and Gerhard Casper, eds., *Landmark Briefs and Arguments of the Supreme Court of the United States: Constitutional Law* (Frederick, Md.: University Publications of America, 1975), 58:305.

26. Interview with Fred Shuttlesworth, Cincinnati, Ohio, December 29, 1989; interview with Fred Grey, Tuskegee, Alabama, June 27, 1990.

27. Schwartz, *Super Chief,* 531.

28. J. Thornton, "The Montgomery Freedom Rider Riots of 1961" (paper delivered at the annual meeting of the Alabama Historical Association, Montgomery, April 28, 1984), 5.

29. *New York Times,* March 29, 1960, 25.

30. The first paragraph of the ad described the efforts by "Southern Negro students" acting "in positive affirmation of the right to live in human dignity as guaranteed by the U.S. Constitution and the Bill of Rights." The second paragraph asserted that more than four hundred students in Orangeburg, South Carolina, had been forcibly ejected, teargassed, arrested en masse, and herded into a barbed-wire stockade when they attempted to sit in at a lunch counter. The third paragraph spoke directly to the events at Alabama State College in Montgomery, while the fourth paragraph noted similar student activity in other major southern cities. The fifth and sixth paragraphs praised Martin Luther King for his leadership of the civil rights movement and charged that "Southern violators" had answered King's peaceful protests with intimidation and violence. The final four paragraphs called for "moral" and "material" support. See *New York Times,* March 29, 1960, 25.

31. Ibid.

32. Hopkins, *Actual Malice,* 76.

33. See "L. B. Sullivan Testifies in Times Suit," *Alabama Journal,* November 2, 1960, reprinted in 5 Record 2077, *New York Times Co. v. Sullivan,* 376 U.S. 254 (1964).

34. J. Thornton, "The Montgomery Bus Boycott and the Pattern of Montgomery Municipal Politics" (paper presented to the Department of History, University of Florida, March 14, 1988), 7.

35. Ibid., 7–9.

36. Ibid., 8–9.

37. 321 U.S. 649 (1944).

38. Thornton, "The Montgomery Bus Boycott," 11.

39. 374 U.S. 483. For a full discussion of Birmingham's and the machine's motivations, see Thornton, "The Montgomery Bus Boycott," 12.

40. The Mobile Plan provided that, unlike in Montgomery, drivers of the city's buses were not required to unseat black passengers as whites entered the bus. Rather, whites were seated from the front to the back, blacks from the back to the front. When riders left the bus, the line of division separating whites and blacks was adjusted, but no rider was required to surrender his or her seat. See Catherine Barnes, *A Journey from Jim Crow: The Desegregation of Southern Transit* (New York: Columbia University Press, 1983).

41. Thornton, "The Montgomery Bus Boycott," 11–12.

42. Garrow, *Bearing the Cross,* 11–82.

43. Thornton, "The Montgomery Bus Boycott," 20.

44. Thornton, "The Montgomery Freedom Rider Riots," 3a.

45. See, e.g., on reporting, *New York Times,* February 24, 1956, 1, 10. On

the reaction to this reporting at the time, see interview, Roland Nachman, lawyer, Montgomery, Alabama, March 24, 1989.

46. *New York Times,* February 24, 1956, 20–21.

47. On June 1, 1956, Patterson secured from Montgomery Circuit Court Judge Walter B. Jones an order barring the NAACP from operating in Alabama. Judge Jones and Patterson were close personal and political friends. For the next eight years, the NAACP was out of business in Alabama, until the Supreme Court finally voided these sanctions. See *N.A.A.C.P. v. Button,* 371 U. S. 415 (1963), but see also the Court's earlier treatment in *N.A.A.C.P. v. Alabama,* 357 U.S. 449 (1958).

48. Thornton, "The Montgomery Bus Boycott," 21.

49. Ibid., 21–22.

50. The material on Sullivan comes from obituaries in the *Alabama Journal,* June 13, 1977, and the *Montgomery Advertiser,* June 13, 1977. In addition, see interview with N. Roland Nachman Jr., March 24, 1989; interview with Ray Jenkins, editor, *Baltimore Evening Sun,* March 23, 1990; and interview with William McDonald, media consultant, Montgomery, Alabama, June 26, 1990.

51. Interview with N. Roland Nachman Jr., March 24, 1989.

52. Branch, *Parting the Waters,* 237–38.

53. As quoted in Thornton, "The Montgomery Bus Boycott," 23.

54. Governor Patterson in early 1960 directed state revenue authorities to charge King with tax evasion and perjury in completing his Alabama state income tax forms. The authorities claimed that King had diverted money raised for SCLC into his own pockets. An all-white jury in Montgomery eventually acquitted King shortly before the trial phase of *Sullivan* began. At that point, Patterson brought a $1 million libel suit against King. Branch, *Parting the Waters,* 277, 288–89.

55. Thornton, "The Montgomery Freedom Riders Riot of 1961," 8a–8b.

56. As quoted in Garrow, *Bearing the Cross,* 157.

57. Branch, *Parting the Waters,* 152.

58. Interview with Ray Jenkins, editor, *Baltimore Evening Sun,* Baltimore, Maryland, March 25, 1990.

59. Interview with William MacDonald, media consultant, Montgomery, Alabama, June 26, 1990.

60. Ibid.; interview with Ray Jenkins, March 25, 1990.

61. Interview with Ray Jenkins, March 25, 1990. As Jenkins points out, of course, blacks gradually became critical of both paternalism and violence-backed segregation. Leaders such as Martin Luther King Jr. eventually concluded that moderates offered little hope for real change, and that strategy simply left white moderates isolated.

62. Interview with Ray Jenkins, March 25, 1990.

63. Ibid.

64. *Montgomery Advertiser,* April 17, 1960.

65. Ibid.; interview with Ray Jenkins, March 25, 1990.

66. Interview with N. Roland Nachman Jr., April 25, 1989; interview with William MacDonald.

67. Interview with N. Roland Nachman Jr., April 25, 1989.

68. Ibid.

69. Ibid.

70. Ibid.

71. Ibid.
72. Ibid.
73. Ibid.
74. *Montgomery Advertiser,* April 7, 1960, 1.
75. Interview with N. Roland Nachman Jr., April 25, 1989.
76. *New York Times,* April 9, 10, 1960, 1.
77. Harrison Salisbury, *Without Fear or Favor: The New York Times and Its Times* (New York: Times Books, 1980), 381.
78. *Birmingham News,* April 10, 1960, 1.
79. *Montgomery Advertiser,* April 17, 1960, 1.
80. Lewis, *Make No Law,* 13.
81. *Montgomery Advertiser,* May 22, 1960, 1.
82. Lewis, *Make No Law,* 13.
83. Interview with N. Roland Nachman Jr., April 25, 1989.
84. There is extensive information on Judge Jones in the Walter B. Jones Biographical File, Alabama Department of History and Archives, Montgomery, Alabama.
85. "Off the Bench," undated clipping, No. 904, *Montgomery Advertiser,* Judge Walter B. Jones Biographical File, Alabama Department of History and Archives, Montgomery, Alabama. *Brown v. Board of Education,* 349 U.S. 294 (1954).
86. Judge Walter B. Jones Biographical File, Alabama Department of History and Archives, Montgomery, Alabama.
87. Ibid.
88. Ibid.
89. Judge Walter B. Jones Biographical File, Alabama Department of History and Archives, Montgomery, Alabama.
90. Salisbury, *Without Fear or Favor,* 385.
91. Hopkins, *Actual Malice,* 75. Hopkins argues, correctly I believe, that the so-called minority rule was actually the majority rule. He shows convincingly that most states actually allowed false statements about public officials as long as they were not done with actual malice. His argument, of course, makes all the more impressive the degree to which Montgomery and Alabama officials were isolated in their views of what should be the proper basis of political discourse.
92. 181 Ala. 439 (1913).
93. The states were Alabama, Arkansas, Florida, Georgia, Louisiana, Mississippi, and Texas. For a discussion of these states and the case law, see id., at 76–86, 193–98.
94. Interview with William MacDonald. Jones was also the architect of Governor Patterson's career. The alignment with the future governor began during the Phoenix City cleanup and continued thereafter. It was Jones, for example, who urged Patterson to become an early supporter of John F. Kennedy, and it was Jones, a circuit court judge, who took the place usually reserved for the chief justice of the Alabama Supreme Court to swear in Patterson at his first inaugural.
95. Judge Walter B. Jones Biographical File, Alabama Department of History and Archives, Montgomery, Alabama.
96. Prior to the federal rules, the practice was to appear specially to challenge the jurisdiction of the court. See Charles A. Wright and Arthur Miller, *Federal Practice and Procedure* (St. Paul, Minn.: West Publishing, 1969), sec. 1344.

97. Order and Opinion on Motion to Quash, 1 Record at 49, *New York Times.* The beginning of the trial may also have been delayed in part because of the presidential election. Governor Patterson had been one of the earliest and most vocal supporters of John F. Kennedy's candidacy for president; indeed, Patterson had come out so early and so strongly for Kennedy that the future president worried that his connection with the segregationist Alabama governor would hurt his chances with white, northern liberals. Patterson had his own political problems in Alabama, not the least of which was proving that in his attachment to the Catholic Kennedy he had lost none of his enthusiasm for segregation, the principal means by which the Alabama Democratic Party had maintained its strength. The *Sullivan* trial became a symbol for the idea that even with a liberal, Catholic Democrat at the head of the national ticket, it was still safe to vote Democratic in Alabama. See interview, Judge John Patterson, Montgomery, Alabama, June 26, 1990.

98. Lewis, *Make No Law,* 32–33.

99. *Montgomery Advertiser,* September 25, 1960, 1.

100. Ibid.

101. Transcript of Proceedings on Merits, 2 Record at 930, *New York Times.*

102. Transcript of Proceedings on Merits, 2 Record at 602–69, *New York Times.*

103. See Oral Charge and Exceptions Thereto, 2 Record at 836, *New York Times.*

104. Transcript of Proceedings on Merits, 2 Record at 787–804, *New York Times.*

105. The four black ministers had little choice in contesting the decision of Sullivan and the two other plaintiffs to select the Montgomery County Circuit Court as a forum because all the ministers were Alabama residents. Moreover, Nachman had joined the action against the ministers in order to keep the *Times*'s attorney, Eric W. Embry, from removing the case to the federal courts. See, 28 U.S.C. $ 1441(b) (1982); interview with N. Roland Nachman Jr., March 24, 1989; and interview with Thomas Eric Embry, lawyer, Birmingham, Alabama, March 25, 1989. In April 1961, after the trial juries in Montgomery had awarded damages in the Sullivan and James cases, the *Times* succeeded in removing the actions brought by Parks and Patterson to the federal courts. Judge Frank Johnson, of the Middle District of Alabama, upheld the removals, but the United States Court of Appeals for the Fifth Circuit reversed Johnson. See *Parks v. New York Times Co.,* 195 F.Supp. 919 (M.D. Ala. 1961), rev'd, 308 F.2d 474 (5th Circ. 1962).

106. Interview with N. Roland Nachman Jr., lawyer, Montgomery, Alabama, June 25, 1990.

107. Post, "Defaming Public Officials," 556.

108. Hopkins, *Actual Malice,* 161–68.

109. Post, "Defaming Public Officials," 555.

110. Randall P. Bezanson, Gilbert Cranberg, and John Soloski, *Libel Law and the Press: Myth and Reality* (New York: Free Press, 1987), 111–44.

111. Post, "The Social Foundations of Defamation Law," 691.

112. Ibid. As Post argues, the question of how these concepts have been formed historically is complex and not entirely understood.

113. Much more research needs to be done on the attitudes of northern and southern judges toward reputation, but the findings are suggestive of important differences. See Hopkins, *Actual Malice,* 81.

114. On the differences between the North and the South, see Bertram Wyatt-Brown, *Southern Honor: Ethics and Behavior in the Old South* (New York: Oxford University Press, 1982).

115. Ibid., 97, 88–114.

116. Ibid.

117. Robert Bellah, "The Meaning of Reputation in American Society," *California Law Review* 74 (May 1986): 743–51. Bellah is writing generally and not specifically about the South, although his insights seem altogether applicable.

118. Post, "The Social Foundations of Defamation Law," 710–11.

119. Ibid.

120. Ibid., 716.

*Part III*

# New Directions in American Constitutional History

*Chapter Ten*

# "Words as Hard as Cannon-Balls": Women's Rights Agitation and Liberty of Speech in Nineteenth-Century America

Sandra F. VanBurkleo

In 1875, the prominent Missouri suffragist Virginia Minor, in collaboration with her husband, attorney Francis Minor, submitted a brief in the case of *Minor v. Happersett,* in which the U.S. Supreme Court considered the extent to which the Reconstruction Amendments had federalized woman suffrage. Among other arguments, the Minors fielded two particularly intriguing constitutional claims: they characterized the ballot as a form of public speech protected by the First Amendment; and, in alleging that state legislatures had violated liberty of speech, they implied that at least one article of the Bill of Rights had been incorporated into the federal Constitution by means of the newly minted Reconstruction Amendments.[1] "The first amendment . . . declares," wrote the Minors, "that Congress shall make no law abridging freedom of speech or of the press, thus incorporating into the organic law of this country absolute freedom of thought or opinion."

> We presume it will not be doubted that the States are equally bound with Congress by this prohibition. . . . [I]n the very nature of things, freedom of speech or of thought can not be divided. It is a personal attribute, and once secured is forever secured. To vote is but one form or method of expressing this freedom of speech. Speech is a declaration of thought. A vote is

> the expression of the will, preference, or choice. Suffrage is one definition of the word, while the verb is defined, to choose by suffrage, to elect, to express or signify the mind, will, or preference, either *viva voce,* or by ballot. We claim then that the right to vote, or express one's wish at the polls, is embraced in the spirit, if not the letter, of the First Amendment, and every citizen is entitled to the protection it affords. It is the merest mockery to say to this plaintiff, you may write, print, publish, or speak your thoughts upon every occasion, except at the polls. There your lips shall be sealed.[2]

Ignoring the Minors' First Amendment arguments, the Waite Court ruled that the Reconstruction Amendments did not mandate sex-neutral election laws. But, more than a century later, we are left with the puzzle of the free speech claims. Historians typically ignore them, characterizing the Minors' position, in one scholar's words, as an invocation solely of "the citizenship and privileges or immunities clauses of the Fourteenth Amendment, the Guarantee Clause . . . ; the Due Process Clause of the Fifth Amendment, and the prohibition against bills of attainder."[3] But what if the Minors actually thought of ballots, oratory, and writing as alternative ways of "speaking" *in a constitutional sense* and thus as incidents of federal citizenship? We might wonder, too, whether heightened regard for liberty of speech antedated World War I, when the First Amendment supposedly took center stage in rights consciousness and in constitutional law.[4]

These possibilities would not surprise historians of women. As Sara Evans once explained, "[T]hemes of finding a voice and a place in which to speak and be heard resonate through the early literature of the women's liberation movement,"[5] and indeed through centuries of resistance to patriarchy. Certainly the struggle to find a common language for self-emancipation lay at the heart of "second-wave" feminism; a list of books employing speech tropes in their titles—for example, *Essentially Speaking, Talking Gender, Excitable Speech, In a Different Voice*—forms a basic reading program in women's studies. To be sure, regard for the female "voice" in a lay sense has not led historians of women to appreciate the importance of speech freedom *in a constitutional sense,* despite evidence of rights consciousness among "first-wave" activists. But reticence is understandable: neither the state nor its historians have served women very well. Among feminists, moreover, late-century suffragists have been blamed for the movement's supposed capitulation to "law talk" by 1900, and for a commensurate loss of same-sex solidarity and feminist social criticism in the shift toward ballots and political individualism.[6]

In recent years, feminism's ongoing sensitivity to words has converged with mounting academic interest in speech as an agent of self-constitution and cultural change. Although scholars caught up in the "linguistic turn" still lead the way, the playing field is increasingly diverse. Anthropologists have been scrutinizing the practice of "speaking for others" and its consequences for identity formation. Political scientists, rhetoricians, and sociologists regularly characterize speech as a primary tool in the citizen's quest for selfhood and sovereignty. The flood of new writing includes accounts of the role of speaking and listening in what Susan Bickford calls "communicative interaction," the imprint of gender in reform discourses, the importance of a citizen's "voice" (to use Sandra Gustafson's words) as a "practice and signifier of an emerging national identity" in the nineteenth-century shift from "spoken to written argument," and the role of constitutional texts in perpetuating sex-based inequality. Robert Jensen and Alvira Arriola, to give an example, conclude that First Amendment jurisprudence "helps create the illusion of 'free speech' in a society where so many know or believe that they cannot speak freely."[7]

Despite a tradition that gives pride of place to the First Amendment, constitutional historians have contributed remarkably little to this discussion. Few scholars would dispute Bickford's claim that citizenship is more than a "legal status"; among other attributes, it involves "a communicative engagement with others in the political realm."[8] Historians know, too, that before the first third of the twentieth century, the majority of Americans had limited access to the forum. Yet, when scholars consider impairments of liberty of speech, they think of modern wartime persecution of typically male anarchists, socialists, and saboteurs, not the removal of antebellum women from convention lecterns and pulpits, the arrest of National Woman's Party picketers outside Woodrow Wilson's White House, or (even more remotely) crusades for the constitutionalization of women's electoral voice.

To some extent, these points of blindness reflect the steady narrowing of the path that civil liberties historians have followed since the 1940s. As the First Amendment narrative has come to be synonymous with an account of the Supreme Court's post-1937 speech and press rulings, it has become progressively more difficult for historians to "see" premodern women and the layers of texts, activities, and beliefs that together expressed popular understandings of what liberty of speech, press, or conscience entailed.[9] Both Paul Murphy and Michael Les Benedict have noted this constriction of the arena and related erasure of the record of human experiences of freedom (or its opposite). Yet, despite mountains of writing in adjacent fields about informal constitutionalism, republican rights discourses, and law's central role in culture formation, premodern women still enter the constitutional history narrative mainly as foremothers of modern constitutional "facts" —in other words, not as prospective speakers barred from lecterns because of a web of socially enforced belief about who ought to speak politically but as the progenitors of the Nineteenth Amendment, the Equal Rights Amendment, and other recognizably "constitutional" texts. Even David Rabban's pathbreaking study of the politics of speech before World War I, while subverting the idea that First Amendment concerns first entered public consciousness during the war, largely ignores the "first wave" as a seedbed of modern regard for liberty of speech—although, in a revolutionary move, Rabban does insist that free speech fights *ignored* by courts, struggles against Anthony Comstock, and state court rulings might be fit subjects for civil liberties history.[10]

Three habits of mind make it difficult for historians to associate the story of women's experiences of liberty of speech with the history of the First Amendment. First, there is the tendency to conceive of the state (and evidence about it) as unitary, formal, and primarily federal. Families, parishes, municipalities, and civic associations fall by the way; scholars see constitutional culture, as well as testimony about citizens' encounters with constitutionalism, as *context* rather than as part of their *subject*. In other words, because scholars look first to judicial opinions, amendments, and statutes rather than to reform convention proceedings, newspapers, and popular fiction, they find little of *constitutional* significance in a poet's claim that a woman possessed only the "right his every joy to double, /

The right to save him every trouble, / The right to clothe and teach the young, / The perfect right to hold her tongue."[11]

Disinterest in the ways in which informal governments controlled women and other subordinate classes is especially troubling. In the past, the power to curtail liberty of speech and many other basic freedoms (e.g., the right of locomotion; the right of assembly; the right to represent a constituency) has been lodged in unofficial gatekeepers such as ministers or temperance society officials, and in men who have been designated family heads—fathers, husbands, masters. Even as gendered spheres of public and private concern crystallized in post-Revolutionary America, lawmakers periodically affirmed the authority of unitary heads to maintain order and speak for household members.[12] Thus, while the term "private sphere" indeed denoted a feminized zone, the state most certainly was *present*. Family heads embodied constitutional sovereignty and claimed numerous responsibilities and powers at home—among them, powers of physical and verbal curtailment—with express judicial and legislative permission. Benevolent men could choose to blink at the letter of the law, and, as the ideal of companionate marriage took root, many did just that. But, in the end, the law of marriage powerfully shaped women's ability to speak and move about freely in public, if only because husbands and fathers voted on behalf of household dependents, controlled the public forum, and impinged mightily on freedom of locomotion. This was hardly a secret. In 1888, for instance, when an ex-senator from Chicago proposed giving each male voter two ballots so that he might properly "represent his family," the writer Catherine Stebbins noted that, a century after the creation of a republic, a "doubly empowered citizen-master" still "spoke" for women at the polls and elsewhere.[13]

Second, historians rarely consider the possibility that, notwithstanding sex-neutral language, the framers' assumptions about race, sex, and class differences formed part of the fabric of the First Amendment. In demanding access to the public forum, women's rights activists sought to replace original meanings with gender-neutral alternatives, thereby framing elements of a "constitution of aspiration."[14] Madison's colleagues had in mind gentlemanly public exchanges, with women participating indirectly as Republican Mothers, writers, or providers of logistical and moral support. On the one hand, the framers believed, after the influential Cato, that there could be "no such Thing as publick Liberty, without Freedom of Speech," which denoted a right to talk about politics and scrutinize public officials. On the other hand, in keeping with the precepts of enlightened paternalism, they assumed that "publick liberty" inhered most perfectly in men. Speech freedom thus was "the Right of every Man, as far as by it he does not hurt and controul the Right of another," by which Cato's American readers likely meant the masculine sex, not a generic mankind.[15] White women's identification with domesticity and sentimentality ensured that they would talk about public matters primarily at home or in sex-segregated settings, and that distinctly public liberties would be off limits except as grants of privilege—as when officials invited women to address legislatures, march in parades, or "speak" in school elections.

Third, even when Americans evicted women from lecterns or jailed female picketers, historians have not attached constitutional (much less First Amendment) significance to such events. Women's words, unlike Eugene Debs's, did not ordinarily resound in Supreme Court chambers until the mid-twentieth century; and women, unless engaged clearly in treason or sedition, typically have been seen as extensions of home and church rather than of the polity.[16] Thus, if historians need record only free speech battles that address what Alexander Meiklejohn once called "the general welfare" (as distinguished from words expressing only "a private intellectual curiosity") and conceive of women's demands for access to lecterns as sex-specific rather than general, as "private" rather than political, and as remote from state action, then women's dissenting speech acts—including candlelight vigils and other symbolic utterances—need not be included in histories of liberty of speech. The "public-private" distinction has been a powerful instrument of exclusion. As Meiklejohn once put it, "The guarantee given by the First Amendment is not . . . assured to all speaking. It is assured only to speech which bears, directly or indirectly, upon . . . the consideration of matters of *public* interest. *Private* speech, or *private interest* in speech, . . . has no claim whatsoever to the protection of the First Amendment,"[17] and by extension scant claim to inclusion in the master narrative. For these and other reasons, women's experiences as transgressive speakers (and the experiences of those vested with responsibility for maintaining order at home and in civic spaces) have been relegated to political or women's history; First Amendment jurisprudence, the public welfare, political dissent, formal government, and constitutionalism itself all seem to be absent.

The historical record, however, amply supports a more complex view of the landscape. Arguably, the Minors' articulation of a broad-gauged right to "speak" politically straddled two constitutional cultures—on the one hand, a face-to-face, speech-centered culture in which sex-specific voices resounded on convention platforms and courthouse lawns, and, on the other hand, an impersonal, ballot-centered culture characterized by subvocal expressions of political opinion and the loss of gender identity in the depths of the ballot box. Historians of woman suffrage regularly note the "first wave's" late-century decision to emphasize electoral politics and attribute it to political expediency, social conservatism, professionalization, or (least often) male duplicity. But suffragists also succumbed to muscular forces reshaping political life throughout the Western world. When organized women's rights agitation first appeared in the United States, possession of the right to vote had not yet emerged as the sole marker of the republican citizen. Among entrepreneurs, what Dana Nelson calls "capitalist citizenship" competed with political conceptions of civic identity, and law talk gradually eclipsed other discourses as the lingua franca of public exchange. By century's end, such changes had altered the rules of the game. Increasingly, patriotic contribution came to be synonymous with wealth production, voting, and campaigning, and expansions of freedom with lobbying or lawsuits.[18]

Given these dramatic cultural shifts, antebellum women's early fluency in the language of law is a good deal more surprising than a later decision to single-mindedly pursue citizenship rights in legislatures and courtrooms. Notwithstanding portrayals of first-wave women as amateurs shoved offstage by a new class of Gilded Age professionals,[19] many antebellum writers and orators "spoke" law as one component of a complex language of emancipation and regularly demanded access to the public forum in explicitly constitutional terms. During the Civil War, many lay elements of this discourse fell away, leaving law talk at center stage. The 1876 Declaration of Rights that Susan B. Anthony read at Independence

Hall, unlike the more familiar 1848 Seneca Falls Declaration, closely resembled a lawyer's brief. By century's end, suffragists sometimes characterized the ballot as a variety of speech freedom—that is, as an alternative way to speak politically *in a formal constitutional sense.* To some extent, then, the Minors' demand for an electoral voice can be seen as a bridge connecting the "first wave" to modern suffragism and eventually to "second-wave" speech communities. If experiences of freedom deserve space in the historians' narrative—and, given scholarly distrust of "soft" elements of the constitutional past, the point is far from settled—women's struggle for a public "voice" surely constitutes a vital chapter in the history of liberty of speech in the United States.

When Roger Taney tried to explain in *Dred Scott v. Sandford* (1857) exactly how he knew that the framers had permanently excluded blacks from the constituent power, he thought first of the power of words. Surely Madison's colleagues had not imagined that bondsmen would be allowed to express opinions authoritatively and raise their voices against tyranny. Yet full citizenship meant just that. Not only did it allow individuals to "enter every other State whenever they pleased" and "to go where they pleased at every hour," but it also extended "full liberty of speech in public and in private upon all subjects upon which its own citizens might speak; to hold public meetings upon political affairs, and to keep and carry arms." In Taney's view, promiscuous grants of a political voice inevitably produced "discontent and insubordination," jeopardizing "the peace and safety of the State."[20]

Analogous fears underlay opposition to the mingling of male and female voices in public settings. Before the Civil War, women's customary public silence was a familiar, if not universally observed or accepted, feature of the American democracy. In an age given over to verbal combat, silence was a sobering prospect. Reformers assumed that speech acts undertaken according to the rules of rhetoric could locate truth, mold public opinion, and construct new social realities; citizens whose voices resounded mainly at home and within household economies effectively entrusted the republic's future to other classes.[21]

Revolutionary movers and shakers had confronted the possibility of a mixed-sex public forum and essentially rejected it: as

Judith Sargent Murray explained in the 1790s, the Sons of Liberty "gradually and deliberately" cut women out of public conversations and ratified masculine constitutions.[22] But women did not go quietly. Writing allowed white middle- and upper-class women to exert considerable influence, so long as they avoided masculine topics and stopped short of scandalizing readers. In 1780, for example, Abigail Adams told John Adams that he had turned her into a "politician"—not as a voter but as a "writer of notes."[23] Often, women characterized publication as an alternative form of political action: as the British journalist Harriet Martineau said, "I want to be doing something with the pen, since no other means of action in politics are in a woman's power." In 1798, Murray predicted that outpourings from women's mouths and pens would usher in "a new era in female history"; decades later, Stanton and Susan B. Anthony listed female fiction writers as "among the forces of the complete revolution a thousand pens and voices herald at this hour."[24]

Into the 1830s, an accelerating battle for access to the forum led to what Mary Ryan has called "the proliferation of democratic publics."[25] Progressive education sometimes propelled young women into lecterns and newspaper offices. In the wake of revolution, rigorous new schools for young women appeared, alongside campaigns to revise established curricula; occasionally, girls with access to lecterns rose to assume the "separate and equal station to which the laws of nature and their *own talents*" entitled them.[26] Much as workingmen's groups encouraged ordinary citizens to advance "rational knowledge, . . . increase their power," and "extend their influence in the Republic" through study and oratory,[27] so women imagined carving out a space in the public forum for themselves. And, as the Second Great Awakening advanced, women "trained to think and write and speak" rose to occupy convention lecterns and pulpits, much as they had done during the late colonial awakening. Rhode Islander Paulina Wright Davis, for instance, had been "roused to thought," as Elizabeth Cady Stanton put it, in parish discussions of women's right to "speak and pray in promiscuous assemblies"; when revivalism abated, Davis was "not so easily remanded to silence."[28]

By at least 1837, then, women's rights activists had begun to construct what historian James Epstein has called "a distinct political culture and public sphere" among and for other women. Many reformers migrated to women's rights from abolitionism, temperance societies, experimental religious groups, or health and education reform. Women who had been excluded from or silenced in civil society often sought havens *between* the masculine polity and the woman-friendly domestic sphere—notably in women's rights conventions (one historian of antebellum women's assemblies calls them "the heart of the movement")[29] but also in newspapers and reform or religious societies. An increasing number of women earned a living as peripatetic lecturers. As Sara Payson Willis Parton explained in 1869, a woman with too little money "teaches, or . . . lectures, or . . . writes books or poems," not only to make ends meet but also to "fee[l] well and independent."[30]

Within their new speech communities, women set about remapping republican citizenship. They did not lack ambition. In an 1852 convention, for instance, an orator demanded "knowledge, sound judgment, and perfect freedom of thought and action," as well as woman's "equal freedom with her brother to raise her voice and exert her influence directly for the removal of all the evils that afflict the race." Another woman thought that the "first great step" would be to "clear away the rubbish of ages from the pathway of woman, to abolish the onerous restrictions which environ her in every direction, to open to her the temples of religion, the halls of science and of art, and the marts of commerce, affording her the same opportunity for education and occupation now enjoyed by man." Often, religious aspirations merged with secular claims. "Could his spirit look down upon us," wrote an Ohioan in 1851, "he would see those synods . . . assembling all over the land, not to restore an age of semi-barbarism, but to hasten the advent of a new and far more golden era . . . ; namely, freedom for woman to exercise every right, capacity, and power with which God has endowed her."[31]

Within women's "synods," liberty of speech soon emerged as a primary constitutional aspiration and norm. And, while activists rarely named the related right of assembly, they surely understood the power of large gatherings of vocal women and had come to associate public silence with banishment from the constituent power. In "disseminat[ing] the principles" of women's rights, the leadership aimed to whet the public appetite for more talk;

and, because the vast majority rising to contest sex-based exclusion were comfortably situated white women for whom the problem was *not* what critics of workingmen's groups called "ignorance," gender emerged unambiguously as the main bar to a serious exchange between the sexes about issues of great moment, including women's rights. Without direct access to public speech, policy makers might never come to regard women as sovereign *individuals.* In Stanton's words, speech freedom was the key to woman's migration from collective "silence and subjection" into "individualism" and public responsibility.[32]

Sometimes women defined First Amendment freedoms more expansively than did judges and scholars, for whom liberty of speech, in Jack Rakove's words, was more "a privilege of legislators than of citizens," tightly controlled by community elites. Women's rights activists frequently assumed that the right of speech included not only a woman's absolute natural right to express ideas without paternal interference but also the right to speak symbolically in street parades, demonstrations, exhibits, and the like, and liberty to *be* in forbidden spaces, whether as a participant or as a listener capable, by virtue of her presence, of gathering information essential to forming sound opinions or being powerful.[33] As late as 1870, a *Revolution* correspondent described the relegation of women to the sidelines in Congress as an impairment of women's right to hear what other citizens had to say: "The gallery is good enough for women. Men smile at the idea. . . . 'You can see there.' Yes, but then the day has passed when women are satisfied with *seeing.* They must hear and know." Editors encouraged women to form local associations to "awaken discussion, . . . circulate information, . . . develop sympathy," and "prepar[e] public opinion for the reform which is inevitable."[34] When Harvard medical students objected to the college's decision to admit Boston's Harriot Hunt to lectures in 1844, the issue was not whether Hunt could speak in the lecture hall—for the most part, all students passively absorbed information—but whether she might "listen to the discussion of the subjects" of interest to medical students without contaminating or "unsex[ing]" herself, destroying "respect for the modesty and delicacy of her sex," and (because her presence ruled out talk about body parts and gore) impairing male students' speech freedom.[35]

By midcentury, women's newspapers had proliferated; at the same time, orators and journalists charged mainstream papers with tightening the "vise" of woman's sphere by omitting news about women's views and fanning the flames of reaction. It was hard to retaliate effectively when influential editors blasted a gathering (as did the *New York Herald* after the 1850 Worcester convocation) as a "motley gathering of fanatical radicals, of old grannies, male and female, of fugitive slaves and fugitive lunatics."[36] But writers and printers persevered, sometimes by inserting convention resolutions about liberty of speech in mainstream prints: in 1860, for instance, the National Woman's Rights Convention in New York resolved to encourage "consciousness of responsibility" for increased "writing and speaking." Time and again, activists tied public utterances to personal independence; self-possession at the pen presaged a new kind of woman—even when words advanced a cause other than women's rights. Amelia Bloomer's temperance paper made the point eloquently: "It is WOMAN that speaks through the LILY."[37]

But citizens could choose to ignore women's newspapers. Not so with mixed-sex lecturing: by the late 1830s, women regularly locked horns with men at the boundaries of, and then within, spaces taken to be central to public life. Audiences expanded, sometimes for the spectacle of watching women talk about scandalous subjects. As early as 1831, African-American lecturer Maria Stewart, the first woman known to have addressed both sexes in the United States, took white men to task for compelling bonded women to "commit whoredoms and fornications" and for the obstructions put in the way of women "pleading in public for our rights."[38] When the utopianist Frances (Fanny) Wright came to the United States from Britain in 1818 and 1824 and commenced a lecture series, she caused a firestorm. Newspapers assailed her for traveling without a male escort, espousing free love, and addressing promiscuous audiences. Words like "Wrightisms" and "Wright-ish" came to be hurled like spears at noisy women. In 1836, Wright was driven off a Masonic stage with raucous cane pounding, stink bombs, and cries of "whore" and "harlot." Catharine Beecher impeached Wright's femininity: "[W]ho can look without disgust and abhorrence upon such an one as Fanny Wright, with her great masculine person, her loud voice, her untasteful attire, going about unprotected, and feeling no need of protection, mingling with men in stormy debate,"

> and standing up with bare-faced impudence, to lecture to a public assembly. . . . There she stands, with brazen front and brawny arms, attacking the safeguards of all that is venerable and sacred in religion, all that is safe and wise in law, all that is pure and lovely in domestic virtue. Her talents only make her the more conspicuous.[39]

In the same year, when the Polish-Jewish emigré Ernestine Rose tried to debate a Kentucky minister at New York's Broadway Tabernacle, shouts of "Throw her down!" and "Drag her out!" and "She's an infidel!" drowned out her remarks. Newspapers called her "lewd" behavior a "forewarning of some terrible calamity, that a woman should call a minister to account, and . . . in a church."[40] In 1837, amid escalating warfare between male and female members of reform societies, Sarah and Angelina Grimké established the first white women's abolitionist society, the Anti-Slavery Convention of American Women. Charleston officials exiled Angelina for her inflammatory pamphleteering and oratory; South Carolina postmasters publicly burned her eloquent *Appeal to the Women of the South.*

Reform society lecterns and presses thus served as training grounds for public life;[41] and, while more than one working-class or black woman expressed impatience with endless talk about issues only tangentially related to *their* lives,[42] orators insisted that speech ensured freedom and mental health. In 1852, Stanton confided to Anthony that she was "at the boiling point! If I do not find some day the use of my tongue on this question, I shall die of an intellectual repression, a woman's rights convulsion!" Said delegates at the 1848 Rochester meeting, "only by faithful perseverance in the practical exercise of . . . talents, so long 'wrapped in a napkin and buried under the earth,' . . . will [woman] regain her long-lost equality with man." Five years later, Stanton made the point forcibly, naming liberty of speech: "We have been obliged," she explained at a meeting of the New York Woman's State Temperance Society, "to preach woman's rights, because many, instead of listening to what we had to say . . . , have questioned the right of a woman to speak on any subject." It was wholly unclear whether a woman had "a right to stand on an even pedestal with man, look him in the face as an equal, and rebuke the sins of her . . . generation. Let it be clearly understood," said Stanton, "that we are a woman's rights Society; that we believe it is woman's duty to speak whenever she feels the impression to do so; that it is her right to be present in all the councils of Church and State."[43]

Dozens of aspiring speakers were condemned. In the wake of the 1837 temperance convocations, writers thought it "not coincidental" that "heretics" (especially Quakers) should be the first to give voice to ideas about male-female equality. While sympathetic journalists in the wake of the 1852 Syracuse convention noted that "daring women" held the platform with uncommon skill, others saw heresy. One particularly hostile clergyman found the entire "infidel" affair "tainted with the unholy doctrine of woman's rights." Four years later, hecklers in Rochester, New York, denied Susan B. Anthony access to the podium on the ground that the "spirit" of their constitution precluded female speech. The abusive crowd made Anthony feel like a Salemite: "If all the witches that had been drowned, burned and hung in the Old World and the New had suddenly appeared on the platform," she said, "threatening vengeance for their wrongs, the officers of that convention could not have been thrown into greater consternation."[44]

In response, reformers increased the pressure for liberty of speech and press. Angelina Grimké, for one, urged each woman to "do all that she can by her voice, and her pen, and her purse, and the influence of her example" to smash slavery *and* to secure "the right of women to unite in holy co-partnership with man in the renovation of a fallen world."[45] Some women even viewed active living as a form of utterance, capable in itself of reshaping social reality. Witness the 1850 convention at Salem, Ohio, where delegates refused to allow men to speak, resolved to regard "those women who content themselves with an idle, aimless life" as perpetuators of the "guilt as well as the suffering of their own oppression," and lauded "those who go forth into the world, in the face of the frowns and the sneers of the public, to fill larger spheres of labor, as the *truest preachers of the cause of Woman's Rights.*"[46] Black women, whose enforced silence in slavery white women could scarcely imagine, so prized the right to express emotions and ideas freely that they gave speech freedom pride of place in the 1832 constitution of the Female Anti-Slavery Society of Salem, Massachusetts, the first such women's society in the United States. Members resolved that "the meetings of this Society shall commence and conclude with prayer and singing. Any member who wishes to speak, is allowed the privilege: when any member speaks, there shall be no interruption."[47]

Women's political oratory could be barbed. Asked the Grimkés' friends in 1837, "Are we aliens because we are women? Are we bereft of citizenship because we are the mothers, wives and daughters of a mighty people? Have women no country—no interest staked in public weal . . . ?" At Lynn, Massachusetts, in perhaps the best-known example of public resistance to female oratory, the Grimkés and other women caused a riot (as well as a much-publicized instance of arson) when they tried to address a large mixed-sex audience at an abolitionist meeting. Afterward, Angelina declared a victory for both abolitionism and female speakers: "It is wonderful how the way has been opened for us to address mixed audiences, for most sects here are greatly opposed to public speaking for women, but curiosity and real interest . . . induce the attendance at our meetings." Woman required "a voice in all the laws and regulations by which she is to be *governed*," if only to prevent unconstitutional takings of property in rights—the "violent seizure and confiscation of what is sacredly and inalienably hers."[48]

When delegates barred women from addressing the annual convention of the New York Sons of Temperance in early 1852, and then denied seats to Antoinette Brown and others a year later, women promptly formed the Woman's New York State Temperance Society, which allowed both sexes to speak but reserved offices for women. In an 1852 address before the mixed-sex group, Stanton caused an uproar when she linked temperance to women's rights—partly to recognize ties between alcoholism and domestic violence but also because temperance women *as women* claimed the right to speak, to be present at councils, to be agents of the society, and to exercise basic civil and political rights.[49] And while scholars know that the "Woman Question" ultimately divided organized abolitionism, it is important to note that women described exclusion in *constitutional* as well as political terms.

Once evicted from rented halls, "lovers of free speech" (as one woman put it) lamented shortages of alternative spaces, the injustice of exclusion from the public, and municipal officials' failure to protect "the right of free speech" for men and women alike. Said one publicist, "What we want for women, is the *right of speech.*"[50] William Lloyd Garrison understood why the right mattered so much: if women were allowed to speak in public as a matter of right rather than by permission, "they might speak elsewhere for another object" and "proceed to occupy a pulpit and settle over a congregation." There was "no knowing where such a precedent might lead." Opinions evinced authority. If women regularly spoke in public, said one activist in a revealing allusion to property law, Americans would have to grant women "title" to other rights, as well as to their own bodies and minds.[51]

Women's autobiographies not only reveal women's sense of the importance of speaking, hearing, and being heard in mixed-sex settings but also show how informal governments restrained uppity women. Firebrand Abigail Kelly encountered "scorn, ridicule, violence, and mobs" and "all kinds of persecutions, still speaking whenever and wherever she gained an audience." In the wake of a controversial speech in Boston, the *Christian Mirror* denounced as immoral a woman who would allow herself to be "closeted with . . . men" in preparing convention documents, sacrificing "her honor, her loveliness, her glory." Sarah Grimké, rejoicing that Kelley had not been "dismayed at the opposition," thought that she had done "more toward establishing the rights of woman than a dozen books." Until 1870, Kelley moved restlessly from state to state, inspiring other women to do the same; when she died, Samuel May credited her with steeling a generation of women for battle at the podium. Her words "startled and aroused the land"; while defending human rights, she "hewed out a path over which many women are now walking toward their equal political rights." Lucy Stone testified that Kelley and members of a debating club at Oberlin College had inspired her to speak in public: "The movement for the equal rights of women began . . . with her. Other women had spoken in public . . . , [but] it was left for Abby Kelley to take on her young shoulders and to bear a double burden, for the slave's freedom, and for equal rights for women."[52]

Antoinette Brown similarly tested the limits of words as agents of change. While studying theology at liberal Oberlin College in 1848, Brown told "best friend" Lucy Stone that she had been discussing a woman's "right to public labors" and women's "*speaking* in particular" with progressive ministers, who grew fainthearted at the prospect of authoritative female theologians. One such critic said that women had "a right to speak in public [g]atherings" but "no right to preach." Brown found "hardly . . . any one to *talk with*," and fewer still in agreement with her. Although the famous theologian Charles Finney initially had opposed female oration, students were "all required to tell their religious experience" in his classes. When a fellow student brought Antoinette and another woman student to his attention, he ignored the suggestion: "Once he looked as though he did not know what to say," wrote Brown, "& the next time said 'O we dont call upon the ladies.'" But once Finney learned that the women were "members of the department," he relented and indeed "seemed to forget that he was talking with a woman." When Finney at length asked her to address a prayer meeting, Brown spoke of her "determination to preach & speak in public"; listeners were "surprised & pleased too at my speaking my views so plainly," and that she was "really expecting to speak."[53]

At Oberlin, however, social conventions had been suspended. Elsewhere, Brown and other vocal women ran aground. In 1852, for example, temperance workers at the New York state convention had resolved not to "listen to the voice of woman in legislating upon great public questions," on the ground that the "constitution of the female mind" rendered woman "incapable of correctly deciding upon the points involved" in statutory reform. When they ejected a number of female delegates, the women roundly condemned a society "in which woman is voted not of the world!"[54] Then, at New York City's World Temperance Conference in May 1853, presiding officers decided that those who had "something else more at heart than temperance" would be excluded. Brown therefore presented her credentials and, as the official delegate of two New York temperance societies, demanded access to the podium. Although the presiding officer accepted her letters and granted her the floor, other delegates refused to let a woman speak. For two consecutive days, Brown's colleagues shouted her down; on the third day, as William Henry Channing and others later testified, delegates "succeeded in silencing her voice." The Reverend John Chambers of Philadelphia reportedly "stood stamping until he raised a cloud of dust around him, pointing with coarse finger and rudely shouting 'shame on the woman.'" After Brown and a distinguished black delegate had been "crowded off the platform," outraged supporters called an alternative *Whole* World Temperance Convention in another hall. Brown's retrospective account merits attention. "I went there," she explained, "to assert a principle . . . relevant to the circumstances of that convention, and one which would promote *all* good causes and retard *all* bad ones. I went there, as an item of the world, to contend that the sons and daughters of the race, without distinction of sex, sect, class or color, should be recognized as belonging to the world, and I planted my feet upon the simple *rights of the delegate.* I asked no favor as woman, or in behalf of woman; . . . but I claimed, in the name of the world, the rights of a delegate in a world's convention."[55]

Horace Greeley's conservative *New York Tribune* predicted that the "*gentlemen*" responsible for Brown's ouster would "live to understand their own folly." They had managed a "very different thing from what they now suppose." Had they aimed to "strengthen the cause of Woman's Rights, they could not have done the work half so effectively. . . . Many who question the propriety of woman's appearing in public will revolt at the gagging of one who had a right to speak. . . . There is in the public mind . . . an intuitive love of fair play and free speech and those who outrage it . . . bestow a mighty power on the ideas they . . . would suppress." Stanton later characterized the affair as a "great battle for free speech and human equality" won handily by Brown's allies. But activists knew that "gagging" by a civic body stripped her of essential attributes of citizenship in an important region of "the public." Brown, in fact, had attended the Half World Temperance Convention (as it came to be called) partly to test "the speech principle." Once there, she refused to "utter words of flattery" by which she might win the battle and lose the war.[56]

The swift, negative response to women's demands for equal time at the lectern and on reform society committees persuaded numerous reformers to join the movement, embodied in dozens of women's rights conventions called after 1848–50. Few women doubted that the restoration of a woman's birthright commenced with public debate. At the 1852 Westchester, Pennsylvania, meeting, Ann Preston invited "magnanimous men and true women" to "examine th[e] subject" of women's rights "in the spirit of a generous and candid investigation." Two years later, Ernestine Rose asked "man to meet us . . . in the spirit of inquiry, in the spirit of candor and honesty, as rational human beings ought to meet each other, face to face, and adduce arguments, if they can, to convince us that we are not included in that great Declaration of Independence." And again: "If they can convince us that we are wrong, we will give up our claims; but if we can convince them that we are right . . . , then we expect them in a spirit of candor . . . to acknowledge it."[57]

Even Frederick Douglass, who viewed the ballot as *the* badge of civic empowerment, discerned the importance of public speech for women. In several post–Civil War orations supporting woman suffrage, he recalled that men once had "shuddered at the thought of daughters, wives, sisters, and sweethearts standing before a multitude of men and women and making themselves heard in speech. Skeptics poured all manner of ridicule upon women's conventions and other demonstrations." Douglass thought he detected a "vast and wonderful change" in the "public mind" on the subject; there now was "no language nor speech where woman's voice is not heard." But it had not always been so. Although Douglass had trouble reconciling his priorities with women's, he granted speech its due. The "boldest pioneers . . . did not think, at first, of asking for the right of suffrage," he said. "To this great height, they had not been lifted." Rather, they sought freedom of expression: "What they wanted, first of all, and most of all, was that greatest of all rights, the right of speech, the right to utter their pent up feelings and . . . convictions . . . ; to make a fiery protest against the fetters with which custom, bigotry and superstition had . . . bound them." He also identified the nub of opposition. "[T]heirs was to the common ear, the wild alarm cry of revolt, a shout of defiance from the barricades of rebellion to the forts . . . of social order and conservatism. It was the uprising of one half of the human race against the opinions and customs of the other half." Within "the most stupendous revolution the world has ever witnessed," words served as a "lever" to pry open the forum.[58]

In short, as Virginia and Frances Minor implied in their *Minor* brief, first-wave leaders and their allies in associated reform groups often characterized the multifaceted right to gather, listen, speak, and be heard in civic spaces as a freedom upon which other elements of a public personality depended. In Stanton's words, women had been "compelled" after centuries of muzzling to "defend the right of free speech for themselves"; the ability to claim and use liberty of speech (variously called "speech freedom," "the right of speech," and "the speech principle") prefigured the search for what rights activist Mariana Johnson called "knowledge, sound judgment, and perfect freedom of thought and action." When Stanton and Susan B. Anthony edited the first volume of the landmark documentary edition, *The History of Woman Suffrage,* they peppered it with praise of female wordsmiths, devoted long chapters to the "clerical attempt to silence women" and female orators' attempts to "defend free speech for themselves," and pointed repeatedly to the transformative power of words, for speakers and listeners alike. Lucretia Mott's mesmerizing lectures, to give one example, supposedly reconstituted Mott as an authoritative woman while eliminating "padlocks on our lips."[59]

Given the stakes, violent resistance was unsurprising. In the difficult year of 1837, the Reverend Jonathan Stearns of Massachusetts published a pamphlet admonishing women to seek "influence" rather than publicity. "It is her province," he wrote, "to *adorn* social life, to throw a *charm* over the intercourse of the world." He then addressed the right of speech: "That there are ladies who are capable of public debate, who could make their voice heard from end to end of the church and the senate house, that there are those who might bear a favorable comparison with others as eloquent orators, and who might speak to better edification than most of those on whom the office has hitherto devolved, I am not disposed to deny. The question is not in regard to *ability,* but to *decency,* to order, to Christian *propriety.*" In the same year, Hubbard Winslow, pastor of Boston's Bowdoin Street Church, delivered a hammerlike sermon in which he coincidentally identified many of the elements of citizenship to which women aspired:

> [W]hen females undertake to assume the place of public teachers . . . ; when they form societies for the purpose of sitting in judgment and acting upon the affairs of the church and state; when they travel about from place to place as lecturers, teachers, and guides to public sentiment; when they assemble in conventions to discuss questions, pass resolutions, make speeches, and vote . . . ; when they begin to send up their names to gentlemen holding official stations, gravely declaring their own judgment . . . , and informing them, with solemn menace what they [will] do, if they do not yield . . . ; when they attempt the reformation of morals by engaging in free conversation and discussion upon those things of which the apostle says, "it is a shame even to speak"; when they encourage meetings and measures . . . by their presence, countenance, or service;—in short, when the distinguishing graces of modesty, deference, delicacy, and sweet charity are . . . displaced by the opposite qualities of boldness, arrogance, rudeness, indelicacy, and the spirit of denunciation of men and measures, . . . it is then no longer a question whether they have . . . violated the inspired injunction which saith, "Let the woman learn in silence with all subjection, but I suffer not a woman to teach, nor to usurp authority over the man, but to be in silence." . . . [W]hether they appear in the name of avowed infidelity, or of civil and human rights, . . . their tendency is ultimately the same— . . . the destruction of the domestic constitution, the prostration of all decency and order, the reign of wild anarchy and shameless vice.[60]

Christianity thus was a double-edged sword. On one side, revivalism had promoted social criticism, community building, and self-assertion. Throughout the century, a staunch handful of female preachers stood their ground in the face of withering criticism. Evangelical women launched tract societies, moral reform clubs, and study groups to circulate new ideas, in the process remaking themselves; itinerant pastors—many of them African-American—vaulted cultural barricades on the lecture circuit. Inspired in part by experimental Protestantism, Stanton, Matilda Gage, and other scholars painstakingly described historical linkages between political governments, organized religion, and the subjugation of women.[61]

But, on the other side, opponents regularly castigated active Christian women. In September 1869, the *Revolution* told of a woman in Mount Pleasant, Iowa, who launched a public appeal after her Presbyterian church expelled her for refusing to maintain silence in church. "I claim that I have the right to speak or pray as the spirit of God may direct or inspire me," she said, "for in the spiritual church, or in Christ, there is neither male nor female, but all are one in Him. And, in conclusion, I am determined, by God's grace, to continue to speak in public as power is given me." *Revolution* insisted that, because oratory achieved "its highest reach . . . in religious discourse," women ought to insist upon it: "If there is one place more appropriate than another for a woman to use her native faculty of public speech, that place is the religious meeting. Three-fourths of all the members of our churches are women, and three-fourths of the ministers of these churches should be women likewise." The idea was not that the "priest should be hushed to silence, but that the priestess also should be suffered to speak."[62]

Criticism was unremitting. In the notorious 1837 pastoral letter published in the *Liberator,* ministers condemned the "mistaken conduct of those who encourage females to bear an obtrusive and ostentatious part in . . . reform," and all women who "forget themselves" and "itinerate" as "public lecturers and teachers." They especially regretted the "promiscuous conversation of females" about "things 'which ought not to be named,'" such as rape or body parts.[63] Some years later, an urban clergyman urged his excessively active female parishioners "not to vote but to *be;* not to dabble in politics, but to acquire personal and moral power; not to strut and storm on platforms and fill the papers with echoes of their rantings, but to fill themselves with ennobling culture and make the world better. . . . The emancipation of woman is not to come from her getting something but from her being somebody."[64]

The battle for the pulpit raged into and beyond Reconstruction. In 1876, to give one example, Presbyterian elders tried the Reverend Isaac See for the "crime" of allowing two women to talk about temperance from his pulpit. In a four-hour, Bible-thumping speech, the Reverend Dr. Craven tied women's speech to attacks on male sovereignty: "I believe the subject involves the headship and crown of Jesus. Woman was made for man and became first in the transgression. My argument is that subordination is natural, the subordination of sex." Dr. See (who lost the case) had "admitted marital subordination, but this is not enough; there exists a created subordination . . . of woman as woman to man as man. . . . The proper condition of the adult female is marriage. . . . Women without children, it might be said, could preach, but they are under the general rule of subordination. . . . Man's place is on the platform. It is positively base for a woman to speak in the pulpit."[65]

Activists condemned such criticism as antirepublican and un-Christian. At issue was nothing less than the promise of the Revolution and Second Great Awakening for women. Could the female majority move about freely and participate in civic undertakings as active members of the constituent power? On one hand, a fully vocal woman destabilized the fiction of female dependency and, with it, the polity; on the other hand, citizens had rights and responsibilities in the forum. Frances Gage recalled that, during the ado over Antoinette Brown at the World Temperance Convention, in the absence of the presiding officer, the Reverend Samuel Carey presented a resolution that recognized women "as efficient aids and helpers in the home, but not on the platform." When tumult erupted at the Broadway Tabernacle, Ernestine Rose reminded her sisters of linkages in other lands between silence and tyranny: Could it be that, in America, "tyrants" violated the "individual right to express opinions on any subject? And do you call yourselves republicans? No; there is no republic without freedom of speech."[66]

Hence, women repeatedly demanded places on platforms from which they had been ejected, to remake the world through speech and to reconstitute themselves as citizens. Frances Gage thought that convention oratory expressed the "Spirit of the Age," through which the "thoughts and feelings of the masses are known. . . . Let them speak out. Let those who think and feel, act."[67] At an Akron, Ohio, meeting, Gage demanded that men "allow women to be heard" and then explained why liberty of speech was so important. "Let woman speak for herself," said Gage, "and she will be heard. . . . Let her claim with a calm and determined, yet loving spirit, her place, and it will be given her. . . . Woman must act for herself. . . . Oh, if all women could be impressed with the importance of their own action, and with one united voice, speak out in their own behalf, . . . they would create . . . [a] revolution without armies."[68]

Such ideas persisted well beyond the Civil War. When the *People's Journal* of Greenwich, New York, noted with some surprise that advocates of women's rights had made their case in the pages of *Revolution* "in language of force and reason," Stanton could only agree: "Yes, sir, it is 'something new under the sun' for women to talk about finance, capital, labor, politics, religion and social life." But the "time ha[d] come." The idea, she said in another place, was "not to reflect, but to make, public sentiment." To help secure both woman suffrage and "a revolution in our political, religious and social systems," journalists would purvey "words . . . as hard as cannon-balls." In 1870, the new publisher observed that *Revolution* was nothing less than "woman's voice speaking from woman's heart."[69]

Occasionally, supportive publicists interpreted women's demand for freedom of speech as a simple assertion of the right to petition government, or as an attempt to secure the legal remedies supposedly guaranteed to citizens when government abrogated rights. Thus, the *Syracuse Standard* affirmed in 1852 that, if "any of the natural rights belonging to women are withheld from them by the laws and customs of society, it is due to them that a remedy should be applied," adding that aggrieved citizens had an unassailable right to "give free expression to their opinions."[70] But "first-wave" strategists had in mind a good deal more than the relatively decorous lodging of grievances. Stanton viewed oratory and planned "disturbances" at men's meetings as positive obligations of women; they were avenues to social refabrication and exercises in self-ownership. However inexperienced or terrified speakers might be, however life-threatening the arsonists gathered outside the hall, women were urged to speak, to affirm the fact of self-rule and to reject collaboration with patriarchal masters. Antoinette Brown regularly compared "enforced silence" to "slavery";[71] and, while Frederick Douglass, the black poet Frances Harper, and others rightly noted that such comparisons slighted important differences between white and black women's experiences, Brown clearly hoped that the struggle against enforced silence and passivity would cut across racial lines, reconstituting *all* women.

The campaign sometimes triggered cultural change. Consider Stanton's report of a determined New Yorker's triumph in 1869. Unscheduled, a "pale, sad woman, mad with oppression," had risen from a mixed-sex audience "claiming her right to speak," only to be "seized by the Police" and "dragged from the platform." The "impatience of the audience with her injuries was hushed at once in pity for the woman in the strong arm of the law"; the "cry of 'Put her out' from many a manly voice was drowned in the nobler one, 'Let her be heard.'... As soon as the officer in uniform laid his hand on the woman, she raised herself up to her full proportions, tall and stately, and, with keen satire, said, 'I deny your authority, I had no voice in the law that made you my ruler.' Her ready wit was greeted with loud applause, and she turned contemptuously from the officer to the audience, who gave her a patient hearing."[72]

Women's rights convention participants encouraged women to exercise vocal chords loudly and continually. In 1853, Frances Gage urged delegates at the fourth national convention in Cleveland to extend "perfect liberty here to speak upon the subject under discussion, both for and against; and that we urge all to do so." She aimed to ensure that the *convention*, and not hostile newspapers or pulpits, became the recognized forum for talk about women's rights, rather than merely a curiosity that skeptics might ridicule. Indeed, for most women, the notion of a party line was anathema because it diminished the volume of speech. In 1854, for instance, women went toe-to-toe with William Lloyd Garrison and other advocates of a "house organ" for the movement. After long debate, Lucy Stone, Lucretia Mott, and others defeated proposals for a movement newspaper modeled after abolitionist prints, on the ground that, while they valued "organization," they also favored "individual freedom and responsibility." Woman was *not* to be viewed as a mass speaking sotto voce.[73]

Occasionally, women silenced men. At the Salem convention of 1850, for example, delegates recalled that no man had been "allowed to sit on the platform, to speak or vote. *Never did man so suffer.*" When men tried to interject comments, they were ruled out of order. Organizers noted that, for the "first time in the world's history, men learned how it felt to sit in silence when questions in which they were interested were under discussion." The Woman's State Temperance Society of New York, founded in the wake of savage physical and rhetorical attacks on its members, resolved that, while men could join their organization, only women could address the membership. But, into the Civil War era, others maintained an open forum. Indeed, in May 1863, when delegates tried to silence a man at a Loyal League convention, Susan B. Anthony condemned their efforts: "Some of us . . . have many a time been clamored down, and told that we had no right to speak, and that we were out of our place in public meetings; far be it from us, when women assemble, and a man has a thought in his soul . . . to retaliate upon him."[74]

For such women, oratory was a vital ingredient in the shaping of new women and a new society; mere attendance at meetings had salutary but quite different effects. When the clergy "place[d] its hands on woman's lips" and silenced her, women decided at Syracuse in 1852, the antidote was dogged female preaching. Reverend Samuel Longfellow of Brooklyn, brother of the famous poet, made clear that speech *did* have the desired effect. "It might seem, that on a platform like this," he said in 1860, "when a woman speaks, her presence is not merely a plea and an argument, but also a proof. When a woman speaks, and speaks well, speaks so as to interest and move and persuade men, there is no need of any argument . . . to prove that she has the liberty . . . , and that it is a part of her sphere to do it. She has done it; and that of itself is the whole argument. . . . And I think if there were none but men present here, it would be better that only women should speak." Critics said that, if men were to "grant this claim of woman's right to make her own sphere, . . . all women will immediately rush into public speaking, and be crowding to the platform, or into the pulpit, or writing books, . . . or painting pictures." But why not? Surely talented women "ought to be there."[75]

Demands for a public voice interacted with and reinforced a parallel interest in "freedom of action"—an umbrella term denoting the right to move about and act independently, through speech and otherwise. Women often denigrated the right of petition as the embodiment of "servility" and the antithesis of action, noting that the right to humbly entreat male governors was the *only* freedom granted easily to women. When using the term "action," reformers sometimes had in mind the relatively simple right to pursue the ends toward which abstract rights aspired: as Frederick Douglass put it, "[W]oman must practically as well as theoretically, assert her rights. She must *do* as well as *be.*"[76] More often, though, women linked "action" to other rights claims. In Angelina Grimké's *Appeal to the Women of the Nominally Free States* (1838), she explained the decision to speak out against sex and race subjugation in terms of both "action" and liberty of speech, both of which were protected by "our national Bill of Rights and the Preamble of our Constitution. The denial of our duty to act is a bold denial of our right to act; and if we have no right to act, then may *we* well be termed 'the white slaves of the North'—for like our brethren in bonds, we must seal our lips in silence and despair."[77]

Women aimed big guns at impediments to action. Said Ernestine Rose in 1856, women were "taxed but not represented, authorized to earn property but not free to control it, permitted to prepare papers for scientific bodies but not to read them, urged to form political opinions but not allowed to vote upon them." Elizabeth Jones, a keynote speaker at the Salem, Ohio, gathering in 1850, urged her sisters to "demand their true position as equally responsible co-workers with their brethren in the world of action." As Harriet Martineau put it in 1851, "Women, like men, must be educated with a view to action." She denounced the notion that a smart woman could "study anything that her faculties led her to, whether physical science or law, government and political economy," so long as she agreed to "stop at the study." When she "entered the hospital as physician and not nurse," took her place "in a court of justice, in the jury box, and not the witness box," or "brought her mind and her voice into the legislature, instead of discussing the principles of laws at home," she would be "feared, lose her influence as an observing intelligence, standing by in a state of purity 'unspotted from the world.' . . . [A]n intelligence never carried out into action could not be worth much."[78]

Time and again, the act of speaking brought individual women to self-sovereignty. In her 1887 autobiography, for instance, Mary Livermore wrote movingly of her epiphanic passage during a wartime speech into the realm of action. In 1863, Livermore traveled to Iowa to encourage patriotic work among women; upon arrival, she was appalled to learn that organizers had invited hundreds of men and women to hear what she had to say. "I am *not* a public speaker," a terrified Livermore told a dignitary; "I have never made a speech in my life, and never have addressed any but companies of women. . . . *I cannot do it.*" Organizers persuaded governor-elect William Stone to make the speech for her. But, at the last minute, he reminded Livermore that *her* voice would advance the cause as nothing else could. Suppressing terror, Livermore navigated the passage from "woman's sphere" into a sex-integrated public forum. "I followed him down the aisle of the church to the platform, erected in front of the pulpit," she recalled in 1887,

> The ladies of the Aid Society looked their astonishment. . . . I rose by a supreme effort, trembling in every fibre of my being. . . . Shutting out all thought of the expectant multitude before me, I concentrated my mind upon what I had to say. For the first ten minutes I talked into utter darkness. . . . I did not even hear the sound of my own voice—only a roaring, as if ten thousand mill-wheels were thundering about me. . . . But gradually it began to grow light about me. I began to hear my own voice.

Thereafter, Livermore proudly "did whatever was necessary" to raise money for the war effort and the cause of women's rights.[79]

Dozens more braved platforms to address what the Seneca Falls organizers called "the Social Civil and Religious Condition of Woman,"[80] to establish public personalities, to pry open the forum for other women, and to secure citizenship rights. Well into the Civil War, women acted on the knowledge that public oratory, especially when listeners *knew* the speaker, was a form of self-defense at least equal in power to periodic utterances at the polls. Indeed, when Stanton ran for Congress in 1866 (she received twenty-four votes), she offered a "creed" of "*free speech, free press, free men, and free trade*—the cardinal points of democracy."[81] To participate in the forum, women required access to the related freedoms of assembly and locomotion; without a "coeval" right to speak one's mind in "promiscuous assemblies" and to be where men gathered, women's civil and political rights would be matters merely of "law" rather than of social "fact."[82] At an 1860 convention, Wendell Phillips drove the point home: "Why talk? We have done a great deal besides talk! But suppose we had done nothing but talk? . . . [T]hirty millions of thinking, reading people are constantly throwing it in the teeth of reformers that they rely upon talk! What is talk? Why, it is the representative of brains. And what is the characteristic glory of the nineteenth century? That it is ruled by brains, and not by muscle; that rifles are gone by, and ideas have come in; and, of course, in such an era, *talk is the fountain-head of all things.*"[83]

Antebellum women's rights activism thus commenced with demands for liberty of speech. Only by expressing views in public, and forcing men through structured conversation to see the irrationality of law and custom, would women be able to experience their otherwise abstract identity as members of the constituent power. As Elizabeth Clark once noted, ballots did not "automatically take pride of place in the panoply of rights sought . . . before the Civil War, but stood as one goal among many," and much of the time "not the most important" goal. Even after the war, suffragists still said that ballots were not ends in themselves; in Brown Blackwell's phrase, the vote was only one of the "powers of self-protection" denied to women.[84]

The experience of Civil War and Reconstruction, in fact, finally persuaded a good many reformers of the inadequacy of face-to-face oratory as the sex's main "lever" in the women's rights battle. For some women, the outcome was unsurprising: Stanton, for instance, had long suspected that the strong medicine of ballots would be *necessary*—that rational discourse might not prevail. She had so argued at Seneca Falls, and after the 1850s continued to make the case for the suffrage, although mounting skepticism about the value of all political "gifts" increasingly colored her writing and oratory. "We who have spoken out," she told Gerrit Smith in 1855, "have declared our rights, political and civil; but the entire revolution about to dawn upon us by the acknowledgment of woman's social equality, has been seen and felt but by a few. The rights to vote, to hold property, to speak in public, are all-important; but there are great social rights, before which all others sink into utter insignificance." Neither words nor votes altered women's deplorable situation at work, in the streets, and in the bedroom. "The cause of woman," she said, "is . . . a deeper one than any with which you compare it; . . . It is not a question of meats and drinks . . . , but of human rights—the sacred right of a woman to her own person, to all her God-given powers of body and soul." Only when women stood "on an even pedestal with men"—when the sexes were bound together "not by tithes of law and gospel, but in holy union and love"—would Americans experience coequality and co-sovereignty.[85]

To be sure, thousands of antebellum women had given voice to fears, aspirations, and political views, reconstituting themselves as citizens and as co-sovereigns within marriage; and politicians sometimes had responded to women's demands, notably in the area of economic liberty. During the war years, moreover, women worked doggedly behind the scenes, sometimes chastising men for their ongoing lack of regard for women's voices. Words still served as potent weapons in the women's rights arsenal. As Mary Livermore explained, "Everywhere there was a call for women to be up and doing, with voice and pen, with hand and head and heart"; the female patriot developed "potencies and possibilities of whose existence she had not been aware, and which surprised her, as it did those who witnessed her marvelous achievement."[86] Individual women and agents of state organizations vigorously exercised the right of petition, pelting Congress with dozens of letters and memorials demanding, with varying degrees of decorum, a declaratory act, new federal legislation prohibiting state impositions of sex-specific disabilities, and (by the mid-1870s) a Sixteenth Amendment guaranteeing woman suffrage. Women armed "with speech and pen" demanded that Congress proclaim black freedom and enfranchise women, thus training themselves for public life; woman-centered newspapers continued to remind Americans of moral failings, unconstitutional denials of freedom, and women's ongoing struggle to be heard. As New Hampshire's Clarissa Olds wrote in 1863, "The right to take any responsibility in [public reform] was denied to woman; it was out of her sphere; it ran into politics, which were unfit for woman. . . . But this painful hour of warfare crowds home upon us the conviction that woman's interests equally with man's are imperiled—private as well as public, individual as well as social."[87]

Yet, as Reconstruction advanced, lawmakers on both sides of the partisan divide dismissed calls for divisions of sovereignty and public responsibility, on the ground that a few "unsexed" women spoke only for themselves. Opponents of women's rights sometimes connected suffragism to oratory and condemned them both, as when the *Albany Evening Journal,* in January 1867, rued the transfer of women "from the drawing room and the nursery to the ballot-box and the forum." In the same year, Lucy Stone confessed to Stanton that she hoped no man would "be asked to speak" at a convention; she was tired of being on her "knees" begging Wendell Phillips and others to make good on past promises.[88] Too often, activists occupied "separate-but-equal" platforms within mainstream reform societies and, in the case of many women's meetings, the back pages of newspapers.

To make matters worse, disagreements emerged within the movement itself about objectives and strategies.[89] And, when Republicans in Congress refused to draw women under the umbrella of new civil rights legislation and constitutional amendments, movement leaders noted with horror that the female class had been written *out* of constitutional texts. Piles of male-centric constitutional language laid waste to women's political aspirations: by 1870, Republicans had constitutionalized old legal and customary bars to female participation in public life; as Richard Brown puts it, women were "more uniformly excluded from electoral politics than black men"—or, for that matter, than any other class of native-born adults. What is more, judges and state legislators mostly blocked reformers' attempts to put new amendments (and the federal government's apparent interest in liberating oppressed classes) to the task of cementing what Linda Kerber calls the woman-citizen's "connection to the political community."[90] By 1868, Susan B. Anthony could say unequivocally that women were "the only class of citizens wholly unrepresented in the Government."[91]

As Reconstruction advanced, anxieties about liberty of speech resurged. Congress continued to relegate women to the galleries and to construct invitations to prominent female speakers like Victoria Woodhull either as spectacle or as examples of women who approximated a male standard of oratorical excellence. Into the 1890s, women cast illegal ballots, demanded places on juries, ran for minor public posts, and condemned the gag in female mouths. In 1869, after praising a convention audience's patience, Stanton added that a people who "have never known despotism, who fear not its dangers, are apt to be too hasty in putting checks on liberty of speech."[92] One of the *Revolution*'s correspondents noted that men still took it to be "strictly man's sphere to be the biggest toad in the puddle, and if any feminine toad dares to warble a note, to annihilate her on the spot." A minister's wife described women's situation this way: "Keep the holes darned, the buttons on, the babies quiet . . . , *hardly ever talk* in meeting, never make stump speeches or muddy coffee, guide the house . . . ; in short, do just as my husband . . . has always thought and taught that good women should."[93]

Susan B. Anthony provided perhaps the best-known example of Reconstruction-era uses of speech to resist oppression before, during, and after her trial in June 1873 for the federal crime of casting a ballot in the presidential election of 1872. Before trial, Anthony doggedly rode the lecture circuit in New York; during and after the event, she wrote petitions, demanded restitution, and eventually secured a congressional apology in lieu of an appeal to the U.S. Supreme Court. At trial, the fear of womanly speech (and speech on woman's behalf) extended even to jurymen. As Hunt labored to curtail both her movements and her prepared statements, Anthony openly defied him; he repeatedly ordered "the prisoner to sit down" and fairly bellowed that he would "not allow another word" from Anthony in self-defense. Dispensing with the jury, Hunt offered an opinion, likely prepared in advance, against Anthony's constitutional right to vote. Stanton and Anthony also deplored the silencing of jurymen: "The jury with freedom now to use their tongues, when too late, also canvassed the trial and the injury done. 'The verdict of guilty would not have been mine, could I have spoken,' said one, 'nor would I have been alone. There were others who thought as I did, but we could not speak.'"[94]

Pressure increased—from the comparatively moderate *Woman's Journal,* for example—for activists to "play on one string" and "sing suffrage songs, and nothing more; no solos on 'side issues,' especially on marriage, divorce, or other social oppressions."[95] The complicity of Republicans in wartime reversals served as a particularly powerful spur toward suffragism and the language of law, which men were wielding to such great good effect against women. In the 1867 Kansas campaign, said Stanton, studiously silent men "did not grasp the imperative necessity of woman's demand for that protection which the ballot alone can give; they did not feel for *her* the degradation of disfranchisement." As conversation across gender lines waned, references to speech multiplied. "The fact of their silence deeply grieved us," she said for the National Woman Suffrage Association,

> but the philosophy of their indifference we thoroughly comprehended for the first time . . . that only from woman's standpoint could the battle be successfully fought. . . . Our liberal men counseled us to *silence* during the war, and we were *silent* on our own wrongs; they counseled us again to *silence* in Kansas and New York, lest we should defeat negro suffrage, and threatened if we were not, we might fight the battle alone. We chose the latter, and were defeated. But standing alone we learned our power; . . . and solemnly vowed that there should never be *another season of silence* until woman had the same rights . . . as man.

Only when a woman "stands on an *even platform* with men, . . . with the same *freedom to express herself* in the religion and government of the country, . . . can she safely take counsel with him . . . ; for not till then will he be able to legislate as wisely and generously for her as for himself."[96]

To some extent, these shifts reflected changes in movement leadership; but, more fundamentally, women's rights activism yielded decisively to legalization and secularization. Reformers settled *into* the world, absorbing and often embracing the intellectual systems of the broader culture in a single-minded crusade for political equality. Convention resolutions bristled with talk about recent Supreme Court rulings, constitutional amendments, remedies for civil wrongs, and impediments to female office holding. The idea of woman's "voice" came to be synonymous not with physically transgressive oratory but with relatively ladylike utterances at the polls. As women (and most Americans) embraced electoral speech, the radical constitutions of aspiration at the heart of antebellum communities more or less collapsed, at least within the mainstream movement. Women's voices would merge anonymously with men's at the polls; face-to-face exchanges of views (and the dynamic construction of solutions across gender lines) would largely cease—especially if women found themselves possessed *only* of ballots, without the ancillary rights (e.g., jury service) customarily extended to voters.

Reformers sensed the passing of an age. Wrote Mary Livermore in retrospect, "I firmly believed it was only necessary to present [men] the wrongs and injustice done to women, to obtain prompt and complete redress. . . . [W]hen we lay before them our need of enfranchisement, they will be prompt to confer on us the ballot. . . . Alas! Experience has taught me a very different lesson. In the present composition of political and legislative bodies, no cause, whose claims are based *only* on eternal right and justice, need appeal to politicians, legislatures, or congresses, with expectations of success." She promptly put her husband's newspaper to the task of securing woman suffrage.[97] In the 1870 convention celebrating the twentieth anniversary of the first national convention at Worcester, Paulina Wright Davis pointed to miscalculations. It was a "fitting question to ask," she said unflinchingly, "if there has been progress; or has this universal radical reform . . . been . . . but a substitution of a new error for an old one; or like physical revolutions, but a rebellion? Has this work, intended . . . to change the structure of the central organization of society, failed and become a monument of buried hopes? . . . We answer, in many things we have failed, for we believed and hoped beyond the possible. . . . Women are still frivolous; the slaves of prejudice, passion, folly, fashion, and petty ambitions, and so they will remain till the shackles, both social and political, are broken, and they are held responsible beings. . . . Men are still conceited, arrogant, and usurping, dwarfing their own manhood by a false position toward one half the human race." In 1850, women had known that "it would take a generation to clear away the rubbish, to uproot the theories of ages"; by 1870, only a few had been "brave enough to do more than touch the fringe work." Because a "peaceful revolution" had not come to pass, women sought direct "participation in government."[98]

Disappointment sometimes merged with a sense of political and racial degradation. "When a mighty nation, with a scratch of the pen, frames the base ideas of the lower orders into constitutions and statute laws," lamented Stanton on the eve of adoption of the Fifteenth Amendment, "and declares every serf, peasant and slave the rightful sovereigns of all womankind, they not only degrade every woman in her own eyes, but in that of every man on the footstool." No amount of well-crafted oratory would win the day. "A moral power that has no direct influence on the legislation of a nation," she wrote in 1881, "is an abstraction, and might as well be expended in the clouds as outside of codes and constitutions, and this has too long been the realm where women have spent their energies fighting shadows. The power that makes laws, and baptizes them as divine at every church altar, is the power for woman to demand now and fovever."[99]

The postwar shift toward suffragism was a matter of degree: as early as 1856, Ernestine Rose had argued, with many other men and women, that the franchise was "the focus of all other rights, . . . the pivot upon which all others hang," and the only way that woman would be able to "protect her person and her property." But, as the war advanced, the tide began to run strongly and consistently away from face-to-face oratory toward electoral speech and legal reform. Increasingly, activists blasted recalcitrant judges, proposed new amendments and statutes, condemned outmoded legal doctrines, and urged women to bang at the doors of law schools. Delegates at the 1869 National Woman's Rights Convention in Washington, D.C., devoted seven of their nine resolutions to "impartial suffrage" and related questions; the American Equal Rights Association meeting of that year declared that "any party professing to be democratic in spirit or republican in principle, which opposes or ignores the political rights of woman, is false to its professions, shortsighted in its policy, and unworthy of . . . confidence." As a disheartened Stanton explained, women needed to secure "every right which the spirit of the age demands. . . . In an age when the wrongs of society are adjusted in the courts and at the ballot-box, material force yields to reason and majorities."[100]

The burden placed upon political freedom was heavy. Elizabeth Blackwell hoped that ballots might open college doors, secure equal pay for equal work, dignify the marriage relation, and make woman an equal partner in society. Surely, women were being "disregarded" for want of constitutional legitimacy. "Having *failed* to secure her legal rights by virtue of her disfranchisement," said Clarina Nichols, "a woman must look to the ballot for self-protection." A Cincinnati convention resolved to achieve woman suffrage "as a basis for all legal and political rights, as the only *effective* protection of their interests, as a remedy against present oppression, and as a school for character." Women had labored to secure the "right to be heard," only to be shunted off ("irrationally") to speak in pristine isolation. Electoral speech was the "key to the situation"; when women "had a voice in the laws," they would be "welcomed to any platform."[101]

To be sure, old ideas about the power of oratory persisted: as late as 1888, when suffrage speakers appeared for the first time in New Albany, New York, mainstream newspapers gave activists "some very complementary notices," in Mary Caldwell's words, particularly when female speakers blended "logic and reasonableness with ideas and feelings truly womanly." In 1884, a newly enfranchised woman in Washington Territory invited men to confront suffragists in face-to-face, winner-take-all verbal combat: "We wish to meet you on the platform of equality, and demand that you give just reasons for withholding the franchise from your women or acknowledge yourselves in the wrong and make haste to do justice." But, by 1880, and with important exceptions (such as paid Chautauqua lecturing), surrogates—municipal elections, newspaper columns, parades, and the like—often took the place of trans-gender oratory. The spontaneity that was so much a part of reform culture began to dissipate. Women's newspapers bore the mark of such changes—as when the *Woman Voter* declared in 1910 that it was "not designed to be a newspaper," but rather a "Bulletin to announce what is coming."[102]

These were portentous developments: as political scientist Susan Bickford explains, face-to-face exchange "makes collective action possible. We have the capacity to hear something about the world differently through the sounding of another's perspective; we are able to be surprised by others and by our own selves. Speech is spontaneous, action is unpredictable."[103] But the tide was strong. On one occasion, Stanton went so far as to describe *Revolution* merely as a "mouthpiece" for feminist debate.[104] Hundreds of suffragists fell behind goals advanced in the 1850s by law-minded reformers: surely political power would allow women to remake society as insiders. Said Frederick Douglass in 1867, "[T]he ballot . . . means bread, intelligence, self-protection, self-reliance and self-respect; to the daughter it means diversified employment and a fair day's wages for a fair day's work; to the wife it means the control of her own person, property and earnings; to the mother it means the equal guardianship of her children; to all it means colleges and professions, open, equal opportunities, skilled labor and intellectual development."[105] "What personal influence may be exerted by tongue or pen," wrote Mary Putnam-Jacobi in 1894, "can be done by the unenfranchised full as well as by those who possess the . . . ballot." Women needed to *rule*: "According to the theory of a Republic, the sovereignty lies, with such Public Opinion as shall prove itself, through superior virtue and intelligence, to be not only the best, but the strongest." Among the inequities in "present distributions of Sovereign Power" was the fact that men governed solely by "physical force"; she therefore demanded "the association of women with men for such functions of sovereignty as they are able to exercise."[106]

The question, then, was not whether women wrongly sacrificed speech communities to ballot boxes—the handwriting was on the wall for everyone[107]—but whether class solidarity would survive campaigns for political individualism, whether female voters would be allowed to "speak" on questions of real moment, and whether public officials would concede that the division of household sovereignty implied in grants of suffrage had placed men and women on an equal footing. Republican senator and antisuffragist James Doolittle of Wisconsin certainly knew that enfranchisement divided household sovereignty and mandated a female presence in the constituent power. In a republic, he told his colleagues in 1866, "every man is king, every woman is queen; but upon him devolves the responsibility of controlling the external relations of his family, and those external relations are controlled by the ballot; for the . . . vote which he exercises goes to choose the legislators who are to . . . govern society. Within the family man is supreme; he governs by the law of the family, by the law of reason, nature, religion. . . . I am not in favor of conferring the right of suffrage upon woman."[108]

Women sometimes thought of ballots as an alternative way to

*speak* on questions of importance to their sex; for some women, some of the time, speech communities had not been relinquished so much as transmogrified. The idea of the ballot as an utterance was anything but new: during the Revolution, for example, Abigail Adams linked voices to votes when she promised that women would not be bound by laws in which they had "no voice, no Representation."[109] Time and again, women said that the act of voting allowed them to interject "voices" into realms otherwise unavailable to them, without making themselves "conspicuous." In a petition read in the Senate in 1877, a total of 202 Californians demanded votes for women so that they might "express opinions upon public affairs" without once raising their voices.[110]

Antisuffrage forces certainly feared women's words: on one occasion, "MEN OF THE SOUTH" warned readers, "Heed not the song of the suffrage siren! Seal our ears against her vocal wiles."[111] In mid-1867, Horace Greeley's *New York Tribune* confessed discomfort with promiscuity of all kinds—that is, with mixed-sex speech and sex-neutral balloting—and linked oratory directly to the willy-nilly blending of voices at the polls. "We only insist," he wrote, evoking powerful images of female oratory before mixed audiences, "that she shall speak and be heard distinctly as woman, not mingled and confused with men." As an alternative to promiscuity, he proposed a "separate-but-equal" convention to be composed solely of women. In "wholly private" debate, delegates would decide "what department of legislative government may be safely assigned and set apart to women. We would suggest all that related to the family . . . , the control and maintenance of children, education, the property rights of married women, inheritance, dower. . . . A female legislature, a jury of women, we could abide; a legislature of men and women, a jury promiscuously drawn from the sexes we do not believe in."[112]

When woman suffrage champions confronted antisuffrage diatribes, they sometimes portrayed electoral speech acts as the least obtrusive way for woman to speak in public. The *Revolution* noted that antisuffrage women lecturing against the extension of suffrage to other women "probably do not see that taking the rostrum is a fatal step in that direction. When a woman so far oversteps her prescribed sphere as to express her opinion in a mixed assembly of men and women, it will not be very difficult for her quietly to slip it into the ballot-box in the presence of four inspectors." In 1884, a Kentucky woman asked state lawmakers merely for the right to approve or disapprove of decisions made by others: "Why should women not vote, since voting is *merely an authoritative expression of an opinion* of how those affairs of life should be managed in which women have as deep a personal interest as men?" Four years later, Frederick Douglass—by that year a supporter of woman suffrage—lambasted the idea that women, simply because they did not have large biceps, should be denied the "right to express her thought, and give effect to her thought by her vote." Later still, Virginians circulated a catechism portraying ballots as a decorous way to "speak":

> I believe that it is my inherent right to express my opinion directly and effectively through the ballot.
>
> I believe that it is not only my right but my *duty* to use my influence for the betterment of the world . . . and that my influence depends on my personality and the opportunity to express my character—an opportunity that the ballot will give me.
>
> I believe that suffrage is the quietest, most dignified, and least conspicuous way of exerting my influence in public affairs.[113]

Voting thus was an avenue by which anxious women might be heard politically and remain ladies. In September 1888, prohibitionist Annie Diggs observed that, although words had a "mighty power for good or ill," the days of rhetorical bombast at party-sponsored "parades . . . and barbeques" had passed. "We shall hereafter have less of sound and more of sense," she said, "less of shouting and more of serious thought and action, as becomes a civilized and dignified people." Another woman associated the pre-suffrage era with "half-wild Territories," and predicted that dignified suffragism would transform both the United States and England into "higher" forms of civilization.[114] Examples abound, some of them early, of the absorption of the ideal of comparatively raucous, face-to-face debate *by* and *into* a mass democracy. At Pennsylvania's first woman's rights convention in June 1852, convention president Mariana Johnson suggested that ballots constituted a second method by which woman might "raise her voice." In 1853, Anthony described a ladder of oratorical steps from the "discipline of declamation" directly into "departments of science and mathematics," the "government of the church," parish elections, and, finally, a "voice in the laws."[115] Thirty-five years later, a *Woman's Journal* correspondent noted much the same progression: oratory and symbolic speech paved the way to ballots. The "persuasive power of womanly speech," heard first in third-party conventions, had migrated into mainstream parties and finally to the polls in a few territories. In 1888, Americans seemed to accept "the marching clubs" in which women and girls "dress in uniform and march in parades" at politicians' invitation. "The right to parade in political processions was . . . never demanded in the most radical, fanatical woman's rights platforms."

> Ten, yes, five years ago, the suggestion, "Imagine a female political parade!" would have been regarded as a clincher against woman suffrage. . . . [But now, young women] tramp in line up and down the streets . . . , crowded, jostled, stared at, coming in contact with the worst elements. . . . Women are in politics unquestionably, and the query will intrude as a logical sequence, would they be more out of place or any less womanly and ladylike as voters?[116]

Into the new century, suffragists and feminists continued to exhibit a keen interest in the right of speech; the 1917–18 skirmishes between White House picketers and Woodrow Wilson's administration are a familiar example. Scholars sometimes argue—indeed, I might argue—that the unidirectional "statements" offered at the polls represented a significant setback for republicans as they struggled to create an electoral democracy. But, to suffragists' credit, the idea of a powerful female voice continued to shape and enrich the century-long push toward universal suffrage. Women testified repeatedly to the radically transformative power of electoral voices. Scholars tend to think of such imagery as a demand for release from "deep silencing" in a cultural sense; yet, a century ago, the ballot could be conceptualized in a constitutional sense as an alternative to (or as an aspect of) liberty of speech, and therefore as a way to remake both individual women and republican society without incurring the wrath of social conservatives, and without sacrificing the whole of women's cultural inheritance.

What might be said about the brief in *Minor v. Happersett*? First, and most obviously, it resounds with antebellum women's demand for a direct "voice" in public life. At issue was not merely an electoral presence but a radical reconstitution of the polity and perhaps of the First Amendment itself in both jurisprudential and cultural terms. Historians will have to decide whether these demands form part of the history of the First Amendment or of civil liberties history. Free speech tropes formed part of a received common-law tradition; well before the First Amendment had been drafted, lawyers recognized a common-law right of public speech, particularly in Parliament. Because we rarely know exactly which discourse undergirded rights talk, it might be safest to say only that women's claims form a chapter in civil liberties history. But, however labeled, a number of nineteenth-century reformers clearly conceived of the right to speak, listen, and print political opinions as an underpinning of republican citizenship *inclusive* of the right to vote, and properly a subject of federal constitutional and political superintendence. Activists also couched ideas about the good citizen's "voice" in explicitly constitutional terms. These realities, in turn, provide a foundation for reconsidering the architecture and content of the master narrative of American civil liberties (and perhaps of First Amendment) history.

Second, were Victorian women allowed to speak on their own behalf, they probably would urge scholars to look to the nineteenth century for the origins of modern sensitivity to First Amendment freedoms. Women's rights champions, no less than post–World War I jurists, thought of liberty of speech as a precondition for the practice of republican citizenship. First-wave women might say, too, that historians have grossly underestimated their fluency in constitutional law, including the tropes that lawyers had long associated with liberty of speech and press. These time-honored words and phrases provided hard-hitting "cannon-balls" and a legitimizing cultural terrain upon which women could write "alternative visions and accounts" of social reality.[117]

Third, it is possible, although by no means demonstrated in this chapter, that the brief in *Minor* bridges a period in which women's demands for face-to-face discussion came to be elided into a demand for ballots. Minimally, the weblike quality of women's rights claims suggests a need to rethink rigidly partitioned, formalized categories of analysis in constitutional history writing. Consider the progression—from speech to wealth production to the polls—in Elizabeth Oakes Smith's midcentury speech at Syracuse, in which personalized, gender-laden words give way to a sex-neutral electoral "voice." For more than a few decades, many women's rights activists would have understood the progression to be about liberty of speech. "*We should have a literature of our own, a printing-press, and a publishing-house, and tract writers and distributors, as well as lectures and conventions,*" Smith said in 1852; "and yet I say this to a race of beggars, for women have no peculiar resources. Well, then we must work, we must hold property, and claim the consequent right to representation, or refuse to be taxed. Our aim is nothing less than an overthrow of our present partial legislation, *that every American citizen, whether man or woman, may have a voice in the laws by which we are governed.*"[118]

## Notes

Longer versions of this chapter were presented at the meeting of the International Federation for Research in Women's History at the University of Melbourne, Australia, in July 1998, and at the thirty-second Modern Literature Conference at Michigan State University in October 1999. I benefited greatly from exchanges with participants at both meetings. Paul Murphy gave me eyes to "see" liberty of speech in odd places. I also thank Paul Finkelman, Kermit Hall, Linda Kerber, Marc Kruman, Nick Kyser, Jill Norgren, Norm Rosenberg, Harry Scheiber, Phillipa Strum, the late Edward Wise, and members of The Group (a Wayne State University colloquium in legal history) for perceptive readings of drafts. Debra Viles provided eleventh-hour research assistance.

1. Given what David Kyvig calls the "misogyny" of the Reconstruction Amendments, reliance on the First Amendment was to some extent an end run around the word "male"; Kyvig, *Explicit and Authentic Acts: Amending the U.S. Constitution, 1776–1995* (Lawrence, Kans., 1996), 168. Yet incorporation was in the air. Scholars have not looked closely at the extent to which the doctrine shaped strategies and outcomes among suffragists. On the doctrine's currency, see Michael Kent Curtis, *No State Shall Abridge: The Fourteenth Amendment and the Bill of Rights* (Durham, N.C., 1986).

2. *Minor v. Happersett*, 88 U.S. Reports (1875); brief reprinted in Elizabeth Cady Stanton, Susan B. Anthony, and Matilda Joslyn Gage, eds., *History of Woman Suffrage*, 2:732–33 (hereafter cited as *HWS*).

3. Ward E. Y. Elliott, "Minor v. Happersett," in *Oxford Companion to the Supreme Court of the United States,* ed. Kermit Hall (New York, 1992), 551.

4. On this point, see note 10.

5. Sara Evans, "Afterword," in *Talking Gender: Public Images, Personal Journeys, and Political Critiques,* ed. Nancy Hewitt, Jean O'Barr, and Nancy Rosebaugh (Chapel Hill, N.C., 1996), 190.

6. On women's history and the state, see Sara Evans, "Women's History and Political Theory: Toward a Feminist Approach to Public Life," in *Visible Women: New Essays in American Activism,* ed. Nancy Hewitt and Suzanne Lebsock (Urbana, Ill., 1993), 119–40; and Linda Kerber, "Separate Spheres, Female Worlds, Woman's Place: The Rhetoric of Women's History," reprinted in Kerber, *Toward an Intellectual History of Women* (Chapel Hill, N.C., 1997), 159–99. On the loss of solidarity, see Estelle Freedman, "Separatism as Strategy: Female Institution Building and American Feminism, 1870–1930," *Feminist Studies* 5 (fall 1979): 524; Aileen Kraditor, *Ideas of the Woman Suffrage Movement, 1890–1920* (New York, 1981), which explores "expediency" in suffragism; or Nancy Cott, *The Grounding of American Feminism* (New Haven, Conn., 1987). Joan Hoff reinforces disillusionment in *Law, Gender and Injustice: A Legal History of U.S. Women* (New York, 1991), by arguing that women secured grants of political or economic right only when men no longer had use for the rights in question.

7. Judith Roof and Robyn Wiegman, eds., *Who Can Speak? Authority and Critical Identity* (Urbana, Ill., 1995), 98; Sandra M. Gustafson, *Eloquence Is Power: Oratory and Performance in Early America* (Chapel Hill, N.C., 2000), xviii; Robert Jensen and Alvira Arriola, "Feminism and Free Expression: Silence and Voice," in *Freeing the First Amendment: Critical Perspectives on Freedom of Expression,* ed. David Allen and Robert Jensen (New York, 1995), 196. On the antebellum loss of energy in public discourse, see Kimberly K. Smith, *The Dominion of Voice: Riot, Reason, and Romance in Antebellum Politics* (Lawrence, Kans., 1999), 118. For examples of fresh writing, see Susan Bickford, *The Dissonance of Democracy: Listening, Conflict, and Citizenship* (Ithaca, N.Y., 1996); Linda Lumsden, *Rampant Women: Suffragists and the Right of Assembly* (Knoxville, Tenn., 1997); Sylvia Hoffert, *When Hens Crow: The Woman's Rights Movement in Antebellum America* (Bloomington, Ind., 1995); Leslie Dunn and Nancy Jones, *Embodied Voice: Representing Female Vocality in Western Culture* (New York, 1994); Karen Foss, Sonja K. Foss, and Cindy L. Griffen, eds., *Feminist Rhetorical Theories* (Thousand Oaks, Calif., 1999); Christine L. Krueger, *The Reader's Repentance: Women Preachers, Women Writers, and Nineteenth-Century Social Discourse* (Chicago, 1992); Jane Kamensky, *Governing the Tongue: The Politics of Speech in Early New England* (New York, 1997); Jennifer Coates and Deborah Cameron, eds., *Women in Their Speech Communities* (New York, 1988); and Catherine MacKinnon, *Only Words* (Cambridge, Mass., 1993). Nancy Isenberg, *Sex and Citizenship in Antebellum America* (Chapel Hill, N.C., 1998), gives prominent place to women's rights conventions as sites of self-emancipation through speech, but she does not present speech freedom mainly as a *constitutional* aspiration. Two documentary editions emphasize speech; see Karlyn Kohrs Campbell, ed., *Women Public Speakers in the United States, 1800–1925: A Bio-Critical Sourcebook* (Westport, Conn., 1993); and Dawn Keetley and John Pettegrew, eds., *Public Women, Public Words: A Documentary History of American Feminism,* vol. 1 (Madison, Wis., 1997). For a general account of the struggle for a public personality, see Glenna Matthews, *The*

*Rise of Public Woman: Woman's Power and Woman's Place in the United States, 1630–1970* ( New York, 1992). For a fuller account of the themes addressed in this chapter, see Sandra F. VanBurkleo, *"Belonging to the World": Women's Rights and American Constitutional Culture* (New York, 2001), esp. parts 2 and 3.

8. Bickford, *Dissonance of Democracy*, 11.

9. Scholars of "hate speech" and pornography seem uninterested in how male and female speakers have interacted historically in public settings—as if history properly includes only an account of formal governmental suppression of "harmful" speech, and as if sex-specific, speech-related harms have been limited to pornography and hate speech. For example, see Kent Greenawalt, *Speech, Crime, and the Uses of Language* (New York, 1989); Greenawalt, *Fighting Words: Individuals, Communities, and Liberties of Speech* (Princeton, N.J., 1995); Nicholas Wolfson, *Hate Speech, Sex Speech, Free Speech* (Westport, Conn., 1997); Owen Fiss, *Liberalism Divided: Freedom of Speech and the Many Uses of State Power* (Boulder, Colo., 1996), which treats sex- and race-related suppression as quite recent in origin; Fiss, *The Irony of Free Speech* (Cambridge, Mass., 1996), which associates gender-related speech with pornography; and Nadine Strossen, *Defending Pornography: Free Speech, Sex, and the Fight for Women's Rights* (New York, 1995), which argues against censorship. Craig Smith's supposedly comprehensive essay collection, *Silencing the Opposition: Government Strategies of Suppression of Freedom of Expression* (Albany, N.Y., 1996), ignores even the Comstock crisis. Classic histories of the First Amendment include Zechariah Chafee, *Free Speech in the United States* (Cambridge, Mass., 1941); Leonard Levy, *Freedom of Speech and Press in Early American History: Legacy of Suppression* (New York, 1963); Paul L. Murphy, *Meaning of Freedom of Speech: First Amendment Freedoms from Wilson to FDR* (Westport, Conn., 1972); and Murphy, *World War I and the Origin of Civil Liberties in the United States* (New York, 1979), which identifies World War I as the seedbed for sustained encroachments on the First Amendment and modern rights consciousness.

10. See Paul L. Murphy, "Time to Reclaim: The Current Challenge of American Constitutional History," *American Historical Review* 69 (October 1963): 64–79; and Michael Les Benedict, "Expanding the Scope of American Constitutional History," published on H-LAW, http://www.hlaw.msu.edu, December 1999. On informal constitutionalism, see Wayne D. Moore, *Constitutional Rights and Powers of the People* (Princeton, N.J., 1996), esp. 3–65, 239–89. See also David M. Rabban, *Free Speech in Its Forgotten Years* (New York, 1997).

11. "S.X.," "The Rights Man Gives to Woman," *Revolution*, April 23, 1868. All citations for this newspaper are to the microfilm edition.

12. For pioneering attempts to link the history of the "private" family to "public" life, see Michael Grossberg, "Crossing Boundaries: Nineteenth-Century Domestic Relations Law and the Merger of Family and Legal History," *American Bar Foundation Research Journal* 4 (1985): 799–847; Grossberg, *Governing the Hearth: Law and the Family in Nineteenth-Century America* (Chapel Hill, N.C., 1985); and especially Hendrik Hartog, *Man and Wife in America: A History* (Cambridge, Mass., 2000). On the decision to perpetuate medieval conceptions of the unitary household sovereign, see Linda Kerber, "The Paradox of Women's Citizenship in the Early Republic: The Case of Martin v. Massachusetts, 1805," *American Historical Review* 97 (1992): 349–78, reprinted in Kerber, *Toward an Intellectual History of Women* (Chapel Hill,

N.C., 1997). On the limits of the idea that Americans translated the ideology of private and public spheres directly into social reality, see Kerber, "Separate Spheres, Female Worlds, Woman's Place: The Rhetoric of Women's History," in Kerber, *Toward an Intellectual History of Women*, 159, which reprints and slightly revises a previously published article.

13. Catherine A. F. Stebbins, "The Head of the Family," *Woman's Journal*, February 25, 1888. All citations for this newspaper are to the microfilm edition.

14. Hendrik Hartog, "The Constitution of Aspiration and the 'Rights That Belong to Us All,'" in *Constitution and American Life*, ed. David Thelen (Ithaca, N.Y., 1988), reprinted from *Journal of American History*. On the lawlike attributes of custom and the layering of legal culture, see Hartog, "Pigs and Positivism," *Wisconsin Law Review* 1985 (1985): 899–935.

15. For Cato, see Mary Beth Norton, "Freedom of Expression as a Gendered Phenomenon," in *The Constitution, the Law, and Freedom of Expression, 1787–1987*, ed. James Brewer Stewart (Carbondale, Ill., 1987), 42–43. On the generic "he," see Susan Moller Okin, *Women in Western Political Thought* (Princeton, N.J., 1979); Mark E. Kann, *The Gendering of American Politics: Founding Mothers, Founding Fathers, and Political Patriarchy* (New York, 1999); Carole Pateman, *The Sexual Contract* (Stanford, Calif., 1988); and Arlene Saxonhouse, *Women in the History of Political Thought: Ancient Greece to Machiavelli* (New York, 1985). See also David Konig, "Principia Jeffersonia: Thomas Jefferson and the Natural Law Tradition" (paper presented at the annual meeting of the American Society for Legal History, Princeton, N.J., October 2000), which brilliantly dissects the frame of mind that allowed both patriarchal mastership within families and an egalitarian system of politics among white men. Cited by permission.

16. The tendency to see women's political speech as un-speech may parallel the judicial tendency to view women's labor as un-labor, even when undertaken beyond the home, because of the sex's primary association with unpaid homework; Reva B. Siegel, "The Modernization of Marital Status Law: Adjudicating Wives' Rights to Earnings, 1860–1930," *Georgetown Law Journal* 82 (1994): 2127–212. My thanks to Harry Scheiber for reminding me of this connection.

17. Alexander Meiklejohn, *Free Speech and Its Relation to Self-Government* (New York, 1948), 45–46, 94.

18. See Jurgen Habermas, *Theory of Communicative Action* (1984), *Structural Transformation of the Public Sphere* (1989), and *Moral Consciousness and Communicative Action* (1990), all available in English editions. See also Dana Nelson, *National Manhood: Capitalist Citizenship and the Imagined Fraternity of White Men* (Durham, N.C., 1998); Alice Kessler-Harris, *Out to Work: A History of Wage-Earning Women in the United States* (New York, 1982), esp. discussions of male-female economic citizenship at 50–52 and elsewhere; Mark Carnes and Clyde Griffen, eds., *Meanings for Manhood: Constructions of Masculinity in Victorian America* (Chicago, 1990); and Judith Schlar's exploration of "citizenship as standing" in *American Citizenship: The Quest for Inclusion* (Cambridge, Mass., 1991). On domesticity and the crystallizing ideology of separate spheres, see Kerber, "Separate Spheres, Female Worlds, Woman's Place." For "judicial patriarchy" and legal-political transformation, see Grossberg, *Governing the Hearth;* for "state patriarchy," Peter Bardaglio, *Reconstructing the Household: Families, Sex, and the Law in the Nineteenth-Century South* (Chapel

Hill, N.C., 1995); Paula Baker, "Domestication of Politics: Women and American Political Society, 1780–1920," *American Historical Review* 89 (June 1984): 620–67, for state usurpation of "feminine" work; and Marc W. Kruman, "The Second American Party System and the Transformation of Revolutionary Republicanism," *Journal of the Early Republic* 12 (winter 1992): 509–37, for the changing role of parties. On the triumph of law talk, see Christopher Tomlins, *Law, Labor and Ideology in the Early American Republic* (New York, 1993). Feminists roundly criticize Habermas but typically for his straitened view of the public sphere, not for his observations about a developing mass democracy; see, e.g., Johanna Meehan, ed., *Feminists Read Habermas: Gendering the Subject of Discourse* (New York, 1995). For the evolution of a suffrage-based democracy, see three competing but ultimately complementary accounts: Eric Foner, *The Story of American Freedom* (New York, 1998); Richard D. Brown, *The Strength of a People: The Idea of an Informed Citizenry in America, 1650–1870* (Chapel Hill, N.C., 1996); and Robert Wiebe, *Self-Rule: A Cultural History of American Democracy* (Chicago, 1995). On the intellectual sources of women's subordination to men, see Rogers Smith, "One United People: Second-Class Female Citizenship and the American Quest for Community," *Yale Journal of Law and the Humanities* 1 (1989): 229–93.

19. E.g., Sara Hunter Graham, *Woman Suffrage and the New Democracy* (New Haven, Conn., 1996), attributing success in the 1910s to strategic modernization; or Steven M. Buechler, *The Transformation of the Woman Suffrage Movement: The Case of Illinois, 1850–1920* (New Brunswick, N.J., 1986), which ties changes in suffragism to professionalization.

20. *Dred Scott v. Sandford,* 19 Howard 393 (1957), 417.

21. On the battle for the forum, see Kenneth Cmiel, *Democratic Eloquence: The Fight over Popular Speech in Nineteenth-Century America* (New York, 1990), which unfortunately pays scant attention to women. See also Joan D. Hedrick, *Harriet Beecher Stowe: A Life* (New York, 1994), esp. chaps. 10 and 12. I do not use the term "speech act" as many antipornography activists do, to designate speech that is beyond the pale of First Amendment protection; rather, I have in mind the antebellum conception of speech as a form of political action that, precisely because it *was* designed to effect change, merited First Amendment protection. In reform circles, neither the modern distinction between speech and action nor the MacKinnon view (which implies that some political speech is *not* action and therefore is properly a subject of First Amendment jurisprudence) would have made sense. For an attempt to buttress the walls of First Amendment theory (including the speech-action dichotomy) against MacKinnon's forces, see Franklyn Haiman, *Speech Acts and the First Amendment* (Carbondale, Ill., 1993); on speech acts as a radically destabilizing political strategy, see Isenberg, *Sex and Citizenship in Antebellum America.* On violent political rhetoric as a species of political action, see the classic article by John R. Howe Jr., "Republican Thought and the Political Violence of the 1790s," *American Quarterly* 19 (summer 1967): 148–65.

22. Judith Sargent Murray, "Sketch of the Present Situation of America" (1794), in *Selected Writings of Judith Sargent Murray,* ed. Sharon M. Harris (New York, 1995), 55–56.

23. Abigail Adams to John Adams, July 5, 1780, in *Adams Family Correspondence,* ed. Lyman Butterfield, vol. 4 (Cambridge, Mass., 1963), 328. Words also permitted revolutionaries to fix the terms in which their achievements would be remembered. Matilda Joslyn Gage, e.g., thought that Mercy Otis

Warren's "burning words" (her history of the revolution) permanently shaped public memory; "Women Revolutionaries," *Revolution,* August 17, 1871.

24. Harriet Martineau quoted in Susan Faludi, "Speak for Yourself," in *Beacon Book of Essays by Contemporary American Women,* ed. Wendy Martin (Boston 1996), 169; Judith Sargent Murray, *The Gleaner,* 3 (1798): 189; *HWS,* 1:42, and 42–49 for publishing history. On the power of female authorship, see also Margaret Fuller, *Woman in the Nineteenth Century,* ed. Bernard Rosenthal (New York, 1971), 93.

25. Mary Ryan, "Gender and Public Access: Women's Politics in Nineteenth-Century America," in *Habermas and the Public Sphere,* ed. Craig Calhoun (Cambridge, Mass., 1992), 286.

26. Litchfield Declaration, 1839, quoted in Linda Kerber, *Women of the Republic: Intellect and Ideology in Revolutionary America* (Chapel Hill, N.C., 1980), 278.

27. Quoted in Brown, *Strength of a People,* 164–65.

28. Elizabeth Cady Stanton in *HWS,* 1:52. See also Reminiscences of Paulina Wright Davis, *HWS,* 1:284.

29. Linda Lumsden, *Rampant Women: Suffragists and the Right of Assembly* (Knoxville, Tenn., 1997), 8.

30. "Fanny Fern" [Sara Payson Willis Parton], "The Modern Old Maid," *Revolution,* September 2, 1869, reprinted from the *New York Ledger.*

31. Speeches of Mariana Johnson and Ruth Plumbly, Westchester Convention, 1852, *HWS,* 1:352–53, 367; letter from Esther Ann Lukens, October 2, 1851, ibid., 311. The term "speech community" derives mainly from sociolinguistics and anthropology. It refers to a community of opinion in which members share a language, assumptions about human nature and prospects for social improvement, and political objectives; such a community need not be coextensive with nation-states or other political entities.

32. Elizabeth Cady Stanton, introduction, *HWS,* 1:53.

33. Jack Rakove, *Original Meanings: Politics and Ideas in the Making of the Constitution* (New York, 1996), 292. Early American press freedom consisted of protection from restriction in advance of publication ("prior restraint"). The right to be where speech occurs to hear or gather information has yet to be recognized as essential to liberty of speech.

34. *Revolution,* April 7, 1870; "Local Agitation," *Revolution,* July 27, 1871.

35. "Harvard Resolutions," in *Second to None: A Documentary History of American Women,* vol. 1, ed. Ruth Moynihan (Lincoln, Neb., 1993), 291–92.

36. For writing, speaking, and press freedom, see, e.g., *HWS,* 1:49, 109, 246, 723; *New York Herald,* October 28, 1850, quoted in Andrea Moore Kerr, *Lucy Stone: Speaking Out for Equality* (New Brunswick, N.J., 1992), 60.

37. *Lily,* January, 1848.

38. Maria Stewart, "Religion and the Pure Principles of Morality, the Sure Foundation on Which We Must Build," October 1831 [published in the *Liberator*], and "Farewell Address to Her Friends in the City of Boston," December 21, 1833, in *Maria W. Stewart: America's First Black Woman Political Writer: Essays and Speeches,* ed. Marilyn Richardson (Bloomington, Ind., 1987), 37–40, 68–69.

39. Celia Morris, *Fanny Wright: Rebel in America* (Urbana, Ill., 1992), 242–73, esp. 249–50.

40. Editors on Ernestine Rose speech, 1836, *HWS,* 1:97.

41. On this phenomenon, see Ryan, "Gender and Public Access"; Sara

Evans and Harry Boyte, *Free Spaces: The Sources of Democratic Change in America* (New York, 1986).

42. Sojourner Truth's reaction to endless speeches at the 1850 convention in Rochester, New York, illustrates this impatience. Harriet Beecher Stowe later recorded this response: "Well, honey, I's ben der meetins, an harked a good deal. Dey wanted me fur to speak. So I got up. Says I, 'Sisters, I a'n't clear what you'd be after. Ef women want any rights mor'n deys got, why don't dey jes' take 'em, an' not be talkin' about it?'" Victoria Ortiz, *Sojourner Truth* (New York, 1974), 167.

43. Stanton to Anthony, April 2, 1852, in *The Elizabeth Cady Stanton–Susan B. Anthony Reader: Correspondence, Writings, Speeches,* rev. ed., ed. Ellen DuBois (Boston, 1981), 55; Stanton, Address, New York Woman's State Temperance Society, 1853, and Rochester Resolutions, *HWS,* 1:495–96.

44. In Matthews, *Rise of Public Woman,* 119, 130; for remarks at or about Syracuse, *HWS,* 1:542–43, 852. For Anthony, see Rochester convention proceedings, 1856, ibid., 513.

45. Angelina Grimké resolution, May 10, 1837, and "An Appeal to the Women of the Nominally Free States," Anti-Slavery Convention of American Women, May 9–12, 1837, in *Turning the World Upside Down: The Anti-Slavery Convention of American Women . . . ,* ed. Dorothy Sterling (New York, 1987), 13, 31.

46. Woman's Rights Convention, Salem, Ohio, April 1850, *HWS,* 1:815 (emphasis added).

47. "Constitution of the Female Anti-Slavery Society of Salem," in *We Are Your Sisters: Black Women in the Nineteenth Century,* ed. Dorothy Sterling (New York, 1984), 113. While black women often encountered many of the same difficulties white women faced, awareness of white men's behavior toward women could inspire generosity. In 1850, male delegates at an Ohio freedman's convention debated the propriety of seating and hearing female delegates, ultimately deciding to set themselves apart from whites and enfranchise the other sex; Proceedings of the National Convention of the Colored Men of America, Washington, D.C., January 14, 1869, in *Proceedings of the Black National and State Conventions,* vol. 1, ed. Philip Foner and George Walker (Philadelphia, 1986), 326.

48. Angelina Grimké, "Appeal to the Women of the Nominally Free States," 1838, in *Root of Bitterness: Documents of the Social History of American Women,* ed. Nancy Cott (Boston, 1986), 194–99; Angelina Grimké to Catharine Beecher, October 2, 1837, in *Public Years of Sarah and Angelina Grimké: Selected Writings, 1835–1839,* ed. Larry Geplair (New York, 1989), 197. This notorious episode, however, is not clearly about *only* female oratory; while gender clearly was implicated, abolitionists of both sexes often met with violent resistance.

49. Elizabeth Cady Stanton address [and Stanton letter read by Susan B. Anthony], 1852, *HWS,* 1:472–513; Rendall, *Origins of Modern Feminism,* 257.

50. For "lovers" and speech right demand, *HWS,* 1:333, 142; for the apparent refusal of the mayor of New York and "a large police force" to protect speech, ibid., 547. See also Mary Ryan, *Women in Public: Between Banners and Ballots* (Baltimore, 1990).

51. William Lloyd Garrison, World's Temperance Convention, 1853, *HWS,* 1:160.

52. Sterling, *Ahead of Her Time,* 69–70, 373, 387; Stanton and Anthony, *HWS,* 1:40.

53. Antoinette Brown to Lucy Stone, winter 1848, in *Friends and Sisters:*

*Letters Between Lucy Stone and Antoinette Brown Blackwell, 1846–1893,* ed. Carol Lasser and Marlene Deahl Merrill (Urbana, Ill., 1987), 33–34; Brown to Lucy Stone, June 1848, ibid., 42–43.

54. Proceedings of the Brick Church meeting, New York City, May 1853; John Marsh of American Temperance Union; testimony of Brick Church delegates; speech at state temperance convention, New York, 1852; *HWS,* 1:483, 502, 508–9.

55. "The Half World's Temperance Convention" [reported testimony of Antoinette Brown], *HWS,* 1:507; for her own version, see ibid., 153–58. Brown also drew upon Christian doctrine to justify behavior condemned by reformers as (at least in an informal sense) unconstitutional. A hostile delegate from Washington apparently had asked, "Do you think Christ would have done so?" Brown turned the question on its head. "I claimed nothing except that which inhered in a recognition of the human brotherhood; and which must therefore be sanctioned by the impartial Father," she wrote in 1853. "There was a principle within, above, and all around stronger than all else. Thanks to the Washington delegate, I was sustained by the sublime conviction, Christ would have done so!" See Brown, *Una,* October 1853 (microfilm edition).

56. [Horace Greeley], *New York Tribune,* September 9, 1853, *HWS,* 1:575; [Elizabeth Cady Stanton], headnote to "*New York Tribune,* September 3, 1853," ibid., 511; for "gagging," Horace Greeley [newspaper article excerpt, September 7, 1853], ibid., 507; Antoinette Brown narration, 1853, ibid., 152–60.

57. Ann Preston, Westchester Convention, 1852, *HWS,* 1:364; Caroline Severance, New England Convention, May 1859, ibid., 262; Ernestine Rose, National Convention in Philadelphia, October 1854, ibid., 377.

58. Frederick Douglass, "Address Before Bethel Literary Society," [post-Civil War, n.d.], in *Frederick Douglass on Women's Rights,* ed. Philip Foner (Westport, Conn., 1976), 126–27.

59. Stanton, *HWS,* 1:53; Mariana Johnson, Presidential Address, Westchester Women's Rights Convention, June 2, 1852, ibid., 352; for praise of wordsmiths, ibid., 38, 82–85, 95, 206, 152–53, 160, 184, 218, 476. The "padlocks" imagery recurs. See, e.g., an article reprinted from *The Trained Nurse,* "Holy Speech for Women," *Women's Journal,* August 3, 1889 ("These miserable padlocks on the gracious lips of women ought to be unlocked and broken off and flung away forever").

60. Jonathan Stearns, "Discourse on Female Influence" (1837), in *Up From the Pedestal: Landmark Writings in the American Woman's Struggle for Equality,* ed. Aileen Kraditor (Chicago, 1968), 47–49; Rev. Hubbard Winslow, *Discourse Delivered in Bowdoin Street Church, July 9, 1837, "The Appropriate Sphere of Woman,"* Pamphlets in American History, W04 (Boston, 1837), 14–16.

61. On female preaching, see Catherine Brekus, *Strangers and Pilgrims: Female Preaching in America, 1740–1845* (Chapel Hill, N.C., 1998); for critical scholarship, see, e.g., Elizabeth Cady Stanton, *The Woman's Bible* (1895–98; New York, 1972); and Matilda Joslyn Gage, *Woman, Church, and State* (1893; New York, 1972). On these points, see Isenberg, *Sex and Citizenship.*

62. [Mrs. McGuigan], "A Church in Trouble," *Revolution,* September 23, 1869; "Why Not Rev. Mrs. as Well as Rev. Mr.," *Revolution,* October 13, 1870.

63. "Pastoral Letter of the Congregational Ministers of Massachusetts" [from *Liberator,* August 1837], in Moynihan, *Second to None,* 1:251–52.

64. "City clergyman" quoted in "Being and Doing," *Revolution,* March 2, 1871.

65. The trial is described in Gage, *Woman, Church and State,* 478–79.

66. Frances Gage, *HWS,* 1:119; Ernestine Rose address at Broadway Tabernacle (New York City), September 6–7, 1853, ibid., 572. On "freedom of speech" for women and America as the "only hope . . . for freedom of speech and action," see ibid., 572.

67. Frances Gage, *Lily,* September 1854 (microfilm edition).

68. Frances Gage, Address, Akron Convention, May 1851, *HWS,* 1:113.

69. "We Have Come to the Revolution," *Revolution,* April 30, 1868; "The Old Year Is Gone," *Revolution,* December 31, 1868; "A Most Unjust Charge," *Revolution,* January 6, 1870; "The Revolution: Prospectus," *Revolution,* October 20, 1870.

70. Syracuse (N.Y.) *Standard,* September 13, 1852.

71. For exile and arson, see, e.g., *HWS,* 1:337, 405, 414. For speech as agent of reconstitution and a positive duty, see ibid., 488, 312–13, 95, 459–60, 500, 180. See also Elizabeth Cady Stanton, "Reminiscences," ibid., 459–60; Antoinette Brown Blackwell, speech, 1860, ibid., 723.

72. Elizabeth Cady Stanton, "The Woman's Suffrage Convention," *Revolution,* May 20, 1869.

73. Frances Gage, Fourth Women's Rights Convention, Cleveland, Ohio, 1853, *HWS,* 1:123–24; Proceedings, National Convention in Philadelphia, October 1854, ibid., 378–79.

74. *HWS,* 1:110; debate, seventh annual meeting, 1856, ibid., 648–51; Susan B. Anthony Speech, Loyal League National Convention, New York, May 1863, ibid., 2:66.

75. Speech of Abby Price, Syracuse National Convention, 1852, *HWS,* 1:532; Rev. Samuel Longfellow, Speech, Tenth Annual Convention, New York City, 1860, ibid., 711–15.

76. Frederick Douglass, "Some Thoughts on Women's Rights," *Frederick Douglass' Paper,* June 10, 1853.

77. Angelina Grimké, excerpt from "An Appeal to the Women of the Nominally Free States . . . ," in *Root of Bitterness: Documents of the Social History of American Women,* ed. Nancy Cott (Boston, 1986), 194.

78. Harriet Martineau letter, Worcester convention, 1851, *HWS,* 1:230–31.

79. Mary Livermore, *My Story of the War: The Civil War Memoirs of the Famous Nurse, Relief Organizer and Suffragette,* ed. Nina Silber (Hartford, Conn., 1887; reprinted, New York, 1995), 607–9.

80. Woman's Rights Convention, Wesleyan Chapel, Seneca Falls, 1848, *HWS,* 1:238–39.

81. "Stanton Runs for Congress," 1866, *HWS,* 2:180.

82. Wendell Phillips speech, *HWS,* 1:401; for "promiscuous assemblies," Lucretia Mott, 1838, ibid., 337; for "law" and "fact," Stanton quoting John Stuart Mill in headnote, ibid., 225. See also ibid., 331, 418.

83. Wendell Phillips, tenth annual convention, New York, 1860, *HWS,* 1:703 (emphasis added).

84. Elizabeth Clark, "Religion and Rights Consciousness in the Antebellum Woman's Rights Movement," in *At the Boundaries of Law: Feminism and Legal Theory,* ed. Martha Albertson Fineman and Nancy Sweet Thomadsen (New York, 1991), 188–208, esp. 189. On the irrationality of seeking ballots, see *HWS,* 1:73; on the importance of the suffrage, see ibid., 262. For "powers of self-protection," see Antoinette Brown to Lucy Stone, 1854, ibid., 1: 862.

85. Introduction, *HWS,* 1:13–24, and passim; Stanton to Gerrit Smith, December 21, 1855, in Kraditor, *Up from the Pedestal,* 129–30.

86. Mary Livermore, *The Story of My Life* (New York, 1974), 485.

87. *HWS,* 1:747; *HWS,* 2:882.

88. *Albany (N.Y.) Evening Journal,* January 24, 1867; Lucy Stone to Elizabeth Cady Stanton, April 1867, *HWS,* 2:235.

89. On wartime schisms that prevailed until 1890, see the first two volumes of Stanton, Anthony, and Gage, *History of Woman Suffrage;* Catherine Clinton, *The Other Civil War: American Women in the Nineteenth Century* (New York, 1984); Ellen DuBois, *Feminism and Suffrage: The Emergence of an Independent Women's Movement in America, 1848–1869* (Ithaca, N.Y., 1978); and Kathleen Barry, *Susan B. Anthony: A Biography* (New York, 1988), which offers a clear window into intramovement changes. See also the early chapters in Aileen Kraditor, *Ideas of the Woman Suffrage Movement, 1890–1920* (New York, 1988).

90. Richard D. Brown, *The Strength of a People: The Idea of an Informed Citizenry in America, 1650–1870* (Chapel Hill, N.C., 1996), 183; Kerber, "Separate Spheres, Female Worlds, Woman's Place," 22.

91. Susan B. Anthony, Address to the National Democratic Committee, Tammany Hall, July 1868, *HWS,* 2:341.

92. Elizabeth Cady Stanton, *Revolution,* May 20, 1869.

93. Mrs. Pat Molley, "Biggest Toad in the Puddle," *Revolution,* April 15, 1869; K.C.M., "A Really Good Woman," *Revolution,* July 30, 1868.

94. For a detailed transcription of the trial and its aftermath, see *HWS,* 2:627–715, esp. 686–89.

95. Elizabeth Cady Stanton, "Side Issues," *Revolution,* October 6, 1870.

96. *HWS,* 2:267–68 (emphasis added).

97. Livermore, *Story of My Life,* 481.

98. Paulina Wright Davis opening speech, twentieth anniversary convention, Apollo Hall, New York City, October 19–20, 1870, *HWS,* 2:428–29.

99. Stanton, *HWS,* 2:335.

100. *HWS,* 2:350; ibid., 262, 84, 259, 173, 820, 493, 460.

101. Ibid.

102. Mary E. Caldwell, "Suffrage Lectures in Indiana," *Woman's Journal,* December 15, 1888; Mrs. E. A. Woodruff [of Washington Territory], "A Woman Voter's Address," *New Northwest* [Portland, Ore.], February 21, 1884, 1; *Woman Voter,* May 1910.

103. Bickford, *Dissonance of Democracy,* 162.

104. [Stanton], headnote (1881), *HWS,* 2:319.

105. Frederick Douglass, "Resolution Adopted at First Annual Meeting, American Equal Rights Association, New York City, May 9–10, 1867," in Foner, *Frederick Douglass on Women's Rights,* 83.

106. Mary Putnam-Jacobi, "'Common Sense' Applied to Woman Suffrage . . . ," (1894), in *Public Women, Public Words: A Documentary History of American Feminism,* vol. 1, ed. Dawn Keetley and John Pettegrew (Madison, Wis., 1997), 270–71.

107. On the loss of same-sex solidarity in the rush toward ballot boxes, see Freedman, "Separatism as Strategy," 524.

108. Senator Doolittle, Senate Discussion of Washington, D.C., Suffrage, December 12, 1866, *HWS,* 2:151.

109. Hoff, *Law, Gender and Injustice*, 60.

110. Speech [Mr. Bingham], Syracuse [N.Y.] Convention, 1852, *HWS*, 1:527; *Congressional Record*, 44th Cong., Senate, 2d sess., January 20, 1877, 762.

111. Broadside, "MEN OF THE SOUTH," in Wheeler, *Votes for Women*, 305.

112. Horace Greeley, *New York Tribune*, July 26, 1867.

113. "Opposing Strong-Minded Women," *Revolution*, October 14, 1869; Mrs. James Bennett, *An Appeal for Woman Suffrage Made by Mrs. James Bennett in the Legislative Hall, Frankfort, Kentucky, January, 1884*, Pamphlets in American History, W069, 3 (emphasis added); Frederick Douglass, "The Woman's Cause," *Woman's Journal*, June 2, 1888; Virginia broadside, ca. 1910, in Wheeler, *Votes for Women*, 283.

114. Annie L. Diggs, "Political Change Needed," *Woman's Journal*, September 22, 1888; "Not From the West but From the East," *Woman's Journal*, August 24, 1889 [reprinted from *Boston Journal* ].

115. Mariana Johnson, "The President's Address," June 2, 1852, in *HWS*, 1:352; for "all other rights," ibid., 262; Susan B. Anthony, Tenth Annual Women's Rights Convention, Cooper Institute, New York, May 1860, *HWS*, 1:690.

116. F.M.A., "Women in Politics," *Woman's Journal*, October 6, 1888.

117. Carol Smart, *Feminism and the Power of Law* (New York, 1989), 88.

118. Elizabeth Oakes Smith Address, Syracuse Convention, 1852, *HWS*, 1:524 (emphasis added).

*Chapter Eleven*

# Race, State, Market, and Civil Society in Constitutional History

Mark Tushnet

As the generation that wrote the Constitution developed its political theories on the west side of the Atlantic, the writers of the Scottish Enlightenment were developing a political-social idea that illuminates American constitutional law—the idea of civil society. To writers like Ferguson and Millar, civil society was distinct from both the state and the market.[1] Civil society included institutions like the church and the press, then a small-scale operation not closely connected, at least in its self-understanding, to commerce. Civil society could discipline the state and the market in two ways. It provided people with values they could then deploy in politics and, to a lesser extent, in the market; in this way civil society was a source of inputs into the state and the market. And civil society gave people real resources, both material and conceptual, to resist the expansionist urges of the state and the market.

The institutions of civil society existed in the new United States as well. But the Constitution that created the United States made the distinction between state and civil society more complex than the relation the Scottish philosophers described, because they dealt with a different range of political and social experiences in the more absolutist United Kingdom. The Constitution itself performed some of the roles of civil society. Most obviously, it restrained the government: the free exercise clause of the First Amendment, for example, severely limited the national government's power to regulate churches. Madison's political science explained how a well-designed government could restrain itself, through devices like the separation of powers and federalism in an extended republic.[2] In addition, federalism meant that "the state" in the United States was a complex institution. On Madison's understanding, state governments were institutions of civil society with respect to the national government. So, for example, "the first and most natural attachment of the people will be to the governments of their respective States," which would give the states "the advantage of the federal government."[3]

Slavery further complicated the relation between the government, the market, and civil society. The theory of civil society saw society as a whole in terms we would now call pluralist: it consisted of separate institutions checking each other.[4] The theory of slavery was different in two ways. First, the role of markets in the slave system was always problematic ideologically.[5] True, masters bought and sold slaves, and they went to markets to sell what their slaves produced. But the widespread disparagement of slave traders by slave owners themselves showed that they saw some tension between the market's reduction of human labor to something of value only to the extent it could produce, and slavery's ideological commitment to ownership of one person—in all aspects of the slave's life—by another.[6] Second, and related, the ideology of slavery portrayed slave society as well ordered and hierarchical, far different from the disorderly contention among diverse institutions in market society.

The Constitution papered over the differences between the slave society of the South and the market-oriented society of the North, most suggestively in the circumlocutions the document used to refer to slaves as "Person[s] held to Service or Labour in one State, under the Laws thereof" (Article IV, section 2) and as "Such Persons as any of the States now existing shall think proper to admit" (Article I, section 9), and most notoriously in the compromise that added "to the whole Number of free Persons, . . . three fifths of all other Persons" for purposes of calculating representation in the House of Representatives (Article I, section 2). The differences could not be suppressed permanently, however, and the Supreme Court confronted—but ultimately avoided—the question of the relation between the national government and slavery in cases dealing indirectly with Congress's power to regulate interstate and foreign commerce.

The framers realized that the commerce clause could easily be read to authorize congressional regulation of the interstate and international trade in slaves. They therefore barred Congress from exercising its powers over "the Migration or Importation" of slaves for twenty years, a provision they exempted from the possibility of amendment. Note as well the ambiguity in this clause: its two words do not commit the Constitution to a position on whether slaves act as agents in migrating or being imported into the states. As constitutional contention over slavery renewed, the ambiguity became important: as objects of importation, slaves clearly were articles of commerce subject to Congress's power to regulate, but as agents who migrated, they might not have been.

The Supreme Court's theory of the commerce clause spoke to the issue of slavery in two ways. From the Court's first confrontation with the clause in *Gibbons v. Ogden*[7] through the late antebellum period, the Court struggled to decide whether Congress's power to regulate interstate commerce was exclusive of state authority, or concurrent with it.[8] The argument for exclusive congressional power was largely conceptual. As many justices saw things, the nature of government power was such that a particular power could be held by only one sovereign. They were satisfied that federalism in the large avoided the problems classical political science found in an *"imperium in imperio"*—a sovereign state subordinate to another sovereignty—but they accepted that general conclusion only by insisting that the Constitution allocated powers to separate governments. The theory of exclusive national power meant that state governments could not regulate interstate commerce.[9]

The argument for exclusive national power over interstate commerce might have created severe practical problems if the Court defined that power expansively, as it appeared to do in *Gibbons*. For, after all, there was little chance that the national government would actually exercise its power to regulate on many occasions. That meant, however, that nearly everything falling within the broad domain of interstate commerce would go unregulated, the states lacking power to regulate and Congress failing to do so. To the extent that the justices addressed this difficulty, it was by another conceptual move: states lacked power to regulate interstate commerce, but much of what they desired to do could be characterized as an exercise of a police power that the states held, rather than as an exercise of a power to regulate interstate commerce that Congress held. So, for example, the Court allowed a state to authorize the construction of a dam across a navigable stream—and so, one might think, to interfere with interstate commerce—in order to drain a swamp that constituted a public nuisance, because eliminating public nuisances fell within the scope of the state's police power.[10]

The conceptual line between regulation of commerce and exercises of the police power was difficult to locate, however, and over the antebellum period the Court drifted in the direction of acknowledging the states' concurrent power even to regulate interstate commerce. In 1852 it held that Congress had exclusive power only over subjects that "imperatively demand[ed] a single uniform rule," while states could regulate subjects that "as imperatively demand[ed] that diversity, which alone can meet the local necessities."[11] This preserved state authority to regulate the market, and at the same time sustained the states as locations of power that might stand against overreaching by the national government.

The question of slavery lurked in these cases. It seemed clear, at least for a while, that Congress had the power to regulate the interstate slave trade after 1808. Southern states also sought to regulate the trade, but if Congress's power was exclusive, they could not do so. As sectional tensions over slavery escalated, Southerners began to worry that Congress might actually exercise its power in ways that would undermine slavery. The solution, from the Southern point of view, was obvious: define the subject matter, commerce among the several states, to exclude commercial traffic in slaves. Persons, they began to argue, could not be objects of "commerce" within the meaning of Article I.

A series of cases involving state efforts to regulate immigration from abroad brought the issue to the Supreme Court. *New York v. Miln,* decided in 1837, upheld a New York ordinance requiring shipmasters to post security for indigent passengers.[12] Justice Philip Barbour, a Virginian, said that this regulation was an exercise of the state's police power, and was not a regulation of commerce. He also indicated, however, that "persons" might not be proper objects of commerce, raising the possibility that Congress lacked power to regulate the interstate slave trade. Justice Joseph Story, a strong nationalist from Massachusetts, dissented.

Four years later the Court again avoided deciding whether slaves were articles of commerce. Mississippi's constitution prohibited the importation of slaves. When a commercial dispute over the breach of a contract to pay for slaves brought into Mississippi reached the Supreme Court,[13] the arguments focused on the commerce clause. As Mary Sarah Bilder has argued, the case placed antislavery advocates in an awkward position.[14] Proslavery lawyers could argue without much ideological strain that slaves were not articles of commerce; they were persons, subject to control by their masters and by state law, but not by national law. To sustain national power over the interstate slave trade, antislavery advocates had to treat slaves as commercial objects, quite contrary to their ideological position that people could not be transformed into property. The Supreme Court avoided the underlying problem by holding that Mississippi's constitutional provision had to be implemented by state laws declaring contracts to import slaves void; because the state had enacted no such laws, the contract had to be honored.

By the end of the 1840s, the Court's divisions could no longer be suppressed. The *Passenger Cases* involved state laws similar to those in *New York v. Miln*.[15] This time, however, the Court was sharply divided, with each justice writing a separate opinion. Five agreed that persons were indeed articles of commerce and invalidated the state laws, finding no sufficient police power justification for them. Chief Justice Roger Brooke Taney and other strong defenders of slavery and states' rights disagreed.

The Court's adoption of the view that states had concurrent power to regulate commerce offered a solution to one half of the problem: states could indeed regulate the slave trade without offering police power justifications, at least if the slave trade was one of those subjects that "imperatively demand[ed]" diverse local regulations. The question of Congress's power to regulate the trade remained open, however. The Court's decision in the *Dred Scott* case that Congress's Article IV power to "make all needful Rules and Regulations respecting the Territory . . . belonging to the United States" did not authorize it to bar slavery in the territories suggested that the Taney Court would not look with favor on arguments confirming congressional power over the slave trade.[16]

The onset of the Civil War aborted further doctrinal developments. Antebellum constitutional law found the relation between slavery, the market, civil society, and the Constitution impossible to define. Federalism in particular complicated the relation. With respect to the national government, states resembled the institutions of civil society, serving as centers of offsetting power and sources of diverse values. With respect to the market, however, states were just another institution of government. No solution was likely to emerge so long as states were understood to be relatively independent sovereigns within their proper sphere.

Considered as a constitutional event, the Civil War's outcome did offer a solution, though only briefly: states were clearly subordinate to the national government whenever the national government chose to make them subordinate. Congress's victory over Andrew Johnson in imposing congressional reconstruction—military occupation of the defeated South until Southern governments satisfied Congress's demands for reform—established that proposition. But the political forces supporting a constitutional theory of expansive national power dissipated. Federalism again complicated the outcome by 1883, when the Supreme Court revisited the question of the relation between government and civil society in matters of race.

Most places of public accommodation had duties to serve anyone who sought service. In the common law's language, they were common carriers. By the 1870s, the common law in many states had been interpreted to mean that common carriers could not deny service on the basis of race. The Civil Rights Act of 1875 extended the common-law nondiscrimination principle. It confirmed that places of public accommodation could not deny service on the basis of race, and it defined such places somewhat more broadly than the common law did. In 1883, the Supreme Court held the 1875 act unconstitutional.[17] The Court said that the Fourteenth Amendment provided only that no *state* shall deny equal protection of the laws. There had to be some state involvement with racial discrimination before the amendment gave Congress power to regulate. But, as the Court saw it, the act imposed duties on individuals without regard to whether state law allowed or prohibited racial discrimination. The act applied, Justice Joseph Bradley's opinion for the Court said, "to cases arising in States which have the justest laws respecting the personal rights of citizens, and whose authorities are ever ready to enforce such laws, as to those which arise in States that may have violated the prohibition of the amendment." A decade earlier, Justice Bradley had written a correspondent that a state could deny equal protection of the laws by "the omission to protect, as well as the omission to pass laws for protection."[18] On this view, African-Americans might still be protected against racial discrimination: by state common-law rules where they existed, and by congressional enactment where state law was inadequate.

Yet the *Slaughterhouse Cases,* the Court's most sustained consideration of the relation between the Fourteenth Amendment and federalism, seemed to pose a substantial barrier to that result.[19] Rejecting claims that a Louisiana statute granting a monopoly over butchering to a private corporation violated the Fourteenth Amendment, the Court did say that "the one pervading purpose" of the amendment was to secure "the freedom of the slave race, the security and firm establishment of that freedom, and the protection of the newly-made freeman and citizen from the oppressions of those who had formerly exercised unlimited dominion over him." That might seem to give the national government substantial power to enact civil rights laws. But the *Slaughterhouse* Court articulated a theory of federalism that limited congressional power.

The *Slaughterhouse Cases* did not involve any congressional statute. The Court noted, however, that the Fourteenth Amendment's fifth section authorized Congress to enact laws to enforce the rights its first section defined. According to the Court, if the amendment defined civil rights expansively, it would "transfer the protection of all the civil rights . . . from the States to the Federal government." This formulation echoed with the last sounds of a theory of exclusive national power. Even if the Court had the view that national power to regulate civil rights would be concurrent, it thought that such a power would "fetter and degrade the States by subjecting them to the control of Congress." Preserving the states as autonomous locations of political power, as institutions of civil society vis-à-vis the national government, remained an important constitutional goal.

A generation after Reconstruction ended, the Supreme Court in 1896 thought it understood the relation between constitutional law, the market, and civil society. Federalism concerns disappeared, and the market and civil society more narrowly understood became the objects of constitutional protection. *Plessy v. Ferguson* upheld a state law requiring segregated railroad cars.[20] Put another way, it held that a state's interference with the market in the service of racial segregation did not violate the Constitution. Railroads respond to market demand: if enough riders were willing to pay to support segregated services, the railroads would provide them.[21] Whites favoring segregation circumvented the market to secure the policy they desired through legislation.

The Supreme Court found this entirely constitutional. The segregation statute was justified by the state's police power, which allowed the government "to act with reference to the established usages, customs, and traditions of the people." In the Court's eyes, these usages arose in civil society and then were simply translated into law. Rejecting the view "that social prejudices may be overcome by legislation, and that equal rights cannot be secured to the negro except by an enforced commingling of the two races," the Court said that "[l]egislation is powerless to eradicate racial instincts, . . . and the attempt to do so can only result in accentuating the difficulties of the present situation."

As many have noted, as an analytic matter the Court's understanding is somewhat strained. Those who challenged the segregation statute in *Plessy* were not relying on "legislation" to overcome social prejudices; rather, the statute's proponents were relying on the law to reinforce or entrench those prejudices in a setting where market pressures might contribute to overcoming them. In referring to "legislation," then, the *Plessy* Court must have meant "the Constitution." On its view, ordinary law—statutes like the one at issue in *Plessy*—reflected preferences and prejudices formed in civil society, and the Constitution did not support the market as a bulwark against the expression of those preferences and prejudices.

Within a decade the Court's view of the relation between the Constitution, the market, and civil society changed.[22] *Lochner v. New York* invalidated the state's attempt to regulate the working hours of bakers.[23] Examining the police power justifications for the statute closely, the Court concluded that an hours limitation did not protect the health of the consuming public, and that the health risks to bakers from long hours were not greater than the health risks to workers in all other occupations. The police power, then, could not support the statute. The Court dismissed out of hand the additional argument that the law was justified as "a labor law pure and simple." The distribution of the workers' product between workers' wages and employers' profits was, for the Court, determined solely by the market. Here the Constitution defended the market against prejudices against employers expressed through ordinary law.

The contrast between *Plessy* and *Lochner* is dramatic. The conventional account of the cases finds them compatible because both cases assumed that there was some prepolitical state of affairs that the government could not effectively interfere with.[24] In *Plessy* the prepolitical state of affairs consists of the white majority's "social prejudices" against African-Americans, which dictates social arrangements, while in *Lochner* it consists of the power relations between employers and workers, which dictates the distribution of wealth. Yet the source of the government's ineffectiveness differs in the two cases. Government could not overcome social prejudices in *Plessy* because they were simply too strong, whereas it could not overcome the distribution of power between employers and workers in *Lochner* because the Supreme Court would not let it. In *Lochner* the Constitution was allied with the market against civil society, while in *Plessy* it was allied with civil society against the market. The only difference appears to be racism.

But the conceptual pressure exerted by *Lochner* inevitably affected constitutional doctrine dealing with race. The Court's first forays into the area after *Plessy* led it to strengthen the market against civil society, and to increase the market cost of complying with civil society's demands. Superficially in tension, these two decisions began to erode the racist distinction that led to different outcomes in *Plessy* and *Lochner*.

*Plessy* became the origin of the doctrine that segregation was justified when, and to the extent that, the segregated facilities provided African-Americans were equal to those provided whites. *Plessy* itself did not announce such a rule. The Louisiana statute in *Plessy* required "equal but separate accommodations." The Court tested the statute under a standard of reasonableness and held that segregation was reasonable when the separate facilities were equal.

The "separate but equal" doctrine hardened into a constitutional rule in *McCabe v. Atchison, Topeka & Santa Fe Railway* (1914).[25] The Court seemed to back into its constitutional holding, both because once again it dealt with a statute purportedly requiring separate but equal facilities and because five justices expressed their views on the constitutional question in a case where procedural rules barred them from enforcing the constitutional position they espoused. Oklahoma's segregation statute authorized railroads to provide higher-priced services like sleeping cars to whites but not African-Americans. The reason, the state asserted, was cost: railroads could not afford to provide both types of cars because African-American demand for them was so small that railroads would have to run essentially empty sleeping cars. Rejecting the state's argument by invoking a "constitutional right" to equal facilities, five justices said that this right was "individual" and "personal," and could not "depend on the number of persons who may be discriminated against." The *McCabe* rule provided a solid foundation for serious attacks on segregation. It increased the market burdens of segregation. Louisiana's railroads might have been willing to provide separate facilities if the market could bear the freight, and perhaps conditions in Louisiana in 1896 meant that segregation compelled by law was not much more costly to railroads. But *McCabe* said that railroads had to provide services that were not cost-justified. It made the market an even stronger ally of African-Americans challenging segregation.

Three years later the Court relied on the philosophy of *Lochner* to make the Constitution itself an ally of those challengers. Louisville adopted an ordinance requiring that housing in the city be segregated by race: only members of the majority race on a block could purchase houses on that block. The Supreme Court in *Buchanan v. Warley* held the ordinance unconstitutional.[26] It interfered with the rights of willing sellers and buyers "to use, control, or dispose of [their] property," and therefore exceeded the limits of reasonableness. The Court acknowledged that "there exists a serious and difficult problem arising from a feeling of race hostility which the law is powerless to control." In *Plessy* that understanding led the Court to say that the Constitution had to stand aside while civil society enacted its prejudices into ordinary law. In *Buchanan,* in contrast, the Court found that the Constitution stood with the market against such prejudices. Race was not a special condition authorizing greater government regulation than anything else.

The Court's understanding of civil society in *Plessy* was unduly constricted, and by the 1920s and 1930s it could no longer ignore the true dimensions of civil society. For the Court in *Plessy,* civil society consisted of (white) prejudices and preferences shaped in general social interaction. But civil society is more than that. It consists as well of the intermediate institutions Tocqueville identified —the institutions within which prejudices and preferences are formed. *Plessy* itself illustrated the role of this thicker version of civil society. The litigation was conducted by a loose organization of African-Americans, forming themselves into an intermediate institution.

The persistent self-organization of African-Americans, made possible by a constitutional framework generally tolerating and sometimes encouraging the development of intermediate institutions through a culture of free expression and a right of association, contributed to the erosion of civil society's dominance over the market, or at least the dominance of the *Plessy* Court's constricted version of civil society. Booker T. Washington and W. E. B. Du Bois were the leading voices expressing divergent views within the African-American community over the proper response to white society's efforts to subordinate their community.[27] Washington took a public stance of accommodation while privately supporting attacks on segregation, while Du Bois tried to organize African-Americans and progressive whites into public organizations that would lobby and agitate for change. Du Bois's first efforts were abortive, but in 1909 they resulted in the founding of the National Association for the Advancement of Colored People (NAACP), which took a leading role in attacking the legal foundations of segregation. Notably, the house seller in *Buchanan v. Warley* was active in Louisville's NAACP branch.

The richness of civil society ultimately undermined the *Plessy* Court's narrow vision of civil society. Seeing *McCabe* as the vehicle for increasing segregation's financial costs, NAACP activists planned a litigation campaign against segregated education.[28] Plans for the campaign began to be developed in the late 1920s. The financial exigencies of the Great Depression led the campaign to move in directions its developers had not anticipated. Instead of attacking the undercapitalized material facilities of southern elementary and secondary schools for African-Americans, litigation focused on higher education and on unequal salaries for African-American teachers. In both dimensions, the litigation campaign sought to strengthen the institutions of civil society among African-Americans.

Du Bois had articulated a vision of activism in the African-American community that relied on leadership by what he called a "Talented Tenth," highly educated people who could communicate to the larger community of African-Americans and whites the necessity for social transformation. White institutions in the North produced some of those leaders: Du Bois himself, the first African-American to receive a doctorate from Harvard University, for example, and Charles Hamilton Houston, a graduate of Amherst College and Harvard Law School who became the mentor to a generation of African-American lawyers, including his star pupil, Thurgood Marshall, and who carried out the first stages in the NAACP's litigation strategy. But, Houston thought, white institutions could not develop enough African-American leaders to constitute a Talented *Tenth.* Only institutions rooted in the African-American community could do that. And southern legislatures failed to offer opportunities for graduate and professional education to African-Americans. Houston believed that challenging the absence of such education would be legally easy: *McCabe* itself showed that the "separate but equal" doctrine could not be satisfied if no segregated facilities were offered. The second prong of Houston's attack drew African-American teachers into the NAACP. By showing that the NAACP could provide real material benefits to its members through the higher salaries they received, Houston correctly believed that teachers would join the organization and facilitate its larger purposes.

By the end of the 1930s, the litigation campaign had begun to win its first victories: Maryland desegregated its law school without a substantial fight, a number of school boards in larger southern cities lost salary suits or agreed to increase teacher salaries faced with the threat of litigation, and the Supreme Court held that Missouri had to offer a law school education to its African-American citizens.[29]

These first victories were almost too easy, however. Litigation could affect school boards in larger cities, but the cases had to be brought on a district-by-district basis. They were more time-consuming than many impatient teachers thought appropriate. Bringing suits against rural school boards proved to be beyond the NAACP's limited resources. The malapportionment of southern legislatures gave rural districts disproportionate power in state government. As a result, the NAACP's strategy could not place enough financial pressure on state governments to make maintaining segregation either fiscally or politically infeasible. The attack on segregated higher education faltered as well. Potential plaintiffs were ordinarily draft-age men, who were called into service by the local draft boards during World War II, sometimes in direct response to the draftee's involvement in litigation. Symbolically, Lloyd Gaines, the successful plaintiff in the NAACP's Missouri law school suit, never attended law school; shortly before the Supreme Court's decision in his favor was announced, Gaines disappeared, and the NAACP never located him.

The NAACP's legal challenge to segregation did not reach the Supreme Court again until the late 1940s, but the Court continued to confront the relation between civil society, the Constitution, and race. Intermediate institutions like the NAACP play political roles in providing what economist John Kenneth Galbraith called "countervailing power" to the government.[30] In the form of interest groups these institutions help shape public policy; in the form of social movements they provide the resources that allow people to resist the encroachments of government.

The Supreme Court dealt with civil society's interest groups in its free speech jurisprudence. A key early case, for example, upheld the right of the Congress of Industrial Organizations to hold a political rally in the antiunion city of Jersey City, New Jersey, dominated by political boss Frank Hague.[31] A series of cases involving efforts to exclude African-Americans from effective political participation in the Deep South brought the question of how the Constitution's equality provisions affected civil society more directly to the Court's attention. The Fifteenth Amendment made it clear that African-Americans could not be barred from voting. In 1915, the Court held that the Fifteenth Amendment outlawed Oklahoma's transparent attempt to disfranchise African-Americans by requiring a literacy test only for those whose grandparents had not been eligible to vote at the time of the Civil War.[32] Terrorism and economic coercion kept many African-Americans from voting nonetheless. But the African-American communities in some places, notably the South's larger cities, were self-sufficient enough to support registration by a significant number of African-Americans, whose votes then became attractive to some ambitious white politicians.

State Democratic parties excluded African-Americans from internal party processes such as primary elections to combat the possibility that African-Americans in the South would gain some effective political power.[33] These white primaries posed a serious problem from the perspective of a theory of civil society. They clearly were designed to accomplish effective disfranchisement of a sort barred by the Fifteenth Amendment. But political parties were institutions of civil society. They could not be controlled by the government if they were to be sources of "inputs" into the political system. Primary elections, the Court held in a decision rendered shortly after primary elections became an important part of the electoral process, were not part of the state's formal election system and so were not subject to the restrictions the Constitution placed on state action.[34]

The Court's early forays into the field of race discrimination in white primaries dealt with relatively easy cases. In the first, Texas state law explicitly authorized the white primary, thereby making the party's action in excluding African-Americans clearly the action of a state.[35] Texas tried again, amending its statutes to provide that state party officials could prescribe qualifications for voting in party primaries. Again the Court found the statute unconstitutional, on the ground that the party officials were exercising power given them by the state and not by the party itself.[36] When the Texas Democratic Party convention adopted a rule barring African-Americans from voting in party primaries, the Court finally was satisfied—at least for a few years.[37]

From early in the twentieth century, political progressives had been concerned about boss-controlled political parties. As they saw it, such parties could not serve as the source of independent inputs into politics. A federal investigation of the influence of Huey Long's political machine in Louisiana led the Court to revisit the question of primary elections in 1941. Ironically, the prosecution involved a political opponent of Long, whose misconduct had turned up in the course of the investigation.[38] Precisely because the Long machine dominated Louisiana politics, the Court saw that party primaries were tightly bound up with the general election: winning the primary meant winning the general election. It followed that conducting primary elections was state action, and the Constitution had to be honored in such elections.

Three years later the Court applied that understanding to the Texas white primary.[39] The Court's opinion in *Smith v. Allwright* blended several analytic strands: the Democratic Party primary in Texas was the effective locus of political decision; state law made the results of the party primary legally significant by making it difficult for someone who lost a primary to appear on the general election ballot. And, in the midst of World War II, the antidemocratic implications of the white primary could hardly escape notice: "The United States is a constitutional democracy. . . . [The] grant to the people of the opportunity for choice is not to be nullified by a State through casting its electoral process in a form which permits a private organization to practice racial discrimination in the election."

Nine years later the Court wrote the final word for a generation on political parties and civil society. But the clarity of the earlier white primary cases disappeared. In *Terry v. Adams*, a sharply split Court required a local Texas party organization, the Jaybird Democratic Association, to admit African-Americans to its "preprimary" ballot, in which the Jaybirds decided which candidate to endorse in the "real" primary.[40] In one sense, and to some justices, the "preprimary" *was* the real primary: almost always the candidate who received the Jaybird endorsement won the primary election, and then the general election. The question that split the Court was that the Jaybirds, no matter what their political power, did look like a purely voluntary association, one of those institutions of civil society that the government ought not control. As some justices wondered, would requiring the Jaybirds to admit African-Americans imply that political associations of Catholics or Polish-Americans were constitutionally suspect? And if so, how could civil society's institutions be sources of countervailing power when they were themselves subject to, and structured by, government power?

The Court in *Terry* did not provide an explicit answer. Implicitly, however, the Court treated the problem of race and civil society as unique. The special political history of the United States meant that legal doctrine could single out those institutions of civil society that contributed to the subordination of African-Americans for treatment that would be unacceptable for any other institutions.

When the NAACP's attack on segregation returned to the Court in the late 1940s and early 1950s, the Court's understanding of the relations among the Constitution, race, and civil society again played an important role. And, just as World War II made the justices aware of the anomalies of boss-dominated political parties, so the early cold war made them acutely aware of the tension between the ideological image of the United States as an open, pluralist society and the reality of segregation in the South.[41] By the end of the war the Western powers were set on a course leading to widespread decolonization and the emergence of what later came to be called the Third World as an important political actor in world affairs. In 1948 the Department of Justice filed a brief in the Supreme Court calling the justices' attention to the fact that the Soviet Union was competing for the allegiance of these emerging nations by pointing to the persistence of segregation as a demonstration of the hypocritical claims the United States made as a land of equality and freedom. The department reiterated those assertions in its filings in the cases culminating in *Brown v. Board of Education.*

The cold war was the general context in which the Court took up the question of desegregation. But it also brought to the task the conceptual tools associated with the idea of civil society. For the generations that produced the original Constitution and the Reconstruction Amendments, property and contract were the key institutions of civil society: the independent yeoman owning his own farm was the key figure in the republican ideology of Thomas Jefferson and others in the founding era; the fabled "forty acres and a mule" embodied the parallel vision during Reconstruction.[42] By 1954, property and contract had been replaced by education as the foundation for civic participation, as Chief Justice Warren's opinion in *Brown* understood:

> [W]e cannot turn the clock back to 1868 when the [Fourteenth] Amendment was adopted, or even to 1896 when [*Plessy*] was written. We must consider public education in the light of its full development and its present place in American life throughout the Nation. . . . Today, education . . . is the very foundation of good citizenship. . . . In these days, it is doubtful that any child may reasonably be expected to succeed in life if he is denied the opportunity of an education.

Warren understood, of course, that education was a "function of state and local governments," and so did not occupy the same place that institutions of civil society did. But, like the institutions of civil society, education, even public education, was the source of values that later became inputs into political life: segregation, Warren wrote, "may affect [children's] hearts and minds in a way unlikely ever to be undone."

The Court's *Brown* decision had little immediate effect on the conditions of education in the Deep South. Gerald Rosenberg and Michael Klarman have used the slow pace of desegregation to argue that Supreme Court decisions purporting to command major social change succeed only when they are supported by the wider social and political system.[43] Rosenberg pointed out that desegregation in the Deep South occurred when Congress armed the federal government with statutory provisions enacted in 1964 directing it to deny financial aid to segregated schools. Klarman noted the ironic path by which the Civil Rights Acts of 1964 and 1965 were enacted: *Brown* shifted political sentiment in the South to the right, reviving the faltering careers of fervent segregationists who had been under assault by white politicians who sought to preserve the southern racial hierarchy through moderate means. These more aggressive segregationists responded to the civil rights movement with violence that made northerners more sympathetic to protests against segregation. Finally, northern political support led to the civil rights acts.

In these accounts *Brown* played only an indirect role, and the Supreme Court's contribution to social change is obscure or at most ironic. Both Rosenberg and Klarman minimized the cultural impact of *Brown* on civil society. Rosenberg surveyed the relatively conservative African-American press and found few references to *Brown* in the press accounts of the civil rights movement. Noting that civil rights protest activities, including boycotts of segregated bus systems, occurred before *Brown*, he discounted the memoirs of civil rights activists, nearly all of whom expressed the view that their work was materially assisted by the Court's decision.

The magnitude of the Court's effects on civil society is hard to assess, but Rosenberg and Klarman seem to understate it. Civil rights rhetoric invoked the Constitution from the beginning: some abolitionists argued that even slavery was unconstitutional,[44] and African-Americans never accepted *Plessy v. Ferguson* as a correct interpretation of the Fourteenth Amendment. But the tension between the positive law—*Plessy* and its progeny—and the idealized Constitution to which civil rights proponents appealed was palpable. *Brown* gave the rhetoric of civil rights real bite. It demonstrated as well that at least one of the nation's governing institutions, the Supreme Court, accepted the movement's view of the Constitution. The psychological boost *Brown* gave civil rights advocates seems quite real, and discounting their own accounts seems unsound. Notably, when civil rights activists planned the Freedom Ride of 1961 as a way of publicizing the failure of interstate transportation companies to comply with existing law that required them to operate integrated facilities, they proposed to arrive in New Orleans, the last stop on the ride, on May 17, *Brown*'s anniversary.[45]

By the 1960s, constitutional law no longer imposed limits on the government's power to regulate the market. Although Robert Bork argued that the Civil Rights Act of 1964 rested on "a principle of unsurpassed ugliness,"[46] the Supreme Court's abandonment of the *Lochner* philosophy in the New Deal constitutional crisis of 1937 meant that the Constitution no longer had anything to say about that, or any other, principle by which the government sought to regulate the market, whether for reasons related to race or otherwise. By the 1980s, however, the Court revitalized the

Constitution as a means of limiting government attempts to restructure the market's treatment of African-Americans.

The doctrinal path was long and tortuous. *Plessy v. Ferguson* held that segregation did not violate the constitutional guarantee of equal protection of the laws because it was a reasonable method of advancing goals governments could legally seek. Civil rights advocates attempted to persuade the courts that segregation was actually unreasonable. But the Court never accepted that view. Its path was set when it upheld the national government's creation of concentration camps to hold Japanese-American citizens during World War II. In the course of doing so, *Korematsu v. United States* stated a new standard: "[A]ll legal restrictions which curtail the civil rights of a single racial group are immediately suspect."[47] This new doctrine made the challenge to segregation easier: as the doctrine developed, to defeat a statute resting on a suspect racial classification, civil rights proponents merely had to show that it rested on racial antagonism or did not serve what the Court called a "compelling" interest in a "narrowly tailored" way.

The strict scrutiny doctrine turned against its original beneficiaries as the civil rights successes of the 1960s expanded. After some false starts, including a number of decisions that approved affirmative action programs in education and public and private employment, the Court came to believe that such programs, which used racial classifications, had to satisfy the strict scrutiny doctrine.[48] Although the Court in the early 1990s did not invoke the doctrine to restrict affirmative action programs adopted by private employers, it did severely limit what cities and states could do in their capacity as employers and, more important, in setting conditions for awarding public contracts, which through the twentieth century had grown to be a major location of economic activity.

Here, too, a civil society perspective may be illuminating. For the Court that decided *Buchanan v. Warley*, race was not a special condition. For the Court that decided *Terry v. Adams*, it was: the Constitution imposed regulation on institutions of civil society where race was involved that would be unacceptable if those institutions involved religion. For the affirmative action Courts of the 1990s, race was again not a special condition. In the Court's eyes the civil rights movement had become a special interest group.

The Court might have taken the position that as a special interest group, civil rights advocates were entitled to no more consideration than any other interest group—but no less consideration either. In that view, civil rights advocates would be relegated to the political process for whatever they could achieve. The Court did not take that position, however. Its affirmative action decisions deprived civil rights advocates of political victories. In a peculiar way, this, too, may represent the triumph of the market over civil society. The New Deal constitutional transformation led the Court to remove itself from the supervision of what it called "social and economic legislation."[49] Why, though, were affirmative action programs not just such legislation? The answer implicit in the Court's position appears to be that affirmative action programs were a *racial* "spoils system," aimed in the first instance at racial goals rather than economic ones. The Court refrained from restricting the government's actions in the economic domain because it believed that such actions resulted from economic motivations that the Constitution stood behind. It believed that affirmative action programs had different, noneconomic motivations. In modern constitutional doctrine, economic motivations are favored, noneconomic ones disfavored. The Court's affirmative action decisions were in this sense a revival of *Lochner* nearly a hundred years later.

Notes

1. For the background of the concept of civil society, including its use in the Scottish Enlightenment, see Marvin B. Becker, *The Emergence of Civil Society in the Eighteenth Century: A Privileged Moment in the History of England, Scotland and France* (Bloomington: Indiana University Press, 1994).

2. See especially *The Federalist Papers,* Everyman's Library ed. (New York: Dutton, 1911), p. 263 (no. 51) (on separation of powers); p. 41 (no. 10) (on the virtues of an extended republic).

3. Id., p. 239 (no. 46); p. 235 (no. 45).

4. The classic modern presentation of this so-called Madisonian analysis is Robert Dahl, *A Preface to Democratic Theory* (Chicago: University of Chicago Press, 1956).

5. For a general discussion of the relation between markets and slavery in Southern ideology, see Mark Tushnet, *The American Law of Slavery, 1810–1860: Considerations of Humanity and Interest* (Princeton, N.J.: Princeton University Press, 1981).

6. See generally Eugene Genovese, *Roll, Jordan, Roll: The World the Slaves Made* (New York: Pantheon, 1974).

7. 22 U.S. (9 Wheat.) 1 (1824).

8. For an example of the Court's difficulties, see *Willson v. Black Bird Creek Marsh Co.*, 27 U.S. (2 Pet.) 245 (1829).

9. Justice William Johnson's concurring opinion in *Gibbons* is the clearest presentation of the "exclusive national power" position.

10. 27 U.S. (4 Pet.) 245 (1829).

11. *Cooley v. Board of Port Wardens*, 53 U.S. (12 How.) 299 (1852).

12. 36 U.S. (11 Pet.) 102 (1837).

13. *Groves v. Slaughter*, 40 U.S. (15 Pet.) 449 (1841).

14. Mary Sarah Bilder, "The Struggle over Immigration: Indentured Servants, Slaves, and Articles of Commerce," *Missouri Law Review* 61 (fall 1996): 808–12.

15. 48 U.S. (7 How.) 283 (1849).

16. *Dred Scott v. Sandford*, 60 U.S. (19 How.) 393 (1857).

17. *The Civil Rights Cases*, 109 U.S. 3 (1883).

18. Quoted in *Bell v. Maryland*, 378 U.S. 226, 309–10 (1964) (Goldberg, J., concurring).

19. 36 U.S. (16 Wall.) 36 (1873).

20. 163 U.S. 537 (1896).

21. Scholars disagree on the extent to which such services were being provided by Louisiana railroads before the segregation statute was enacted. Cf. Charles A. Lofgren, *The Plessy Case: A Legal-Historical Interpretation* (New York: Oxford University Press, 1987), 17, and, with Jennifer Roback, "The Political Economy of Segregation: The Case of Segregated Streetcars," *Journal of Economic History* 46 (1986): 893–917.

22. The following paragraphs summarize an argument made in more detail in Mark Tushnet, "*Plessy v. Ferguson* in Libertarian Perspective," *Law and Philosophy* 16 (1997): 245–58.

23. 198 U.S. 45 (1905).

24. The classic modern expression of this account is Cass R. Sunstein, "*Lochner*'s Legacy," *Columbia Law Review* 87 (1987): 873–919.

25. 235 U.S. 151 (1914).

26. 245 U.S. 60 (1917).

27. For a discussion of these competing views, see August Meier, *Negro Thought in America, 1880–1915: Racial Ideologies in the Age of Booker T. Washington* (Ann Arbor: University of Michigan Press, 1988).

28. For an overview of the campaign, see Mark Tushnet, *The NAACP's Campaign Against Segregated Education, 1925–1950* (Chapel Hill: University of North Carolina Press, 1987).

29. *Missouri ex rel. Gaines v. Canada*, 305 U.S. 337 (1938).

30. John Kenneth Galbraith, *American Capitalism: The Concept of Countervailing Power* (Boston: Houghton Mifflin, 1956).

31. *Hague v. CIO*, 307 U.S. 496 (1939).

32. 238 U.S. 347 (1915).

33. For an overview of the litigation dealing with voting rights from the 1920s on, see Steven F. Lawson, *Black Ballots: Voting Rights in the South, 1944–1969* (New York: Columbia University Press, 1976).

34. *Newberry v. United States*, 256 U.S. 232 (1921).

35. *Nixon v. Herndon*, 273 U.S. 536 (1927).

36. *Nixon v. Condon*, 286 U.S. 73 (1932).

37. *Grovey v. Townsend*, 295 U.S. 45 (1935).

38. *United States v. Classic*, 313 U.S. 299 (1941).

39. *Smith v. Allwright,* 321 U.S. 649 (1944).

40. 345 U.S. 461 (1953).

41. For a discussion of the international dimensions of the segregation issue, see Mary L. Dudziak, *Cold War Civil Rights: Race and the Image of American Democracy* (Princeton, N.J.: Princeton University Press, 2000).

42. See Akhil Reed Amar, "Forty Acres and a Mule: A Republican Theory of Minimal Entitlements," *Harvard Journal of Law and Public Policy* 13 (1990): 37–43.

43. Gerald Rosenberg, *The Hollow Hope: Can the Courts Bring About Social Change?* (Chicago: University of Chicago Press, 1991); Michael J. Klarman, "How *Brown* Changed Race Relations: The Backlash Thesis," *Journal of American History* 81 (June 1994): 81–118.

44. See William C. Weicek, *The Sources of Antislavery Constitutionalism in America, 1760–1848* (Ithaca, N.Y.: Cornell University Press, 1977).

45. Jack Greenberg, *Crusaders in the Courts* (New York: Basic Books, 1994), 286.

46. Quoted in Ethan Bronner, *Battle for Justice: How the Bork Nomination Shook America* (New York: Norton, 1989), 66–67.

47. 323 U.S. 214 (1944).

48. *City of Richmond v. J. A. Croson, Co.,* 488 U.S. 469 (1989); *Adarand Constructors, Inc. v. Pena,* 515 U.S. 200 (1995).

49. *Dandridge v. Williams,* 397 U.S. 471 (1970).

*Chapter Twelve*

# Constitutional History and the "Cultural Turn": Cross-Examining the Legal-Reelist Narratives of Henry Fonda

Norman L. Rosenberg

*Law is a vast construction of representations.*
—Anne Norton, *Republic of Signs*

*[We] shall never understand the meaning of the rule of law in American political life . . . [without] an examination of the ways the imagination shapes political meaning in the American polity.*
—Paul W. Kahn, *The Reign of Law*

Studies of representation and narrative, familiar concerns in cultural history,[1] are becoming part of legal and constitutional history as well.[2] Interest in representation and narrative, in turn, dovetails with broader projects, especially those that bring together legal and cultural studies, and thereby expands the types of sources to be read as "legal texts."[3] The category of "legal writing" now embraces titles from the literary canon, artistic products, popular fiction, motion pictures, television shows, and a variety of textual traces of "the law."[4] As a consequence of this cultural-linguistic turn, "legal reelism," the study of Hollywood films as legal texts, has become a recognized genre of legal-constitutional writing.[5]

The Hollywood film industry has long looked at, and spoken about, law. Much like an appellate court opinion, a film explicates a legal controversy through narrational frameworks and representational codes that, while similar to those found in other types of cultural texts, incorporate their own unique qualities.[6] Few other modes of storytelling have ever reached more people than the Hollywood cinema, and legal reelism might be said to epitomize what Karl Llewellyn once called "jurisprudence for the millions."[7] Even before movies began to talk, the silent cinema told legal tales, including ones set in courtrooms, and the coming of sound made the trial film a Hollywood staple during the 1930s.[8] Most of these films, such as *A Free Soul* (1931), for which Lionel Barrymore won an Academy Award, center on a colorful but corrupt criminal-defense attorney—a "mouthpiece" or "shyster."[9]

To suggest a way of locating the place of Hollywood films in constitutional history, I want to highlight several motion pictures that feature Henry Fonda. A film "Star" (rather than simply a "star") during five decades,[10] Fonda became one of those "representative figures" who help citizens to construct, through mass-mediated imagery, their nation's constitutional culture. Representative figures, the political theorist S. Paige Baty argues, provide "a common means of relaying stories and constructing histories which are easily circulated and imaged across great distances of time and space." They supply these histories with "iconic figures through whom multiple meanings, references and roles are remembered."[11] "Mass-mediated representative characters incorporate citizens into a representational nation, enabling them to interact with a virtual community," Baty concludes.[12] More specifically, Hollywood Stars such as John Wayne, Clint Eastwood, and Henry Fonda can provide enduring symbols around which cultural narratives about the nation's constitutional culture can be represented.[13] Even after their death, these representative figures remain part of an ongoing *process* of cultural production, reception, and reproduction as their iconic images continue to circulate within a mass-mediated mode of information.[14]

The legal-reelist texts of Henry Fonda construct his "populist outlaw hero" as a representative character. As the cultural historian Richard Slotkin suggests, Fonda came to represent "an uncommon common man, laconic, folksy, commonsensical, basically decent, yet quick, skillful, tough, unsentimental, and capable of effective and violent action."[15] Fonda's iconic character articulates what seems to be an intuitive, commonsense vision of justice.[16] This character appears in a number of legal-reelist texts, and I will look at several of these to suggest how Hollywood films might be seen as part of "constitutional history."

To move beyond more traditional sources and look at motion pictures requires cross-examining filmic texts in ways that, initially, may seem strange to constitutional historians.[17] As the law professor Paul Kahn argues, however, "we shall never understand the meaning of the rule of law in American political life if we look only at particular laws and particular [court] decisions." The study of legal-constitutional history involves "an examination of the ways the *imagination* shapes political *meaning* in the American polity."[18] This "imaginary" dimension of constitutional history, this chapter suggests, appears most vividly in Fonda's final legal-reelist role as Clarence Earl Gideon, a leading character in the drama that students of constitutional history know as *Gideon v. Wainwright* (1963).[19] *Gideon's Trumpet* (1980)—a filmic representation of this case, which itself involves multiple issues of legal representation—relies on the meanings that had come to cluster around the Star image of Henry Fonda.

Over time, an iconic film Star such as Fonda accumulates and changes meanings in a way that is roughly analogous to how a legal doctrine, such as the "right-to-representation-by-counsel" issue at stake in the *Gideon* case, accumulates and changes meanings. In the case of both a film Star and a constitutional doctrine, past "performances" are important. Just as the meanings of a doctrinal principle accrue over time, case by case and treatise by treatise, so the meanings signified by a filmic icon such as Henry Fonda are constructed and reconstructed intertextually, movie by movie and role by role.[20] Thus, familiar legal texts such as the Supreme Court's opinion in *Gideon v. Wainwright* or Anthony Lewis's *Gideon's Trumpet*,[21] a journalistic account that inspired the Fonda film of the same name, trace the pre-*Gideon* case law to explain how the Supreme Court came to interpret the right-to-representation-by-counsel doctrine as it did in the *Gideon* decision itself. In much the same way, this chapter focusing on the legal work that the Star image of Henry Fonda performs in *Gideon's Trumpet* will look at pre-1980 films to highlight the "legal-reelist process" through which the law-related meanings of Fonda's iconic image were constructed. Ironically, accounts of the changing meanings of the right-to-representation-by-counsel doctrine and of Fonda's legal image begin at roughly the same point in time, the 1930s. At about the same time that the U.S. Supreme Court was wrestling with the meaning of this doctrine, particularly in the Scottsboro cases, Henry Fonda was emerging as a Hollywood film Star.

Fonda's representative character took shape slowly, as the actor starred in an extraordinary number of legal films. In Fritz

Lang's *You Only Live Twice* (1937), Fonda played a man whom a jury wrongly convicts, and sentences to death, for committing a murder. Eventually, he escapes from prison but is hunted down and killed by the police.[22] Two years later, in 1939, Fonda portrayed both Abraham Lincoln, at the beginning of his legal career, and Frank James at the outset of his extralegal one with brother Jesse.[23] The following year, Fonda became firmly identified with the populist outlaw image when he starred in *The Return of Frank James* (1940) and played John Steinbeck's Tom Joad in John Ford's film version of *The Grapes of Wrath* (1940). During the 1940s, Fonda starred in *The Ox-Bow Incident* (1941), an antilynching drama, and played the famous law officer Wyatt Earp in Ford's *My Darling Clementine* (1946). During the 1950s, he played the title role in Alfred Hitchcock's *The Wrong Man* (1956) and portrayed the pivotal figure in one of this nation's most famous (albeit fictional) trials, the case of *12 Angry Men* (1957). After a number of other legal films (particularly in the western genre) during the 1960s and 1970s, Fonda ended his legal-reelist career with *Gideon's Trumpet* (1980).[24]

As a means of focusing this discussion, I want to use Fonda's iconic image to highlight the differing portrayals of criminal defense attorneys in four of these film narratives. *Young Mr. Lincoln* and *The Wrong Man* seek to translate, through different cinematic forms, a real-life legal cause into a legal-reelist one. Many students of law consider the third Fonda film, *12 Angry Men*, "realistic" enough to be used in undergraduate and even law school classes. And *Gideon's Trumpet* offers a popular dramatization of an important Supreme Court case on the defense counsel issue. Taken together, these four films employ the iconic character of Henry Fonda to help represent a wide range of roles for a defense lawyer.

The kinds of "imaginings" in these four films—textual traces of broader legal-constitutional discourses—can help to give meaning to *Gideon v. Wainwright*. By emphasizing the role of Stars, I want to suggest how the representative character of Henry Fonda has come to shape the popular imagination of this Supreme Court decision on the right-to-representation-by-counsel doctrine. *Gideon's Trumpet* sympathetically employs Fonda's iconic image as the populist outlaw hero to help link, in the nation's popular constitutional culture, the right to representation by legal counsel to the search for justice.

A legal-reelist history of *Gideon v. Wainwright* might begin with Henry Fonda's performance as a criminal defense lawyer in *Young Mr. Lincoln.* Since this film appeared at the end of a decade during which the "mouthpiece" genre dominated legal-reelist filmmaking, the law professor Anthony Chase plausibly sees it as one of the first motion pictures to feature "the positive image of the virtuous lawyer."[25] Other possible readings of the film, however, complicate this judgment.

Fonda's Lincoln confronts a legal-moral dilemma when he takes the case of Adam and Matt Clay, two brothers accused of stabbing to death a frontier ruffian named Scrub White. Each defendant, while knowing that he didn't kill White, assumes that the other did and, therefore, refuses to say anything in court. Lincoln promises their mother, who also refuses to testify, that he will derail the trial judge's plan to save one of the brothers by establishing the guilt of the other. Mrs. Clay would rather lose both sons, she tells the court, rather than allow the law, any more than she, to choose between them. Both of her boys, the innocent along with the guilty one, seem headed for the gallows, and Lincoln appears too inept to represent them effectively.

The legal machinery tests Lincoln's skills. An eyewitness, J. Palmer Cass (Ward Bond), testifies that he can identify one of the boys as White's killer. Still, the brothers refuse to break ranks, and Lincoln's apparent incompetence, on display during a bumbling cross-examination of Cass, prompts the presiding judge to urge the young attorney to seek assistance from the more experienced Stephen A. Douglas (Milburn Stone). Lincoln refuses and, instead, recalls Cass to the stand. After more, seemingly pointless questioning (which filmgoers subsequently discover is designed to disarm Cass), Lincoln suddenly turns on the state's star witness. During a savage verbal grilling, Lincoln reveals that Cass could not possibly have seen, aided only by the light of the moon as he had earlier testified, either of the boys stab Scrub White. The *Farmer's Almanac,* which Lincoln pulls from his top hat, reveals that the moon had already set by the time of White's killing. J. Palmer Cass's lie about having been able to see the killing under the moonlight, Lincoln insists, was designed to conceal the fact that he, and neither of the defendants, had killed Scrub White! Cass, unhinged by Lincoln's brutal cross-examination, sobbingly confesses his guilt.

*Young Mr. Lincoln* does depart, of course, from the mouthpiece films of the 1930s. The young attorney displays total devotion to both his clients and to the larger cause of justice. Despite the absence of any financial reward, he sticks with the boys' case. And in the context of the 1930s, when the Supreme Court of the United States was beginning to consider in what circumstances the Constitution guaranteed a criminal defendant a competent attorney, *Young Mr. Lincoln* might be said to offer a powerful, popular representation of the claim that meaningful defense counsel is essential for a fair trial and the protection of civil liberties, at least in a capital case.[26]

But *Young Mr. Lincoln* also displays dark, brooding, and unsettling representations of the legal process and of the defense lawyer. The camera captures Fonda's Lincoln roaming the edges of the film's frame, as if unsure of his place within the judicial system. Moreover, as a famous essay in the film journal *Cahiers du Cinéma* argues, the film can be seen to represent Lincoln, especially as he overwhelms J. Palmer Cass and then shambles awkwardly from the courtroom, as a castrating figure who resembles the vampire-protagonist of the German expressionist film *Nosferatu* (1922). Lincoln, in this reading, is primarily concerned with demonstrating his own potency and displays only flashes of human emotion.[27] Here, Lincoln may use this power to achieve justice. But what is the broader implication, the film might suggest (especially to audiences of the 1930s), of allowing such a "monstrous" figure to invoke the lethal power of the law?

Modifying this line of criticism, it might be argued that *Young Mr. Lincoln* tries to contain this potentially disturbing discourse about a defense attorney's power. When Fonda's Lincoln first considers law as his calling, for example, he is reading a copy of *Blackstone.* After considering only a few passages of this treatise, Lincoln decides that practicing law is a simple matter: "[T]hat's all there is to it, right and wrong." This cultural narrative, then, consistently plays down the reel-life Lincoln's legal knowledge—learning that the real-life Lincoln clearly did possess—and shows him resolving the Clay case by citing information about the pattern of the moon from the *Farmer's Almanac* rather than by parsing legal precedents.

Fonda's Lincoln displays the natural ability to see what other people might have seen for themselves had they not been blinded by wrongheaded, legalistic assumptions. Only Lincoln recognizes that the narrative scripted by legal authorities has begun with the wrong question. The story should begin by asking *who* killed Scrub White, not *which* of the Clay boys did it. Fonda's defense attorney saves his clients not because of any special legal skills or knowledge but precisely because he lacks the qualities that mark a trained lawyer. In a number of ways, then, this film identifies "its hero as someone who works *within* but is not really *of* the legal machinery."[28]

Fonda's portrayal of Young Mr. Lincoln closely parallels another of his iconic roles, that of Tom Joad in *The Grapes of Wrath*. In the latter film, a corrupt legal-political system forces young Tom, an Oklahoma farmer who has migrated to California, to flee from the safety (and the confines) of his family and to fight for justice. Tom promises his mother—and the film audience—that "I'll be around in the dark. . . . Wherever you can look. Wherever there's a fight so hungry people can eat, . . . wherever there's a cop beatin' up a guy, I'll be there." Fonda's character represents the populist outlaw hero who will fight to restore the natural-law values that the legal system appears to have corrupted. In these films, Fonda is last seen, as both Lincoln and Joad, walking up a hill, out of the filmic frame, and into "history." Taken together, *Young Mr. Lincoln* and *The Grapes of Wrath* underscore, through the iconic image of Henry Fonda, "the essential unity of the populist outlaw and the Great Emancipator," Richard Slotkin argues.[29]

The film *12 Angry Men* (1957), by recalling this iconic image, seeks to re-present Fonda's "Young Mr. Lincoln" and "Tom Joad" as an independent-minded, justice-seeking citizen-hero. Here, Fonda's character convinces other members of a jury to reverse course and acquit a young man of the charge of having murdered his father. As in *Young Mr. Lincoln*, "Fonda's function [in *12 Angry Men*] is to serve as the great unifier, dispelling prejudice, faulty reasoning and uncommon haste to allow others to discover the truth they would not have otherwise seen."[30] And just as most filmgoers are likely not surprised when Abraham Lincoln literally pulls crucial evidence from his hat, they are probably not shocked when the iconic Fonda—the narrative does not even give his character a name until the final minute of the drama—convinces his fellow jurors to change their minds and follow his lead. Fonda's juror, like the young Mr. Lincoln, can notice things that a defense attorney and eleven other jurors, including a savvy stockbroker (E. G. Marshall), overlook.[31] In *12 Angry Men*, then, the image of both Fonda's Joad and his youthful Lincoln seems to inhabit the jury room. From this perspective, Fonda's representative character embodies the populist constitutional ideal that preserving legal forms and protecting rights is not simply the responsibility of legal professionals, judges, and defense lawyers but that of every member of the polity.[32]

The film *12 Angry Men* conspicuously downplays the role of the defendant's attorney. It begins, after final arguments, with the judge instructing the jurors about their duty. The defense attorney's performance, as a consequence, remains outside the filmic frame, and the audience must reconstruct it from the jury's subsequent arguments. During these heated discussions, Fonda consistently spotlights exculpatory evidence that the defendant's court-appointed lawyer has failed to see and assumes, though a layperson, the role of the young man's attorney. As Fonda debates other members of the jury, the narrative valorizes his powers of observation and reasoning over those of the never-seen defense counsel. After Fonda convinces one juror to change his vote from "guilty" to "not guilty," another juror explodes in anger. Even the defendant's attorney did not believe in his client's case, he rages. Right from the beginning, "you could see it!" Yes, Fonda quietly concedes, the defendant's court-appointed lawyer probably wanted no part of a case that would bring neither money nor glory. And, yes, he seems not to have believed in his client's cause. In contrast, Fonda declares, by quiet example, as much as by dramatic exhortation, that citizens must insist that the law operate by a higher standard than the one embraced by this defense attorney.

Although the juror in *12 Angry Men* is not quite the quintessential outlaw hero, his stance toward the law seems consistent with that of the representative character with whom the iconic Fonda has become popularly identified. This juror is someone who, particularly in contrast to the defendant's lawyer, has not been jaded by too much contact with the legal system. Although adopting a pose of cool detachment while framing his arguments, Fonda's character will not stand by while the legal process mechanically grinds out an automatic, possibly unjust result. From a contemporary, intertextual perspective, this character might even be seen as the "Ghost of Tom Joad" in a Brooks Brothers suit.[33]

Fonda's legal performance here also differs in at least one crucial respect from that in *Young Mr. Lincoln: 12 Angry Men* eschews the "who-done-it" framework. Fonda's juror claims no special insight or opinion about the guilt or innocence of the defendant. His primary concern is to ensure that the process works, that the young man receives a fair hearing and the kind of legal representation that his defense attorney has failed to provide. To do this, he simply wants "to talk," he tells the jurors who want to brand him as a bleeding-heart liberal. As the film scholar Bill Nichols observes, Fonda brings closure to the narrative "less by arriving at conclusive certainty, than by eliminating the proclivity to easy answers and quick fixes in a complex world."[34] More important, the narrative of *12 Angry Men* is not resolved—or justice vindicated—through the skills of a professional lawyer but through the commonsense judgment and tenacity of the representative character of Henry Fonda.[35] But what might happen if Fonda's iconic character were not available to represent an innocent defendant, as in *Young Mr. Lincoln*, or to stop the rush to convict, as in *12 Angry Men*?

Arguably, Alfred Hitchcock's *The Wrong Man* asks these questions. Here, a character played by Fonda himself desperately needs a savior, but no human agent, not even a thoroughly dedicated defense attorney, seems of much help. *The Wrong Man*, with its images of entrapment and despair, falls within the cycle of film noir that came to dominate motion picture making about "things legal" during the 1940s and 1950s. The cycle of noir films contains so many texts with legal themes, in fact, that it seems possible to identify a subcycle that I call "law noir."[36]

Law noirs portray defense attorneys in a number of ways. Updating the mouthpiece genre, *Force of Evil* (1948) pictures Joe Morse (John Garfield) as a complex, conflicted lawyer who, by faithfully representing the interests of his mobster client, unwittingly sets in motion the sinister forces that kill the brother he is trying to help.[37] Other law noir defense attorneys seem amoral cynics. Kingsley Willis (Stanley Ridges), who is hailed as "the best defense lawyer in the country," accepts his usual high fee to defend the title character (Barbara Stanwyck) in *The File on Thelma Jordan* (1949). "The world is full of innocent lambs, and I'm their lawyer," Willis assures Thelma. A jury acquits her, though she is—since this *is* a law noir—later revealed to have conspired to kill her wealthy aunt.[38] In *Angel Face* (1952), Diane Tremayne (Jean Simmons), unlike Thelma Jordan, willingly admits that she is guilty of murder. But Frank Barrett (Leon Ames), her attorney, refuses to let her confess this "truth." Truth is "what the jury decides," Barrett tells her, and he orchestrates a courtroom narrative that ends with a verdict of "not guilty."[39]

If Kingsley Willis and Frank Barrett exhibit a world-weary cynicism, defense lawyer Andy Morton (Humphrey Bogart) in *Knock on Any Door* (1949) may not be cynical enough. A fervent civil libertarian who jeopardizes his reputation to defend a vicious punk, Nick ("Pretty Boy") Romano (John Derek), against a murder charge, Morton conducts a passionate, skillful defense.[40] This law noir denies the audience a clear view of who committed the crime for which Romano is on trial, and its narrative encourages viewers to identify with the defense attorney and his handsome, if flawed, young client. Morton pokes numerous holes in the prosecution's case, and a verdict for acquittal seems in the offing.[41] But true to his credo of "live fast, die young, leave a good-looking corpse," Nick Romano recklessly insists on taking the witness stand. There, aggressive questioning by the district attorney (George Macready) cracks his fragile psyche, and he ends up confessing his guilt.[42] At the end of the trial sequence, a high-angle shot depicts Andy Morton, Romano's once confident defense counsel, as a small, insignificant figure who is dwarfed by the majesty of the presiding judge's bench.[43] After investing so much in his representation of Romano, Morton must struggle to place his own personal and professional commitment within a broader legal-moral context.

Fonda's defense attorney in *The Wrong Man* (played by Anthony Quayle) resembles Bogart's Andy Morton, but this law noir shifts the narrative focus away from the defense lawyer to the criminal defendant.[44] *The Wrong Man* represents the ordeal of Manny Balestrero (Fonda), a musician at New York City's swanky Stork Club, who is charged with committing a string of small-time holdups. Piece by piece, coincidence by coincidence, the evidence against Balestrero mounts. Needing money for his wife's dental work, Manny visits a loan office that recently has been robbed by a man who closely resembles him; seeking refuge from the pressures of his hardscrabble life, he pretends to play the horses, a hobby that the police mistake for the real thing and a motive for Manny turning to crime; and while writing a sample hold-up note for the police, Manny makes the same grammatical mistake as the stickup man. Eyewitness identifications—the crucial one, as in *12 Angry Men,* by a woman who wears glasses—convince the police that Manny is the "right man."

*The Wrong Man* creates the haunting vision of an ordinary person trapped within a harsh cityscape and an impersonal legal bureaucracy.[45] A shot of Manny descending into New York City's subway system, for example, lacks a complementary one of him emerging from the city's depths. And when Manny does magically appear above ground, on his own doorstep, he is suddenly whisked away by police officers who do not even allow him to talk to his wife, Rose (Vera Miles). The trio rides to the police station in silence, with Manny jammed between two burly officers. Yet the police, in contrast to those in law noirs such as *Force of Evil,* are not represented as corrupt or mean-spirited. Competent (if uncaring) professionals, they do their job with plodding efficiency. They tell Manny that they are only following "procedure" and that his trip to the station is just a "routine" matter. "An innocent man has nothing to worry about," they assure Manny while persuading him to write the sample holdup note. Once he is booked, the film employs grating sounds and a darkly lit mise-en-scène to represent his isolation. Finally, when Manny is arraigned in a shabby courtroom, a nameless lawyer suddenly pops into the film frame, slinks from a bench, sidles up to his side, enters a plea of innocent, and fails to win a reduction in his bail. The story of *The Wrong Man* derives additional force because it is Henry Fonda—conspicuously playing against his iconic role as the confident, independent, outlaw hero—who portrays the helpless victim. By the time Manny finally gets back home, he is too traumatized even to seek legal counsel. Rose must contact

Frank O'Connor (Quayle), who agrees to handle Manny's defense and assures the couple that his fee "will take care of itself." *The Wrong Man,* by representing O'Connor's role in an ambiguous manner, offers a narrative in which the role of a defense attorney cannot easily be plotted on any simplistic mouthpiece-versus-virtuous lawyer scale.

Recalling an early example of law noir—*The Stranger on the Third Floor* (1940)—the film assigns the burden of gathering exculpatory evidence to a romantic couple rather than to agents of the legal system. In *Stranger,* the fiancée of a man falsely accused of murder saves the day by tracking down the real killer herself. But Manny and Rose, trying to locate people who can substantiate his alibi, discover that potential witnesses have either died or disappeared.[46] In time, Rose even begins to doubt Manny's innocence. "How do I know you're not guilty? You don't tell me everything you do," she accuses him. Finally, she suffers a breakdown and must be institutionalized.[47] *The Wrong Man* cuts directly from a shot of the mental institution, in which Rose will reside, to one of the courtroom in which Manny will be tried.

The film's trial sequence, like those in the police station, represents the legal process as mind-numbing, bureaucratic routine. As the prosecutor mechanically outlines his case, it increasingly appears as if Manny must be guilty. While sympathetic to Manny's plight and committed to his defense, O'Connor dominates his client as completely as the police had done earlier. He, not Manny, first recognizes the psychological toll that this ordeal by legal process has taken on Rose. And O'Connor's legal representation seems of little help to Manny and of scant interest to anyone else in the courtroom. As O'Connor is cross-examining one of the state's eyewitnesses, boredom settles over the proceedings. Not even Manny's relatives seem attentive to O'Connor's attempt to shake crucial testimony against his client. Then, suddenly, a juror who is anxious to convict Manny blurts out, "Your Honor. Do we have to sit here and listen to this?" The result is a mistrial. (Ironically, then, Manny's fate turns on the emotions of a juror who behaves much like those whom Henry Fonda confronts in *12 Angry Men.*) O'Connor must tell his client that he will have to endure another trial. "Can you make it, Manny?" he asks.

Nearly catatonic, Manny seems to need extralegal, perhaps

divine, intervention. "I think I could've stood it better if they'd found me guilty," he tells his mother. She suggests prayer, and he retreats to his bedroom to stare at a picture of Jesus. Then, in a highly stylized sequence that breaks with the film's neodocumentary mode, a close-up of Manny gradually dissolves into that of another man's face.[48] As the camera pulls back, this second man, who resembles Manny, tries to rob a small grocery store but is subdued by the owner. When the holdup man enters a police station, one of the faceless, by-the-book officers who had earlier arrested Manny notices the similarities between this suspect and the "wrong man." Soon the legal bureaucracy sets Manny free. The film ends abruptly with a written text informing viewers that, after two years in an institution, Rose was also released and that the Balestrero family now lives in Florida. A brief long shot captures four people, supposedly Manny and his family, walking away from the camera and down a street lined with palm trees.

Just as students of Hitchcock's films can offer a number of credible, and competing, interpretations of *The Wrong Man*'s enigmatic ending, so can students of law legitimately differ over the film's ambiguous representations of the legal process and of the role of a defense lawyer. In what ways does O'Connor's legal expertise assist Manny's cause? In what ways might a defense attorney's intervention seem irrelevant? And in what ways does the film suggest that even dedicated and well-meaning lawyering may only confuse and immobilize a client already shaken by a nightmarish trip through the legal system?[49]

Legal-constitutional historians once would have dismissed these kinds of questions as ones for film reviewers assuming the role of legal buffs or for lawyers playing at being film critics. But the claim of legal reelism—and, more broadly, of legal-constitutional studies after the cultural turn—is that readings of mass-mediated imagery should not be separated from readings of other forms of legal representation.[50] Paul Kahn's study of *Marbury v. Madison,* after underscoring "the representative character of law's appearance," concludes that law "is a state of mind before it is an order of the state."[51] Going further, William Ian Miller's essay on the legal films of Clint Eastwood suggests how legal-reelist narratives can effectively cross-examine the representations of constitutional government and of the rule of law that are constructed in official, state-sanctioned accounts such as court opinions. "Popular culture just might not be all that wrong in its view of a law blind to its mission of keeping an orderly society in accordance with just principles," Miller's piece maintains.[52] And Carol Clover's work on trial films argues that any account of the relationship between legal and mass commercial culture should recognize an ongoing process of cross-examination: "[T]he legal system has always drawn on the entertainment system, playing to the spectator in us all," and the entertainment system, in turn, "draws on the legal system, playing to the juror in us all."[53] It is in this context, then, in order to underline the cultural dimensions of constitutional history, that I want to suggest one possible way of cross-examining the reel-life cases of Henry Fonda, especially the film version of *Gideon's Trumpet,* and several other, more traditional representations of the real-life cause of *Gideon v. Wainwright*.[54]

To begin, images similar to those appropriate to a law noir such as *The Wrong Man* could be used to tell the story of Clarence Earl Gideon. A middle-aged ex-convict from Florida, Gideon imagines that the Constitution guarantees him an attorney in a criminal case, even if he lacks the money to hire one. After a Florida judge, following state law and the U.S. Supreme Court's decision in *Betts v. Brady*,[55] refuses to appoint a lawyer for Gideon, the defendant ineffectually represents himself during a trial for having allegedly robbed a pool hall. Found guilty of burglary, Gideon is sentenced to five years in prison. Eventually, the case is appealed to the U.S. Supreme Court, which votes to hear arguments on whether or not to overrule *Betts v. Brady* and to hold that the Constitution requires states to provide indigent defendants with an attorney.

The petitioner's brief, from the elite Washington law firm that handled the *Gideon* case before the High Court, does use noirlike imagery that might be found in a law noir, or in a noir-inspired TV police drama, to portray the relationship between the legal-constitutional apparatus of the state and citizens such as Gideon. Only an "experienced lawyer," the petitioner's brief insists, "can possibly know or pursue the technical, elaborate, and sophisticated measures which are necessary to assemble and appraise the facts, analyze the law, determine contentions, negotiate the plea, or marshal and present all of the factual and legal considerations" that "make up a criminal defense." The frequency of guilty pleas "suggests that those who are arrested, particularly the penniless and persons who are members of minority groups, are more likely hopelessly to resign themselves to fate than aggressively to act like the defense counsel portrayed on television."[56] Here, the brief might even be read, in a cultural context, to be arguing for realigning the constitutional law of the state with the "imaginary" justice system represented in commercial mass culture.

Justice Hugo Black's opinion, for the Supreme Court, employs similar imagery. This legal text, like many other constitutional narratives about criminal procedure cases, pictures "the authority of the state [as] no longer aligned with a comprehensive scheme of justice. Instead, it is aligned against the individual, who must be protected."[57] The state spends "vast sums of money to establish machinery to try defendants accused of crime," and it has become an "obvious truth" that lawyers are now "necessities not luxuries," Justice Black's opinion argues.[58] Consequently, this account concludes with an order granting Gideon a new trial—one in which he will be represented by a court-appointed lawyer. But in contrast to a law noir narrative such as *The Wrong Man,* Justice Black's opinion implicitly assumes that a competent, real-life lawyer will provide the expertise needed to realign the legal system and to protect the rights of indigent defendants such as Gideon.

A similar assumption frames another important narrative of the Gideon case: *Gideon's Trumpet,* Anthony Lewis's journalistic history that appeared only a year after Justice Black's opinion. In Lewis's narrative, however, any trace of noirlike imagery disappears. This account begins with Gideon, forgoing the kind of divine intervention that had rescued Manny Balestrero, handwriting his own in forma pauperis petition for the U.S. Supreme Court. Then Lewis's story goes on to detail how Abe Fortas, the prominent Washington, D.C., attorney who was appointed by the Supreme Court to argue Gideon's appeal, mobilizes the resources of his law firm and convinces the Court to overturn Gideon's conviction and to reverse *Betts v. Brady.* The book concludes with Gideon returning to court and, with a lawyer representing him, winning an acquittal on the original burglary charge.

The emplotment of *Gideon's Trumpet,* as with that of any other historical account, requires choices in narrative strategy and representational imagery. Anthony Lewis's decision to represent Gideon's tale in one way invariably suppresses other, equally plausible options. Another history, for example, might see the *Gideon* case as much less dramatic than Lewis's book manages to make it seem. Fortas's role might legitimately be reimagined so as to emphasize the ways in which his performance, similar to that of Frank O'Connor in *The Wrong Man,* seems relatively insignificant, in light of "higher" forces, to legal decision making. An alternative telling of *Gideon v. Wainwright,* for instance, could portray Fortas's role as less compelling than *Gideon's Trumpet* constructs it. By 1963, few "reasonable" people favored retaining the rule of *Betts v. Brady.* Thirty-seven states (though not Florida) and the federal courts had already rejected the *Betts* approach to providing counsel for indigent defendants. Chief Justice Earl Warren had instructed his law clerks to be looking for a petition, such as Gideon's, that could provide the occasion to overturn *Betts.* During oral argument before the Supreme Court, when an attorney representing Florida starts to argue for retaining the rule of *Betts v. Brady,* one of the justices asks, "You don't really expect to win this case, do you?" And some years later, Justice Potter Stewart tells Fortas's biographer that "probably no lawyer could have lost that case."[59]

Thus, much of the drama that Lewis's book imputes to the *Gideon* case, from a literary-rhetorical perspective, depends on constructing a narrative in which it appears that an apparently irreconcilable moral-legal dilemma might cause Fortas to "lose." Fortas, like virtually every member of the elite bar, wants a Supreme Court ruling overturning *Betts v. Brady* and guaranteeing all criminal defendants in Gideon's position an attorney. But his primary responsibility, *Gideon's Trumpet* constantly emphasizes, must be to represent Gideon's own interests, even if this requires an argument that stays within the "special circumstances" discourse of *Betts v. Brady* and does not help the justices address broader constitutional issues. Can Fortas negotiate this dilemma? asks Lewis's book.

This background structure—which parallels that of most classical Hollywood films, including *Young Mr. Lincoln*[60]—yields a narrative in which Fortas must resolve a conflict that would have confounded a less talented legal defense attorney. Lewis's book details how Fortas and his legal team craft an argument that addresses *both* Gideon's personal interests and broader constitutional values so clearly and compellingly that any "rational" lawyer was bound to be "persuaded" by its force and logic.

Lewis's narrative represents the *Gideon* case, then, as an example of textbook-perfect defense lawyering: dedicated attorneys work within a labyrinthine, but principled, legal arena in which advocates as resourceful as Fortas need not choose between achieving the narrow needs of clients and championing expansive constitutional principles. The properly crafted argument can speak simultaneously to the interests of individual litigants and to broader constitutional aspirations. Lewis's book represents the defense lawyer, embodied by Abe Fortas, as a "heroic" figure. In contrast to Fonda's young Mr. Lincoln, however, Fortas need not wander the edges of the filmic frame during the trial sequences of *Gideon's Trumpet* but can confidently operate at the center of the legal arena.

Abe Fortas, while remaining inside the legal machinery, can still assume the heroic mantle of Abraham Lincoln because *Gideon's Trumpet* represents the *Gideon* case very differently than *Young Mr. Lincoln* portrays the prosecution of the Clay brothers. In contrast to John Ford's film, Anthony Lewis's book unequivocally celebrates the legal process itself. It emphasizes how Fortas's well-trained legal staff—and, then, the justices of the Supreme Court—recognize the competing interests and values at stake in Gideon's case. The odd couple, Clarence Earl Gideon and Abe Fortas, also play complementary roles: Gideon intuitively imagines he has a right to an attorney, and Fortas translates this intuition into reasoned, constitutional arguments. His personal legal performance can be represented as meshing smoothly with the workings of the legal system itself. Fortas need not, as did Fonda's youthful Lincoln (or Raymond Burr's Perry Mason), be represented as standing apart from the day-to-day workings of the legal apparatus.[61] *Gideon's Trumpet,* grounded in the liberal legal culture of the Warren era, imagines constitutional litigation as a thoroughly rational, entirely principled enterprise.

During the late 1970s, producer-actor John Houseman, a legal-reelist celebrity because of his portrayal of the law professor Charles W. Kingsfield in the *Paper Chase* (1973), began to plan a made-for-TV film of *Gideon's Trumpet* that would feature Henry

Fonda.[62] Although this drama was to follow the narrative structure and representational economy of Lewis's print version, Fonda's iconic, legal-reelist presence, along with the passage of nearly fifteen years of legal-constitutional history, threatened the cultural meanings that surrounded *Gideon's Trumpet* and the Supreme Court decision it had so skillfully represented.

In this sense, it is interesting to speculate on the casting of Henry Fonda. What role might his representative character play in the drama of Clarence Earl Gideon?[63] Why not, for instance, have young Mr. Lincoln become the twentieth-century legal wizard, Abe Fortas? (Fonda's age would not be an insurmountable barrier, since the role of Fortas, who was a youthful fifty-two when he represented Gideon, eventually went to Jose Ferrer, who was not much younger than Fonda.) Or might Fonda cap his legal-reelist career by portraying a member of the Supreme Court? (These parts were assumed by Fonda's Hollywood contemporaries, including Sam Jaffe, Dean Jagger, and Houseman himself, in the scene-stealing role of Chief Justice Earl Warren.)

But Fonda's iconic image, it can be argued, simply did not "fit" any of these roles. To have cast Fonda as Fortas or as any of the Supreme Court justices was to risk recalling his earlier roles in legal narratives whose representations of the legal process (and especially of the role of a defense attorney) were at odds with the celebratory mode of *Gideon's Trumpet.* Fonda's iconic status as the outlaw hero, in other words, could have disrupted the film's narrative pattern and representational economy if he had tried to portray a legal "insider" such as Fortas, Black, or Warren.[64]

In addition, any film project based on Anthony Lewis's Warren era text had to deal with the passage of time. In 1964, Justice Black, Abe Fortas, Lewis, and other celebrants of the Warren Court could confidently place the *Gideon* case within a cultural-constitutional narrative that inexorably moves toward a triumphant conclusion. Decisions such as *Gideon v. Wainwright,* according to the liberal story frame of Justice Black's opinion and of *Gideon's Trumpet,* represented the legal process at its best: reasoned arguments, learned opinions, and progressive policy making. Wise lawyers and Herculean judges, such "grand narratives" imagined,[65] could use certain parts of the legal machinery to check potential excesses by other parts. If the prosecutorial arm of the state threatened to overwhelm indigent defendants such as Gideon, the legal process itself could provide lawyers who would represent their claims in ways that would guarantee fair trials and social justice.[66]

The film version of *Gideon's Trumpet,* in contrast, took shape at the beginning of the Reagan era. The Warren Court was no longer in session; a new constitutional "regime" seemed to be emerging; and there was sharp controversy over decisions, particularly *Miranda v. Arizona,*[67] which had sought to extend the framework of the *Gideon* case.[68] Popular legal-reelist narratives, especially those such as *Dirty Harry* (1971) and *Death Wish* (1974) in the "revenge" genre, were representing constitutional decisions protecting the rights of criminal defendants "as too narrowly concerned with wrongful acts rather than evil characters."[69] At the same time, lawyers and legal writers still committed to the narratives of the Warren era were acknowledging that the day-to-day operation of the criminal justice system seemed to mock the liberal imagination of the mid-1960s. A few years after the 1980 release of *Gideon's Trumpet,* the film, a number of the same legal observers who had participated in the *Gideon* case—and who had helped to construct the background frame through which so many liberal narratives had initially represented its meanings—participated in several symposia designed to mark the twenty-fifth anniversary of the Supreme Court's decision. Not surprisingly, they expressed scant optimism about the relationship between Supreme Court opinions and the ability of ordinary attorneys to do heroic work on behalf of criminal defendants.[70] The promise of the *Gideon* holding, "that all criminal defendants would eventually receive representation from skilled and adequately funded attorneys," had yet to be realized, Anthony Lewis conceded.[71]

The 1980 film version of *Gideon's Trumpet* tries to negotiate this passage-of-time issue in several ways: by anchoring itself as securely as possible within the constitutional culture of the Warren era; by trying to avoid any reference to post-1964 perspectives; and, most important, by invoking the iconic image of Henry Fonda to smooth over issues related to the historical contingency of the criminal justice system as it had been imagined in Anthony Lewis's view of the *Gideon* case.[72] In contrast to Lewis's book, (Fonda's) Gideon, rather than (Ferrer's) Fortas, seems to center a filmic narrative that looks back, nostalgically, on the era of the Warren Court *and* on the iconic, legal-reelist image of Henry Fonda.[73] Fonda's representative character, who had triumphed, as the outlaw hero, in earlier legal-reelist films, prevails again but as a different kind of champion of the underdog in the film version of *Gideon's Trumpet.*

Fonda's portrayal of Gideon can recall his contrasting legal performances in *The Grapes of Wrath* and *The Wrong Man.* When Fonda first speaks directly to the camera at the beginning of *Gideon's Trumpet,* for example, it might seem as if Tom Joad—now an aged, four-time loser to the criminal justice machinery—has returned from the 1930s for one final battle. Fonda's Gideon stubbornly insists that an ordinary person cannot have a fair trial unless the state provides a lawyer, and he continues to haunt the prison library, in search of legal precedents, much like his Tom Joad had promised to roam the hills of California, in search of justice. The film also draws on Fonda's outlaw image when his character marches defiantly through the prison yard, followed by a crowd of younger prisoners who hope that, by winning his case, Gideon might lead them from bondage to freedom. Yet, at most other times, especially during the lengthy sequence when the camera shows Fonda clumsily trying to conduct his own defense during the initial jury trial, his portrayal of Gideon intertextually invokes his role as Manny Balestrero, another person who becomes dazed and confused when confronting the state's vast legal bureaucracy. The outlaw hero, while still legible in the iconic figure of Henry Fonda, seems as much an anachronism as an inspiration. To improvise on Anthony Lewis's musical metaphor, the "Ghost of Tom Joad" can sound a trumpet, but only the lawyer in the Brooks Brothers suit can conduct a complicated legal-constitutional symphony.

The film version of *Gideon's Trumpet* still, however, manages to employ Fonda's iconic image to bring closure to its representation of the results of Supreme Court decisions. Portrayed economically, with few dramatic flourishes, Gideon's second, lawyer-conducted, trial ends—amid applause from a diegetic, small-town audience—in a swift acquittal. Following the verdict, Fonda's Gideon, as at the beginning of the film, faces the film-viewing audience head-on. And to the question of whether or not he had "accomplished anything" by his struggle, he responds simply, "Well, I did!" Then the film's final sequence reprises the endings of *Young Mr. Lincoln, 12*

*Angry Men, The Grapes of Wrath,* and *The Wrong Man:* once again, Henry Fonda's iconic character walks away from the camera until he disappears, for the final time, into history.[74]

As with most representative figures, Fonda's lives on in medias res and continues to generate popular re-memberings,[75] including those of *Gideon v. Wainwright.* Within the promotional and "taste-making" commentary that now prepares audiences to view *Gideon's Trumpet,*[76] for instance, this legal-reelist narrative has come to center, more firmly than ever before, on the reel-life image of Henry Fonda rather than on Abe Fortas, the Supreme Court justices, Clarence Earl Gideon, or any of the other real-life participants in the original case. The Museum of Television and Radio, while celebrating *Gideon's Trumpet* as its "Movie of the Month" for April 1998, featured comments from John J. O'Connor of the *New York Times* and Tom Shales of the *Washington Post* that emphasize the iconic performance of Fonda rather than any other aspect of the Gideon case.[77]

The graphic design package for a recent video edition of *Gideon's Trumpet* goes even further in its use of Fonda iconography. An elaborate illustration mixes religious and civic republican imagery to suggest a reading of the filmic narrative that literally elevates Fonda's Gideon above the professionals who work within the legal system. Fonda's representative character, now aged but still majestic, flanked by two U.S. flags, looms above a stylized courtroom scene. This iconic image gazes downward, much as one of Tom Joad or Abraham Lincoln might do, presumably judging whether or not the defense lawyer and the other participants in the legal system are pursuing the cause of justice.[78] The case of *Gideon v. Wainwright,* as it is now being represented in popular legal-cultural imagery, can easily appear to be the cause of (the iconic) Henry Fonda.[79]

Notes

I thank Sandra VanBurkleo for her support, patience, and wise (and humorous) counsel while this chapter was lurching forward; Kermit Hall for his unflagging support; Richard Steele for an insightful critique and the many conversations that helped smooth out some of the lurches; and Emily Rosenberg for suggestions that vastly improved what, given the nature of any law-and-film project, remains a work that will likely always be in progress.

1. See, e.g., W. J. T. Mitchell, "Representation," in *Critical Terms for Literary Study*, 2d ed., ed. Frank Lentricchia and Thomas McLaughlin (Chicago, 1995), 11–22; and J. Hillis Miller, "Narrative," in ibid., 66–79.

2. See, e.g., Costas Dougzinas and Ronnie Warrington, with Shaun McVeigh, *Postmodern Jurisprudence: The Law of Text in the Text of Laws* (New York, 1992); Anne Norton, *Republic of Signs: Liberal Theory and American Popular Culture* (Chicago, 1993), 143; and Paul W. Kahn, *The Reign of Law: Marbury v. Madison and the Construction of America* (New Haven, Conn., 1997), 2. On the issues of narrative and representation in historical writing, see, e.g., Hayden White, *The Content of the Form: Narrative Discourse and Historical Representation* (Baltimore, 1987); Robert F. Berkhoffer Jr., *Beyond the Great Story: History as Text and Discourse* (Cambridge, Mass., 1995), esp. 45–137; Keith Jenkins, ed., *The Postmodern History Reader* (New York, 1997); and Karen Halttunen, "Cultural History and the Challenge of Narrativity," in *Beyond the Cultural Turn: New Directions in the Study of Society and Culture*, ed. Victoria E. Bonnell and Lynn Hunt (Berkeley, 1999), 165–81.

3. See, e.g., Sarah Maza, "Stories in History: Cultural Narratives in Recent Works in European History," *American Historical Review* 101 (1996): 1493–515.

4. See, e.g., Paul W. Kahn, *The Cultural Study of Law: Reconstructing Legal Scholarship* (Chicago, 1999); Guyora Binder and Robert Weisberg, "The Critical Use of History: Cultural Criticism of Law," *Stanford Law Review* 49 (1997): 1149–221; Rosemary J. Coombe, "Contingent Articulations: A Critical Cultural Studies of Law," in *Law in the Domains of Culture*, ed. Austin G. Sarat and Thomas R. Kearns (Ann Arbor, Mich., 1998), 21–64. See also Coombe, "Room for Manoeuver: Towards a Theory of Practice in Critical Legal Studies," *Law and Social Inquiry* 14 (1989): 69–121. And for an imaginative reading of the relationship between the "signs" in commercial advertising and law, see Coombe, "Critical Cultural Legal Studies," *Yale Journal of Law and the Humanities* 10 (1998): 464–69; and Coombe, *The Cultural Life of Intellectual Property: Authorship, Appropriation, and the Law* (Durham, N.C., 1998). For a broadly imaginative look at possible relationships between "culture" and "law," see Richard K. Sherwin, *When Law Goes Pop: The Vanishing Line Between Law and Popular Culture* (Chicago, 2000). See also "Symposium: A New Legal Realism? Cultural Studies and the Law," *Yale Journal of Law and the Humanities* 13 (2001): 3–327, esp. Naomi Mezey, "Law as Culture," 35–67.

5. See, e.g., John Denvir, ed., *Legal Reelism: The Hollywood Film as Legal Text* (Champaign, Ill., 1996); Paul Bergman and Michael Asimow, *Reel Justice: The Courtroom Goes to the Movies* (Kansas City, Mo., 1996); "Symposium: Picturing Justice: Images of Law and Lawyers in the Visual Media," *University of San Francisco Law Review* 30 (1996): 891–1247; and Allen K. Rostron, "Book Review: Lawyers, Law and the Movies: The Hitchcock Cases," *California Law Review* 86 (1998): 211–39.

6. For brief, cogent introductions to the use of narrative forms and representational codes in cinema, see Graeme Turner, *Film as Social Practice*, 3d ed. (New York, 1999), chap. 3; and Robert F. Kolker, "The Film Text and Film Form," in *Oxford Guide to Film Studies*, ed. John Hill and Pamela Church Gibson (New York, 1998), 11–23. On the narrative dimension of the appellate court opinion, see, e.g., Peter Brooks and Paul Gewirtz, eds., *Law's Stories: Narrative and Rhetoric in the Law* (New Haven, Conn., 1996); David Ray Papke and Kathleen H. McManus, "Narrative and the Appellate Opinion," *Legal Studies Forum* 23 (1999): 449–65.

7. See Norman L. Rosenberg, "Hollywood on Trials: Courts and Films, 1930–1960," *Law and History Review* 12 (1994): 341–67.

8. Carol Clover suggests that in the "Anglo-American world . . . trials are already movielike to begin with and movies are already trial-like to begin with": Clover, "Law and the Order of Popular Culture," in *Law in the Domains of Culture,* 99. See also Clover, "'God Bless Juries!'" in *Refiguring American Film Genres: History and Theory,* ed. Nick Browne (Berkeley, 1997), 255–77.

9. The "mouthpiece" or "shyster" film, then, features defense attorneys who faithfully represent the interests of their criminal clients while cynically corrupting the legal system. The classic portrayal was by Warren William in *Mouthpiece* (1932). See, generally, Andrew Bergman, *We're in the Money: Depression America and Its Films* (New York, 1971), 18–19; and Roger Dooley, *From Scarface to Scarlett: American Films in the 1930s* (New York, 1979), 310–18.

10. In distinguishing between the "Stars" of classical Hollywood, who assumed the kind of iconic significance in the broader culture I claim for Henry Fonda, and mere "stars," celebrities manufactured by the Hollywood factory system, I am following Jackie Byers, "The Prime of Miss Kim Novak: Struggling over the Feminine in the Star Image," in *The Other Fifties: Interrogating Midcentury Icons,* ed. Joel Forman (Urbana, Ill., 1997), at 198–99. On the power of film Stars, see also Richard Dyer, *Heavenly Bodies: Film Stars and Society* (London, 1987); Dyer, *The Matter of Images: Essays on Representation* (London, 1993); Turner, *Film as Social Practice,* 103–9; and Richard Maltby and Ian Craven, *Hollywood Cinema: An Introduction* (Cambridge, Mass., 1995), 253–57.

11. The use of "representative" characters and "iconic" figures, though associated with postmodern discourse, traces back to Plutarch and Ralph Waldo Emerson. See S. Paige Baty, *American Monroe: The Making of a Body Politic* (Berkeley, 1995), 11. See also Scott E. Casper, *Constructing American Lives: Biography and Culture in Nineteenth-Century America* (Chapel Hill, N.C., 1999).

12. Baty, *American Monroe,* 45. See, generally, Norton, *Republic of Signs;* and Frederick Dolan and Thomas L. Dumm, eds., *Rhetorical Republic: Governing Representations in American Politics* (Amherst, Mass., 1993).

13. On John Wayne, see Gary Wills, *John Wayne's America* (New York, 1997); on Clint Eastwood, see William Ian Miller, "Clint Eastwood and Equity: Popular Culture's Theory of Revenge," in *Law in the Domains of Culture,* 161–202.

14. For a view of this process in film culture, see Barbara Klinger, *Melodrama and Meaning: History, Culture and the Films of Douglas Sirk* (Bloomington, Ind., 1994); for a view of this process in legal culture, see Pierre Schlag, *Laying Down the Law* (New York, 1996); and Schlag, "Normativity and the Politics of Form," in Paul F. Campos, Pierre Schlag, and Steven D. Smith, *Against the Law* (Durham, N.C., 1996). Thus when *12 Angry Men,* a legal drama initially set in the context of the 1950s, was remade in the late 1990s, it became a very different legal text. From a cinematic standpoint, for example, the remake became a vehicle for a series of individual "star performances" by each of the twelve jurors. And in the wake of the Rodney King and O. J. Simpson trials, the remake inevitably becomes, far more than the 1957 version, a film about race. See, e.g., James Sterngold, "A Tense Jury Room Revisited, and Racism Is Given a Twist," *New York Times,* August 17, 1997, H27–H28.

15. Richard Slotkin, *Gunfighter Nation: The Myth of the Frontier in Twentieth-Century America* (New York, 1992), 302.

16. In several of Fonda's later westerns, such as *Once Upon a Time in the West* (1968) and *There Was a Crooked Man* (1970), the filmic narrative and representational codes work against his iconic image, and this reversal helps to anchor the filmic text. His representative character is also deconstructed, though in a very different way, in *The Wrong Man.* See later discussion.

17. For a discussion of the way in which cultural work on law will require new ways of imagining "law" itself, see Austin D. Sarat, "Book Review: Redirecting Legal Scholarship in Law Schools," *Yale Journal of Law and Humanities* 12 (2000): 129–50. And for a broad view of the way in which traditional legal writing has, long before the advent of motion pictures, looked suspiciously at visual representation, see Costas Douzinas and Linda Nead, eds., *Law and the Image: The Authority of Art and the Aesthetics of Law* (Chicago, 1999), esp. 1–15.

18. Kahn, *The Reign of Law,* 2 (emphases added).

19. 372 U.S. 335 (1963).

20. Jeremy G. Butler, "The Star System and Hollywood," in *Oxford Guide to Film Studies,* 342–53.

21. Anthony Lewis, *Gideon's Trumpet* (New York, 1964).

22. See Patrick McGilligan, *Fritz Lang: The Nature of the Beast* (New York, 1997), 241–47.

23. Fonda portrayed the title character in *Young Mr. Lincoln* (1939) and played Frank James to Tyrone Power's Jesse in *Jesse James* (1939).

24. In addition to numerous other legal-reelist roles, such as the protagonist in a free speech fight in *The Male Animal* (1942), Fonda portrayed the famous trial lawyer Clarence Darrow in a one-person play during the 1970s and the defense attorney in the stage version of *The Caine Mutiny Court Martial.* Allen Roberts and Max Goldstein, *Henry Fonda: A Biography* (Jefferson, N.C., 1984), 172–77. Fonda was particularly taken with his role as Darrow, a legal figure he came to admire as a person of "tremendous heart" (175). See also note 63.

25. Anthony Chase, "Lawyers and Popular Culture: A Review of Mass Media Portrayals of American Attorneys," *American Bar Foundation Research Journal* (1986): 282, 283.

26. For a case law counterpart to *Young Mr. Lincoln,* see, e.g., *Powell v. Alabama,* 287 U.S. 45 (1932), one of the Scottsboro cases. For a superb narrative treatment of these cases, see James Goodman, *Stories of Scottsboro* (New York, 1994).

27. Entitled "John Ford's *Young Mr. Lincoln,*" this collectively written essay, a blend of structural Marxist and psychoanalytical criticism, is one of the most influential pieces in the history of film analysis. It is reprinted in Bill Nichols, ed., *Movies and Methods: An Anthology,* vol. 1 (Berkeley, 1976), 493–529. For a critique of the *Cahiers* essay, see Tag Gallagher, *John Ford: The Man and His Films* (Berkeley, 1986), 162–74. Renata Salecl, a criminologist writing from a psychoanalytical perspective, suggests that many of Fonda's characters, because of their presumed perfection, also give off "a sort of insensibility, coldness, and monstrosity." Salecl, "The Right Man and the Wrong Woman," in *Everything You Always Wanted to Know About Lacan but Were Afraid to Ask Hitchcock,* ed. Slavoj Zizek (New York, 1992), 185–94, 194 n. 10.

28. For a fuller treatment of the film's legal themes, see Norman Rosenberg, "*Young Mr. Lincoln:* The Lawyer as Super-Hero," *Legal Studies Forum* 15 (1991): 215–31, quotation on 224.

29. Slotkin, *Gunfighter Nation,* 303.

30. Bill Nichols, "The Unseen Jury," *University of San Francisco Law Review* 30 (1996): 1056. Young Mr. Lincoln, before working his courtroom magic, similarly stops a rush to judgment, by a lynch mob, in the 1939 Ford film.

31. Peter Biskind's different view of the film turns on seeing Fonda's character, identified as an architect, representing "an expert who qualifies for his role [of instructing the juror in cold war, liberal values] by virtue of his superior education." Biskind, *Seeing Is Believing: How Hollywood Taught Us to Stop Worrying and Love the Fifties* (New York, 1983), 18. Fonda's character begins to construct a "liberal center" within the jury room, Biskind argues, by winning over Marshall's Wall Street stockbroker (16). For yet another plausible perspective on the film, see Clover, "'God Bless Juries,'" 266–71; this essay is particularly good on the origins of the film in a 1950 French film, *Justice est faite.*

32. A similar, "populist constitutional" claim is articulated in another classic legal-reelist text, *Talk of the Town* (1942). See Norman Rosenberg, "Professor Lightcap Goes to Washington: Rereading *Talk of the Town," University of San Francisco Law Review* 30 (1996): 1083–95. "Populist," of course, is a highly contested term, and the version of "populism" represented in *Talk of the Town* and in *12 Angry Men* is different than that articulated in other legal-reelist texts such as *The Return of Frank James* or *The Grapes of Wrath.* Indeed, the film scholar Peter Biskind ignores the populist framework and sees Fonda's juror in *12 Angry Men* representing a "corporate liberal" approach to problem solving. Biskind, *Seeing Is Believing,* 10–20. Such a reading—though, again, hardly "wrong"—would seem to ignore what this essay is seeking to highlight: the "iconic" image of Henry Fonda as a site not only of articulation but also of "remembering"—remembering him as "Young Mr. Lincoln," as "Tom Joad," and as "Henry Fonda, the representative character."

33. See Bruce Springsteen, *The Ghost of Tom Joad* (Columbia Records, 1995).

34. Nichols, "The Unseen Jury," 1059.

35. The role of the courageous juror has become, in "popular memory," so identified with Fonda's iconic image that few people know—or remember—that the role was originated, in the 1954 TV production, by Robert Cummings. This performance, on the live drama series, "Studio One," gained Cummings an Emmy award. Anita Gates, "The Original '12 Angry Men' A Mirror of Its Time with a Moral," *New York Times,* August 17, 1997, H27.

36. Norman L. Rosenberg, "Law Noir," in *Legal Reelism,* 280–302.

37. *Force of Evil,* directed by the soon-to-be blacklisted Abraham Polonsky, appeared in 1948. See Abraham Polonsky, *Force of Evil: The Critical Edition,* ed. Mark Schaubert (West Hills, Calif., 1996).

38. For analysis of this film, see Norman Rosenberg, "The 'Popular First Amendment' and Classical Hollywood, 1930–1960: *Film Noir* and Speech 'Theory for the Millions,'" in *Freeing the First Amendment: Critical Perspectives on Freedom of Expression,* ed. David S. Allen and Robert Jensen (New York, 1995), 151–53; and Michael Walker, "Robert Siodmak," in *The Book of Film Noir,* ed. Ian Cameron (New York, 1992), 145–51.

39. See Edward Gallafent, "Angel Face," in *The Book of Film Noir,* 232–39.

40. "Bogie" is another representative character whose iconic, legal-reelist roles bear scrutiny. Images of legal authority, for example, pervade his most famous film, *Casablanca* (1943), in which he portrays an idealistic lawyer

who has become a "saloon keeper." His many other "legal" roles include playing a crusading district attorney, patterned on Thomas E. Dewey, in *Marked Woman* (1937); the defense attorney in *Knock on Any Door;* and a defendant in the courtroom drama, *The Caine Mutiny* (1954).

41. And as Carol Clover notes, trial films often place the film audience in the place of jurors. See Clover, "'God Bless Juries!'" passim.

42. Here, *Knock on Any Door* might be viewed in light of legal-cultural examination of the difficult question, which is related to the right-to-representation-by-counsel issue, of confessions. See Peter Brooks, *Troubling Confessions: Speaking Guilt in Law and Literature* (Chicago, 2000).

43. This shot, it might be argued, underscores the importance of the "architecture" of legal culture. See, e.g., Jonathan D. Rosenbloom, "Social Ideology as Seen Through Courtroom and Court House Architecture," *Columbia-VLA Journal of Law and the Arts* 22 (1998): 463–523.

44. The story of "the wrong man" became well known to readers of *Life* and the *New York Times,* both of which did a number of features on the incident involving Manny Balestrero. There was also a TV show based on the case. Warner Brothers hailed *The Wrong Man* as "the first [Alfred] Hitchcock film taken from life," and it opens with an unusual film appearance by its director, who directly advises viewers that "this is a true story—every word of it." The real-life defense attorney in the case, Frank O'Connor, worked as a technical consultant on the film, and the reel-life courtroom scenes were shot in the same place in which the real-life drama took place. Despite Hitchcock's claim of realism, his reelistic emplotment differs from those in *Life* and the *New York Times.* See Marshall Deutelbaum, "Finding the Right Man in *The Wrong Man,*" in *A Hitchcock Reader,* ed. Marshall Deutelbaum and Leland Pogue (Ames, Iowa, 1986), 207–18.

45. Film critics often debate *The Wrong Man*'s cinematic aesthetic. A common critique focuses on the film's neorealist approach, a departure from Hitchcock's usual style. See, e.g., Slavoj Zizek, "'In His Bold Gaze My Ruin Is Writ Large,'" in *Everything You Always Wanted to Know About Lacan,* 211, 216, 218–19. For views that stress the film's multilayered representation of the policing-judging bureaucracy, see Leslie Brill, *The Hitchcock Romance: Love and Irony in Hitchcock's Films* (Princeton, N.J., 1988), 122–25; Paula Marantz Cohen, *Alfred Hitchcock: The Legacy of Victorianism* (Lexington, Ky., 1995), 124–34; and Cohen, "Hitchcock's Revised American Vision: *The Wrong Man* and *Vertigo,*" in *Hitchcock's America,* ed. Johnathan Freedman and Richard Millington (New York, 1999), 155–72. And for a suggestive view of how the film noir cycle provided a "realistic" view of policing and judging, see J. P. Telotte, *Voices in the Dark: The Narrative Patterns of Film Noir* (Champaign, Ill., 1989), 134–78.

46. In the real-life case, Manny actually did find witnesses who would verify he had been far from one of the robbery scenes, and his attorney took their depositions. Deutelbaum, "Finding the Right Man," 208.

47. In a feminist-framed view of *The Wrong Man,* Renata Salecl contests the "usual reading" of the film: "[A] hero who got trapped in the wheels of the Kafkaesque machinery, is then accused by mistake and, owing to the steadiness of his morals, manages to survive the whole affair, while his wife, because of the feminine weakness of her character, cannot stand the pressure and goes mad." In Salecl's view, it is Manny who is "mad from the very start," primarily because he cannot manage even a single sign of his own "guilt" in the whole

incident. Instead, it is Rose who must, through her incarceration, bear the burden of "guilt." "The Right Man and the Wrong Woman," 193. See also Cohen, "Hitchcock's Revised American Vision," 162–65.

48. In contrast to Fonda's Manny, the real-life Manny apparently was back at work, not in prayer, when the "right man" was apprehended. David Sterritt, *The Films of Alfred Hitchcock* (New York, 1993), 78. This sequence plays with a filmviewer's powers of observation, because the second man, the "right" one, has already appeared, fleetingly, in several earlier sequences in the film!

49. To offer only one other possible interpretation, suggested to me by Richard Steele, *The Wrong Man* might be read as a celebration of the ability of the legal bureaucracy to dispense "blind justice." Once the "right man" came into police custody, the officers move swiftly and efficiently, with no consideration for their own reputations, to release the "wrong" one. For a suggestive overview, informed by film and legal theory, of *The Wrong Man* and two other of Hitchcock's courtroom dramas—*The Paradine Case* and *I Confess*—see Rostron, "The Hitchcock Cases," 221–39.

50. See, for example, Kahn, *The Cultural Study of Law;* Coombe, "Critical Cultural Legal Studies," passim, and esp. 483; Coombe, *The Cultural Life of Intellectual Properties,* 1–39; and Binder and Weisberg, "Cultural Criticism of Law," passim. See also Brook Thomas, *American Literary Realism and the Failed Promise of Contract* (Berkeley, 1997); and Karen Halttunen, *Murder Most Foul: The Killer and the American Gothic Imagination* (Cambridge, Mass., 1998).

51. Kahn, *The Reign of Law,* 177.

52. Miller, "Clint Eastwood and Equity," 200.

53. Clover, "'God Bless Juries!'" 271.

54. These more "traditional" narratives include the Supreme Court's opinion by Justice Hugo Black, the brief written by the law firm of Abe Fortas, and Anthony Lewis's *Gideon's Trumpet.*

55. 316 U.S. 455 (1942). Under the rule of *Betts v. Brady,* indigent defendants received court-appointed attorneys only in "special circumstances"—if they were young, mentally impaired, and so on.

56. *Gideon v. Cochrane, Brief for Petitioner* in *Landmark Briefs of the Supreme Court of the United States: Constitutional Law,* ed. Philip Kurland and Gerhard Casper (Arlington, Va., 1975), 57:342, 355.

57. Paul W. Kahn, *Legitimacy and History: Self-Government in American Constitutional Theory* (New Haven, Conn., 1992), 165.

58. 372 U.S., at 344.

59. Bernard Schwartz, *Super Chief: Earl Warren and the Supreme Court—A Judicial Biography* (New York, 1983), 458–59; "Remarks of Bruce Jacob," in "Conference on the 30th Anniversary of the United States Supreme Court's Decision in *Gideon v. Wainwright," American University Law Review* 43 (1993): 1–48, 41; Laura Kalman, *Abe Fortas: A Biography* (New Haven, Conn., 1990), 183. Many of these structural components of the case are nicely considered in Kalman's brief retelling of the Gideon case, a narrative that seeks, nonetheless, to emphasize the power of Fortas's brief and argument before the Supreme Court. Kalman, *Abe Fortas,* 180–83.

60. The film scholar Robert Ray discusses this background frame, in which a heroic figure manages to avoid the apparent necessity of making a difficult choice, in *A Certain Tendency of the Hollywood Cinema, 1930–1980* (Princeton, N.J., 1985).

61. On representations of the "heroic" attorney in the *Perry Mason* TV series, see Norman Rosenberg, "Perry Mason," in *Prime-Time Law: Fictional Television as Legal Narrative,* ed. Robert M. Jarvis and Paul R. Joseph (Durham, N.C., 1998), 115–28.

62. Houseman had also worked with Fonda on the one-person play based on the career of Clarence Darrow. The film was to be directed by Robert Collins, who had already directed one TV docudrama, *The Life and Assassination of the Kingfish [Huey Long]* (1976) and would do a later one entitled *J. Edgar Hoover* (1988). David Rintels, a fan of *12 Angry Men* and a contributor to the TV legal series *The Defenders,* was to do the screenplay. Rintels had also written the Darrow play for Fonda. See an "E-Mail Interview with David Rintels," ed. Robert J. Elisberg (http://www.wga.org/craft/interviews/rintels.html).

63. In trying to imagine what role Fonda might plausibly play, rather than simply assuming that he would be, as he was ultimately cast, the perfect Gideon, I am following the lead of law professor Pierre Schlag, who once speculated on what role the legal theorist Ronald Dworkin might play on *LA Law.* Pierre Schlag, "Normativity and the Politics of Form," *University of Pennsylvania Law Review* 139 (1991): 852–84. Such an approach is also a recognized device, called the "commutation test," by which better to chart the meanings that become attached to an iconic film image such as that of Henry Fonda. Butler, "The Star System and Hollywood," 352.

64. Fonda's stage performance as Clarence Darrow, another legal "outsider," may have also been a consideration. (This play, entitled *Clarence Darrow,* is available in a VHS edition from Kino Video.) Earlier in his legal-reelist career, Fonda did play, on stage, a legal "insider," the defense attorney in *The Caine Mutiny.* During the play's run, he continually clashed with his director because he felt that his character was represented as being too beholden to the system of military "justice." Roberts and Goldstein, *Henry Fonda,* 172–77. Ironically, Jose Ferrer, who played Fortas in *Gideon's Trumpet,* assumed the lawyer's role, which had so troubled Fonda, for the film version of *The Caine Mutiny.*

65. On the "grand narrative" in historical writing, see Berkhoffer, *Beyond the Great Story,* passim; in legal texts, see Douzinas and Warrington, *Postmodern Jurisprudence,* 92–110.

66. On the "fragmented" manner in which the state is (ideally) "imagined" in criminal trials, see Norton, *Republic of Signs,* 143–50. For a discussion that outlines some of the very different background frameworks that can be used to narrate constitutional controversies over the operation of the criminal justice system, see Erik G. Luna,"The Models of Criminal Procedure," *Buffalo Criminal Law Review* 2 (1999): 389–534.

67. 384 U.S. 436 (1966).

68. On the controversy surrounding criminal cases, see, e.g., Fred Graham, *The Self-Inflicted Wound* (New York, 1970); Liva Baker, *Miranda: Crime, Law, and Politics* (New York, 1983); and Lewis Michael Seidman, "*Brown* and *Miranda,*" *California Law Review* 80 (1992): 673–753. For a suggestive overview of the switch in "constitutional regime" or "constitutional order," see Mark Tushnet, "The Supreme Court 1998 Term Foreword: The New Constitutional Order and the Chastening of Constitutional Aspiration," *Harvard Law Review* 113 (1999): 29–109.

69. Miller, "Clint Eastwood and Equity," 180.

70. See, e.g., "Remarks of Abe Krash," in "Conference on the Twentieth Anniversary," 23–28; and Yale Kasimar, "*Gideon v. Wainwright* a Quarter Cen-

tury Later," in "*Gideon v. Wainwright* Revisited: What Does the Right to Council Guarantee Today?" *Pace Law Review* 10 (1990): 343–78. For a critical assessment at the thirty-fifth anniversary of *Gideon*, see Thomas F. Liotti, "Does Gideon Still Make a Difference?" *New York City Law Review* 2 (1998): 105–36.

71. Anthony Lewis, "To Realize Gideon: Competent Counsel with Adequate Resources," *The Champion*, Web site, http://www.criminaljustice.org/CHAMPIONARTICLES/98maro3.htm.

72. Whatever the intent of filmmakers, or any other text makers, many students of culture insist that the representational economy of any narrative about the past inevitably bears markers from the time of its own production. For an argument along these lines related to legal-reelist texts, see Marjorie Garber, "Cinema Scopes: Evolution, Media, and the Law," in *Law in the Domains of Culture*, 121–59.

73. Nostalgia surrounded the film's TV debut. It was shown as part of the *Hallmark Hall of Fame*, a prestigious TV series that could trace its lineage back to the glory days of live drama in the 1950s. The film's nostalgic aura—heavily indebted to casting of Fonda, Sam Jaffe, and Dean Jagger—was enhanced by a return to the screen, after years of retirement, by Fay Wray. Once the object of King Kong's ardor, Wray makes a cameo appearance in the role of Gideon's landlord, someone who, while conceding his failings, testifies as a character witness at his first trial.

74. The nostalgic tone of this sequence is reinforced by accompanying it with, as a Houseman voice-over, a 1964 comment by Robert Kennedy in praise of the *Gideon* decision. An abbreviated version of the same Kennedy statement appears on the back cover of the paperback edition of *Gideon's Trumpet*.

75. "[E]ven the dead can live forever in *media res*. In the process, in the middle, in the matrix, the media make a virtual world where the living and dead meet." Baty, *American Monroe*, 29.

76. For a view of how films, long after their original release, come to circulate within promotional and taste-making networks of mediated discourse, rather than simply as freestanding works of art, see Klinger, *Melodrama and Meaning*, passim.

77. "The Museum of Television & Radio Movie of the Month" Web site, http://www.mtr.org/exhibit/movie/1998/April/april.htm.

78. The graphic was found on the Web site of Frank Watkins Design, http://www.fwdesign.co.uk/fwd.page/fwooo2.html. One of the graphics at the Museum of Television and Radio site uses a similar design in which Fonda's image also looms above that of the members of the Supreme Court, as they were represented by the actors in *Gideon's Trumpet*.

79. At a summer workshop on rights, I asked participants what the speaker modeled on Abraham Lincoln in Norman Rockwell's iconic *Freedom of Speech* painting might be saying. One respondent, who had seen Fonda's films but not my analysis of them, immediately replied: "It's Gideon asking for a lawyer!" On the "endless recycling" between commercial mass culture and law, see also Mezey, "Law as Culture," esp. 55–57.

# Contributors

MICHAL BELKNAP (Ph.D., University of Wisconsin–Madison; J.D., University of Texas) describes himself as a historian-turned-lawyer. A member of the law faculty at California Western School of Law since 1986 and an Adjunct Professor of history at the University of California, San Diego, Belknap has published, among many other studies, *Cold War Political Justice* (1977); *American Political Trials*, rev. ed. (1994); *Federal Law and Southern Order* (rev. ed., 1995); and *Civil Rights, the White House and the Justice Department, 1945–1968* (1991). He presently is at work on a synthetic account of the Warren Court's place in American constitutional development and a book about the court-martial of Lieutenant William Calley for the My Lai massacre.

KERMIT L. HALL (Ph.D., University of Minnesota; M.S.L., Yale University Law School) is President and Professor of history at Utah State University. His numerous books, articles, and editions include *The Magic Mirror* (1989); *American Legal History: Cases and Materials*, 2d ed. (1996, with William Wiecek and Paul Finkelman); the acclaimed *Oxford Companion to the Supreme Court* (1992); and, with James Ely Jr., *An Uncertain Tradition: The South and the American Constitutional Tradition* (1989). He has labored to make American constitutional history more accessible to the citizenry—for example, by organizing NEH-funded summer institutes for teachers and by editing article and essay collections for nonacademic or precollegiate use. He is completing a study of *New York Times v. Sullivan*, to be published by the University Press of Kansas.

CYNTHIA HARRISON (Ph.D., Columbia University) is Associate Professor of history and of women's studies at The George Washington University. Her book *On Account of Sex: The Politics of Women's Issues, 1945–1968* appeared in 1988. Formerly the Chief of the Federal Judicial History Office at the Federal Judicial Center in Washington, D.C., which she inaugurated, Harrison has contributed to the creation of several documentary and bibliographic projects related to the judicial branch. From 1982 to 1988, she served as Managing Editor of *This Constitution,* a magazine published by the American Historical Association and the American Political Science Association, designed to make scholarship about the U.S. Constitution available to the public. Her many articles and chapters include "A 'New Frontier' for Women: The Public Policy of the Kennedy Administration," *Journal of American History* (1980).

JOHN W. JOHNSON (Ph.D., University of Minnesota) is Professor and Head of the Department of History at the University of Northern Iowa. Johnson has just completed editing the second edition of the massive *Historic U.S. Court Cases: An Encyclopedia* (2001). His other publications include *The Struggle for Student Rights: Tinker v. Des Moines and the 1960s* (1997); *Insuring Against Disaster: The Nuclear Industry on Trial* (1986); and *American Legal Culture, 1880–1940* (1981). Johnson is currently working on a study of *Griswold v. Connecticut* and the right of privacy for the University Press of Kansas.

ROBERT J. KACZOROWSKI (Ph.D., University of Minnesota; J.D., New York University Law School) is Professor of law and Director of the Condon Institute in Legal History at Fordham University School of Law. He was a law clerk for the Honorable A. Leon Higginbotham Jr. of the United States Court of Appeals from 1982 to 1983. Among Kaczorowki's books and articles are *The Politics of Judicial Interpretation: The Federal Courts, Department of Justice, and Civil Rights* (1985); *The Nationalization of Civil Rights: Constitutional Theory and Practice in a Racist Society* (1987); and "To Begin the Nation Anew: Congress, Citizenship, and Civil Rights After the Civil War," *American Historical Review* (1987). Kaczorowski is currently writing a history of federal enforcement of constitutional rights from the 1790s through the nineteenth century.

STANLEY N. KATZ (Ph.D., Harvard) is Lecturer with the rank of Professor at the Woodrow Wilson School of Public and International Affairs, Princeton University, and President Emeritus of the American Council of Learned Societies. The author and editor of numerous books and articles, Katz has served as President of the Organization of American Historians and the American Society for Legal History; recently, he has been Vice President of the Research Division of the American Historical Association. He is general editor of two landmark multivolume series—the *Oliver Wendell Holmes Devise History of the United States Supreme Court* and *Oxford Encyclopedia of Legal History.* His current research focuses on private philanthropy and its effect on public policy in the United States. In collaboration with Benjamin Gidron of Ben Gurion University, Israel, Katz is completing a book about the behavior of nongovernmental peace and conflict organizations in Northern Ireland, Israel/Palestine, and South Africa.

DAVID KONIG (Ph.D., Harvard), Professor of history at Washington University at St. Louis, is the founder and director of WU's Legal Studies Program. He is completing a legal history of Virginia, to be entitled *The Course of the Law in Virginia: Politics, Law, and Power in Tidewater Society, 1585–1705.* His works include *Law and Society in Puritan Massachusetts* (1979) and an essay collection exploring legal development in the early nation, *Devising Liberty: Preserving and Creating Freedom in the New American Republic* (1995). Between 1979 and 1981, he edited the indispensable *Legal Records of Plymouth County, Massachusetts, 1686–1859.* With Michael Zuckert, he is now editing Thomas Jefferson's *Legal Commonplace Book* for *The Papers of Thomas Jefferson,* second series.

NORMAN ROSENBERG (Ph.D., SUNY, Stony Brook) is DeWitt Wallace Professor of History at Macalester College, where he teaches legal-constitutional and recent U.S. history. He is the author of *Protecting the Best Men: An Interpretive History of the Law of Libel* and numerous law-review articles, including "Looking for Law in All the Old Traces: The Movies of Classical Hollywood, the Law, and the Case(s) of Film Noir," in *UCLA Law Review.* He is also the coauthor of *In Our Times: America Since 1945,* 7th ed. (2002). In recent years, Rosenberg has been looking at the mass-mediated dimensions of legal-constitutional culture.

Harry N. Scheiber (Ph.D., Cornell University; D.Jur. (Hon.), Uppsala University, Sweden) is the Stefan Riesenfeld Professor of Law and History, University of California, Berkeley, and a member of the Jurisprudence and Social Policy doctoral program's faculty. He is the author or editor of more than a dozen books and has published more than 120 articles since 1960 in history, law, political science, and economics journals. Principal publications include *The Wilson Administration and Civil Liberties* (1960); *Federalism and the Judicial Mind* (1994); *Ohio Canal Era: A Case Study of Government and the Economy* (1969; 2d ed., 1987); *The State and Freedom of Contract* (ed.; 1998); *Law of the Sea* (2000); and *Inter-Allied Conflict and Ocean Law, 1945–1953* (2001). With Lawrence Friedman, he coedited *American Law and the Constitutional Order* (1987) and *Legal Culture and the Legal Profession* (1997); with coauthor Jane L. Scheiber, he is completing a book about army rule in Hawaii during World War II.

Jane L. Scheiber (A.B., Cornell University) is Assistant Dean for College Relations, College of Chemistry, University of California, Berkeley. After graduate study in American history at Cornell, she served as Public Affairs Laboratory Director at Dartmouth College and then as Editorial Director and Associate Project Director of Courses by Newspaper at the University of California, San Diego. She is editor or coeditor of ten books, including such works as *America and the Future of Man* (1973); *In Search of the American Dream* (with Robert Elliott, 1974); *American Issues Forum* (with Daniel Aaron et al., 1976); and *Crime and Justice* (with Jerome Skolnick and Martin Forst, 1977). Scheiber was associated with Paul Murphy in a number of extended-education programs. She has written about the African-American community and civil rights in World War I and, with coauthor Harry N. Scheiber, is completing a book about civil rights and liberties in Hawaii during World War II.

Mark Tushnet (M.A. and J.D., Yale University), who served as a clerk to Supreme Court Justice Thurgood Marshall in 1972–73, is Carmack Waterhouse Professor of Constitutional Law at the Georgetown Law Center. He is coauthor of two casebooks (*Federal Courts in the 21st Century: Policy and Practice* and *Constitutional Law: Cases and Commentary*) and a coursebook, *Comparative Constitutional Law* (1999). His best-known historical works include *The American Law of Slavery, 1810–1860: Considerations of Humanity and Interest* (1981);

*The NAACP's Legal Strategy Against Segregated Education, 1925–1950* (1987), which won the American Historical Association's Littleton-Griswold Prize; *Making Civil Rights Law: Thurgood Marshall and the Supreme Court, 1936–1961* (1994); and *Making Constitutional Law: Thurgood Marshall and the Supreme Court, 1961–1991* (1997). From 1976 to 1985, he served as Secretary of the Conference on Critical Legal Studies.

SANDRA F. VANBURKLEO (Ph.D., University of Minnesota) is Associate Professor of history and Adjunct Professor of law at Wayne State University and the author of *"Belonging to the World": Women's Rights and American Constitutional Culture* (2001). One of her articles, "'The Paws of Banks': Kentucky's Decision to Tax Federal Bankers, 1818–1821," in *Journal of the Early Republic* (1989), won that journal's Best Article Prize for 1989. In 1981–82, she served as assistant editor for the first volume of *The Documentary History of the Supreme Court, 1789–1801* (1984). She is finishing a book about renegotiations of citizenship rights as Washington Territory moved from constitutional dependency to statehood after 1879.

G. EDWARD WHITE (Ph.D., Yale University; J.D., Harvard Law School) joined the University of Virginia law faculty in 1972 after a clerkship with Supreme Court Chief Justice Earl Warren. He is University Professor and John B. Minor Professor of Law and History. Of his eleven published books, four have won Gavel Awards from the American Bar Association, one received the James Willard Hurst Prize from the Law and Society Association, and another won the American Historical Association's Littleton-Griswold Prize and the Scribes Award. In 1996, White was awarded the Triennial Coif Award for distinguished scholarship from the Association of American Law Schools. His most recent book is *The Constitution and the New Deal* (2000).

WILLIAM M. WIECEK (Ph.D., University of Wisconsin–Madison; LL.B., Harvard University Law School) is Professor of law and history at Syracuse University, where he holds the Chester A. Congdon Chair in Public Law and Legislation. He is the author of *The Lost World of Classical Legal Thought: Law and Ideology in America, 1886–1937* (1998); *Equal Justice Under Law: Constitutional Development, 1835–1875* (1982, with Harold Hyman); and many other significant studies.

# Index